John Gill and the Cause of God and Truth

JOHN GILL D.D.

John Gill and the Cause of God and Truth

George M. Ella

Go Publications
The Cairn, Hill Top, Eggleston, Co. Durham, DL12 0AU, ENGLAND.

© Go Publications 1995
First published 1995

British Library Cataloguing in Publication Data available

ISBN 0 9527074 0 3

Printed and bound in Great Britain at the Bath Press, Avon.

This book is dedicated to Bob and Veronica Campen, not forgetting their daughter Elizabeth.

Contents

Foreword and Recommendation

After reading *William Huntington, Pastor of Providence*, George Ella's masterful biography, of a much maligned and misunderstood gospel preacher, I wrote to commend him for his scholarly, well-researched work by which one of God's faithful servants was set forth in much better light than history has given him. Since then, Mr Ella and I have become friends by correspondence. After reading his manuscript on *John Gill and the Cause of God and Truth*, I was so delighted to see the name of another faithful servant of God lifted from the muck and mire that has been heaped upon it that I volunteered to write this foreword to it and make my recommendation of it.

I began reading the works of John Gill when I was an eighteen-year-old Bible college student. My first introduction to him was through his *Body of Divinity*. It is to this day the best theology book I have read. Next, my heart was lifted in the knowledge and worship of Christ by his *Exposition of the Song of Solomon*. By this time, I was hooked on Gill. On the day my daughter was born, being assured that she was to be a boy, I ordered *Gill's Commentary on the Old and New Testaments* for my 'son'. (Bible college students use whatever excuse they can for buying books.) In subsequent years, as I could find them, I have read with great spiritual profit Gill's *Tracts and Treaties* and his *Cause of God and Truth*.

From the beginning, men who obviously never read Gill warned me of what they call his 'tendencies toward Hyper-Calvinism and Antinomianism'. Having read almost everything Gill wrote, I am still searching for even a hint of those 'tendencies'. Instead, I have found in all his writings the most faithful exposition of Holy Scripture, a consistent Christ-centred, Christ-exalting theology, and a constant, robust declaration of God's free and sovereign grace in Christ. Very few days have passed since my first introduction to Gill in which I have not read something from his pen. He is, by far, my favourite writer.

Until now, no biographer (to my knowledge) has treated Gill fairly, except his successor in the pastorate, John Rippon. Rippon's work was very good, but far too brief. George Ella has been used of God to give the Christian public an opportunity to understand and appreciate one of the giants of church history in this thoroughly researched biography. As I recommend Gill's writings to anyone who wants to understand the Bible, I heartily recommend George Ella's biography, *John Gill and the Cause of God and Truth*, to anyone who wants to understand Gill.

Don Fortner,
Pastor of Grace Baptist Church,
Danville, Kentucky, USA

Acknowledgement

I am deeply grateful for the cheerful assistance and advice given me by Mrs Sue Mills of the Angus Library, Oxford, and Mrs Irene Ferguson of Edinburgh University Library. Special thanks are also due to the staff of the Evangelical Library, London; the Central Library, Darlington; and the Duisburg University Library, whose help procured for me many an indispensable book and hand-written manuscript.

I am also indebted to the highly constructive international help in scrutinizing my manuscript given by Mr Malcolm Pickles, Mr J. R. Broome, Mr Greg Fields, Mr Wylie Fulton, pastors Don Fortner, Henry Sant, Graham Miller and James North. My grateful thanks also go out to farmer Frank Thirkell for his prayer and book support, and also his many long-distance telephone calls and encouraging fellowship.

My special and most heartfelt thanks go to Mr Stephen Pickles of Oxford, a most meticulous historian, whose parcel of 130 A4 pages of hand-written comments on my MS convinced me that he would have been the better man to write this book. His suggestions caused me to replan three chapters and make some fifty alterations to the rest of the text, leaving my work all the richer for his careful, brotherly yet scholarly, attention.

One initial obstacle to my research was that the existence and where-abouts of the Goat Yard/Carter Lane Church Books, which I urgently needed for the history of Gill's pastoral work, were entirely unknown to Gill's pastoral successor and his church officers at the Metropolitan Tabernacle, London. Extensive enquiries throughout the British and American libraries proved fruitless. After a year's detective work during which the Angus Library, the Baptist Historical Society, the Baptist Union, Evangelical Press, the Metropolitan Tabernacle trustees, Pastor Dr Peter Masters, his Administration Officer Mr Andrew Wyncoll, The Baptist Standard Bearer Inc. and some twenty personal friends in Britain and the

USA all came to my assistance and pooled their resources, the tremendously important documents were found in a private household complete and undamaged apart from the invariable signs of age. They had been lost for some fifteen years. Mr Bob Campen, working on clues which I had from American friends, was able to reclaim the documents which are now in the hands, or rather in the strongroom, of the Metropolitan Tabernacle.

My special thanks are also due to the late Pastor Kenneth Matrunola whom I approached in the initial stages of my work, knowing that he was a true lover of Gill and an expert on his works. Ken had just been let down by a scholar who had solicited a good deal of Gill material from him but had not bothered to thank him on receiving it and had used the material in an attempt to discredit Gill. In spite of this negative experience, Ken accepted me in true Christian love and understanding, encouraged me enormously and we were able to share our views and our bibliographies concerning Gill in a number of letters. I had hoped that Ken would be able to receive and check my finished MS but the Lord called him home in keeping with his gracious timing.

I am especially grateful to God for the kind gesture of Pastor Don Fortner of Danville, Kentucky, in providing this book with a foreword. It is refreshing to know Gill is being rediscovered in the States, as in Europe, and his teaching is also seen in the New World as a needy antidote against the old downgrading heresies of preaching a gospel improperly, void of biblical teaching concerning sin, the Fall, the efficacy of Christ's atonement, the vicarious, substitutionary, penal nature of Christ's sufferings and death, the imputed righteousness of Christ, the unity of will and purpose in the Godhead, the teaching of the two Adams and the doctrines of sovereign justification and sanctification.

Biographical Table

1697	Born, 23 November, o. s., Kettering, Northamptonshire
1709	Conversion through preaching of William Wallis
1716	First public confession of Christ; baptism; becomes church member and occasional preacher
1717	Assists John Davis at Higham-Ferrers
1718	Marriage to Elizabeth Negus Nominated by John Noble for a grant from the Particular Baptist Fund
1719	Further grant from the Particular Baptist Fund Supplies at Goat Yard Chapel, Horselydown, Southwark Called to pastor the Horselydown church Received into membership 15 November
1720	Inducted as pastor on 22 March
1721	Reorganizes pastoral and evangelistic outreach of the church
1723	Severely ill for many months
1724	Begins preaching series on the Song of Solomon First publication, sermon on Romans 5:20, 21 at death of his deacon, John Smith

1725   Publishes *The Urim and Thumim found with Christ*,
          Deuteronomy 33:8

1726   *The ancient mode of baptism by immersion* in reply to Mattias
          Maurice's *The manner of baptizing with water, cleared up
          from the Word of God, and right reason &c.* published the year
          before

1727   *A defence of the ancient mode &c.* published at the request of
          American friends and against pamphlets by Maurice and his
          followers

1728   *Exposition of the Song of Solomon* published with a translation
          of the *Chaldee Targum*. Also *The Prophesies of the Old
          Testament respecting the Messiah, considered and proved to be
          literally fulfilled in Jesus.*

1729   Draws up a new Confession of Faith
          Great Eastcheap lectures commenced

1730   Lime Street lectures commenced

1731   *Treatise on the Doctrine of the Trinity* against Sabellianism in
          the Baptist churches

1732   Lime Street lectures published

1733   Works published on *Prayer* and the *Singing of Psalms*

1735-38   *Cause of God and Truth* published in instalments

1736   *Truth Defended* published against Job Burt's *Some Doctrines
          in the Supralapsarian Scheme examined, &c.* in which Gill
          argues for the doctrine of God's everlasting love, the eternal
          union and the biblical doctrine of justification

1737-39   Various pamphlets on the baptism controversy published as a
          result of the anti-Baptist writings of Samuel Bourne, a
          Presbyterian minister

1737   *The Doctrines of Grace cleared from the charge of licentious-
          ness*

1738   *The necessity of good works to Salvation*
Also *Remarks on Mr Chandler's Sermon preached to the
societies for the reformation of manners, relating to the moral
nature and fitness of things*
Death of Elizabeth, John Gill's daughter, aged 13, on 30 May
Gill preaches her funeral sermon on I Thessalonians 4:13-14

1740   *A Vindication of the Cause of God and Truth* against
Heywood's Arminian objections to the *Cause of God and
Truth*

1746-48   *Exposition of the whole New Testament* in three folio volumes

1748   Receives the degree of Doctor of Divinity from Marischal
College, Aberdeen University, for his knowledge of the
Scriptures, oriental languages and Jewish antiquity

1749   *The divine right of Infant-Baptism examined and disproved*
against the New England writer, Jonathan Dickinson

1751   Revises, writes a preface to and publishes John Skepp's
Divine Energy. Also publishes new extended edition of Gill's
*Song of Solomon, The Arguments from apostolic Tradition in
favour of infant-Baptism, with others, &c. considered.* His
*The Dissenter's Reasons for separating from the Church of
England* was written in this year for the Baptist churches in
Wales who published the pamphlet in a Welsh translation

1752   Escapes being killed when a stack of chimneys crashes
through the roof of his study
Writes *The Doctrine of the Saints' Final Perseverance*
against John Wesley's *Serious Thoughts upon the Perseverance of the Saints.* This was followed by Wesley's *Predestination calmly considered* which Gill refuted with *The
Doctrine of Predestination, Stated and Set in the Scripture
light*

1753   *Antipædobaptism: or, Infant-sprinkling an innovation* published

1754   Various writings of Gill on baptism published at Boston,
North America

1755   Publishes Dr Crisp's *Works* in two volumes, adding a Memoir
         and explanatory notes

1756   Preaches his farewell sermon at the Wednesday evening
         lecture at Great Eastcheap on 24 March
         Publishes proposals for a work on the prophets

1757-58 Publishes his *Expositions of the prophets, both the larger and
         smaller* in two folio volumes adding a *Dissertation concern-
         ing the Apocryphal writings*

1757   Moves to new chapel in Carter Lane, St Olave's Street,
         Southwark
         Publishes *Attendance in places of religious worship, where
         the divine Name is recorded, encouraged*

1761   First proposals for his *Exposition of the Old Testament*
         published

1763-66 *Exposition of the Old Testament* published in four volumes

1765   *A reply to Mr Clark's Defence of the Divine right of Infant-
         Baptism* published with several reprints of Gill's on baptism
         caused by North American controversial writings
         Mr Carmichael of Edinburgh visited Gill to be baptized and,
         on his return to Scotland, founded a Baptist church
         Published *Baptism a divine commandment to be observed*
         and *Infant-Baptism a part and pillar of Popery*

1764   10 October, Elizabeth Gill dies aged 67 being married to Gill
         46 years

1767   *Dissertation on the Antiquities of the Hebrew Language,
         Letters, Vowel-points, and Accents* published
         Third edition of Gill's *Song of Songs* published with further
         additions

1769   *Body of Doctrinal Divinity* published in two volumes

1770   *Body of Practical Divinity* in two volumes published including a
         Dissertation concerning the Baptism of Jewish Proselytes

1771   Dies 14 October at his home in Camberwell, aged 73 years
         10 months

1.
Introduction

The church of the Lord Jesus Christ in the present day has been enriched by many recent reprints of the works of leaders of the eighteenth-century revival and many biographies have been written about their authors. The emphasis, however, has been placed almost solely on the work of Anglicans such as Whitefield, Toplady, Newton, Cowper and Venn leaving the unavoidable impression that Dissenting churches, such as the Baptists, played no part in these revivals. Though this is largely true of the General Baptists,[1] who had, to a very large extent, become Unitarian by the 1770s, it is far from true regarding the Particular Baptists.

John Gill, a Particular Baptist through and through, must certainly be listed with the earliest and greatest pioneers of the work of the Holy Spirit in the eighteenth century. Gill's widespread influence from 1719-1771 was immense by any standards. In general, the Baptist churches of his day were going through a most difficult time owing to a lack of definitive doctrinal standards and when Gill became pastor of the Goat Yard church in Southwark, the Baptist churches were still finding their feet after the Restoration persecutions and the severe anti-Dissenting laws that followed.

Gill was not only a tower of strength to the Baptists but was also greatly appreciated by 'many in other churches, of different denominations',[2] and especially by Anglican Evangelicals.[3] James Hervey (1714-1758), who was one of the very first eighteenth-century Evangelical pastors to enter into the revival work, did so some ten years after Gill had started his ministry in London and depended very much on Gill's works in his own expository preaching. Hervey, who is himself commonly known as 'the prose poet' because of the lyrical quality of his language, likened Gill to Milton for the way in which he combined theological teaching with a language marked by beauty and variety. Hervey, the Anglican, whose books went into three editions per year, leaned so heavily on Gill, the Baptist, that he sent him his manuscripts before publication with such pleas as 'Let me beg of you to run over it with your pen in hand, and to minute down whatsoever is unevangelical in doctrine; inconclusive in argument; obscure, ambiguous, or improper in expression'.[4] Writing to Gill in 1755 concerning a volume of Vitringa the Baptist pastor wished to borrow, Hervey told him that he would prefer Gill to spend his time correcting his *Theron and Aspasio* first, instead of reading Vitringa, which Hervey would send as soon as his corrected MS came back. In the same letter, Hervey mentions especially Gill's work on Christ's ransom, on faith and his funeral sermon on Mr Seward's death which had all been for him 'sweet to my taste, and I trust have been a blessing to my soul'.

Augustus Montague Toplady (1740-1778), another Anglican, was, if possible, more attached to Gill than Hervey and allowed Gill's thoughts to influence his own to a great extent, looking up to him as his personal monitor in the faith. Of his Baptist teacher, he testifies:

'Perhaps, no man, since the days of St. Austin, has written so largely, in defence of the system of Grace; and, certainly, no man has treated that momentous subject, in all its branches, more closely, judiciously, and successfully. What was said of Edward the Black Prince, that he never fought a battle, which he did not win; what has been remarked of the great Duke of Marlborough, that he never undertook a siege, which he did not carry; may be justly accommodated to our great Philosopher and Divine: who, so far as the distinguishing Doctrines of the Gospel are concerned, never besieged an error, which he did not force from its strongholds; nor ever encountered an adversary, whom he did not baffle and subdue.'[5]

Anglican leaders of the Awakening were drawn to Gill because he brought back the teachings of the Reformation which had been widely abandoned in their denomination in favour of the Restoration duty-faith teaching based on the natural religion of Tillotson, Tindal and Toland and the rationalistic, moral philosophy of Hugo Grotius. Faced with such non-theological humanism Gill emphasized the biblical doctrines of the total depravity of man, penal redemption, justification by faith as the gift of God and the imputed righteousness of Christ.[6] Sadly these doctrines were again dropped like hot cakes by the main body of Baptists after Gill's death, fearing that they encouraged Antinomianism. This led to a massive turning again to the doctrines of Tillotson, Grotius and the Deists with an even greater stress on the universality of fallen man's knowledge of his 'duties' and basic abilities for carrying them out. This emphasis on man's alleged natural powers has become the mainstay of widespread Arminian methods of modern evangelization with their stress on human decisions for Christ rather than God's respect for the law man has broken and Christ's loving death for his church. The doctrines of grace were to be continually taught, however, by those believers of all denominations who associated them-selves with such preachers of righteousness as William Romaine, Augustus Montague Toplady, William Huntington, J. C. Philpot, William Gadsby, Robert Hawker and David Alfred Doudney.[7]

This latter writer's testimony to the value of Gill's teaching is an inspiration in itself. Doudney, who was editor of the *Gospel Magazine* from 1840-1893, was an Anglican curate in a tiny, mainly Roman Catholic, village in Ireland. He was so thrilled with the clarity of Gill's teaching that he determined to set up a printing press so that he might reprint as much of Gill as he could lay his hands on. When his landlady heard of his plan, she forbade him to erect the press on her property as she wanted to be of no assistance whatsoever to the enemies of the pope. Doudney persevered and in rapid time trained the local unemployed ragamuffins to run the press and obtained support from over 1,100 friends who were prepared to finance the undertaking. The copies of Gill that Charles Haddon Spurgeon treasured were from this tiny Popish-Ireland press and it is mainly Doudney's excellent productions that have provided the basis of modern reprints.

When Doudney the Anglican encountered the Baptist scholar's works, he confessed they had 'a savour and power for which we were scarcely prepared'. He goes on to say, 'We love sound, full, so-called high-doctrine; but where the grace and the dew of the doctrine is there too, under the teaching, power and application of the Holy Ghost, it fixes that doctrine in the heart and conscience; and we defy men or devils thence to uproot it. An unctuous word dropped by the Holy Ghost upon the heart is like "cold water to a thirsty soul"; and whilst it exalts and endears a precious Christ, in his person, work and office, it is the most deadly artillery with which Satan and all the powers of darkness can be attacked. We are of the opinion that many of these savoury sweets, beloved, will drop from this honey-comb into your heart; and thus make

"Sovereign mercy dear to you,
And Jesus all in all."'

These words were prefaced to Doudney's edition of Gill's commentary on the *Song of Solomon* which is couched throughout in the language of Eden and heaven. In producing Gill's works, Doudney testifies that he is following God's call to 'print, preach, and practise (as God shall give you grace) the truth, the whole truth, and nothing but the truth. Let press, and pulpit, and parlour, echo and re-echo, with a living testimony for covenant love, covenant blood, and covenant salvation: and this shall be found the most effectual means of counteracting the artifices of Satan, and the cunning devices of pope, Puseyite, and all such sanctimonious but hypo-critical pretenders.'

Times have changed and any biographer attempting to write a 'life' of Gill, particularly in this modern age of doctrinal confusion and distaste for Reformed theology, is in danger of putting his foot into a hornet's nest of controversy. Anyone who speaks his mind as clearly and, at times, as sternly as did John Gill must be expected to cause opposition and resent-ment in those who feel their fur is being brushed the wrong way. The surprising fact, however, is that during the entire period of Gill's ministry few within his own denomination reacted violently against him and Gill was able to unite many on a sound doctrinal basis who had formerly been at sixes and sevens on doctrinal issues. Ivimey, the Baptist historian, claimed that Gill's words were universally accepted as 'almost oracular among the Baptists'.[8] Outside of Baptist circles there was also little marked opposition from evangelicals. Even John Wesley, who campaigned against Gill's teaching on the need for Christ's imputed righteousness, election and the perseverance of the saints, kept a good opinion of his strongest contestant. After firing a few broadsides against Gill's Calvinism which Gill more than adequately debunked, Wesley hoisted the white flag and retired from combat. Talking one day to Toplady, Wesley affirmed of Gill, 'He is a positive man, and fights for his own opinions through thick and thin.'[9] If Gill's most ardent enemies spoke of him in this positive way, one can imagine how high an opinion his many friends must have had of him.

One of these friends and admirers was John Collet Ryland, a Baptist minister who asserted a strong influence for good on eighteenth-century Baptist church life. Ryland was convinced that God had specially chosen Gill to lead the Particular Baptists out of oblivion and doctrinal disunity. In 1777, when dealing with the falling away of the Arminian Baptists, Ryland, the Calvinist, wrote: 'At present blessed be God, we believe there is no apparent apostasy in our ministers and people from the glorious principles we profess.' He goes on to say, 'Much of the credit for this unswerving allegiance to the doctrine of Scripture, under God, must be attributed to John Gill, known affectionately as Dr Voluminous.'[10]

Much of the uniting influence Gill exercised during his lifetime was not only because of his doctrines but because of his life which gave those doctrines credibility and authority. Writing a 'Life' of Gill, however, is a truly arduous task, fraught with many difficulties. Writing the lives of William Cowper and William Huntington was very easy in comparison. There are almost 1,500 extant letters from the pen of Cowper which provide a detailed, often day by day, view of every corner of his life. Similarly, many hundreds of letters to and from Huntington have been preserved and Huntington did his biographers the good turn of writing several autobiographical volumes. On starting my work on Cowper, I was pleased to find that almost fifty authors had written detailed biographies before me. Huntington had only one major biographer, Thomas Wright, but his was a very sound piece of work, both biographically and in its theological assessment. There are, however, some dozens of short biographies and appraisals of the Immortal Coalheaver and the Huntingtonians. As the latter were highly recommended by Dr Martyn Lloyd-Jones, a continuing modern interest for Huntington by Christian writers is guaranteed.[11]

When turning to Gill, the situation is quite different. There are very few known extant personal letters from the scholar-pastor's pen. There are hints to be found that there may be private collections in existence, but I have been only meagrely successful in following up these clues, rediscovering three or four letters which were said either to have disappeared or their existence was not known. Nor is there much biographical information to be found in Gill's works which are mostly of an expository nature. Nor has there ever been a fully detailed biography of Gill's life printed. A very short account was written in 1772 by an anonymous author and prefaced to Gill's *Sermons and Tracts* with an even shorter biography by Toplady. In 1786 Erasmus Middleton, an Anglican Evangelical, placed Gill next to Whitefield in vol. iv of his *Bibliographia Evangelica* and devoted eighteen pages in praise of Gill's life and work. John Rippon's 'Life' of Gill written in 1800 is true to its full title *A Brief Memoir of the Life and Writings of the Late Rev. John Gill, D.D.*[12] It is only 141 tiny pages long and touches very lightly on many parts of Gill's life, leaning very heavily on the earlier accounts and quoting Toplady's brief 1772 biography in full. Rippon's work is, however, doubly valuable. Rippon was Gill's successor at Carter Lane after his death. He was thus able to discuss with people who had known Gill for many years and find out at close hand about his true character. Because of Rippon's close friendship with Andrew Fuller, Gill's major critic, one would have feared that Rippon may have been biased against Gill especially as a large number of Gill's followers left the church when Rippon took over. Gill's successor did not let these facts deter him from being objective to a large degree and he has faithfully painted a picture of Gill which puts to flight most of the criticisms of modern Fullerites. Charles Haddon Spurgeon wrote a brief biography of Gill in his *History of the Metropolitan Tabernacle,* depicting Gill as a grim preacher without a sense of humour, although the anecdotes of Gill which Spurgeon quotes indicate that the humour was certainly there but Spurgeon somehow was unable to grasp the point!

Apart from these brief works, little general research has been done into Gill's life. A few university essays and theses have been written, but these are, on the whole, most unsympathetic to his cause. One is amazed to find that our universities award Ph.D.s to those prepared to write almost a thousand pages of persiflage on the life and teaching of John Gill. In recent years there has been a short biography written by Mr J. R. Broome of the Gospel Standard Baptists who has the abilities and the doctrines to write further on his subject. Graham Harrison gave the annual Evangelical Library lecture in 1971 on 'Dr John Gill and his Teaching' which will be commented on in due course. Several excellent articles have appeared from time to time in the *Baptist Quarterly Magazine* run by the Baptist Historical Society, supplying much information omitted in the older biographies. Indeed, I have found the research of Dr B. R. White of the Baptist Historical Society invaluable in writing on Gill's early years as a pastor and Dr Raymond Brown of the same society has done some excellent background work. Alan Sell's *The Great Debate* also contains a more balanced evaluation of Gill's life and work than the usual modern tirades against Gill.

There are two outstanding recent American works on Gill. Thomas J. Nettles' chapter entitled 'Bridge Over Troubled Waters' in his book *By His Grace and for His Glory* is one of them. Nettles seeks to present 'a correction to modern caricatures and misrepresentations' concerning Gill and puts to flight all accusations of Hyper-Calvinism and Antinomianism levelled at him. Even more notable is Timothy George's evaluation of 'Gillism' in his joint production with David Dockery under the title *Baptist Theologians*. This work indeed reinstates Gill as the great, orthodox, Baptist leader he was. Important, too, is the fact that George and Dockery are obviously not writing from a High-Calvinistic point of view, nor have they an obvious theological axe to grind. On the whole, however, the way the churches have treated Gill's memory, or rather neglected to treat it, is highly blameworthy. Recent British works have, with few exceptions, merely underlined the maxim that a prophet is not honoured in his own country.

When one turns, however, to the theological works of Gill rather than purely biographical matter, no present-day writer could complain of a lack of material. Indeed, one encounters a veritable embarrassment of riches. Toplady wrote of Gill's immense energies as a reader and writer: 'If any one man can be supposed to have trod the *whole circle* of human learning, it was Dr Gill. His attainments, both in abstruse and polite literature, were (what is very uncommon) equally *extensive* and *profound*. Providence had, to this end, endued him with a firmness of constitution, and an unremitting vigour of mind, which rarely fall to the lot of the sedentary and learned. It would, perhaps, try the constitution of half the *literati* in England, only to *read*, with care and attention, the whole of what he *wrote*.'[13]

It is this immense mind-stretching aspect of Gill's works which perhaps poses the major problem for a present-day appraiser. Anyone approaching Cowper with an eye for good prose and an ear for good poetry can immediately get down to the task of writing about him. Anyone with a working knowledge of the Bible is immediately at home in Huntington's works. One can also read their works in a comparatively short length of time. Gill's works, however, are far more extensive and time-consuming. Coupled with their vast breadth is their awe-inspiring, deep profundity. Though Gill is a master of prose and attains to poetical heights, especially in his commentary of the *Song of Songs*, he also wrote many extremely scholarly theses which require of the reader a detailed understanding of theological problems, a working knowledge of at least Greek, Hebrew and Latin and also a compendious familiarity with Classical writers and the Christian writers of the 1700 years up to his day. Any discrepancies in the learning of a would-be recorder of Gill's life and works, as I have learnt to my dismay, has to be supplemented by a prodigious use of dictionaries, encyclopaedias, history books, theological works and linguistic tomes. The reward for such toil, however, is enormous. The more such a student-writer digs in the mines of past saints' thoughts, the more he discovers true gems which are a veritable blessing to his soul. Cowper taught me a better language with which to praise my God. Huntington taught me how the sinner needs and can obtain a true holiness without which no one can see the Lord. My time spent at Gill's feet has shown me most profitably how a servant of God must 'study to show himself approved unto God, a workman that needeth not to be ashamed, rightly dividing the word of truth'.

C. S. Lewis has much to say about reviewers' reconstructions of the genesis of an author's work and invariably an author trembles every time a new review of one of his works is put into his hands. So often, it is not the book itself which aids or hinders sales but the personal, subjective comments of the reviewers. Though reviews in general of my Cowper and Huntington biographies were highly positive, from one particular corner came the comment that I was highly biased in my work. This, of course, was no great feat of insight on the part of the reviewers as I had freely confessed this in my books. I can hardly imagine an author writing a life of a Father in Israel with whom he was in full disagreement! Furthermore, it is quite obvious that an author, biased in one direction, can hit upon facts that those biased in the opposite direction have ignored. In the case of Gill, as in the cases of Cowper and Huntington, it is impossible to give an assurance of no bias and would be a claim no writer could uphold.

Opinions concerning Gill differ widely and those on each side of an argument tend to believe that the other side argues inconclusively or even in an exaggerated way. If we take modern positive appraisals of Gill, leaving aside those who are obviously against him for the moment, it is plain to see how glaringly they still contradict one another. This leaves the

impression that someone must be exaggerating somewhere as the conflicting arguments from within the pro-Gill camp cannot possibly be reconcil-
able. This is illustrated by the positive appraisals of Broome and Nettles
referred to above. Broome sees Gill as a pioneer of the movement which
came to be known as the Gospel Standard Churches.[14] This group of
Particular Baptist churches, unlike many other so-called Reformed
churches, still holds to the Five Points of Calvinism and looks upon the
doctrinal U-turn amongst Baptists initiated by Andrew Fuller after the
death of Gill as a leap back into rationalism and humanism and a
forewarning of the liberalism that followed in its trail. This is a position
with which I, though not a Strict Baptist, can sympathise and find entirely
comprehensible, though I also believe that Gill's doctrines appeal to a far
wider field of believers. Nettles, in his ardent praise for Gill, sweeps aside
almost all that distinguishes him from Andrew Fuller, concluding that
there was only 'slight' or 'little substantial difference' between the
doctrines of the two men.[15] This view I find incomprehensible for obvious
reasons. If this were true, one is left with the unanswerable question as to
why Fullerites react so violently against Gill's teachings and why modern
Fullerites are so enthusiastic in their denunciation of all that Gill stands for.
Such a view would indicate that Fuller has been as badly misunderstood by
modern Fullerites as Fuller misunderstood Gill.[16]

Another embarrassing aspect of a biographer's work, particularly in the
realms of theology, is the degree of agreement he is thought to show or not
to show with his subject. Is the biographer objectively presenting his
subject or is he using his subject to put over his own views? In my case, I
feel it will be best to come clean and state my own agreements and
disagreements. I feel that in general Gill's works were a very marked
improvement on Baptist theology up to date, with the possible exception
of those of John Bunyan. Gill, however, covered far more ground than did
Bunyan. Amongst Dissenting theologians in general, I rank Gill with John
Owen. Gill, however, is far more analytical in his exposition of doctrine
than Owen and often far more moving in his language. He combined the
scientist and theologian with the poet. I feel that Gill's doctrine of the
eternal love of God for his people has never been put so well since biblical
times. His doctrine of justification is as convincing as it is scriptural and
puts to flight modern pseudo-evangelical teaching that justification only
comes to those who first practise the Neonomian course of believing, faith,
and sincere righteousness. His teaching on law and gospel shows a
harmony which I believe reflects true Christianity. His doctrines of the
atonement and redemption show clearly a suffering Husband dying vicariously for the Bride he loved, loves and always will love. Few have depicted
this truth better than Gill. His doctrine of the imputed righteousness of
Christ is perhaps not put over with the depth of detail that Hervey and
Huntington used but Hervey and Huntington built solidly on Gill.

I would have wished Gill had given more theological attention to such points as the law, baptism, the universal church and sanctification, though he was far clearer on these matters than the bulk of his Baptist brethren and I find his views far sounder and better documented. I do, however, find that Gill never managed to apply his own theological, linguistic and historical findings critically enough to his doctrines of ordinances or sacraments and, at times, adopted foibles contrary to true Dissent and very similar to those in the Establishment he rightly criticized. But perhaps no man can cover the whole field of doctrine in a lifetime. Gill left room for others to take up his mantle and continue his work. It must not be forgotten that he was a pioneer Reformer after the spiritual and theological doldrums of the Restoration period. Though he left several things to be done, what he did was enormous by any standards and has an almost unequal grandeur about it. I have thus restricted my comments on Gill's numerous works on baptism to matters which will be of general interest and edification to both the dipped and sprinkled and help the church in general to put Christ before churchmanship. A detailed examination of Gill's views on the sacraments would completely burst the limits of such a biography as this and would be a work which I am quite incapable of carrying out. I trust that especially my Baptist friends will show patience with me here as I have truly endeavoured to show what an enormous contribution to the development of sound theology and true gospel preaching in general Gill and his denomination, the Particular Baptists, have made. Readers will look in vain in this biography for comments on Gill's very few articles on eschatology which I have left alone as being completely beyond my ken and powers of analysis.

It may disturb some readers to note that I name Gill's traducers and seek to refute their works. This is a sad duty indeed. This biography, however, is, first and foremost, a vindication of a very maligned man of God. Gill's solid Christian testimony vouchsafed through his works and contemporary reputation has been so overshadowed in recent years by absurd reports concerning his life, witness and moral integrity that I feel it my duty as a Christian to play the part of a lawyer and examine the quality of the evidence brought against him. I wish to stand by the Baptist pastor's side in defending the cause of God and truth. What Gill — and truth — has suffered through recent attacks on his reputation cannot be put down to the efforts of a few religious cranks with a personal mission to criticize the 'big names'. It is the work of a large group of highly qualified people, mostly from within Gill's own denomination, with the highest aims, though of questionable theology, who are unwittingly undermining the faith once committed to the saints. They are substituting it for a humanistic system of duties which they mistakenly term the 'gospel of salvation' and which they believe every man is naturally capable of receiving. The sanctifying work of the Spirit is being substituted by psychological appeals to man's 'better part'. Christian fundamentals are in jeopardy and must be defended. The witnesses against Gill must be prepared to be as open to the case against them as they are open and verbal in their long list of indictments against Gill. This biography of Gill will provide the Counsel for the Defence with a dossier against the plaintiff cries of the false witnesses against him.

I thus unreservedly concur fully with Toplady's words written soon after Gill's death, 'This age has not produced a more learned, pious and profound divine, than the late Dr Gill. He was, I believe, the greatest man the Baptists ever enjoyed.'[17] It is this shared conviction which makes me feel sure of my calling to attempt a new and fuller biography of Gill's life and works. I feel it as a very strong compulsion backed up by many signs of the Lord's guidance in the undertaking. More than mindful of my failings in attempting the task, I feel like my mentor Cowper when he suddenly became aware that God had called him to be a monitor poet to the nation. Of this calling, which cut him across the grain as none had a less praiseworthy view of himself, Cowper said:

> But when a poet, or one like me,
> Happy to rove among poetic flow'rs,
> Though poor in skill to rear them, lights at last
> On some fair theme, some theme divinely fair,
> Such is the impulse and the spur he feels
> To give it praise proportioned to its worth,
> That not t'attempt it, arduous as he deems
> The labor, were a task more arduous still.[18]

In this confidence, realizing that my 'fair theme' *The Cause of God and Truth* given me by God commands me to write, I am no longer troubling myself to be silent but must speak and spell out what I believe the Lord has laid on my soul concerning the life and teaching of Christ's faithful follower, John Gill. My next chapter provides an overview of the international political, literary and spiritual state of the world into which Gill was born. Readers who wish to delve into the facts of Gill's life and work immediately are advised to reserve this chapter for later reading and start with chapter 3 'The birth of an infant prodigy'.

2.
The world of 1697

As John Gill was so very much a child of his times and addressed himself to the spirit of the age in which he lived, something must be known of the political, cultural and spiritual turmoils of the era into which he was born before a correct assessment of his life and work and its relevance for today can be made.

Our subject began his days in 1697 when the Dutch king, William III, was sitting on the throne of England. It was a turbulent year of political and religious struggles which were to limit severely the Protestant powers and pave the way for a Romanizing of Europe. On the Continent, the Thirty Years War had officially ended in 1648 with the Peace of Westphalia. Though, on the face of things, the war had proved a modest victory for Protestantism with the Swedish King Gustavus Adolphus being declared the saviour of Germany, the Roman Catholic forces were far from spent and were licking their wounds only to strike again in other areas.

In eastern Europe, Leopold I, the Holy Roman Emperor, was busily consolidating his Habsburg titles and domains, strengthening the hand of his Vienna Court and systematically purging Austria, Bohemia and rebellious Hungary of all that was Protestant. Leopold saw himself as the supreme leader of the Roman Catholic Counter Reformation. In his realms, however, Protestantism was no longer his fiercest enemy. The Turks with their vast Ottoman Empire were knocking at the gates of Vienna and it looked as though all that was left of the once worldwide Holy Roman Empire would be blotted out by Islam's warrior missionaries. After the siege of Vienna in 1683, the scales turned and Leopold's generals defeated the Turks in one battle after another. Finally, in the year of Gill's birth, the valiant Eugene of Savoy, fighting on the side of the Austrians, triumphed completely over the Ottoman hordes in three crushing victories at Zenta. Soon most of former Protestant Hungary was delivered from the Turks but only to be placed firmly under the Roman yoke. Protestant Britain was so enamoured by this Counter-Reformation hero that she backed Eugene of Savoy as joint-commander with the Duke of Marlborough against France in the ensuing wars of the Spanish Succession.

Northern Europe, still Protestant, began to suffer troubled times in 1697 when Charles XII of Sweden succeeded his father Charles XI. On Charles' accession, Sweden was immediately attacked by Denmark, Poland and Russia which led to the Great Northern War. Sweden's enemies had thought that the young teenage king would be helpless in the face of their concerted aggression but they were to be bitterly disappointed. The boy king rallied his forces and succeeded in completely defeating Denmark and her Norwegian vassals in less than two weeks. He then went on to destroy Peter I's Russian army completely in a blinding snowstorm in Estonia and then forced Poland and Saxony to sue for peace. When Russia began to revive, however, Charles allied with the Mohammedans against her. The Turks skilfully absorbed Charles' power and then dropped him. This proved the end of Sweden as a political power in Europe but it also proved her end as a strong source of Protestant influence.

Western Europe with her growing overseas possessions was in political chaos in 1697, although what came to be called the War of the Grand Alliance came to an end that year. The Roman Catholic monarch Louis XIV of France, commonly known as the Sun King, wanted a Stuart on the British throne and had begun to make claims on Protestant William's Dutch and Canadian domains. He obviously saw himself as having better rights to the French-Jacobite inheritance of James II than William. Louis had particular ambitions of bringing the lucrative Hudson Bay Company under his control and also to colonize at least part of Hispaniola, the second largest island in the West Indies. The League of Augsburg thus entered the fray led by the Anglo-Dutch king and battles were fought at Beachy Head, La Hogue, Steenkerke, Neerwinden, Port Royal, Quebec, Maine and Nova Scotia but with no major gains for either side.

By the summer of 1697, the French under Iberville had captured the Hudson Bay territories from the English, forced England to give up Nova Scotia and compelled the Spaniards to surrender San Domingo. Vendôme had defeated the Spaniards on their own soil and taken Barcelona. The Swedes intervened as mediators and the British signed a peace treaty at Ryswick putting a very indecisive end to the wars. Much went wrong on the British side. There is the story, for instance, that, after the notorious Captain Kidd had finished his years of lucrative privateering along the African coast, he began looking for further treasure troves. The British Government came to his help and decided to send him to plague the French and help defend the Hudson Bay territories. On his way past New England, freebooter Kidd was unavoidably delayed by the number of opulent merchant ships which he could not resist boarding and sinking in search of booty. The result was that though Kidd's coffers were full, he arrived too late for the fight with Iberville who scorned the weak British resistance. Negative as the Ryswick peace treaty was for England, the French now at least recognized William as the true king of England, although they did their level best in the following years to take that title from him. William was now too worn out by ill health and overburdened by the political difficulties of carrying on a permanent war to show much strength and the diplomats had to take over from the warriors.

When William invaded England at Torbay in November 1688, he had sent out his spies far and wide to find publishers who could print his propaganda handbills and pamphlets appealing for a peaceful revolution. They found printers few and far between, mainly due to the fact that the Stuart kings had kept a tight control on the press, forcing many printers out of business. This move had invoked massive protests from Puritans and Whigs and especially John Milton who wrote at length against censorships of this kind. In 1695 the House of Commons refused to renew the old Licensing Act which virtually meant the freedom of the press in England. This move resulted in printing presses being set up all over the country.

This freedom coincided with a new impulse in fictive literature and writing in general which was quickly spreading throughout Europe. Until that time oral storytelling had been cultivated as an art and most popular legends, fairy stories and folk-tales were to be heard from the tongues of grandparents and professional storytellers but hardly ever found in print. Now there was a great urge in Europe to collect all these tales and produce them in printed form. 1697, for instance, marked the year of the first appearance in print of Charles Perrault's *Contes de temps passe*, better known in England under the title *Mother Goose Tales*. This collection included such stories as Little Red Riding Hood, Cinderella, Sleeping Beauty and Puss in Boots. Soon the great demand for fiction of this kind produced John Gay's fables, Mary Cooper's *Nursery Rhymes* and John Newbery's *Goody Two-Shoes* (now thought to have been written by Goldsmith) in England, the Grimm brothers' stories in Germany and similar collections in Scandinavia by Asbjornsen and Moe with Hans Christian Anderson taking up the challenge many years later.

As everyone likes a good fairy story the Continental collections were translated into English. These influenced the development of the English language considerably and have provided a staple diet for nursery and primary school education ever since.[1] The English language, unlike the French, has always been free of the strict laws of linguistic conformity enforced by academies and other governors of the people's speech. The Englishman is free to speak as he wishes, providing he accepts broad rules as to what is socially acceptable and what is not. As the so-called common people began to read these fairy stories and nursery rhymes, their language was gradually influenced by the, for them, new syntactic, grammatical and lexical forms which were void of local dialect colour. There is no doubt that this enriching of the English language played an enormous part in purging it of the low vulgarities prevalent in educated speech and fostered by the fops, dandies and court jesters of the Restoration. George Colman, himself a playwright and editor of the *Connoisseur*, confessed, 'A man might as well turn his daughter loose in Covent Garden, as trust the cultivation of her mind to a circulating library.' Evangelicals played a large part in changing this situation and fostered the reformation of language and manners through the literary works of such writers as Edward Young, James Hervey, William Cowper, John Newton and Henry Venn. John Ash the Baptist and John Wesley the Anglican-cum-Methodist wrote grammars and dictionaries that were of enormous influence. Even Dr Samuel Johnson's epoch-making dictionary relied greatly on the works of Christian writers such as William Law for its vocabulary.

Polished manners, however, are no proof of a cleansed heart and soon things began to go wrong. It was steadily assumed that those who strove to be gentlemen and were clean in thought, word and deed must be doing, by reason of their behaviour, all that God required of them. Gradually the new emphasis on clean language, high morals and gentlemanlike duties was seen as the sum total of the Christian way of life, a development which had dire theological consequences. These new ideas were widely published in books such as *The Whole Duty of Man*,[2] *Christianity as Old as Creation*,[3] and *Christianity not Mysterious*.[4] *The Whole Duty of Man* was placed in churches all over the country and virtually took the place of the Bible for many churchgoers. Such books maintained that faith in Christ was merely the following of moral laws and convictions which were governed by reason and natural religion and which every man knew inherently he ought to follow. The gospel was reduced to reminding man of his moral duties, totally leaving aside the fact that man was physically, rationally and morally depraved and quite unaware of spiritual things because of his fall from spiritual contact with God. In fact, teachers of this system tended to de-spiritualize the doctrines of the gospel and look upon them merely as moral law-bound duties well within the natural abilities of fallen man.

We thus find none other than Archbishop Tillotson (1630-1698) speaking of the natural duties of man in a sermon entitled 'The Wisdom of Being Religious',[5] and arguing that the knowledge of duty is the image of God in man. Of this awareness of duty, he says: 'For to know our duty, is to know what it is to be like God in *goodness*, and *pity*, and *patience*, and *clemency*, in *pardoning injuries*, and *passing by provocations*; in *justice and righteousness*, in *truth* and *faithfulness*,[6] and in hatred and detestation of the contrary of these. In a word, it is to know what is the good and acceptable will of God, what it is that he loves and delights in, and is pleased withal, and would have us to do in order to our perfection and our happiness.'[7]

Tillotson defined 'religion' as a coming to God through obeying one's duty. Whether one 'came' or not indicated whether one was dutiful or not. He argued in this way because he believed that one could find the full gospel in the law and if one obeyed the law, one automatically obeyed the gospel. Here Tillotson has lost sight of the Fall and the need for justification through faith which is a gift of God who approaches man by grace. He sees duty-faith rather as a matter of natural religion and within the scope of man's natural powers.

On the more positive side of the development in language research, scholars began to work out the relationship between various languages which pointed to a common source and common human way of thinking shared by all peoples. This enabled them to work out rules of translation and language laws in order to facilitate the necessary translation work that was going on and explain these developments in the vernacular language. It is commonly assumed that the pioneers of this linguistic work were to be found in Denmark (Rask and Verner, hence Verner's Law) and Germany (the Grimm brothers, hence Grimm's Law), but John Gill played a major role in working out sound shifts and rules of linguistic development some fifty years earlier than his Continental counterparts. This pioneer work by Gill has still to be generally recognized by scholars. Gill became a linguistic scholar of great abilities and incorporated the rules of language development he discovered into his Hebrew and Greek studies and biblical exegesis.

Some time before Gill made a name for himself as a Christian scholar, Christian authors of Dissenting persuasions were busy proclaiming gospel morals, as opposed to humanistic morals, through the avenue of literature. These writers had suffered the most from the restrictions placed on the press by the Stuarts who wished to give tit for tat with interest for the persecution Anglicanism had suffered during the Commonwealth. John Bunyan had published his *Pilgrim's Progress* in 1678 (Part I) and 1684 (Part II) some years before the popular demand for fiction spread and was facilitated by more generous laws on censorship. Now a number of other Dissenting writers took up their pens to create Christian fiction and non-theological writings to improve the times. In 1697 one of the major earlier writers in this field, Daniel Defoe, wrote *An Essay Upon Projects* and went on to write his ever famous *Robinson Crusoe*, which was published in 1719, the year when Gill began his London pastorate. When, however, Defoe used his biting satire as a defence of the Dissenting way, he found that, in spite of the Toleration Act of 1689 called by some Baptists 'The Magna Carta of Dissenters',[8] and the annulling of the Licensing Act,

Dissenting writers were still not socially acceptable. Defoe thus found himself chained to the pillory by the Public Prosecutor where the angry mob rid itself of its anti-Dissenting frustration by bombarding him with rotten fruit and bad eggs. The same lot was assigned to Benjamin Keach, pastor of Goat Yard church and John Gill's predecessor, who reaped the wrath of the Establishment for writing a children's book with a Dissenting background.

Defoe is rightly claimed as the most prolific Dissenting fiction writer of his age but John Gill can equally be claimed as the greatest Dissenting theological writer of that time. Defoe's *Crusoe* is still widely read but Gill's vast one-man exegeses of the Old and New Testaments is an unrivalled effort and also still in print.

After the Restoration, the Cavaliers swore that the Anglican Church should never again be humiliated as under the Commonwealth administration and looked upon all Dissenters as traitors to the cause of the monarchy. This gave rise to the Corporation Acts and Clarendon Codes which maintained that all holders of municipal offices should take communion according to the practice of the Church of England thus abjuring the Solemn League and Covenant of 1643 whose subscribers had sworn to replace the Anglican Church by Presbyterianism as the established religion. After the Act of Uniformity in 1662 all the Baptists and Presbyterians who had taken over Anglican livings and endowments but refused to subscribe to the Thirty-Nine Articles were replaced by orthodox Church of England clergy. As a result of these 'purges' but also because of quite voluntary withdrawal, motivated by political factors and an aversion to the Book of Common Prayer, some 2,000 ministers found themselves without a church and without an income. Of these ministers some thirty were Baptists but a number of their ejected brethren became Baptists or founded churches which eventually became Baptist.

Not content with this measure the Restoration powers passed the Conventicle Act of 1664 which penalized those attending Dissenting religious services. As if this were not severe enough, the Five Mile Act of 1665 prohibited those clergymen who would not subscribe to the Act of Uniformity from even living within five miles of their former parishes. This political move on the part of the Stuarts actually defeated its own aim of forcing departed sheep back to the Anglican fold. Most of the evicted clergy refused to acknowledge the Anglican Church as their 'mother' and formed free churches in various stages of legitimacy. Under the Commonwealth the established church had been governed by a committee of pastors representing the various denominations so that one could find Presbyterians, Baptists and Independents in fellowship together. This state of affairs was reflected in the newly-formed churches which were gathering-places for various non-Anglican Christians rather than separate religious bodies with a common-held creed. It was only very gradually that they formed into independent denominations and associations or were merged into the older Dissenting denominations some of which were long established.[9] Most of the Presbyterians departed from biblical Christianity and became Unitarians which meant the virtual death of Presbyterianism in England. The remainder were divided into Congregational churches who believed in baptism as the covenant duty of believing families, including their children, and those who practised a baptism of adult believers only. Until the end of the eighteenth century the terms 'Congregational' and 'Baptist' were used interchangeably by a number of free churches and those who stressed adult baptism shared communion with those who baptized infants. In the same way, there was no standard form of church government practised by these Dissenters and church offices set up, such as that of a bishop, elder and deacon, were virtually the same as those in the Anglican Church. Some churches added the office of apostle or messenger, a title which denoted a kind of liaison officer between churches in fellowship with one another. Other churches looked on the apostle as a kind of bishop who even had authority to excommunicate.[10] This variety in Dissenting unity was also found in many churches with traditions reaching back before the Great Ejection, as especially was the case amongst the General Baptists.[11]

Acting too late, the Church of England sought to keep her doors open for Dissenters by granting them far-reaching concessions in the Toleration Act of 1689. This act granted Dissenters a kind of auxiliary membership. They received the right to their own places of worship, provided they were duly registered. They were exempted from subscribing to the first part of Article XX of the Church of England referring to her power to decree rites and ceremonies and also from that part of Article XXVII which referred to the baptizing of young children. They were also free to withdraw subscription from Articles XXXIV concerning the authority of the national church, Article XXXV concerning the Second Book of Homilies and Article XXXVI concerning the appointment of ministers. Thus the act 'legalized' what had long been a practice as known through the testimonies of, for instance, Richard Baxter and Philip Henry who used their freedom in Christ to commune with both Anglicans and non-Anglicans.

As a result of the act many Dissenters remained closely attached to the Church of England but, over the next century, such churches gradually forbade their members to partake in Anglican services and ordinances. Pamela Russel records that Particular Baptists were even disciplined for taking communion with George Whitefield at the Tabernacle, i.e. communion with an Anglican though in a Dissenting church.[12] Even in the eighteenth century, there were Dissenters such as William Jay who were prepared to grant Anglicans similar concessions regarding fellowship in their churches, but they were frowned upon by the movement as a whole. Gradually those Dissenting members who felt that a local church was a church-state (rather than a State church) of believing baptized adults formed their own congregations. These Baptist churches soon divided themselves into two separate blocks according to their beliefs or disbeliefs concerning election, predestination and the perseverance of the saints. Those who argued for a limited atonement gradually took on the name of Particular Baptists and those who could not accept the 'once saved always saved' view came to be called the General (or Arminian) Baptists. The latter-named brethren were far more lax in doctrine than the former and it was obviously considered a greater heresy amongst them to be a Calvinist than deny either the deity or manhood of Christ.

In 1697, the year of Gill's birth, the Arminian Baptists formed a General Association, one of its aims being to expel heretics. They were not very successful. The first preacher to be accused was Matthew Caffyn who had already been accused of heresy several times, but the General Baptist ministers had defended him, claiming that his accusers were uncharitable. Though strong accusations and proof were brought forward, this time by a Mr Amory, the association refused to discipline Caffyn who, by this time, had gained a large following. It is noteworthy that Caffyn, who was so strict as a pastor that he excommunicated Richard Haines for being worldly enough to take out a patent for one of his inventions, could not understand why he should be criticized for denying his Lord. Eventually the General Baptists split over the controversy with many member churches and pastors opting for Unitarianism. This splitting up of the churches on fundamental doctrinal grounds ought to have been a warning to both the General Baptist and the Particular Baptist churches as both sides were vainly maintaining that being members of a joint organization would reduce splits amongst the Baptists. The Particular Baptists, however, always made it quite clear in their joint pronouncements that they sought organizational unity with their General Baptist brethren, believing against the odds that they would somehow, someday, find doctrinal unity.

A National Assembly of Particular Baptist churches was instituted on General Baptist lines and did good work for several years. One of the leading pastors in this work was Benjamin Keach. At Keach's instigation the Particular Baptist Assembly drew up a fine confession of faith in 1678 but the will to follow it faithfully waned in the following years. The assembly gradually lost members and momentum and split into local fraternities. This seems to have been because of the difficulty in organizing a national association and also because of differences of opinion regarding the authority of a common creed. Keach was now looked on with suspicion by many brother elders, particularly after he introduced singing into church worship and strove to exert authority over the General Baptists. After a

number of warnings from his fellow ministers that he should stop interfering with their churches and cease trying to enforce his unwanted ideas on
them, Keach kept aloof from his ministerial brethren and became something of a lone runner. In 1697 Keach's church at Goat Yard asked for a
confession of faith. Instead of giving them the 1678 confession he prepared
a shortened, less specific, though still highly evangelical, version. This
'low church' rendering was, however, supplemented by 'high church'
clauses on the laying on of hands as an essential part of the baptismal
ceremony, and singing as a Christian duty and church ordinance. This
rather mixed confession remained the doctrinal standard of Goat Yard until
Gill took over the pastorate.

The difficulties found in adopting a common creed prevented the
Particular Baptist churches and their General Baptist brethren from enjoy-
ing true fellowship with one another but a number of pastors believed that
if they could only persuade their fellow office-bearers from the various
Baptist churches to meet in fellowship, eventually some form of church
unity could be worked out. The venue chosen for these ministers' fraternals
or clubs, sometimes meeting within the denomination, sometimes together, were not the Baptist chapels but the many coffee-houses springing
up at the time in London and other major towns.

These coffee-house fraternals of special approved pastors (club members determined who could join them, not the churches) gradually became
the true governing bodies of both the General and Particular Baptists in the
years between 1697 and 1720 when Gill succeeded Benjamin Keach's son-
in-law Benjamin Stinton as pastor of Goat Yard. Their unifying aim was
made clear right from the start as, when the Hanover Coffee House club
was founded by Keach and like-minded brethren, it was done so with the
recorded determination to seek union with the General Baptists. Thus by
the time of Gill's 'preaching with a view' at Goat Yard, it had become
generally recognized by the average church members that the coffee-house
brethren were their central body of elders who were to officiate at the
ordinations of local deacons and pastors. In effect the coffee-house
fraternals had become not churches *within* churches, but governing church
bodies *outside* of the churches. These 'elders' had formerly criticized the
House of Bishops for their aloofness from and authority over the Anglican
churches but they had, in effect, become a House of Bishops themselves.
The only difference was that the Anglican bishops met in Lambeth Palace
whereas the Baptist bishops met over a bowl of tobacco[13] provided for the
occasion in a London coffee-house of far more humble nature.

It would seem most odd that the London coffee-houses should be so
closely associated with the development of Baptist history. Whitely argues
that as the armed forces, civil administration and municipal services — he
could have added much of the academic world including all of the English

universities — were closed to Baptists, they had only farming and commerce left to turn to as a means of livelihood.[14] A number of Baptists, including pastors and the widows of pastors, thus set up coffee-houses in London to rival the taverns and also provide meeting-places for the numerous clubs and societies which were springing up at the time. James Jones of Southwark, a Baptist pastor and contemporary with Keach, combined being a tailor and coffee-house keeper with his quite enormous pastoral duties.

This brief survey of the world in general and the Baptist situation in particular is not full enough to give a complete view of the organizational and doctrinal turmoils that the Baptist churches were in at the time of Gill's birth and youth. The intention behind it is rather to show clearly how badly the churches needed the reforming hand of a strong, godly leader. They needed a shepherd who could build the churches up in the faith, provide them with a new evangelistic zeal and give them a unity based on scriptural principles. It is the aim of this biography to show that, in the providence of God, such a man was indeed raised up for the edification of the churches. This man was John Gill, the scholar-pastor whose life and writings not only put Baptists of his day onto the right paths but are equally capable of showing a better way to the weak and doctrinally shaky would-be evangelicals of all denominations today.

3.
The birth of an infant prodigy

John Gill was born in Kettering, Northamptonshire, on 23 November o.s. 1697,[1] the son of Edward and Elizabeth Gill née Walker. Almost nothing is known about Gill's ancestry as the Kettering parish records perished in the fire of 1795. Nor do the extant records left by John Gill himself throw much light on his own parents. They were obviously God-fearing people who were in good, though not affluent, financial circumstances because of the small textile business they ran. The Gills were in membership at a local Dissenting chapel founded by the Rector of Kettering some years after his 'ejection' from the Church of England in 1662. There, at what they called the 'Great Meeting', they shared fellowship with people who, in spite of their various views on church organization, existed together in the bond of peace and fellowship in Christ. Schaff-Herzog informs his readers that Edward Gill occasionally preached to a 'mixed congregation of Dissenters' but no sources are given.[2]

As is seemingly inevitable in such an ideal gathering, discussions on modes of entrance into the true church and methods of local church government emerged from time to time and gradually the members found themselves in dispute concerning the nature and practice of baptism, the nature of the church universal and whether God's kingdom on earth, represented by the local church, included covenantal children or was merely an adult-only fellowship.

The church had a pastor who served as a ruling elder but also at least one teaching elder, William Wallis, who was responsible for counselling the minority in the church who felt they ought to be baptized (or re-baptized as other church members saw it) as adult believers. Wallis also openly questioned the biblical status of the church he was in. This annoyed a number of influential members who challenged Wallis' views and their significance concerning church membership. Those who agreed with him found themselves in very trying circumstances in the church. They were troubled by their own doubts concerning whether they were indeed members of a New Testament congregation and upset about the protests from the other members.

It was gradually thought best that Wallis and his followers should form a church of their own which could then be run completely according to Baptist principles. Thus the 'Little Meeting' was formed at Bailey's Yard, Kettering, with Wallis as its first pastor. In time this became known as the Particular Baptist Church. The word 'particular' refers to a belief in the Reformed doctrine of particular atonement as opposed to the General Baptists' belief in a general and even a universal atonement. The term is thought to have first been used as an official name by those Baptist leaders who drew up the rules for the Particular Baptist Fund in 1717, thus distinguishing themselves from the General Baptists who were not allowed to take part in the maintenance of the fund.

The newly-formed church, according to Gill's first biographer, saw itself as a church state. He does not go into detail as to how such a church state is formed and what its particular beliefs are[3] but we may obtain some idea of what was meant by the term through examining the Baptist creeds and confessions prior to the founding of the Kettering church. In 1646 seven Baptist churches in London drew up a doctrinal confession dealing with fifty-two aspects of their common faith. Paragraph 33 reads:

> Jesus Christ hath here on earth a spiritual kingdom, which is his church, whom he hath purchased and redeemed to himself as a peculiar inheritance; which church is a company of visible saints, called and separated from the world by the word and Spirit of God, to the visible profession of the faith of the gospel, being baptized into that faith, and joined to the Lord, and each to other, by mutual agreement in the practical enjoyment of the ordinances commanded by Christ their head and king.[4]

The new Baptist church at Kettering prospered and grew, practising open communion.[5] Eventually Edward Gill was elected as one of its deacons and he is recorded as possessing a good witness because of his 'grace, his piety, and holy conversation'.[6]

During the unrest leading up to the separation of the two groups of Christians, Edward met, wooed and won his Elizabeth and the two were married. When Elizabeth told her husband that they were expecting a baby, Edward became at once convinced that his wife would bear a son who would become a household word amongst the Baptists. This view was strengthened by an experience that Edward had on the day the child was born. On seeing his new-born son, Edward ran out of the house in great joy, ready to tell the world of the good news. The first person he saw was a man called Chambers who had brought a supply of wood to the house and was unloading it in the yard. Edward wasted no time in telling the woodsman that his wife had been delivered of a healthy bouncing boy. As he was relating the good news, a complete stranger passed by. The man, overhearing Edward's words, came over to him and said, 'Yes, and he will be a scholar, too, and all the world cannot hinder it.' The stranger then went on his way and was never seen again.

Both Edward and Elizabeth watched young John's earliest development from babyhood to boyhood closely, always looking for special signs of great intellect in him. They, of course, gave young John every encouragement and soon had proof enough that their son was indeed of far more than average intelligence. John was sent to the local grammar school at a very early age and soon surpassed those who were considerably older than himself. Before he was eleven years of age, John had become very proficient in Greek and Latin and had a wide knowledge of classical literature, Virgil being his great favourite. He thus became the wonder of the neighbouring clergy who encouraged him as much as they were able. One of these local ministers was a Richard Davis, pastor of the Independent Church at Rothwell (otherwise called Rowel), just a few miles away. Gill said of Davis in 1748, 'His memory has been always precious to me, partly on account of his great regard both for my Education, for which he was heartily concerned, and also for my spiritual and eternal welfare.' Davis was one of the first instruments of God to convince Gill of the one thing needed in his life, telling him, 'If you know Christ well, it is no matter though you are ignorant of many other things; if you are ignorant of Christ other knowledge will avail but little.'[7]

Soon John came to be known generally far and wide as a boy scholar of note. Every market day he could be seen by all, sitting in the local bookshop, reading whatever informative work he could lay his hands on. It was at this bookshop that he usually entered into conversation with the more learned people of the Kettering area and they delighted in discussing various books with the young expert. It became a common expression in Kettering that when a person wished to affirm that anything was true, he would say, 'It is as sure as John Gill is to be found in the bookseller's shop!' John Gill's grammar school days were, however, numbered due to the narrow denominational views of his father. John's schoolmaster took his religion seriously and encouraged his pupils to attend prayers at the local parish church during weekdays. The Baptists who had children at the school decided that their consciences could not allow them to put their children into the care of a non-Baptist, no matter how pious that man was, so, in a joint effort, they withdrew their children from the school. The more affluent of the Baptists sent their children far away from Kettering to be boarded out with tutors or in private schools which were not too pronouncedly Anglican. The clergy of all denominations in and around Kettering came to the assistance of John's parents in finding a suitable school for him. Applications were made in London and specimens of John's work were sent off in the hope that they would earn a scholarship for the young protégé. It was John's youth and learning, however, which proved a difficulty as the bursaries which were sought for him were for older boys and youngsters who had not yet reached John's proficiency. The schools were obviously unwilling to have a bright pupil such as John amongst them as they maintained he would leave all the other boys far behind and finish his studies years before being able to take up an occupation and fend for himself. Edward Gill had not given up hope that his son would one day become a notable Baptist minister but the Dissenting academies and colleges he applied to agreed that John was far too precocious for them and would finish the courses long before he was old enough to become a minister. It was useless for the Gills to apply for early entrance to the universities on John's behalf as they were closed to non-members of the Anglican Church. Denominational bigotry worked both ways!

Now it seemed that the words of the stranger indicating that the world might wish to hinder John's progress were coming true. From eleven years of age to nineteen, John helped in his father's business as no suitable school was found for him. His understanding parents, however, gave him ample time to continue his studies autodidactically. John improved his Latin and Greek systematically and then, after purchasing Buxtorf's Grammar and Lexicon, went on to learn Hebrew. He then tackled logic, rhetoric, moral philosophy and science. Languages proved to be his greatest delight and through reading the Latin writers, he developed a great interest in theology.

John Gill spent most of his childhood in bouts of severe torment and great joy. Though blessed with a loving family and with friends all around, he would often feel pangs of horror and fear. This may have been due to the nervous fevers which often assailed him, but more likely to the pangs of conscience he received on contemplating the indwelling sin which he knew was there and had to be dealt with. At other times, even as a young child, he would be full of the joys of heaven and experienced deep insight into spiritual truths. At twelve years of age, when it seemed certain that a higher education would be refused him, John went to hear Mr Wallis preach. The text was Genesis 3:9: 'And the Lord God called unto Adam, and said unto him, Where art thou?' During the following weeks and months John was accompanied by an inner voice saying, 'Where are you? What a wretched state and condition you are in!' 'You will remain miserable living and dying in an unconverted state.' Gill turned to his pastor for help and ever afterwards looked on him as his spiritual father, but William Wallis died soon after the spark of conviction was struck in John's life. Nevertheless, encouraged by his parents and the church members, John saw the exceeding sinfulness of his own sin and the need for another righteousness to take its place. He was enabled, through the gift of faith, to believe in Christ who promised to indwell him, and to trust in him for his eternal hope.

John Gill was greatly loved by the members of his church and the change in his life did not go unnoticed. After William Wallis' death, his son Thomas took over the pastorate of the church but only on a part-time basis. This state of affairs troubled the church members who invited many good speakers to relieve their pastor of some of the work but would have preferred someone from their own church. After a few years the members, seeing how John was growing in grace, began to feel that he was the youth called of God to assist their pastor. John, however, had not yet testified openly to a saving work in him and thus had not been baptized.

That time was soon to come as John realized that he must confess with his mouth what the Lord had done to his soul. He also believed that once he started to make a public confession of Christ, he should continue to do so as a minister of the gospel. Thus on the first day of November 1716, nineteen-year-old John was baptized in the local river. Already proficient at writing, John composed a hymn to be sung at the ceremony. As he passed through the waters a large crowd of believers and onlookers sang his words:

> Was Christ baptiz'd to sanctify
>   This ordinance He gave?
> And did his sacred body lie
>   Within the liquid grave?
>
> Did Jesus condescend so low
>   To leave us an example?
> And sha'n't we by this pattern go;
>   This heavenly rule so ample?
>
> What rich and what amazing grace!
>   What love beyond degree!
> That we the heavenly road should trace,
>   And should baptized be.
>
> That we should follow Christ the Lamb,
>   In owning his commands;
> For what we do, He did the same,
>   Tho' done with purer hands.

And does this offer to my faith,
>   How Christ for me did die,
And how He in the grave was laid,
>   And rose to justify?

Then how should this engage my heart
>   To live to Christ that died;
And with my cursed sins to part,
>   Which pierc'd his precious side?

On the following Sunday, 4 November, John Gill was formally admitted as a member of the Kettering Particular Baptist Church and was invited to take part in the Lord's Supper. During the same evening, at a private house meeting, he opened his Bible at Isaiah 53, read the text and commented on a few verses. After the meeting several members told John that their hopes had been confirmed and they believed that their young friend had now started on his true calling as a minister of the Word. John was asked to return to the home the next Lord's Day evening and preach a full sermon, his very first, to those gathered there. At that meeting, Gill turned to I Corinthians 3:2: 'For I determined not to know any thing among you, save Jesus Christ, and him crucified.' Rippon records that this sermon ushered in 'a charming season to the godly people'.[8] Present at the meeting was a young lady named Mary Bayly who not only heard Gill's first sermon but was to hear his last sermon preached in London over fifty years later. The odd thing is that this lady, though an experienced sermon-taster, made no profession of faith throughout all these fifty years until she joined Gill's London church soon after his death. Because of her gentle nature Gill's old congregation called her Mary the Lamb.

After preaching for several weeks in the homes of believers, Gill was officially asked by his church officials to assist Wallis in his work and he was soon preaching regularly in the chapel and at meetings in neighbouring areas. Just as Charles Haddon Spurgeon over a century later was viewed as a boy wonder and preacher of ability though still in his teens, so John Gill now quickly gained a reputation as a faithful servant of God and a more than average preacher and it was not long before he was well known and loved even in the capital.

Gill, though happy to be serving the Lord, was less than happy about his own lack of education and suitability as a Bible expositor. Influential friends in London, however, were planning the next step in Gill's divine calling. They felt he should lodge with a learned Baptist minister John Davis who had recently founded a new work at Higham-Ferrers some six miles from Gill's home. This would mean that Gill would come under expert guidance and be able to witness to a wider field without breaking ties with his home church. Gill was particularly taken up with the idea that he would have access to Davis' library and skill in Hebrew and Greek and thus be able to deepen his biblical studies with the help of his new friend.

Davis proved something of a disappointment to Gill who did not receive the time and opportunities to deepen his studies he had hoped for. The Higham-Ferrers area proved to be unevangelized and barren of spiritual life, not only outside of the Baptist church but within. Instead of finding time for studies, Gill was taken up fully with the work of evangelizing the neighbourhood, a task for which he showed an unmistakable calling as many were converted under his ministry. Thus Gill soon found full confirmation that he had been called to Higham-Ferrers for reasons other than scholarly. There was another, obvious reason why Gill had been sent to what he called 'a place of great darkness and ignorance'. After a year of working under Davis' guidance, Gill met a young woman a year or so older than he was, who was reputed to be rather odd and was constantly being jeered and scoffed at by her family and neighbours. On closer inspection, Gill found that the young lady had been soundly converted for several years and maintained an earnest witness to gospel truths both in word and deed. It was this that had caused her to be ridiculed by her fashionable friends. Gill found that the young lady, for want of an able ministry in the area, did not know of the doctrines of grace which she received from her new friend as a means of great comfort. Within no time, Gill realized that the young lady, whose name was Elizabeth Negus, was the Lord's chosen one for him and, after a very short courtship, the two were married, young as they were. This 'capital blessing', as Gill always referred to his marriage to Elizabeth, happened in 1718 after which Gill moved with his wife back to Kettering where his home church needed his assistance.

Help for Gill's studies came from the same quarter as his Higham-Ferrers appointment. The London Particular Baptist churches did all they could to produce well-educated pastors, hindered as they were by not being able to send suitable candidates to the universities. In 1717 the Particular Baptist Fund was founded to provide money for books and educational facilities for men intended for the ministry, but it was also used to help support poorly-paid ministers. This fund, which was the first of its kind to be raised by Baptist churches, has proved so successful that it is still in existence today. A London minister, John Noble, nominated Gill for a grant in 1717-18 and a further grant followed a year later in recognition of the good work Gill was doing at Kettering. With the aid of the money supplied by the grant Gill was able to purchase a fine collection of lexicons, grammars and Hebrew works and eventually procure a scholarly library left by a deceased Baptist minister and friend.[9]

The brethren in London, only too well aware of Gill's talents and abilities, were reluctant to leave their young friend at the call of a small church in the provinces. Gill was thus often asked to preach in London. Early in 1719, Benjamin Stinton, the pastor of Goat Yard, Horselydown, Southwark, died. Stinton was the son-in-law of the famous Benjamin Keach who had died fifteen years earlier, and his successor to the pastorate. Stinton, however, had in no way stood under Keach's shadow and made a name for himself as a preacher and pastor of note. It was Stinton's writings on the Baptists which formed the basis of Thomas Crosby's history of the movement. Crosby was a local schoolteacher and also a member of the Horselydown church. This church was now looking for a pastor who could carry on the great traditions of good preaching and scholarly work which had made their former pastors famous and added many souls to their church. Stinton was hardly buried before letters were sent to Gill, inviting him to preach at Goat Yard. The young pastor's assistant did not hesitate to go and preach under circumstances which would have awed much older and more experienced men, and in April and May of 1719 he expounded the Scriptures in the London chapel.

The 'Church of Christ Meeting At Horsely Down', as they called themselves, were not in agreement about calling a new pastor and several meetings were held in rapid succession to consider how the church was to continue its witness. As no solution was forthcoming, a Mr Abraham Atkins came up with the suggestion that the church should merge with Mr Edward Wallin's people at Maze Pond, thus reuniting the two churches which had split during the ministry of Benjamin Keach. A committee was formed and a meeting was arranged for Monday 27 April to talk the matter over with representatives from Mr Wallin's church. The meeting was to be kept secret from the church until something concrete could be offered the members but the news leaked out and a number of the brethren were so offended that plans for a merger had to be dropped.

Though the church records are rather vague at this point, it is clear that differences of opinions were so strong that there was even talk of meeting in two different localities under a plurality of pastors, yet remaining one church. By June of the same year two names were being mentioned as possible pastors, a Mr Scarney, who was recommended by a member named Mr Morgan, and John Gill, backed by Thomas Crosby. It appears that Morgan put his case very badly and Crosby was able to gain considerable attention for his Gill proposal. Thus a formal church meeting was called on 29 June and it was decided to invite both men to preach. This meeting, however, did not proceed peacefully and Mr Morgan resigned his office of speaker, threatening opposition against any plan to invite Gill. After a member called Mr Cobb had taken over the chair, the church decided that Scarney should preach throughout July, followed by Gill in August. Invitations were then sent out and both men accepted.

Meanwhile, the bonds of peace in the church were rapidly being strained and soon pressure on the committee appointed to organize the preaching was so great that they resigned *en bloc* and five other men were appointed to replace them. The new trouble was probably due to the fact that Scarney failed to turn up on the first Sunday in July though he put in an appearance on 19 July. Crosby records in his *Journal* that Scarney's preaching 'was acceptable to very few, his voice was so low that great attention was needed to hear him', after which Scarney 'went into the country and returned no more to us'. This was perhaps not so surprising as Scarney, according to the records, had never preached before, was not even a Baptist, had never even professed to having a call to the ministry and was not a member of any church.

It was Gill's turn to preach on 4 August of which Crosby writes, 'His preaching was very acceptable and so numerous was the Auditory that the place though a large one could hardly contain them.'[10] As soon as Gill started preaching, the church was particularly impressed by his evangelistic fervour and held a meeting at which more members were present than there had been for many years. It was decided to write to Kettering asking for a report on Gill's character and invite him to continue preaching until the end of September. The matter continued to be debated in the church until a meeting was called on 10 September where, after heated discussion, votes were cast concerning whether Gill should be invited to the Horselydown pastorate or not. The vast majority of the members voted for Gill with only six votes against him. A further vote was then taken concerning whether Gill should be officially asked to become pastor on the following Sunday. This was rushing things too much for a number of members and though the Gill faction won, twelve voted against the motion. Expressing his strong objection to the results of the vote, Mr Atkins, the deacon in charge of the chapel's purse, resigned his office. Crosby blamed Atkins for inviting Scarney to preach and Atkins' disappointment at Scarney's performance may have deepened his prejudice against the better man.

Thus, though still only twenty-one years of age, Gill was asked to pastor one of the most notable Dissenting churches in the country. Gill thought and prayed over the matter for some time before recognizing the call as being from God and thus accepted it unconditionally. However God's ways are not always the smoothest. As soon as Gill accepted the offer, he was plunged into a hornets' nest of intrigues and inner-church quibbling which were none of his making but which were to daunt and damage his ministry for a number of years to come. No pastor could have had a more trying introduction to the flock he was supposed to shepherd.

4.
Making his calling and election sure

Though Gill had been called almost unanimously to the pastorate of the Horselydown church, a few influential wealthy members had rebelled at Gill's forthright preaching on God's all-sufficiency and man's insufficiency and it was rumoured that if Gill became pastor, they would not be so free with their money in keeping him. Perhaps this is another reason why Atkins joined the rebel group as he was responsible for raising money for both the pastor's wages and the Baptist Fund. Now the minority faction, with Atkins as their chosen leader, made a 'great cavilling' and asked the church on Sunday 13 September to reconsider their choice and allow other candidates to preach. This suggestion displeased the members and they showed by 'a very great majority', through raising their hands, that they wished for Gill to be ordained as soon as possible. In particular the widows and families of Keach and Stinton spoke for Gill and Thomas Crosby defended the formal decision of the previous church meeting. The meeting broke up with tempers raised and the rebels demanded that Gill should meet them the following day at Blackwell's Coffee House and have the matter out with them. The records are almost unbelievable. After laying various stumbling-blocks before Gill, obviously of the financial kind, which did not move him one inch, they produced a list of twenty-one names of members who, they argued, were dissatisfied with the church proceedings. When the list of names was openly disclosed in the church a few days later, many were the protests of members who found their names on the list though their sympathies were with Gill. It must have come as no surprise for the rebels, then, to find that on the following Sunday, when Gill was officially asked whether he would pastor the church, he answered in the affirmative, believing that the great majority of the church was behind him.

On Tuesday 22 September Atkins, disregarding the fact that he had resigned his office, gathered together a number of dissidents who did not normally attend church meetings. After sending one back home who had been suspended by the church because of fornication, the splinter group gathered in the name of the church, elected a new preaching committee and reversed the church's decision concerning Gill. They then sent two brethren to inform Gill and also to tell him that should any members of the church wish to have Gill as their pastor, they would have to worship elsewhere with him. This view was presented to the whole congregation the following Sunday but, again, the majority of the members would have nothing to do with such irregular conduct, though now the majority of deacons were behind it. Crosby's comment was 'How unjust, nay how ridiculous' Atkins' efforts were.

In order to understand the motivations and tactics of the rebel minority, it is necessary to know something of the position of the ladies in the Baptist church life of the day. It had been the custom at Goat Yard, as amongst Baptists in general, to accept women into membership with full voting powers. Deaconesses had been chosen and ordained in the various churches at least since the 1640s. These sisters were 'set apart' to visit the sick, whether male or female, and could be instructed not only to tend to their bodily needs but also to 'speak a word to their souls, as occasion requires, for support or consolation, to build up in a spiritual lively faith in Jesus Christ'.[1] The Horselydown congregation under Benjamin Keach's pastorate had taken the initiative in Particular Baptist churches and encouraged women 'to speake and sing, to teach and admonish in the Worship and servis of God in his Church'.[2] When one sister in the congregation protested that this was contrary to the Word of God, Keach accused her husband of exercising too much authority over his wife and teaching her to say intolerable things! It could thus hardly be argued by the Horselydown minority that sisters should be considered less than full members of the churches they served. This, however, was the line the tiny minority who had not voted for Gill took. It is not difficult to see why. This minority had always been critical of Keach's and Stinton's innovations. They believed that it was wrong to place women in authority in the church. When they saw that the pro-women lobby, i.e. the Keach-Stinton supporters, had voted for Gill *en bloc*, they felt that their chance had come to make a firm protest and get back to basics. The number of members' votes cast showed that a large majority of the women had voted for Gill but the men's votes for him were two less than those against him. Gill's opponents thus began to complain that women ought to have no say in such important matters as choosing a pastor. The majority of men were against Gill, they explained, so the church had not called him to be their pastor. It was as simple as that, in their view. They argued further that as the Goat Yard church was a church state, women had to keep silent in its affairs and thus could not possibly be given the right to vote.

The majority who had voted for Gill were deeply shocked at Atkins' strategy and were at a loss to know what to do to keep the peace. The minority had no scruples in forcing their ill-gotten decisions onto the church but the majority wanted to end the matter peacefully and with no room for doubt. They also feared that if Mr Atkins could not be pacified, he would lead a number of members out of the church to join Mr Wallin's. As the question could not be solved internally, Thomas Crosby, backed by the widows of Keach and Stinton, decided to appeal to the Hanover Coffee House fraternal for arbitration.[3] The majority thus met at Crosby's school to word the letter as they could not meet in peace at the chapel for such an undertaking. Sending such a letter to the coffee-house fraternal may have been a sensible thing to do in the circumstances but it put a question mark on their faith in the sovereignty of the local church in the eyes of others. Gill took no initiative in this infighting and held his peace, though it is obvious from the records that he was fully convinced of his calling to the church.

The Horselydown majority worded their letter to the 'Elders of the Baptized Churches' in terms which today would seem highly inappropriate and exaggerated. They addressed the gathering of pastors as 'Next unto God himself' and continued, 'We look upon it to be our Duty to make our appeal unto you, who are his chosen ambassadors, and qualified by him for the good of his people and therefore as we hope your prayers have not been, nor will be wanting for us, so we likewise trust you will give us all the Christian direction you are capable of, and Judge impartially with respect to the Differences betwixt us and our Brethren.' The letter was signed by Crosby, John Jones, William Deall, William Allen, Thomas Cutteford and John Thompson.

The ministers duly consulted one another, weighing up both sides of the quarrel. They came to a conclusion which shocked Gill's supporters and made them change their minds quickly about their advisors being 'next unto God himself'. The coffee-house fraternal came down fully on the side of the Horselydown minority arguing that such an important matter as calling a minister should be dealt with by the men in the church and by them alone. The majority, they argued, had thus acted 'contrary to the Constitution and Discipline of the Church'.

Crosby and his brethren wasted no time in writing back to the fraternal in quite a different tone, stating that they were not arguing against any generally accepted idea of a constitution and discipline. Every church, they maintained, is authorized to decide what rites and ceremonies it ought to perform itself. They also explained that it had been the custom of the sisters to vote in the church for many years and this had even been encouraged by the group that were now against it. This time, the fraternal adopted a more conciliatory tone and they suggested that Gill should be invited to preach each Lord's Day, say in the evening, and a candidate of the opposition should be invited to preach each Lord's Day at a different time until the church could come to a solution which would please all. This letter was signed by the moderator, Pastor Wallin, which probably explains the compromising tone. Wallin could hardly afford to get mixed up in the quarrel as Mr Atkins and his followers had been keen on splitting up and joining his church. Actually the minority group were now talking of joining Mr Parks' church at White Street.

The new coffee-house suggestion pleased none. The minority group were convinced that they were in the right and had no need of any kind of compromise; those who wanted Gill for their pastor were equally convinced that they were the true church at Horselydown; and a tiny minority (which had now grown to almost a third of the church) had refused to accept the verdict of the vote and thus broken fellowship with their church. The unanimous reaction of the majority was that the advice ran 'contrary to the Interest and honour of the Church'.

The two sides could not and would not agree, so they decided to split up in October 1719, with the minority staying on at Goat Yard and the majority meeting in Thomas Crosby's school for the time being as they thought it wiser not to be 'caught up in the snare' of prolonging the controversy. Several pro-Gill members had not the heart to leave their former brethren, nor their church building, and so did not make the move with the Keach-Stinton party. Once settled down in new premises the now somewhat depleted majority, under the leadership of Crosby until Gill should be installed, recorded in their church book that they were the true church as formerly pastored by Keach and Stinton and that they were in fellowship within the terms of the Solemn Covenant which was drawn up by Keach in 1697, interestingly enough, the year of their new pastor's birth. Twenty-six brethren signed the document and sixty-eight sisters so there was truly a majority of ladies in the church. It was not long before the new church had rented an abandoned meeting house for £10 a year after having 'conveniently fitted it up for publick worship'. Meanwhile the minority were calling their majority brethren 'Scismatics, Fools, Beggars and the like'.[4]

The other Particular Baptist churches in London were greatly alarmed by this move as their pastors had disapproved of the vote taken in the Goat Yard chapel. With hindsight it can be said that the worst thing Gill's supporters could have done was to appeal for arbitration from those who held no office in their church as this resulted in their being outlawed by all and sundry. It was obvious, however, that the opposition to the actions of Gill's supporters was in no way directed against Gill's person. The opposition admitted that Gill was a humble man who would probably make a good pastor in time. Furthermore, they had no candidate of their own in mind. It appears now that the minority's only reasons for remaining antagonistic to Gill were ones of policy and an effort to justify their men-only method of voting.

As Gill was still in fellowship at the Kettering church, his would-be flock needed to apply there for a transfer of his membership. With much fear and trembling they thus sent off their written request. If Kettering refused to comply on the grounds that the voting majority at Horselydown did not represent a true church, their future looked very bleak indeed. They would be seen as a renegade split-off of a church with a pastor who was not even a member of either of the opposing sides. The Kettering church, however, replied with a beautiful display of brotherly love and a deep understanding regarding the situation. They also made it quite plain how much Gill meant to them personally. Nevertheless, in the interests of the spread of the gospel and edification of the churches, they realized that they must part with Gill as a member. Their letter is too important as a key-link in the development of Gill's call not to quote it in full.

> Dearly beloved in the Lord we received your Letter sent to us dated ye 15th of October, 1719, Wherein you desire and request of us to give up our Dear Brother in Christ Mr. Jno. Gill to you. We have also his desire to be dismist to you made known to us. This may certify you that we having taken the Matter into Consideration do think it our Duty to grant his and your request as judging that a Church ought not to be made a prison to any of its members so as to detain them against their wills though we are deeply sensible of the great Loss we sustain thereby, and cannot but acknowledge the Frowns of Divine Providence upon us in this regard. But seeing it must be so in order to your and his contentment and spiritual advantage we do dismiss him unto you discharging him from his near relation and obligation unto us and commit him to your particular Watch and Care as a person whom we doubt not partakes of the Grace of God in Christ and hath walked in all good Conscience and Holy Conversation amongst us Desiring you to receive him in the Lord and that you will be every way helpfull to him to the promoting to his Edification and Comfort and that he in the hand of Christ may be a blessing to you for which spiritual ends we commend you and him with you to the Lord and the Word of his Grace who is able to build you up and to give you an inheritance among all them that are sanctified Declaring withal that upon his actual joining with you we shall look upon his particular relation as actual member with us to cease. We salute you in the Lord and rest your Loving Brethren in Gospell Bonds.

Such a loving letter must have come as a real comfort and means of assurance to the alleged renegade church. They were also now supported by Mark Key, the veteran minister at Devonshire Square, and a Mr Curtis who were prepared to administer the Lord's Supper to the reconstituted 'old' church. Those ministers, however, who professed any kind of sympathy with the new church were sent anonymous, threatening letters and efforts were made to stir up trouble in Key's and Curtis' churches against their pastors. On the more positive side, there were also at this time moves by the Goat Yard brethren to seek a compromise with Gill's flock within the terms of the Hanover Coffee House decision. Probably because they were now free to accept Gill into full membership, which indirectly meant that the influential Kettering church viewed them as a true church, Gill's supporters refused to concede to their opponents' wishes. Such a move might also have been mistaken as evidence that they did not accept themselves as a properly formed church. The fact that they were slowly being recognized as a true church by other London churches must also have influenced this decision.

Gill was officially received into full membership on 15 November 1719 with two other brothers and one sister. The church also decided that Gill should be ordained as pastor on 28 December and that no further church meetings should be accepted as such unless the pastor and at least twelve members were present. As soon as Gill started ministering, there were many conversions and Gill's congregation grew so quickly that there was talk of building a new chapel. Now several other pastors decided to support Gill's flock though they received harsh criticism from the Horselydown remnant who were going through a number of internal difficulties of their own and were prepared to risk further trouble by taking disciplinary steps against those ministers who associated themselves with their cast-off brethren.

Up to this period there had been no attempt on the majority side to elect new deacons to replace those who had opposed Gill's nomination to the pastorate. As it now seemed obvious that reunification was impossible, two meetings were held in November to pray for guidance and Thomas Stone, John Jones, John Smith and Thomas Crosby were appointed deacons subject to a later ordination.[5] Thomas Crosby, who was also elected as secretary and treasurer, had proved a tower of strength during the fight for recognition. He had taken over most of the correspondence of the church during the struggle and had served, in effect, as a ruling elder in lieu of a proper pastor. Now invitations were sent out to sympathetic neighbouring pastors, inviting them to officiate at the ordination ceremony. To make quite sure that all conventions were met, Crosby wrote a formal letter to both the Hanover and Blackwell's Coffee House elders informing them of the move and requesting their official approval. Meanwhile, a number of people applied for membership including several from White Street but Mr Parks, their pastor, formally disowned Gill's church and would not grant those who wished to leave their release. One can understand his disappointment. Parks had been expecting his membership to be increased by a merger with the pastorless Goat Yard people but now his own people were wishing to join the Goat Yard majority under another man's pastorate! Opposition to Gill's ordination was, in fact, still widespread and none of the invitations were accepted. Crosby complained that when it came to a question of decision-making, the coffee-house fraternal always sided with the more well-to-do in the controversy.[6] Not only was no approval forthcoming from the coffee-houses, they did not even bother to reply. Pastors such as Mark Key and John Curtis, who had even preached and presided over the Lord's Supper at Gill's church, now backed down, somehow frightened of going the whole way and appointing Gill as minister to the church which they had, in all respects but this, approved of. It seemed now that the group of believers who looked upon Gill as their pastor would never be allowed to worship in peace and in harmony with their brethren in other churches.

Then Gill's followers received an ally from a most unexpected quarter. The Goat Yard meeting-house was not the property of the church and only leased. That lease ran out in the summer of 1719 and the remaining remnant of the church, who regarded themselves as the lease owners, bargained for an extension. The owner, however, was obviously in sympathy with the former majority of the church members who had been compelled to meet elsewhere. He also regarded Gill's supporters as the true representatives of the church and wished to work out a new lease with them. He thus told the remnant church to quit, but generously gave them a year's notice. Perhaps he felt that this would give the two sides time to patch up their differences. However, as it was soon obvious that such a hope was in vain, the owner began to negotiate with Thomas Crosby who was chosen as spokesman by Gill's congregation. Then, early in 1720 it was unanimously agreed by Gill's supporters that they would return to their former chapel under the trusteeship of Crosby and five other members. They opted for a new lease of 40¾ years, promised to keep the chapel in good repair and to take out a fire insurance costing £300. The owner demanded a mere 20 shillings as a deposit. When the remnant who had to leave heard of this, they immediately told the owner that they knew of tenants who would be prepared to accept conditions which would be far more lucrative for him and that he had allowed himself to make a bad deal. On hearing this, the owner sent the deposit back to Gill's church, begging them to tear up the agreement. Crosby intervened and again peace was restored and the deal was settled. Going back to Goat Lane meant for Gill's flock that half their battles were over.

Various efforts were now made to secure some form of agreement with those who were still at Goat Yard, hoping that they might not go off and form another church but stay and be reunited with their former friends and brethren. Still hoping for a display of sympathy from the all-powerful Hanover Coffee House fraternity, Gill's supporters decided to send a delegation to them, asking them to reconsider their decision.[7] It seems that they received some form of favourable reply as a number of the coffee-house pastors now openly threw in their weight to persuade the two factions to give each other the right hand of fellowship. It seems that Crosby's insistence that 'two churches were better than none'[8] won the day as it was becoming apparent that the controversy was doing neither of the sides any good. Gill's delayed induction was arranged for the coming March and his deacons suggested, rather tactlessly at this point, that he should be ordained at Goat Yard. If the minority church still occupying its premises had agreed to this, it would have been tantamount to burying the hatchet, but the Goat Yard people refused to comply. The coffee-house fraternal now decided that Gill's church ought to be recognized as a true church and they not only withdrew their opposition but promised to send a number of ministers to Gill's March induction. When that day arrived, no less than ten Baptist ministers turned up for the occasion.

At the induction service[9] John Skepp (c. 1670-1721), pastor of the Cripplegate church,[10] presided and called upon Crosby as acting church secretary to give an account of the church's dealings including how Gill came to be called as a minister and how he became a member of the church. This was all known by everyone present but belonged to the formal protocol of such an occasion. The solemnities were rather disturbed when John Noble required the church members to stand around the communion table to confirm their choice of Gill as pastor. The small chapel was filled to bursting point and the members, spread around the hall, could not force their way to the table. Noble had to tell them to stay where they were but stand up while the rest of the congregation remained seated. He then asked them to confirm their interest in Gill as their pastor by raising their hands. On taking note of the great display of hands, Noble asked Gill formally if he were prepared to accept the recommendation of the church. Gill affirmed his calling and promised the church to abide by four principles in his new office. He would take the Word of God for his rule, the Spirit of God for his guide, the promises of God for his support and Christ's fulness for the supply of all his wants.

After this solemn declaration, Gill was ordained by Curtis and Key through the laying on of hands. Then it was the deacons' turn to have their calling confirmed by the church members after which Gill joined the pastors who had ordained him in laying his hands on the deacons and officially ordaining them to their office. Noble then went on to address the new pastor and his deacons from Acts 20:28, pointing out to them what their various duties were. Next John Skepp addressed the church from Hebrews 13:17 and told them of their responsibilities as members to their church officers, to one another and to their common work as ambassadors for Christ. To conclude the induction meeting, Gill led the church in prayer, Psalm 133 was sung and then the new pastor dismissed the assembly with a benediction. Charles Haddon Spurgeon, in recording briefly the facts of Gill's ordination, adds, 'Little did the friends dream what sort of man they had thus chosen to be their teacher; but had they known it they would have rejoiced that a man of such vast erudition, such indefatigable industry, such sound judgement, and such sterling honesty, had come among them.'[11]

Now the church had official recognition but their joy was not complete. The Goat Yard opposition that day registered in their church book that Gill had been ordained over a flock that was officially still in fellowship elsewhere and had never been dismissed according to acceptable Baptist standards. Now, however, the separated minority was more or less alone in their opinions with the bulk of the local pastors and their churches backing Gill.

The records of Gill's ordination service have provided church histori-ans with a complete picture of how the Particular Baptists were organized at the beginning of the eighteenth century. It is clear that they only elected one elder per church, who was also their pastor, who then presided over a number of deacons.[12] Though many pastors were present at Gill's ordina-tion ceremony, they were referred to by Crosby in his records as 'elders'. This might indicate that the Baptists had some idea of a church universal with elders belonging to it which were not members of the local church but fellow members of the body of Christ. In their confessions of faith, however, they tended to define the local church as if it excluded any membership of a wider church concept. This wider church concept, however, in many Baptist churches, had begun to take the form of fraternals, associations, societies and unions. They, in turn, tended to isolate the normal church members from fellowship with the other churches as only representatives called 'messengers' took an active part in inter-church dealings. Gradually these associations and unions, with their representative membership only, elected non-church-based hierarchies with no doctrinal creeds who saw themselves as ruling bodies over local churches.[13] Gill was to do much in his pastorate to curb this downgrading of a true church conception but he was very much a lone voice and his successor John Rippon went back to the old para-church policies. By the time Charles Haddon Spurgeon became pastor of Gill's church after Rippon, over a hundred years later, the situation had become so bad that a doctrineless Baptist Union dominated the majority of local churches, ruling them from outside. Churches founded abroad by British missionar-ies were ruled by a committee of men in the Baptist Missionary Society who opened their membership to anyone who would pay 10/6^d, irrespec-tive of their beliefs. Declaring that he was taking up the mantle cast down at Gill's death, Spurgeon took up the postponed fight again for the rights of the local church over external organizations, patronages and societies. Spurgeon had a measure of success in his reforming plans for the Baptist Missionary Society but he failed sadly in his opposition to the Baptist Union who continued to put organizational unity sealed by the rite of baptism before a common faith.

Be that as it may, Gill's church could now breathe freely and get on with the task of evangelizing the neighbourhood. His preaching and the testimonies of the church members were soon rewarded by a good number of new converts being added to the church. One of these was William Jerome Joseph Dean Benjamin Stinton, the second son of the late pastor. Other newcomers had been dissatisfied members of Keach's and Stinton's churches who had left to become Quakers or Presbyterians, others had moved to London from the Provinces or even as far away as Wales. The numbers that were added to the church were truly large, but as there were many old people in the church, deaths, too, were numerous. Nevertheless, for every member who died or left for some other reason there were at least two who were added to the church in its early years and three to four in later years. Membership did wane somewhat towards the end of Gill's life when he became rather feeble but that was all over fifty years in the future and up to then the church prospered in leaps and bounds. On 27 May a most warm and loving letter was sent from Higham Ferrers on Elizabeth Gill's account, dismissing her from the fellowship there and recommending her to the London church because 'her Conversation hath been as it becometh the Gospel of Christ'. Mrs Gill was then duly accepted as a member of her husband's church at Fair Street.

During the summer of 1720, Gill and his church moved back into their old premises at Goat Yard and the still irreconcilable, pastorless remains of the old congregation founded a church in Unicorn Yard. Gill's followers had to roll up their sleeves and start painting, decorating and doing general odd jobs around the chapel as the fabric of the church had been greatly neglected since Stinton's death. This, however, welded the church members more firmly together and gave them a stronger feeling of being at home at Goat Yard. £117.9s 6ᵈ was quickly raised by the members to cover the costs. Gill's congregation does not seem to have been a particularly wealthy one though there were one or two donations running into two figures, quite a sum in those days. The new Unicorn Yard church did not leave without a strong protest and a full-scale row. They insisted that the fittings in the church did not come under the lease contract and were thus their property. This was indeed partly the case as the Goat Lane chapel was originally built with standing room only, private people having pews built into the chapel for their own use.[14] Gill's followers argued that this was not true as the majority of people who had formerly sat on the pews were now back to sit on them again. This logical argument did not work with the Unicorn Yard people and Gill's flock had to pay the departing brethren £10 for the pews to preserve the peace.

After several months at Unicorn Yard the church there invited William Arnold to become their pastor. Arnold was ordained towards the end of 1720 but he seemed powerless at first to instil a new vision into the church and heal them of the wounds caused by the break-up. On the contrary the church, finding themselves once again firmly established with a regular pastor and church government, began to lick their wounds and thus keep them fresh. They soon found a new cause for strife. Benjamin Keach had always campaigned for the setting up of a joint fund amongst Particular Baptists to provide for books and education for poor pastors. Stinton had fostered this interest and the Horselydown church had contributed generously to it. Gill had found at first hand how admirable and necessary this fund was. The zealous engagement of the Horselydown congregation in fostering the fund had gained for them the right to send their pastor and three 'messengers' to the managerial meetings. One of these managers was Abraham Atkins who had remained at Goat Yard and had been one of the loudest voices against Gill's nomination. Now that Gill's congregation had settled down at Goat Yard and the minority church had received a new home at Unicorn Yard with a new pastor, the other churches represented on the fund's managerial committee suggested that both churches should now have their say in the support and management of the fund. At first the Unicorn Yard church would have nothing to do with the idea although pressed to consider it by other coffee-house-controlled churches throughout 1720 to 1722. At last the managerial committee approached Gill's church directly, formally inviting them to contribute to the organization and financing of the fund. At a church meeting Gill's congregation decided to maintain a joint claim with Unicorn Yard to their rights regarding the fund suggesting that each church should send two messengers to the committee meetings. The Goat Yard church offered to stock up the fund by donating £50. The matter was not settled until two years after, as further trouble was brewing up between the two 'Yards'. It all had to do with Thomas Crosby and his Keach-Stinton relations.

The summer of 1720 had brought problems enough to twenty-three-year-old Gill and his wife. One major blow was that the young couple were expecting their first child but Elizabeth miscarried and, as a result of the complications which set in, was ill for seven or eight months. This was the first of very many difficult pregnancies and the young couple saw one child after another stillborn or die in early infancy. Only two children, John, who became a goldsmith, and Mary, who married her father's bookseller, reached adulthood. These occasions of sadness and suffering always bore down on Elizabeth and made her doubt her usefulness in the Lord but her husband looked after her with great attention and sought the best medicine and professional care for her. Instead of spending all his time in his study, Gill sat by his wife's side in the living room when preparing his sermons, to be at hand when needed. The faithful attention Gill showed his wife angered Benjamin Keach's widow who felt that Elizabeth was acting like a spoilt child and should do what all young women do after a miscarriage — forget it and get on with the household chores. Soon rumours were being spread by the Keach-Stinton members that Elizabeth only pretended to be ill so that she could keep the bulk of her husband's attention for herself and away from his pastoral duties. Mrs Keach lived with Thomas Crosby and his family and probably discussed the matter with him at length as he decided to represent the troubled faction in the church and have the matter out with his pastor. He thus invited Gill to meet him at a local tavern of all places and there accused Gill to his face of spoiling Elizabeth who was faking illness and had merely a 'vapourish humour'.

Crosby took this step, obviously thinking that his leading position in the church gave him the right and the responsibility to do so. In fact, up to this incident, it had been Crosby who had led the congregation in its fight for recognition and had carried the burdens of organizing and finding funds for the new church. He also campaigned for so-called lay people to be members of the governing coffee-house body. Perhaps this willingness to shoulder many burdens had made him unduly critical of Gill's inactivity in matters of church politics. Though Crosby was critical of Gill, many of the members had become critical of Crosby, feeling that he was throwing his weight about too much and trying too hard to literally buy Gill's friendship by his use — or misuse — of church funds which were set apart for the minister and for the poor. He had also been criticized by a sister for overlooking the 'crimes and misdemeanours' of another female member of the church. Crosby reacted by resigning his position as treasurer on 17 July 1722 but this did not stop him being accused some time later of deliberately trying to defraud the church in various ways. Those who looked into the matter found several pages torn out of the accounts book and now everyone was convinced that Crosby was a crook. There was, however, a natural but rather unusual explanation for the deed. One of the elders, appointed to look through the books, had a small daughter who was fond of making paper patterns. She had espied the accounts book and, seizing the opportunity, tore out a number of pages in order to make new patterns. When this fact was discovered, Crosby was quickly cleared of every hint of fraud. He could not, however, forget that he had been wrongly condemned.

These matters angered Crosby and the Keach-Stinton families so much that they began to make plans to leave Goat Yard and rejoin those members of the former Goat Yard church. The odd thing about this intended move was that it was the Keach-Stinton faction who had wanted to separate from the other members in the first place, and now they could not wait to be rejoined with them.

Crosby, being 'uneasy and dissatisfied', was the first to threaten resignation and records that Gill visited him to ask him to stay. Instead of leaving the matter at that, Crosby demanded that a special vote of confidence should be given him at the next church meeting because of all the wrong that had been committed against him. Gill argued that he had already received a vote of confidence and been cleared of fraud before the church and had received the open support of his pastor so the matter should be left there. As there were no further charges against Crosby, it would be wrong to bring the matter up again for official comment. Crosby was not satisfied with this and became outraged. He told the brethren in anger at the next meeting that he was seeking membership in another church and stormed out before the day's matters were concluded. Some time later, however, Crosby decided that he had acted wrongly and asked to be taken back into the fellowship of the church.

The reasons given by Crosby for changing his mind, however, had nothing to do with his personal sorrow. He actually justified his wanting to stay at Goat Yard in a letter with the argument that if he went, the whole Keach-Stinton family, who had now inter-married, would go with him. On 26 March 1723 the church meeting discussed the matter of Crosby's change of opinion and his threat. Crosby did not turn up at the meeting and so brothers Berwick and Stinton were sent to his house to fetch him. The two, however, found no one at home. This time Gill spoke out firmly against Crosby's lack of assurance regarding where he belonged spiritually and even mentioned his high-handedness in criticizing Elizabeth Gill. Elizabeth had suffered greatly from the harsh criticism of Crosby and his relations. She was a very humble, sensitive person, always convinced that she was the least of all saints and always striving to live as to give no offence. Gill was shocked to see that what he knew to be true in his wife's experience was seen as an 'I am holier than thou' attitude by her critics. This caused Elizabeth much soul-searching and self-criticism followed by doubts and fears of which her critics knew nothing.

After hearing all manner of complaints against Crosby, including the startling facts that he had resumed the offices he had given up without the consent of the members, and that he had spread scandalous reports about the pastor and his wife, he was formally discharged from his offices and banned from communion until he showed signs of repentance. He was ordered to report to the next church meeting. The required repentance was not shown and thus Crosby was excommunicated and eventually received into membership with his family at Unicorn Yard.[15] The family left in great rage, the ladies calling Gill 'a monster' and the church 'a giddy ignorant company'. Crosby complained that the church's decision was 'the most base and ungrateful action hardly to be paralleled in this age!'.

Crosby's dismissal had grievous consequences for his entire family, many of whom could not really make up their mind which 'Yard' they belonged to. Crosby himself was soon accused of negligence in financial matters in his new church and eventually excommunicated. Several female members of his family proved themselves as adept at spreading gossip in their new church as they had been in their old and were dismissed for 'spreading evil rumours'. After some years, Crosby's wider family split up. Several, including Crosby himself, were accepted back at Unicorn Yard and several, whom Crosby had defrauded in business, returned to Goat Yard. When writing his *History of the Baptists*, Crosby chose to forget that he had ever been a member of Gill's church and wrote as if Unicorn Yard was the true and only successor to Benjamin Stinton's old church.[16]

Sad as the occasion was, Gill's congregation was the happier for not having the trouble-makers amongst them. It was to take some time, however, before the strife between the two Yards stopped. The Unicorn Church, for instance, applied to Goat Lane for the transference of several members of the Crosby clan. Gill's church explained that they thought this was an odd move on the part of Unicorn Yard as that church had not yet recognized Goat Yard as a true church. Furthermore, they argued, Crosby's wider family were not in good standing with Goat Yard so how could they recommend them? It was not until 1727 that the two churches, this time on the initiative of Unicorn Yard, decided to recognize each other formally and offer each other the right hand of fellowship. The Unicorn Yard congregation, in fact, began to go through a period of growth and spiritual blessing once they put away their differences with Goat Yard.

There was a further reason why it was beneficial to the Goat Yard church not to keep the Keach-Stinton family in fellowship. Keach and to a greater extent, Stinton, had kept a door open for their Arminian brethren and had set great store by associations and fraternals with them. Keach had emphasized that these ministers' associations should have no jurisdiction or authority over individual churches, but he did not keep to this resolution himself and was often censored for trying to exert authority over the General Baptists. The Annual Baptist Church meetings had been looked on by the member churches as a general governing body and by Stinton's time, the coffee-house fraternals certainly regarded themselves as having such authority. This is why Crosby made no hesitation to apply for arbitration to the Hanover Coffee House meeting, which was largely a creation of Stinton, following Keach's initial ideas, when trouble arose at Goat Yard. This is also why Gill did not take part in these appeals at all as he was beginning to see them as a breach of New Testament church principles.

Crosby's views were even more 'open' than Stinton's and he made himself unpopular in his new church for expressing sympathy with a member who was excommunicated for denying the Trinity. Now that this more liberal faction had left, Gill was able to concentrate on building up a church according to true gospel methods. Part of this reconstruction work was not only to reform the church's inner life but also to reform the church's outside relationships to the Hanover Coffee House.

Gill showed an uncommon interest in becoming a member of the coffee-house fraternal as soon as he was recognized by them. This eagerness was unexpected as it clashed considerably with his usual behaviour. It is all the more surprising when one learns that one of the main aims of the Hanover Coffee House was to seek union with the General (Arminian) Baptists,[17] a union which was already partly accomplished as the Hanover Coffee House party was now meeting once a month with the Arminian Coffee House fraternal. The General Baptists had refused to discipline pastors who doubted the doctrine of the Trinity[18] and argued for a belief in 'the doctrine of universal redemption',[19] giving their members virtually a *carte blanche* to believe what they liked. This apparently made no difference to the Particular Baptists' wooing of them.[20] Gill certainly became a member of the Hanover Coffee House group for the sake of fellowship with other pastors but his main purpose soon became evident. It was Crosby who gave him the opportunity he had been waiting for.

Crosby was most enraged at the treatment he had received at Goat Yard and demanded that his good name be re-established. He was obviously prone to such bouts of self-justification in the face of all evidence as, several years later, after defrauding his own son-in-law of a large amount of capital and after arbitration the courts and the church had shown him the folly of his ways, he still wrote letters to all and sundry proclaiming his innocence. As was his custom, Crosby now wrote a very long letter to the Hanover Coffee House demanding the justice which he refused to believe he had received. The letter was read before the assembly, and Gill was amongst the hearers. The ministers solemnly asked Gill to give his side of the quarrel so that they could pronounce their official opinion. Gill calmly told the august gathering that they were a mere fraternal of pastors, gathered together for fellowship and they had no authority whatsoever over the inner affairs of local churches. His church, he claimed, was sovereign over its own actions under God and as his church had decided on a course of action regarding Crosby, it was not to be questioned by an external body. The coffee-house brethren had to accept this truth, whether they liked it or not. After this action on Gill's part, it was merely a matter of months before the Hanover Coffee House brethren ceased to exist as a para-church form of 'eldership'.[21] A new venture, however, was started up on a less formal and official basis at the Gloucestershire Coffee House in 1724.

Crosby's faction would not give up and retorted by arguing that the local church had no jurisdiction over deacons. They argued that Crosby had been ordained as deacon of the Goat Yard church by elders who were outside of their church state, i.e. the coffee-house brethren. They then argued logically enough, but hardly theologically enough, that only those elders who ordained Crosby had the authority under God to take his office from him and the Goat Yard church members could not therefore legally do so. If this had been true, it would have meant that the coffee-house fraternal held absolute authority over all the churches which supplied them with pastors and messengers. Gill had, however, shown the coffee-house 'elders' what their limitations were and, as the majority of church members at Goat Yard did not believe in rule by remote control, Crosby and his followers thus found themselves outvoted and cast out.

Another reform which Gill did not hesitate to encourage was long overdue. Unlike most Dissenting ministers, Keach, though entirely evangelical in his doctrine, defended views of the pastoral office which differed little from those held by the Anglo-Catholic Church and the papal system. Raymond Brown says of him, 'Neither Keach nor his son, Elias, had time for interfering lay busy-bodies, comparing them with those in the Old Testament times who "meddled with the priest's work and office".'[22] The Baptist historian Whitley says that Keach was 'intolerant of meeting others as equals'[23] and he was very impatient with 'lay-men' such as the Amsterdam trader and jeweller Isaac Marlow, one of his members who believed in 'the priesthood of all believers'. Marlow protested strongly against Keach's ritualism, especially on his insistence that only those who receive the laying on of hands are properly baptized. At least one major split in the church had developed because a number of the members felt that Keach was over-pontifical and the deacons and members were not allowed to share in the general witness of the church.[24] Indeed, when speaking of the lack of money given to the pastor and the lack of ceremony and splendour in the Baptist churches, Keach did not so much refer to the biblical maxim of not muzzling the ox which treads the corn but referred favourably to the pomp of the pontifical priesthood.[25] Striving to be fair in his assessment of Keach, Brown says, 'Keach might well have exaggerated the role of the minister but, at the time, his emphasis may have been necessary. For too long the churches had been without a well-educated or adequately supported minister.'[26] Gill, who was too well-supported and respected to have to spend his pastoral time pleading for such ministerial recognition, always stressed the responsibility of each member to spread the gospel, often likening the bringing in of new converts to harvesting, where the full-time workers (pastors) had to bring in their thousands and the part-time workers (the 'laity') were to bring in their hundreds.

Towards the autumn of 1721 Gill began to organize the spiritual life of the church, making sure that every member was taken care of and instructed in the faith. Gill then encouraged ordinary members of the church to take on some of the pastoral duties such as electing messengers to visit those who wished to join the church or those who were negligent in their duties. Gill divided the area covered by the Goat Yard witness into four parts with two brethren responsible for each section, making sure that all the members in that area were regularly visited. Coupled with this, Gill encouraged most members to be active and usually had jobs for them such as visiting the sick, calling on absentees or distributing charity from organized bursaries. Though there were very few well-to-do people in Gill's congregation, the church records show that their giving to the poor was extremely generous. Often Goat Yard relieved those living on very low parish aid such as 'Sister Haines' who received two shillings a month from the bursary and 'Sister Morris' who received four shillings monthly. Poor members of the church were given well-paid caretaking jobs to do in the chapel[27] so that they would keep their self-respect and not feel they were a burden to charity. Church meetings were held at least once a month so that the work of the church could be discussed and planned. These were also times for church discipline and the records show the loving care with which Gill and his deacons exercised this duty. Acute scandals were rare, though one member was tried and convicted for highway robbery! Drinking was obviously a problem but these were the days of the terrible 'gin craze'. The church meetings were also times to hear the testimonies of the recently saved and new members. It is heart-warming to read how often such testimonies are recorded. A quarterly Day of Humiliation and Prayer was set up and new deacons appointed. Now that the Crosby clan had left, no appeal was made to the coffee-house fraternal for them to send 'elders' to ordain the new deacons. It was seen as a matter for the local church and no one else.

Contemporary accounts say that the Goat Yard chapel was a spacious building, usually quite full during meetings. It had a large courtyard in front with an alley of lime trees leading up to the main entrance. Ivimey says that though the chapel was only built of wood it could house almost a thousand people. Estimates of membership during Gill's fifty-one years as pastor vary greatly from between 150 and 1,000 members, the figures at both ends of the scale obviously needing qualification. The most conservative estimate was that of John Ryland Senior who recorded that 150 members were at Goat Yard in 1753. This is the number most critics give to show that Gill attracted but few hearers in comparison to Keach and Stinton. They do not note that when Gill was called to Goat Yard, the sum total of those both for and against him did not amount to more than 150 church-going members, as the records show. There were 210 actual members but some 60 did not attend regularly and church discipline had been slack. Even when Atkins drummed up as many dissident members as he could, only

160 attended. Ivimey, otherwise always wary of attributing too much evangelistic fervour to Gill, feels Ryland's figures are too low. What Gill's critics do not point out is that Ryland also states that Gill's church had the largest membership in London in 1753, at a time when there was supposed to be an average of a mere 50 members per church even in the other larger London Baptist churches![28] Ivimey suggests that Ryland's numbers must be increased by a third to obtain a more accurate estimate of membership and then increased by two-thirds to find out how many hearers attended the churches. This would mean that Goat Yard had a regular attendance of some 330 hearers at a time when the churches were at a comparatively low ebb. Ivimey, however, gives no reasons for his criteria. For at least twelve weeks every year, the numbers of young people in the congregation must have increased radically as the Horselydown charity school marched its pupils off to the church services. The collections on these days went towards the upkeep of the school. This practice was continued by Dr Rippon until well into the next century. Pamela Russel, after carefully studying the statistics available, states that in 1746 the Southwark Particular Baptist churches had an individual membership which ran into a plurality of hundreds with the majority of members being women.[29] It thus may well be that Ryland listed male members only. An entry in Gill's church book for 30 September 1757 which lists the members 'at their Removal from Horselydown to Carter Lane' shows no less than 235 names. An earlier list in the records gives 400 names but a number of these had died before other names were added. Another possible interpretation of the number 150 that reoccurs time and time again in references to Gill's congregation is that it refers to hearers only, a separate group who were not formal members. The Carter Lane minutes distinguish between members and hearers who were present at meetings. So when Seymour, for instance, mentions critically, without quoting sources, that Gill had only 150 hearers at the end of his life, this need not be interpreted as negatively as Seymour sees things.[30]

Shortly before Gill died, a number of young hearers started attending other churches. When Gill passed away, there was something of an exodus from the church. A number of members joined neighbouring churches and when it was rumoured that Rippon was to take over the church officially, a further thirty-five to forty members separated to form a church of their own. When Rippon counted the members left on 10 January 1774, the date of his ordination, there were no less than ninety. This means that, at a very conservative estimate, Carter Lane at Gill's death probably had a membership of 150-200 which was still relatively large in comparison with other Particular Baptist churches. If 150 hearers still attended the meetings besides members, there is little room for criticism. Gill's successor Rippon says, 'Mr Gill's "preaching had been very acceptable from the beginning", and his "auditory became so numerous, that the place of worship, though a large one, could hardly contain them". And now being settled, "his people were very zealous in manifesting their affections towards him, and, to the utmost of their abilities, raised him a suitable maintenance".'[31]

Several other churches had fellowship at times with Gill's congregation at Horselydown. This was partly due to Goat Yard having joint oversight and ownership of a large registered baptistery[32] with a chapel attached at nearby Fair Street. This was used by a number of churches who had no such facilities themselves.[33] Gill also helped to organize joint monthly services between the churches, a practice which was carried out for many years. He was in particular demand at Cripplegate and that church did their best in 1728 to persuade Gill to become their joint pastor with Goat Yard. Though Ivimey rarely lists Gill and the Goat Yard church in his index, one comes across many references to them in his volumes, showing that there was a lively inter-church fellowship practised at the time.

Way up on Gill's list of priorities for establishing himself as pastor and putting the church in his charge on a sound basis was the need for a confession of faith anchored in the Scriptures. Gill knew it was little use his preaching sound doctrine when his hearers had no standards by which they could test the validity of his message. Such a standard was all the more necessary as the Baptist churches, on the whole, were scorning creeds, convinced that they restricted renewal in the churches; besides, they did not believe in having laws like the Medes and the Persians.[34] One of the major voices against 'explicit' creeds was Thomas Crosby who, in his history of the Baptists, had striven to tone down the difference between the General and Particular Baptists. Ivimey, a Particular Baptist himself, rebukes Crosby for not including the signatures of the persons responsible for the Orthodox Creed of 1679 so as to make it impossible to know if the creed was occasioned by Arminians or Calvinists. Of this omission Ivimey says, 'This is one of many instances of his attempting to amalgamate all the Baptists into one denomination, and therefore he has endeavoured to prevent the General and the Particular Baptists from being distinguished.'[35] Ivimey himself, however, adds to the confusion here. The Orthodox Creed has been widely seen as a General Baptist creed intended to make it easier for Calvinists to join the Arminian churches.[36] Ivimey, however, finds that, 'This Creed is what is termed Calvinism, and all its parts are supported by a great variety of scriptural references.' It is significant to note that Ivimey does not dwell on the articles on predestination and reprobation which truly go a long way to appease the Calvinists but he finds the points of agreement highlighted in the article on baptism which was never a real stone of stumbling between Arminian and Calvinist Baptists.[37]

As yet, the 'renewal' which confessions of faith were supposed to hinder had resulted in the Baptist brethren being ill-taught in matters of doctrine and many creedless churches were going the way of all flesh and denying Christ's divinity and man's total fall. For fifty years Gill's confession of faith put an end to the downgrading in doctrine going on in his own church and served as a standard for churches throughout the country until his death in 1771 and long after. A creed which was so successful in stemming the tide of heresy and rallying the faithful is worthy of a detailed study.

5.

The Goat Yard Declaration of Faith

Earlier creeds had been drawn up by the Baptists as a defence mechanism against accusations levelled at them by non-Baptists. This was especially true of John Smyth's confession of 1611, which earned for him the title of 'Father of the General Baptists', but also very much true of the 1646 Particular Baptist confession whose full name was *A Confession of Faith of seven congregations, or Churches of Christ in London, which are commonly, but unjustly called, Anabaptists; published for the vindication of the truth, and information of the ignorant, likewise for the taking off those aspersions, which are frequently, both in pulpit and in print, unjustly cast upon them.* This would explain why their language is highly polemic and dialectic and, especially in the case of Smyth's confession, highly rationalistic.

Coupled with this apologetic function of creeds,[1] declarations of faith were used to facilitate unity with other churches. It is thus no accident that the 1677-1688 Particular Baptist creed which bears the signature of denominational pioneers such as Knollys, Kiffin and Keach resemble the Westminster Confession fairly closely. Though Keach's confessions were, on the face of things, Calvinistic, there were, however, statements in them that could be interpreted by Arminians as overtures to them. Indeed this had obviously been Keach's intention in the creed he drew up for the Goat Yard church in 1697. Such a unifying intention was also true of the 1678 General Baptist confession mentioned above which was published as *An Orthodox Creed; or a protestant confession of faith; being an essay to unite and confirm all true protestants, in the fundamental articles of the Christian Religion against the errors and heresies of the church of Rome.* This was nothing but an attempt to define basic doctrines which all denominations could agree to, leaving good will and tolerance to take care of the rest. It stands to reason that Gill, who was no Presbyterian and the last man in

England to favour Arminianism, could no longer tolerate such declarations of faith which were mere compromises at best. One of the Goat Yard's main interests in their new confession of faith was to guard themselves against wrong views concerning election and the meaning of regeneration.

Another reason why the older creeds needed urgent revision were the anachronistic political views they reflected, including statements implying that governmental powers were persecuting bodies.[2] Gill's church, however, existed at a time of peace when it would have been most inappropriate to open the old political wounds of the past. This is why, when it was broadcast that Crosby was about to publish a history of the Baptists, many Baptists begged him not to do so as this would rekindle old political strifes and perhaps give people who lived in peace with the Baptists fresh cause to disagree with them.

One of the most pressing reasons why a new confession was advisable was the fact that Gill had been called to the pastorate of Goat Yard in 1719, the year of the Salters' Hall[3] Trinitarian controversy. A large number of Baptist ministers, including Dr John Gale (1680-1722) whom Ivimey says was the most zealous non-subscriber, preferred to withhold their signatures from the pro-Trinitarian declaration drawn up at the Salters' Hall conference. Some of them argued that they believed that Christ was truly God but did not believe in subscribing to creeds worded in non-biblical languages. They also protested that they had never been guilty of Arianism[4] so they had no need to prove their orthodoxy where this had not been challenged. Gale's views were too well known for him to hide under the mantle of orthodoxy and he and a number of other Baptist leaders were unusually shy of being put into a doctrinal corner, protesting that in a true church 'mutual forbearance and brotherly love' should be the key factors.

Gale, pastor of Paul's Alley, Barbican, had earned his doctorate at Leyden University whilst only nineteen years of age and was considered by many Baptists as *the* theologian of the movement, chiefly because of his writings on baptism. According to the Baptist historian Whitley, Paul's Alley was 'the most learned, the wealthiest, the most progressive of the London Particular Baptist Churches'.[5] This statement, though true concerning its wealth, is highly misleading concerning the title 'Particular' as Gale's church was certainly not Calvinistic in any sense of the word. In 1695 a remnant of the General Baptists of Turner Hall had amalgamated with Paul's Alley, and by Gill's day the Arminian-Arian views of the General Baptists prevailed in that church until it was disbanded in 1768 after Gale, Burroughs and Foster had 'served' it as pastors. Historians always stress that Gale was the leader of the 'advanced party' amongst the Baptists, 'advanced' being obviously a euphemism for 'highly liberal'. Ivimey paints a positive picture of Gale with reference to his works on baptism but finds him otherwise 'anti-evangelical'. Such a title is rather a misnomer as Gale, besides rejecting the doctrine of the Trinity, rejected almost all Reformed doctrines including justification by faith. Soon Gale, like his co-pastor Burroughs and successor Foster, became an out and out Socinian[6] who preached mere rational and humanistic moralism.

Strangely enough, it is the custom of evangelical Baptist scholars and historians to speak favourably of Gale's views on baptism though they reject his other doctrines. This is an extremely risky business indeed as Gale's view of baptism is an integrated feature of his entire theology. One cannot be sound on baptism if one is unsound on justification, salvation and the doctrine of the church. As Christian baptism is in the name of the Trinity, the baptism of an Arian can hardly be called Christian, nor can it truly be called biblical. The Socinian doctrine of baptism is even more radical as Socinians deny altogether that baptism is a seal of faith and look upon it as a mere symbolic turning away from Jewry or paganism by first generation Christians who are not obliged to baptize their offspring be they infants or believers. It was thus absolutely necessary that a new leader should come and put the Baptist churches back on a sure theological foundation.

This necessity, however, is not seen by many a Baptist who believes that a set standard of doctrine does away with the liberty that is so much a part of the Baptist churches. Baptists, they believe, must remain non-creedal as an adherence to any formative creed would distract the believer from following the Word of God as his only standard and authority for right belief. Creeds can therefore never have a permanent usage but are, at best, creations of the moment to meet particular and temporary needs. This very Baptist argument is explained by William Lumpkin in his *Baptist Confession of Faith*, where he says, 'Periods of controversy and crisis have been most productive of Baptist confessions, which have appeared in each century since the sixteenth, though in greatest numbers in the seventeenth. Therefore Baptists have freely made, used, and discarded confessions of faith, which have appeared in the name of individuals, of single churches, and of groups of churches or denominations. For them confessions have ever been simple manifestos of prevailing doctrine in particular groups. No confession has ever permanently bound individuals, churches, associations, conventions, or unions among Baptists. Even when issued, the confessions have allowed for individual interpretation and perspective, so that each signatory was made to feel that the statements spoke of him.'[7] This view is echoed by J. J. Goadby in his *Bye-Paths of Baptist History*. He quotes a messenger of a member church who drew up the General Baptists' Orthodox Creed as saying, 'They were men who composed it; and men may err. They expounded as well as they could, and imposed upon nobody, but left others to judge for themselves, and to receive their well-meant interpretations, if they could understand them, if not, to let them alone.'

Goadby adds, 'In other words, they were, like the other Confessions, expositions of sentiments, not articles of belief, and expositions that were accepted or refused as men might individually determine.' Baptist creeds, according to this view, are for the moment only and binding to no one.[8]

On realizing that Gill's declaration of faith was meant to be taken seriously and permanently as a testimony of belief, it is thus hardly surprising that many Baptists viewed, and still view, Gill's action as being highly 'un-Baptist' and an unnecessary reform. It is argued that the pastor's deed was a rigid break with the past and a break with the faith and practice of his Baptist fathers. They also point out that the churches were only too eager either to get back to the old usage of creeds after Gill's death or take on more liberal ones or do away with creeds completely.[9] Those that argue in this way accuse Gill of thrusting his own authoritative, un-Baptist ideas on his church, implying that the church was unwilling to take on his more definite and positive and less apologetic declaration of faith. Against such an accusation it is sufficient to point out that Gill's breaking with doctrinal traditions, or rather the lack of them, can only be seen as a positive move on his part. If churches under his influence turned away from that influence after his death, it in no way speaks for those churches and shows how much those sheep still needed a good shepherd of Gill's calibre. Furthermore, Gill's policy with his church was never to bully them into adopting any measure as his relationship with his flock had shown up to 1729 when the creed was entered into the church book. Interestingly enough, Lumpkin never bothered to list Gill's confession in his collection at all and seems not to know of its existence. He claims that the eighteenth century produced no notable Baptist confessions and mentions that Gill's church used a local confession in 1764, not realizing that they had been doing so since 1729.

It is obvious that Gill's modern accusers use the argument that confessions of faith are 'un-Baptist' as a camouflage for the fact that they cannot accept his Calvinistic doctrine. Particularly Gill's teaching concerning fallen man's state and Christ's imputed righteousness is a stone of stumbling for them. Their conviction that Gill's reforming views failed to be of lasting service to the churches is also highly exaggerated and backed by dubious evidence.[10] John Rippon (1750-1836), Gill's successor, was still using Gill's declaration of faith in his church well into the nineteenth century.[11] Writing in 1800, Rippon records that new members were only accepted into fellowship on giving their full assent to the 1729 declaration. S. F. Paul tells of the forming of a new church in 1842 which professed its 'unflinching adherence' to Gill's declaration of faith.[12] Many Baptists, Anglicans and Presbyterians still read Gill with joy and edification as witnessed by the fact that his works are still kept in print by several publishing houses. Furthermore, the Particular Baptist confessions of the mid-nineteenth century show a remarkable similarity to the Horselydown declaration, indicating the lasting nature of Gill's influence. Gospel Standard Baptists attribute much of their doctrine to the teaching of John Gill and a good number of their articles of faith are almost verbatim reproductions of Gill's articles.[13] The Gospel Standard brethren have kept to the standards of their confession throughout many generations and so put to flight the idea that a creed can only be a declaration of a fleeting, passing faith.

Against modern criticism of Gill's supposed high-handedness in drawing up the Goat Yard confession, it is sufficient to say that the congregation called Gill to pastor them, thus indicating that they were prepared to accept his leadership. The church book also states categorically that the new confession was the will of the members as witnessed by an entry written seven weeks before Gill drew up the declaration stating: 'yt (that) a Declaration of ye faith & practice of the Church be drawn up by Bro. Gill to be read & assented to by members at their admission, instead of yt which was formerly called ye Church Covenant.'

Moreover Dr Rippon affirmed that the church was 'cordially one' with their pastor in this venture. Rippon stresses that Gill's declaration is a positive testimony of how he, right from the start of his ministry, united *faith* with *practice*. This statement by Rippon is of great importance in the face of modern criticism that Gill's theology taught passive rather than active faith. Rippon adds in his presentation of the declaration, 'Few are the formulas which have at any time been more closely united with duty. The term and the thing are remarkable, in this confession — and no man was more fond of either in their proper place, and fairly understood.'

These 'formulas' were entered in Gill's hand in the church book under the title 'A Declaration of the Faith and Practice of the Church of Christ at Horsely-down, under the Pastoral Care of Mr. John Gill, &c.' The preamble states: 'Having been enabled, through divine grace, to give up ourselves to the Lord, and likewise to one another by the will of God; we account it a duty incumbent upon us to make a declaration of our faith and practice, to the honour of Christ, and the glory of his name; knowing, that as with the heart man believeth unto righteousness, so with the mouth confession is made unto salvation.'

Here the church affirms strongly that their creed is first and foremost a testimony of what they believe and what they feel obliged to convey to others in their everyday witness. It was thus not merely a 'statement of faith' but a course of Christian action, outlining what the church's ministry was to the outside world. Former creeds had spoken much of 'faith and order'. Gill's church spoke of 'faith and practice' or 'faith and works'.

Article I
The first article concerning the 'incumbent duties' of this church was: 'We believe that the Scriptures of the Old and New Testament are the word of God, and the only rule of faith and practice.'

This was, historically speaking, a very necessary statement for the Horselydown church to make. One of the main reasons why the Baptists had formed churches of their own was their distrust of the emphasis the Anglican Church placed on certain traditions which they felt were to the detriment of a *sola scriptura* faith. Most Baptist creeds therefore emphasized a trust in the Word of God alone, but their aim to keep Scripture free of 'new revelations of the Spirit or traditions of men' (1689) was not always met with the same efficiency. Because of the particular situation to which the declaration addressed itself, doctrines were at times omitted which definitely belonged to a Christian's statement of faith. Because of prevalent unorthodoxy, statements sometimes crept in which were not in keeping with a belief in *sola scriptura*. The Particular Baptists made a constant effort to keep their creeds within the scope of Scripture as is seen by their altering Chapter XXXIII of the 1644 declaration. Here their view of the church had been far too narrow and local and their view of being baptized into the faith open to too many interpretations. These doctrines are put on a more firm basis in the 1677 declaration.[14] A similar case is the 1644 statement in Chapter XXV disdaining the preaching of the terrors of the law as part of the work of the gospel, which could be interpreted as Neonomian. The correction in the 1677 declaration is on a sound Reformed, scriptural footing and must have greatly agitated Andrew Fuller and the so-called moderate Calvinists who have a different view of the Covenant of Works and the work of the law.[15] Such corrective work is plainly missing from the General Baptist creeds. *A Short Confession, or a Brief Narrative of Faith* of 1691 with its insistence in Chapter xxi. 5 that 'We believe, that God hath not decreed the reprobation of any infant, dying before the commission of actual sin' is in stark contrast to the scriptural 'all have sinned' and the 1677-89 Particular Baptist declaration which acknowledges all born of Adam to be sinners and only elect children dying in their infancy will be saved.[16] When Thomas Grantham and Joseph Wright presented their General Baptist *Standard Confession* to Charles II in 1660, Article 10 stated:

> That all children dying in infancy, having not actually transgressed against the law of God in their own persons, are only subject to the first death, which comes upon them by the sin of Adam, and not that any one of them dying in that state shall suffer for Adam's sin eternal punishment in Hell (which is the second death), for to such belongs the kingdom of heaven (1 Cor. xv. 22; Matt. xix. 14); not daring to conclude with that uncharitable opinion of others, who, though they plead much for the bringing of children into the visible Church here on earth by baptism, yet nevertheless by their doctrine, that Christ died but for some, shut a greater part of them out of the kingdom for ever.[17]

Here the General Baptists are striving to kill two birds with one stone: those who believe in particular atonement, including their fellow Baptists of the 'Particular' kind; and those Calvinists amongst Anglicans, Presbyterians, Congregationalist, and Dissenters in general who believe in the role of baptism within covenant families. One can imagine how the playboy king, who had Rome as his first choice, Anglicanism as his second choice and the Dissenters as no choice at all, would have been impressed by this infighting amongst those who maintained they represented true churches in opposition to Charles' favourites!

Eighteen years later Chapter XLIV of the General Baptist Orthodox Creed of 1678 still quoted Matthew 19:13 as 'proof' that children dying in infancy are 'members of the invisible church'. This is strange exegesis indeed as the children mentioned in that particular verse were very much alive! This interpretation must have surprised Anglicans and Independents as they were constantly being criticized by Baptists for using the verse as a grounds for baptism. Obviously if Matthew 19 viewed children as members of the church, then nothing could stop them being baptized! Gill argued in his various works on baptism that Matthew 19 referred to those believers who were childlike at heart, not to children as such.

A *sola scriptura* testimony was also essential because of the contrary claims of the 'Ranters' and the French Prophets of whom both the General and Particular Baptists had their share, the latter still plaguing the churches. These were people who felt that they were so enwrapped in God that they identified themselves as God and put themselves over the Scriptures and over their pastors. These heretics were quickly bundled out of both groups of churches but their claim to have intimate revelations from God which discarded Scripture remained present in the faith of many an otherwise orthodox believer. One can see ranting tendencies in the 1611 General Baptist creed. The sixty-third and sixty-fourth articles leave one with the impression that the 'outward Scripture', i.e. the written Word, must take second place to the 'inner Word', i.e. Christ, which is 'better than all Scripture'. This would mean that those who believe Christ indwells them are above the Word of God.

One member of William Kiffin's church,[18] who repented of his ranting days, confessed that when the ranting fever came over him, his first thoughts were to disdain Scripture as being mere ink and paper and as they testified to Christ, he was driven to disbelief in Christ, too.

Finally, the Word of God as the final court of appeal needed to be emphasized as contemporary Grotians and Latitudinarians were enthusiastically preaching the *pia antiquitas* i.e. a trust in the decrees and traditions of the early church rather than Scripture, and the Quakers were spreading the teaching that the Word of God was completely subservient to the feeling of the Spirit within.[19]

Article II

After establishing the Word of God as the source of the congregation's doctrine, Gill went on to outline what was their first and foremost belief which he stated in the words: 'We believe that there is but one only living and true God; that there are three Persons in the Godhead, the Father, the Son, and the Holy Ghost, who are equal in nature, power, and glory; and that the Son and the Holy Ghost are as truly and as properly God as the Father.'

Here again we see evidence of a new broom sweeping. Gill's predecessor Stinton had been on very close terms with the renegade Baptist church at Paul's Alley, Barbican, whom he wished to see as members of the Particular Baptist Fund. This was obviously because of the wealth of the members there and Stinton was prepared to compromise on doctrine in order to raise funds. He thus protested that the fund should not be an 'Inquisition for the Tryal of mens principles in Religion'.[20] The fact that Crosby was also very sympathetic regarding anti-Trinitarians, and especially Gale, went back to the time of his close friendship with Stinton. The majority of the Particular Baptists, however, refused to have anything to do with the Barbican church because of their anti-Trinitarian stand and Stinton had to give up his plans for a mixed fund for doctrinally mixed churches.

This former affinity with heretics was ground enough for Goat Yard to make a clear statement of the Trinity as a testimony to its fellow churches and a sign that Gill was steering a straight biblical course. Such a clear signal was urgently needed in the Baptist churches as former confessions were often very confusing in their efforts to define the doctrine of the Trinity. The General Baptists' 1678 'Orthodox Creed' was highly metaphysical and was preserved in many forms of more or less modalistic nature as witnessed by Goadby's version in his book *Bye-Paths in Baptist History* which he presents as the official one. Here Article 3 is given as: 'In this Divine and Infinite Being, or unity of the Godhead, there are three persons, or subsistences, the Father, the Word or Son, or the Holy Spirit, of one subsistence, power, eternity, and will; each having the whole Divine essence, yet the essence undivided.'[21]

To say that the Trinity is three subsistences in one subsistence is hardly clarifying the matter and to affirm that this subsistence is at times the Word *or* at times the Spirit, if not a misprint — as it surely must be — is sheer heresy. Even if Lumpkin is followed and the text reads 'three subsistences . . . of one substance' it hardly explains the full divinity of each person. In claiming that each subsistence has 'the whole Divine essence, yet the essence undivided', the Orthodox Creed was merely echoing the Particular Baptist Confession of 1677. Here the confession lacks the clarity and, indeed, simplicity of the Goat Yard declaration. Such wording could be misunderstood as paving the way for a modal teaching concerning the Trinity[22] and it is hardly surprising that the main heresies which sprang up amongst the Baptists of this period were to do with an insufficient understanding of the Godhead. Many did indeed come to view the Father, Son and Holy Spirit as three manifestations or modes of appearance of one God. Several Baptist churches came to deny the eternal Sonship of Christ and others affirmed that Christ was eternally human and thus did not take on himself 'the form of a servant' at the Incarnation. Thomas Crosby was one Particular Baptist who was more than shaky on his doctrine of the Trinity and his lengthy defence of Matthew Caffyn, who virtually led the General Baptists into Unitarianism in his *History of the English Baptists,*[23] did untold damage in the churches of his denomination. Gill effectively combated these heresies during his fifty years of strong influence amongst the Baptist churches.

The previous Baptist confessions, in an effort to guard against numerous misinterpretations of the Trinity, had not made the doctrine any easier to understand and had departed from the simple definitions of the early church. Tertullian at the beginning of the third century had argued that God was one 'substance' but three 'Persons'. The Goat Yard confession was a very successful attempt to return to the simplicity of Tertullian's wording which was more in keeping with Scripture than that of the older creeds.[24] Gill's creed is also nearer the Westminster Confession's description of the Trinity and Article I of the Church of England than former creeds in his denomination. The Church of England article had been drawn up to protect the Church from Anabaptist, Arian and Socinian teaching and here Goat Yard were proclaiming that they, too, abhorred such heresies. It is worthy of note that when the Dissenters drew up the pro-Trinitarian document to be signed by subscribers at Salters' Hall in 1719, they chose Article I of the Church of England as their doctrinal basis.

The case of Matthew Caffyn shows how great was the need for a clearer statement of faith regarding the Trinity. He had been declared to be 'the battle-axe and weapon of war' of the General Baptists because of his wit and learning and skill in debate. It was his popularity that caused his liberalism to be adopted throughout the movement and the majority of the General Assembly ministers became anti-Trinitarian and finally Unitarian. It is interesting to note that both sides in the Caffyn controversy argued that there was no scriptural warrant for making creeds which could be used to test orthodoxy. It is thus no wonder that the Baptist historian Carlile comments: 'While attention was centred in doubtful disputations the light of true godliness burned dim.' When Dan Taylor was asked to give the reason for the decline in the General Baptist churches, he is quoted as saying, 'They degraded Jesus Christ and he degraded them.'[25] This could also be said of a relatively small number of Particular Baptists, particularly

Dr Sayer Rudd, and his brother John. The Baptist historian Underwood, following Ivimey, chides Crosby, for instance, because he failed completely to distinguish between General and Particular Baptists.[26]

As anti-Trinitarian heresies came and went in rapid succession during the eighteenth century, Article II was amended from time to time to keep up its usefulness in correcting wrong doctrine. The minutes of a church meeting at Gill's chapel held on 24 July 1768 show that a heresy was spreading which touched the very heart of Christian faith. A member named Isaac Harman who had been in fellowship since May 1757 had declared that 'He had long been at Enmity with the doctrine of the Eternal Sonship of Christ by the Generation of the Father.' As a result of the subsequent unrest caused by this teaching in the church, Gill had the following words added to the article on the Trinity:

> These three divine persons are distinguished from each other by particular relative properties: The distinguishing character and relative property of the first person, is *begetting*; he has begotten a Son of the same nature with him, and who is the express image of his person; and is therefore with great propriety called the *Father*: The distinguishing character and relative property of the second person is that he is begotten; and he is called the only begotten of the Father, and his own proper Son; not a Son by creation as angels and men are nor by adoption as saints are, nor by office as civil magistrates are, but by nature, by the Father's eternal generation of him in the divine nature; and therefore he is truly called *the Son*: The distinguishing character and relative properties of the third person is to be *breathed* by the Father and the Son, and to proceed from both, and is very properly called the *Spirit* or Breath of both: These three distinct divine persons, we profess to reverence, serve and worship as the one true God.[27]

Article III

Now Gill went on to tackle the much debated topic of election which was the supreme stumbling-block between the two main bodies of Baptists and which had caused these two groups to modify their beliefs to make unity possible. There was no sign whatsoever that Gill was prepared to tone down what he and his church believed was the full testimony of Scripture merely to suit the feelings of other religious bodies. Gill therefore wrote in the third Article:

> We believe that, before the world began, God did elect a certain number of men unto everlasting salvation, whom he did predestinate to the adoption of children by Jesus Christ, of his own free

grace, and according to the good pleasure of his will and that, in pursuance of this gracious design, he did contrive and make a covenant of grace and peace with his Son Jesus Christ, on the behalf of those persons, wherein a Saviour was appointed, and all spiritual blessings provided for them; as also that their persons, with all their grace and glory, were put into the hands of Christ, and made his care and charge.

Though Gill believed that God's saving grace also extended to elect children dying in infancy, he could not accept the Arminian Baptist view that infants were without sin and thus not in need of salvation. Critics of Gill have always maintained that they side with John Owen's Calvinistic doctrines which they allege were different to and milder than Gill's. Owen, however, was one with Gill in condemning the idea of a general election of infants due to their innocence. He looked on the doctrine as sheer Arminianism as it denied the universal effects of the Fall. In his *A Display of Arminianism*, Owen points out that though the Scriptures say 'By the offence of one judgement came upon all men to condemnation,' (Romans 5:18), Arminians such as Boræus affirm that 'Adam sinned in his own proper person only, and there is no reason why God should impute that sin unto infants.'[28] The next article to be recorded by Gill, quite in keeping with Owen, stressed that 'all Adam's posterity sinned in him'.

Article IV
Article IV of the Goat Yard declaration reads:

> We believe that God created the first man, Adam, after his own image, and in his likeness; an upright, holy, and innocent creature, capable of serving and glorifying him; but, he sinning, all his posterity sinned in him, and came short of the glory of God: the guilt of whose sin is imputed, and a corrupt nature derived, to all his offspring, descending from him by ordinary and natural generation: that they are by their first birth carnal and unclean, averse to all that is good, incapable of doing any, and prone to every sin; and are also by nature children of wrath, and under a sentence of condemnation, and so are subject not only to corporal death and involved in a moral one, commonly called spiritual, but are also liable to an eternal death, as considered in the first Adam, fallen and sinners; from all which there is no deliverance but by Christ, the second Adam.

Gill stressed clearly and definitely the full and total depravity of man. This depravity was physical, bringing corporal death with it. It was moral because man was now averse to all that was good. It had taken hold of the will as man now wished to do evil rather than good, but it also affected his entire mental, rational and spiritual capacities leaving him completely incapable of responding to God in any way. John Smyth had objected to the idea of original sin and argued that the Fall did not rob Adam of his 'natural power or faculty' and that salvation was merely a matter of willing.[29] Gill put the total depravity of man or a total Fall back on the theological map, denying that fallen man could attain to spiritual insight regarding his own state. This doctrine was attacked from time to time, for instance by Yorkshireman Alvery Jackson in 1751, but during Gill's lifetime few dared to challenge his biblical competence. It was not until after his death that Andrew Fuller took up and combined Smyth's and Jackson's views in his doctrine of man's natural capacity to exercise duty faith savingly.[30] The doctrine of sin as a mere Grotian volitional lapse, however, had no place in the Goat Yard declaration.[31] The words 'fallen and sinners' in the last sentence of Article IV were added in later years to this paragraph in view of the heresies in the 1730s concerning a limited Fall and a denial of original sin.

Article V
The fifth article in the Goat Yard declaration deals more specifically with the person of Christ in the Trinity and is a further guard against the modal theory. It was drawn up with a particular view to Sabellianism,[32] which was making large inroads into the Baptist churches at this time, and, together with Socinianism, eventually providing a breeding ground for what has become known as 'the Sonship controversy'.[33] Gill fought against this heresy throughout his Christian life and one of his very last publications was his *Dissertation concerning the Eternal Sonship of Christ* which he penned in 1768. The controversy waned but rose again some seventy years later when it was contended successfully by J. C. Philpot who leaned very much on Gill's works for guidance. Now, in 1729, putting the axe to the root of all faulty teaching on the person of Christ the Goat Yard congregation maintained:

> We believe that the Lord Jesus Christ, being set up from everlasting as the Mediator of the new covenant, and he, having engaged to be the surety of his people, did, in the fullness of time, really assume human nature, and not before, neither in whole nor in part; his human soul, being a creature, existed not from eternity, but was created and formed in his body by him that forms the spirit of man within him, when that was conceived in the womb of the virgin; and so his human nature consists of a true body and a reasonable soul; both which, together, and at once, the Son of God assumed into union with his divine Person, when made of woman, and not before;

in which nature he really suffered and died as their substitute, in their room and stead, whereby he made all that satisfaction for their sins, which the law and justice of God could require, as well as made way for all those blessings, which are needful for them both for time and eternity.

This article was altered from time to time during Gill's pastorate so that it continually reflected the testimony of the church to the various heresies as they arose. For instance the words following 'did in the fullness of time really assume human nature' and before 'which nature he really suffered and died', etc. were added in 1768 when the Sonship controversy was invading Gill's church.

At times, not only was Christ's position in the Trinity challenged but some believers went to the other extreme and affirmed that Christ's human nature was eternally part of the triune nature, i.e. part of God's nature even before the Incarnation. Again, after Gill's death, these heresies became so prevalent that even the Particular Baptists, who were far more careful about doctrinal matters than many other churches, were split in two because of the ensuing debates.[34]

Article VI

Article VI of the declaration was a broadside against the doctrine of universal redemption as proclaimed by Arminians of all kinds. Writing on behalf of his church, Gill states: 'We believe that that eternal redemption which Christ has obtained, by the shedding of his blood, is special and particular, that is to say, that it was only intentionally designed for the elect of God, and sheep of Christ, who only share the special and peculiar blessings of it.'

This paragraph was of vital importance to the Horselydown church as it provided them with sound biblical teaching for future use both against the Arminianism of Wesley and the 'Modern Question' interpretations of Alvery Jackson[35] and Andrew Fuller who taught an unlimited atonement from within the Particular Baptist churches and, in effect, sought for a compromise between Calvinists and Arminians. It also served as a bulwark against the teaching of Robert Hall who is attributed with taking Fullerism to its logical conclusion. Hall, who professed to be an evangelical Calvinist, is recorded as saying affirmingly, 'I consider the fact that "Christ died for all men" as the only basis that can support the universal offer of the Gospel.'[36] Hall was a master at arguing backwards, maintaining that as saving grace should be offered to all, Christ must logically have died to save all. As Scripture and experience teach that there are sheep and goats amongst fallen man and the sheep alone represent the scope of the atonement, Hall's statement is at best misleading. Gill, supported by his church, denied completely that such teaching had anything to do with the gospel of the Lord Jesus Christ. It is no wonder that Hall thought that Gill's works were 'a continent of mud',[37] probably wishing to correct John Ryland's remark that they were 'an ocean of Divinity'.[38]

The truths embodied in Article VI have been dropped by many a Particular or Strict Baptist today. Peter Naylor, for instance, coming from a Calvinist background, nevertheless complains that 'one of the most puzzling features of Gill's idea of faith' is that he 'denied emphatically that Christ intended seriously to save some who, in event, were not saved'.[39] Fuller, who insisted all his life that he was a Calvinist and a 'strict' one at that, taught, contrary to Calvin, that Christ died for all men irrespective of any covenantal standing with them, and referred to Owen, as Naylor points out, for confirmation of his views. Owen, however, would have been the last person to have backed up such a notion and his words on the subject must be quoted in full here to show that John Gill's church stood fully in line with him and the interpretation of the gospel which has come to be known as Calvinism. As it is Gill's adherence to the doctrine of limited atonement which is the main reason why he is called a Hyper-Calvinist today, Owen's remarks on the subject are of special importance. In his *A Display of Arminianism* he argues:

> First, The death of Christ is in divers places of the Scripture restrained to his 'people', and 'elect', his 'church', and 'sheep', Matt. i. 21; John x. 11-13; Acts xx. 28; Eph. v. 25 ; John xi. 51,52; Rom. viii 32, 34; Heb. ii. 9, 14; Rev. v. 9; Dan. ix. 26; — and therefore the good purchased thereby ought not to be extended to 'dogs', 'reprobates', and 'those that are without'.
>
> Secondly, For whom Christ died, he died as their sponsor, in their room and turn, that he might free them from the guilt and desert of death; which is clearly expressed Rom. v. 6-8 'He was wounded for our transgressions, he was bruised for our iniquities: the chastisement of our peace was upon him; and with his stripes we are healed,' Isa. liii 5, 6, etc. 'He hath redeemed us from the curse of the law being made a curse for us,' Gal. iii 13. 'He hath made him to be sin for us, who knew no sin,' 2 Cor. v. 21. Evidently he changeth turns with us, 'that we might be made the righteousness of God in him'. Yea, in other things, it is plain in the Scripture that to die for another is to take his place and room, with an intention that he should live, 2 Sam. xviii. 33; Rom. v. So that Christ dying for men made satisfaction for their sins, that they should not die. Now, for what sins he made satisfaction, for them the justice of God is satisfied; which surely is not done for the sins of the reprobates,

because he justly punisheth them to eternity upon themselves, Matt. v. 26.

Thirdly, For whom Christ 'died', for them also he 'rose again', to make intercession for them: for whose 'offences he was delivered', for their 'justification he was raised', Rom. iv. 25, v. 10. He is a high priest 'to make intercession for them' in the holy of holies for whom 'by his own blood he obtained eternal redemption', Heb. ix. 11,12. These two acts of his priesthood are not to be separated; it belongs to the same mediator for sin to sacrifice and pray. Our assurance that he is our advocate is grounded on his being a propitiation for our sins. He is an 'advocate' for every one for whose sins his blood was a 'propitiation', 1 John ii. 1, 2. But Christ doth not intercede and pray for all, as himself often witnesseth, John xvii.; he 'maketh intercession' only for them who 'come unto God by him', Heb. vii 25. He is not a mediator of them that perish, no more than an advocate of them that fail in their suits; and therefore the benefit of his death also must be restrained to them who are finally partakers of both. We must not so disjoin the offices of Christ's mediatorship, that one of them may be versated about some towards whom he exerciseth not the other; much less ought we so to separate the several acts of the same office. For whom Christ is a priest, to offer himself a sacrifice for their sins, he is surely a king, to apply the good things purchased by his death unto them, as Arminius himself confesseth; much more to whom he is a priest by sacrifice, he will be a priest by intercession. And, therefore, seeing he doth not intercede and pray for every one, he did not die for every one.

Fourthly, For whom Christ died he merited grace and glory, faith and salvation, and reconciliation with God; as I shall show hereafter. But this he hath not done for all and every one. Many do never believe; the wrath of God remaineth upon some; the wrath of God abideth on them that do not believe, John iii. 36. To abide argueth a continued, uninterrupted act. Now, to be reconciled to one, and yet to lie under his heavy anger, seem to me ασυστατα — things that will scarce consist together. The reasons are many; I only point at the heads of some of them.

Fifthly, Christ died for them whom God gave unto him to be saved: 'Thine they were, and thou gavest them me,' John xvii. 6. He layeth down his life for the sheep committed to his charge, chap. x. 11. But all are not the sheep of Christ, all are not given unto him of God to be brought to glory; for of those that are so given there is not one that perisheth, for 'he giveth eternal life to as many as God hath given him', chap. xvii 2. 'No man is able to pluck them out of his Father's hand,' chap. x. 28, 29.

Sixthly, Look whom, and how many, that love of God embraced that was the cause of sending his Son to redeem them; for them, and so many, did Christ, according to the counsel of his Father, and in himself, intentionally lay down his life. Now, this love is not universal, being his 'good pleasure' of blessing with spiritual blessings and saving some in Christ, Eph. i. 4, 5; which good pleasure of his evidently comprehendeth some, when others are excluded, Matt. xi 25, 26. Yea, the love of God in giving Christ for us is of the same extent with that grace whereby he calleth us to faith, or bestoweth faith on us: for 'he hath called us with an holy calling, according to his own purpose and grace, which was given us in Christ Jesus,' 2 Tim. i :9; which, doubtless, is not universal and common unto all.[40]

This rather long quote ought to show clearly that Gill was in no way more or less of a Calvinist because he taught that Christ did indeed save those whom he intended to save.

Article VII
Article VII reflected a doctrine which was to become the central teaching of the Evangelical Awakening and was fundamental to the preaching of Gill, Hervey, Toplady and Whitefield. Gill, however, had been preaching this doctrine some fifteen years before it was taken up by Hervey and Whitefield. This makes Gill one of the very first pioneers of the Great Awakening in Britain and America.[41] The article reads: 'We believe that the justification of God's elect is only by the righteousness of Christ imputed to them, without the consideration of any works of righteousness done by them; and that the full and free pardon of all their sins and transgressions, past, present, and to come, is only through the blood of Christ, according to the riches of his grace.'

Gill and Hervey were to come under heavy fire from John Wesley who could not accept the term 'the imputed righteousness of Christ' as being biblical, arguing with Arminius that Abraham was saved by his own righteous act in believing and that this faith had no reference to Christ's righteousness.[42] Soon after Gill's death, this doctrine was modified greatly by Andrew Fuller who took a middle position between that of Gill and the Anglican Calvinists on the one hand, and the Wesleyans on the other. He did not go as far as Gill in believing that a literal imputation of both our sins to Christ and Christ's righteousness was man's only claim of acceptance before God. Nor did he deny outright, as Wesley, that the concept was un-biblical. Instead he claimed that the imputed righteousness of Christ should be regarded as a metaphor referring to the moral influence Christ had on the believer. In arguing this way, Fuller joined Wesley in leaving the question 'How can a man be found righteous before God?' open and unanswered and, in so doing, left the mainstream of the revival champions. William Huntington, a contemporary of Fuller's, ably defended the crucial doctrine of Christ's imputed righteousness against both Wesley and Fuller and thus ensured that the true revival witness was carried on.

Article VIII

In Article VIII Gill stated: 'We believe that the work of regeneration, conversion, sanctification, and faith, is not an act of man's free will and power, but of the mighty, efficacious, and irresistible grace of God.' This statement is the biblical and logical conclusion of Article IV concerning the total depravity of man. If man is dead in trespasses and sins, if he cannot discern any spiritual thing, then any infusion of spiritual life in him must be the work of God. It was becoming popular in Gill's day to say that justification was an act of God but its efficacy regarding the believer's position before God was dependent on the believer's progressive sanctification through his obedience to the law. This would mean that justification and sanctification were relative to the deeds of man rather than outright gifts of God. Gill thus maintained that justification *and* sanctification were gifts of God which led the Christian to perform good works. A Christian can be known by his fruits. It is extremely hard to understand why this teaching caused Gill's critics to accuse him of Antinomianism especially as Gill constantly emphasized the need for his flock to live a life pleasing to God and full of good works — which, he maintained, was the very purpose of his declaration.

Article IX

The General Baptists openly maintained that a truly converted man could become truly lost. Article IX was designed to confront this heresy with the biblical norm. 'We believe that all those who are chosen by the Father, redeemed by the Son, and sanctified by the Spirit, shall certainly and finally persevere, so that not one of them shall ever perish, but shall have everlasting life.'

It was inevitable that when Wesley started to lead the Arminians in their anti-Calvinist campaign, he was to view Gill as one of the main contenders for traditional Calvinism. His writings against the perseverance of the saints and his pamphlet war with Gill on the subject will be dealt with in the chapter entitled 'Laying the axe to popery's roots'.

Article X

There was nothing didactically new in presenting Article X. Nor did it refer to any controversy in the Baptist churches of the time. Nevertheless, no creed is complete without a statement of the glorious outcome of Christ's atonement. Thus Gill can affirm, knowing that he has the full backing of the Word of God: 'We believe that there will be a resurrection of the dead, both of the just and unjust; and that Christ will come a second time to judge both quick and dead, when he will take vengeance on the wicked, and introduce his own people into his kingdom and glory, where they shall be for ever with him.'

Article XI
Article XI of the Goat Yard Declaration of Faith was another matter. It was a topic fraught with controversy both within and without the Baptist churches and Gill needed to tread cautiously in order to prevent a major row. On the subject of ordinances the declaration maintains: 'We believe that Baptism and the Lord's Supper are ordinances of Christ, to be continued until his second coming; and that the former is absolutely requisite to the latter; that is to say, that those only are to be admitted into the communion of the church, and to participate of all ordinances in it, who upon profession of their faith, have been baptized by immersion, in the name of the Father, and of the Son, and of the Holy Ghost.'

There is much of the old Baptist creeds in this statement, although it is free of much of the earlier sacramentalism of Gill's predecessors such as their talk of baptism being the gateway to the church or being baptized into the faith, and that baptism, accompanied by the laying on of hands, is a purveyor of the Holy Spirit or leads to a work of the Spirit. Throughout the history of the Baptists there have been debates on the modes and methods of baptism, its relevance to church membership and the worthiness — or otherwise — of partakers of the Lord's Supper. The waters which should unite those of 'one faith and baptism' have often divided the 'open' churches from the 'closed', i.e. those who are willing to join all believers in partaking of the Lord's Supper and those who hold that a certain mode of baptism must be performed before the recipient, no matter how evident his faith is, is invited to join the saints around the communion table. These inner- and inter-church debates have been a major cause in the perpetual splitting up of Baptist churches and, even today, much is written and debated over this topic. Baptist brethren can be fully united in all the five points of Calvinism and all the doctrines of the Bible, pray with one another and share glorious experiences of the presence of God with one another but still refuse to sit at the Lord's Table together. Such an approach is not restricted to Baptists but blights the wider fellowship of believers in membership with different denominations. This is shown by the life and witness of Rowland Hill, an Independent eighteenth-century minister. William Jay, pastor of a 'mixed' church, explains how Hill was invited to speak at an Association meeting at Bath. Instead of using the opportunity to edify the brethren from the Word of God, Hill started to rail against the Baptists, criticizing them ardently. This caused the pastor of the local Baptist church to stand up and walk out in protest. Once Hill was present when the Baptists broke bread and expected to be invited to join in but he was refused permission. 'It is our table,' explained the Baptist brethren, perhaps thinking of the above-mentioned blameworthy event. 'Oh,' said Hill, 'I thought it was the Lord's.'

All that can be said at this stage[43] is that Gill was a pioneer in ridding his church of false doctrine and bigotry and he was far more open concerning his non-Baptist evangelical brethren than many who went before him and came after him. He prepared the way for a clearer understanding of the relationship between faith and practice but many of his successors reverted to a ritualistic and sacramental view of baptism which can only be described as 'High Church'.[44]

One major difference in the Goat Yard article on baptism to former Baptist creeds was the total omission of directions concerning the laying on of hands. The thirty-second Article of the Orthodox Creed, for instance, added to its instruction on baptism the highly questionable advice, 'Prayer with the imposition of hands by the bishop or elder, on baptised believers, as such, for the reception of the holy promised Spirit of Christ, we believe is a principle of Christ's doctrine, and ought to be practised and submitted to by every baptised believer in order to receive the promised Spirit of the Father and Son.' Gill's predecessor Keach, though a Particular Baptist, held very closely to the sentiments of this General Baptist article. He first made his views public in 1675 in a book entitled *Darkness vanquished, being an answer to Danvers on laying on of hands* and two years later provided his church with a supplement to the 1689 confession to harmonize it with General Baptist ritualistic views on baptism. From then on, until Gill took over the pastorate,[45] it was demanded of candidates that they should submit themselves to the rite of laying on of hands at baptism. Those already baptized and seeking membership with the church were narrowly questioned as to whether they had been 'correctly baptized' or not. If no laying on of hands had taken place, either the candidates had to submit to this ceremony or they were refused membership.

Gill was the last to believe that the laying on of hands at baptism brought with it the Spirit whom a believer was supposed to possess before baptism. Rather than see an otherwise biblical practice abused in this way, he decided not to include it in the new confession.

Article XII

Article XII must come as a major surprise to anyone familiar with the older Baptist creeds, or the creeds of any denominations, for that matter. The article declares: 'We also believe that singing of psalms, hymns, and spiritual songs, vocally, is an ordinance of the Gospel to be performed by believers; but that as to time, place, and manner, every one ought to be left to their liberty in using it.'

One cannot imagine a modern church meeting deciding to put such a statement into their creed and this entry would appear to tone down the high quality of the declaration, ending it with a remark that is almost amusing in its bathos. The reasons for this statement will become clear when one considers the historical circumstances in church life at the end of the seventeenth and the beginning of the eighteenth centuries.[46]

Hymn singing was almost unknown in Baptist church services up to the end of the seventeenth century. The psalms were sung in metrical versions in the Anglican Church but most Dissenting churches had given up this practice in their efforts to rid themselves of all that was attached to Anglicanism. Baptist churches who continued the Anglican practice were looked upon by other 'purer' churches as if they had opened the doors to the devil and all his works. Anti-singing Baptists, who were taken by surprise in a meeting where psalms were sung, would immediately put their hats on to indicate that as this was not a display of true worship,[47] they need not doff their caps.

Psalms were sung by some churches to impress the authorities that they were not far removed from the 'established church'. This ruse sometimes took the oddest forms. During times of persecution, the Baptist preachers would preach behind a curtain, unseen by the congregation. Whenever the approach of government spies was feared, the congregation would start singing a metrical psalm and when the spies arrived they were met with nothing but a crowd of keen 'Anglicans' faithfully singing something out of the Prayer Book. All this tended to make singing in the Dissenting churches a mere sham or at best a thing not to be taken seriously.

One of the Baptist pioneers in the field of singing, if not *the* pioneer, was Benjamin Keach, the former pastor of the Goat Yard congregation. One day he startled his flock with the news that hymns or psalms were to be sung to enhance the worship at the Lord's Supper. Next, he tried introducing singing on public thanksgiving days. This caused so much opposition that Keach held his peace and did not urge his musical opinions openly on his church, though he obviously campaigned in the background for what his opponents called 'confused singing', that is, a mixture of words and artificial music. In 1690, a group of members at Horselydown decided they had had enough of Keach's 'musical madness' and they formed themselves behind Isaac Marlow, a craftsman member of the church, and looked to him to rid their church of their pastor's new-fangled idea. Marlow rose to the occasion and published a book which he called *Discourse Concerning Singing*, which was a discourse against singing. Not to be outdone, Keach retaliated with a book entitled *Breach Repaired in God's Worship; or Singing Psalms, Hymns, and Spiritual Songs, proved to be a holy ordinance of Jesus Christ.* Much of his argument would appear rather a weak defence of singing today, as it no doubt did to his church members, some of whom reacted violently against the publication. Keach started by arguing that the angels sung at creation and that the devil hates singing, and developed his argument by declaring that as God has given us a voice to sing it must be our unbounded duty to use that voice in singing his praises in collective worship. He capped his logic by saying that as singing was part of natural religion, it ought to be part of Christian religion too. Soon Keach's followers were even arguing that it was a 'public duty' to sing and if this public duty were not performed in church, there was something wrong with the one who thought he was practising 'sanctified silence'.

The Goat Yard church now entered a period of strife which was to last well over a decade in which Keach argued that 'singing in rhyme' was the 'public duty' of all Christians and Marlow argued just as energetically that the New Testament recognized no such duty. Marlow maintained in a work entitled *The Truth Soberly Defended* that singing was false worship and dangerous to the spiritual well-being of the church. He also argued that it was wrong for a mixed assembly of believers and unbelievers to sing of a salvation which they did not share. Marlow could not understand Keach, who had complained of Anglican 'vain repetitions' in worship, introducing such vanities into Baptist services, and moreover, to the tunes of worldly music. Liturgical prayers were bad enough but liturgical prayers set to music beat the band! The strife was so ferocious and widespread that several Particular Baptist pastors, long retired from scenes of controversy, joined in. Ninety-two-year-old Hansard Knollys (1599-1691) used his pen and voice to assist Keach in his praise of musical words and Marlow was duly dubbed by the songsters 'a person not fit to meddle in divine things, an "ignoramous" in the things of the Lord'. Marlow, however, received the backing of none other than William Kiffin (1616-1701), rightly called the Father of the Particular Baptists, who entered into the fray both orally and in writing to combat what he felt was a false form of worship. The General Baptists sounded the alarm against singing and Dr William Russell, famous for his part in the 1698-99 Portsmouth Debate, entered the contest by saying of Keach's attempt to make singing in rhyme a duty: 'This way of singing has a tendency to your ruin, having begun already to diminish your numbers, and for two congregations to unite into one, to keep up their reputation and supply that deficiency which singing in rhyme has made in their numbers. Nay, further, a great part of your members that remain are so dissatisfied, that, as soon as you begin to tune your pipes, they immediately depart like men affrighted.' Thomas Armitage, who records this quote, adds, 'Possibly with good reason, too.'[48]

The General Baptists, on the whole, kept aloof from the Particular Baptist novelty well into the next century. They saw what was clearly going on in the churches of their Particular brethren. Numbers were diminishing so singing was introduced to liven up the worship and attract a different spiritual clientele. These came in numbers, mostly from other churches, but when they arrived, they frightened off many of the more 'concervative' members in their new congregation. Here a lesson could be learnt by modern churches who are going through the same process. The trouble Keach was having with his old and new members did not, however, cause him to reconsider his views on singing.

On the contrary, to prove his point concerning the utter necessity of singing, Keach introduced what he called 'the ordinance' every Sunday as the result of a quickly called church meeting at a time when most of the non-singers had gone home after the service and the singers were left alone to round off the meeting in song. Another similarly called church meeting decided that the members should not read Marlow's books. Armitage's judgement was that Keach 'resolved to introduce singing into his Church, cost what it might'. General Baptist 'rebels' now made overtures to Keach and it looked as though the church unity that Keach sought with the Arminians was to be found in a common interest in song. Keach now began to emphasize that singing in church services was not only a Christian duty but a sure mark of true spiritual faith.

Marlow was shocked and baffled at Keach's naive argument that singing must be allowed dominance in the church as a Christian duty as it is natural to man. 'Why not laughter, dancing, whistling, shouting and other "natural" human peculiarities, too?' he asked. The Keach party, however, began to go to extremes — if they had not done so already — and argued that rhyming verse in hymns ought to be used in worship as the Hebrew psalms were also in rhyme. Marlow, who had a better understanding of verse-forms than Keach, explained that Hebrew verse was such because of its parallelisms, an observation confirmed by the local Jews.

Marlow found sympathy in the Particular Baptists General Assembly. This was too much for Keach's followers who adopted the same tactic as they had done in their church meeting. They waited until the last day of the General Assembly when most 'messengers' had gone home and pressed for a vote in favour of singing. This time the ruse did not work. The remaining brethren felt they could not take the revolutionary step of ruling that all the Particular Baptist churches should take up singing. Now the assembly began to look down their noses at Keach who, nevertheless, remained pastor of Goat Yard and refused to give up musical worship.

The Keach faction now approached the Jews whom Marlow had consulted and asked them to explain how Hebrew verse was *really* constructed. The outcome of this discussion was that either the Jews decided to do the singing-party a favour and give them the interpretation they wanted, or the wrong questions were asked them, or Keach and company fully misunderstood their answers. The result was that immediately after consulting the Jews it was announced by the songsters that Hebrew poetry was indeed written in rhyme and thus it must be a Christian's duty to sing God's praises in rhyme in public worship.

Of course Hebrew poetry does seem to rhyme on odd occasions but this appears to be purely accidental and due to similar grammatical inflections. It was certainly never aimed at by biblical writers as an essential feature of their poetry.[49] By no stretch of the imagination can it be claimed that Hebrew poetry has the same numbers, feet, metre and verse-forms as in the poetry of, say, Greek and Latin which has influenced English poetry so much. It would be a brave — or very foolish — Hebraist who even dared to say that he knew how the original line endings of the Davidic Psalms were pronounced, let alone prove that they rhymed![50]

Nevertheless, when Keach broadcast that the Jews were on his side, he was pleased to see support for him grow and Marlow was charged with making false claims. Gradually Marlow saw that he was losing the fight. His last word on the subject was that singing would be the downfall of the church and become the be-all and end-all of its existence. One day, he proclaimed, the true churches would see the folly of their ways and repent. Nowadays when singing and music are the main ingredients in many so-called church services, and Bible schools make musicality a sign of a candidate's calling to the ministry, perhaps Christians are prepared to reconsider whether Marlow may have been talking sense.

After a decade of banging his head against a brick wall, Marlow decided to leave the church, which he thought had become a mere place for public singing, and founded a church at Maze Pond.[51] Though the General Baptists still banned singing from their churches, Marlow did not ally with them but kept to his doctrines of free grace and the perseverance of the saints.[52]

The church at Maze Pond existed without 'confused singing' for another thirty-five years or so but their third pastor, Abraham West, went the way of all flesh, in the opinion of a number of the members, and introduced singing, so causing further disruptions in the church and new reasons for splitting up. On looking back at this sorry state of affairs it must be a sobering thought indeed to find that singing in the Baptist churches was finally introduced through ignorance of Hebrew poetry and a conviction that Jews knew best in determining how Christians should worship.

Keach was not quite satisfied with his victory. In order to impress on his church the great importance of singing, he defined it as 'a holy ordinance of Jesus Christ' and as such added it to the church's declaration of faith along with his somewhat ritualistic views of baptism, the Lord's

Supper and the laying on of hands. Perhaps the coining of the phrase 'a holy ordinance of Jesus Christ' is the reason why the Goat Yard church was perpetually debating the difference between 'ordinances of Christ' and 'church ordinances'. To the Goat Yard church, for instance, baptism was an 'ordinance of Christ' but it was not an 'ordinance of the church'.

When Gill took over the Goat Yard church fifty years after the singing controversy had started, he found that the subject was still a matter of debate. Although most, but certainly not all, of the non-singers had gone, those who remained were of highly different opinions concerning what should be sung and when singing should take place. Gill thus had to tread cautiously so as not to upset any of the parties. A number of writers believe that Gill walked fully in Keach's footsteps. Seymour, for instance, says 'Gill heartily approved'[53] of singing both psalms and hymns. Such a statement needs to be qualified strongly. Gill's position seemed to be that a little singing could be of spiritual help but that this soon could develop into too much singing which could do no one any good. The result was Article XII in his declaration of faith showing that he did not consider singing of acute importance to faith and practice but left the matter open to the whims of the congregation which he knew changed considerably from time to time. The subsequent history of the church reflected these changing whims. The minute book records how church meetings were called on several occasions concerning what should be sung during church services. Some were for singing hymns, others for merely singing the Psalms of David to well-established tunes. Sometimes the psalm faction won, sometimes the hymn singers. The words 'as to time place and manner, every one ought to be left to their liberty in using it' were added to the declaration in 1768 showing that the controversy raged all through Gill's period of ministry.

The following story is typical of the delicate position Gill was in as the pastor of a church which could never make up its mind on the singing topic. One elderly lady visited Gill to complain of the precentor's weaknesses in leading the singing and protested at a few new tunes that were being used. The church was probably going through a hymn-singing period at this time rather than singing psalms. Gill asked the lady if she knew much about singing to which she replied that she neither understood singing nor could she sing. She gave proof of her statement by saying that she had tried to learn the Old Hundred all her life but had never managed it. Now Gill had to tread carefully so as not to upset the sister who had confessed absolute ignorance on the subject, though she was keen to give advice on how to improve the singing. 'What kind of tunes would you like us to sing?' Gill asked. 'Why, sir, I should very much like David's tunes,' said the old lady. 'Well, if you will get David's tunes for us, we will try to sing them,' said Gill. Perhaps there were many in the church of the same opinion as the old

lady and this caused the church meeting to revert back to psalm singing
rather than hymn singing. Gill always advised prudence in musical matters
and never came down firmly on either side.

Modern Baptist writers often presume that the pro-singing faction
represented 'evangelical Calvinists' and that 'the warm personal element
in Christian experience was kept alive in eighteenth-century dissent by
hymns'.[54] On the other hand, Hyper-Calvinists or High-Calvinists,
amongst whom Gill is invariably placed, are shown as being against
spreading the gospel in song. Raymond Brown states, for instance, that
when revival songs were sung in Baptist churches 'the influence of high
Calvinist theology was certain to decline'. Gill, in fact, was instrumental
in bringing out a seventh edition of Richard Davis' hymn-book in 1748 and
as early as 1733 he had published a work on singing the Psalms which had
caused a Mr Solomon Lowe to prepare a large piece of it for his intended
Supplement to *Chamber's Cyclopædia*. Concerning Gill's endorsement of
psalm singing under the right conditions, Mr Lowe says, 'I find there is no
dealing with you, as with the generality of writers. The afore-mentioned
piece is all quintessence; so that instead of extracting, I have been obliged
to copy the greatest part of it, to do justice to the article of Psalmody, and
know not where to find any hints for the improvement of it.'[55]

Gill was known to use hymns in his private devotion and even quoted
a verse from Watts, whom he usually thought highly liberal in his theology,
on his deathbed. If allowing singing in church services was a sign of
'evangelical Calvinists' and not 'High-Calvinists' then both Hart's and
Gadsby's hymns should be looked on as perfectly evangelical (as, of
course, they are) though these men, in conjunction with Gill, are also put
into the High-Calvinist camp. The fact that Gill allowed hymn singing in
his church services, however, only proves how far he went to accommodate
himself to the wishes of his brethren in Christ as, left to himself, he would
certainly not have used hymns in the worship of the gathered church.
Speaking to his young people about singing hymns as opposed to psalms,
Gill said: 'I must confess, that I cannot but judge them, in a good measure,
unnecessary, since we are so well provided with a book of psalms and
scriptural songs, indited by the Spirit of God, and suitable on all occasions.'[56]

One obvious omission in the Goat Yard confession was a reference to
the purpose of the law in Christian witness. The London confession of 1644
and those built on it had been most radical in apparently doing away with
the need for a law-work before preaching salvation in Christ. Article XXV
stated dogmatically that: 'The tenders of the Gospel to the conversion of
sinners is absolutely free, no way requiring, as absolutely necessary, any
qualifications, preparations, terrors of the Law, or preceding Ministry of

the law, but onely and alone the naked soule, as a sinner and ungodly to receive Christ, as crucified, dead, and buried, and risen againe, being made a Prince and a Saviour for such sinners.' Erroll Hulse, writing in *Our Baptist Heritage*, regards this factor as evidence that the creed was 'Calvinistic'[57] but this must be doubted on the testimony of Calvin himself who maintained that God's righteousness in his law must first be displayed before the sinner becomes aware of his own unrighteousness and need of salvation. To deny the necessity of the preceding work of the law in gospel preaching smacks of Dr Daniel Williams' Neonomianism i.e. the teaching that the old law is abrogated as Christ has fulfilled the covenant of works for all men — sinner and saint alike. The new law is the gospel which demands faith and conversion producing 'evangelical righteousness' in the believer which, however imperfect, is his ground of acceptance with God and consequently his justification. With this heresy comes the rejection of the imputed righteousness of Christ. The gospel of life, however, is for those who are aware that they are dead in trespasses and sins according to the old, eternal law.[58] It may have been thought that as Gill's declaration of faith was the testimony of those who had escaped the terrors of the law, the topic did not relate directly to a statement of faith. There was, however, a great need for such a doctrinal statement at the time, especially as, only fifteen years before, under the pastorate of Stinton, Goat Yard had agreed at Lorimers' Hall Association meeting to denounce the doctrine of Christ's imputed righteousness and adopt a Neonomian position.[59] Gill saw this need later and took up the subject in numerous works.[60]

Gill rounded off his declaration of faith by affirming the duties and obligations of his church to maintain these doctrines both for the welfare of the church and in view of their evangelistic responsibilities to the world at large. In stressing the purpose of the creed, Gill ends by saying,

> Now all, and each of these doctrines and ordinances, we look upon ourselves under the greatest obligations to embrace, maintain, and defend; believing it to be our duty to stand fast, in one spirit, with one mind, striving together for the faith of the Gospel.
>
> And whereas we are very sensible, that our conversation, both in the world and in the church, ought to be as becometh the Gospel of Christ, we judge it our incumbent duty to walk in wisdom towards them that are without, to exercise a conscience void of offence towards God and men, by living soberly, righteously, and godly, in this present world.
>
> And as to our regards to each other, in our church-communion, we esteem it our duty to walk with each other in all humility and brotherly love: to watch over each other's conversation; to stir up one another to love and good works; not forsaking the assembling

of ourselves together, as we have opportunity, to worship God according to his revealed will; and, when the case requires, to warn, rebuke, and admonish one another, according to the rules of the Gospel.

Moreover, we think ourselves obliged to sympathise with each other, in all conditions, both inward and outward, which God, in his providence, may bring us into; as also to bear with one another's weaknesses, failings, and infirmities, and particularly to pray for one another, and that the Gospel and the ordinances thereof might be blessed to the edification and comfort of each other's souls, and for the gathering in of others to Christ, besides those who are already gathered all which duties we desire to be found in the performance of, through the gracious assistance of the Holy Spirit, whilst we both admire and adore the grace which has given us a place and a name in God's house, better than that of sons and daughters.

Gill knew, however, that a declaration of faith was only of use when the spiritual life of the church could back it up and testify to its truths. Gill now planned a detailed exposition of the Word of God to instruct and stabilize his flock in the faith. Surprisingly enough, his first choice of a biblical book to expound fully was The Song of Solomon. Starting in 1724 he devoted no less than 122 sermons to this majestic love poem of Christ and his Bride.

6.
The voice of the Beloved

Gill had held himself together admirably throughout the first few years of his ministry. Sure of his election and calling, he had not looked back though the ploughing was hard and the ground rough. By 1723, he was clearly established as pastor of his own flock and had gained respect not only from his own denomination but also from church leaders who were not Baptists. Just when Gill was settling down to the everyday routines of a pastor's life he collapsed and was ill for much of the following year. The fevers and fainting fits and great bodily pain which he had experienced in his childhood now came back with renewed strength so that Gill, at times, believed the Lord was about to call him. Times of testing and experiencing the divine rod are also times of growth and inner renewal. Thus Gill came out of the shadows of death with a stronger and more fervent desire to teach his flock about the love of God which passeth all understanding. Feeling his health returning, Gill started out on his long preaching series concerning the voice of the Beloved to his lovesick Bride.

It would appear that Gill was first drawn to 'The Song of Songs which is Solomon's', to give the book its full title, by radical critics of the day who refused to accept it as part of God's revealed Word. Hugo Grotius (1583-1645), the Dutch humanist and founder of the Moral Government theory of the atonement, whom Gill had studied carefully, had denied that the Song was part of holy writ and his dubious mantle had been taken up in England by William Whiston (1667-1752),[1] a Cambridge professor, friend and successor of Sir Isaac Newton. Whiston set himself the task of restoring the text of the Old Testament, assisted by Baptist pastor John Gale, throwing out those books which were not in accordance with his rational ideas and adding books with the strangest of theological content such as the 'Apostolic Canons and Constitutions'. To him this collection of writings was 'the most sacred of the canonical books of the New

Testament'. To most scholars, they were obvious forgeries. Whiston is remembered today for his translation of the works of the Jewish historian Josephus but he was more well known by his contemporaries for his endeavours to reform the church. He felt that Christianity had wandered far from its origins and in his book *Primitive Christianity Revived*, he sought to reintroduce what he thought had been lost. This included less controversial elements as anointing the sick with oil but also the performance of miracles, a trine immersion at baptism, the forbidding of remarriage for widows and widowers, the awaiting of the Second Coming, which Whiston reckoned would be in twenty years time, and an Arian interpretation of the Godhead which caused him to ban 'Athanasian interpretations' from the liturgy.

Oddly enough, considering the great extent of his heresies and speculations, Whiston has always received a sympathetic write-up from Christian writers of all persuasions. High Churchmen Abbey and Overton write:

> Poor Whiston grievously lamented the triumph of interest over truth, which these defections implied. Neither the censures of Convocation nor the falling off of his friends had any power to move him. He still continued for some time a member of the Church of England. But his character was far too honest and clear-sighted to enable him to shut his eyes to the fact that the Liturgy of the Church was in many points sadly unsound on the principles of primitive Christianity.[2]

R. E. D. Clark, writing in the 'evangelical' *New International Dictionary of the Christian Church*, says of Whiston: 'Of his piety and passionate desire to follow Christ whatever the consequences there can be no doubt; his Arianism, if mistaken, was based only on his understanding of Scripture.'

Gill was of a different calibre as he felt that a man who degraded Christ could hardly be called 'pious' in the Christian sense and if one's understanding of Scripture was irrelevant to Christian piety then the door was open to the devil and all his works. Whiston, for instance, judged a man's theological respectability according to whether he included or excluded the Song of Solomon from his canon. Those that excluded the book were 'sound' and those who included it were judged to be 'unsound'. Just a year before Gill commenced his exposition, Whiston had published a small book entitled *A Supplement to Mr Whiston's late Essay towards restoring the true Text of the Old Testament* in which he rejected the Song of Songs as spurious, finding it immoral, of a late date and nowhere referred to in the 'true' canon of Scripture. Gill commenced his series of expositions by taking up Whiston's points one by one and refuting them with an exceptional display of knowledge regarding the times of Solomon and Jewish and Gentile scholars throughout the ages. In Gill's defence of the glories of Christ revealed in the book, Whiston's badly researched ideas fall down like dominoes and Gill even finds quotes from the Song in the very non-canonical works which Whiston added to the canon, claiming that the true canon of Scripture never mentioned the Song.

Whiston's book on primitive Christianity caused such a stir in the Church of England that it was condemned as 'directly opposite to the fundamental articles of the Christian religion'. Whiston then went on to write against the doctrine of the Trinity. With the censure of Convocation against him, Whiston sought long for a new 'spiritual' home and eventually left the Church of England to settle down as a member of Paul's Alley Baptist Church, Barbican, where he was welcomed with open arms. Paul's Alley was the place where, to use Ivimey's words, Dr John Gale 'had laboured' and Dr James Foster had 'entered into his labours'. Foster himself was widely accused of deism and wrote books which gave definite proof to the allegation.[3]

Gill, like William Huntington, who carried on and built on much of Gill's work, has been criticized for being the pastor to the ignorant who would believe anything, rather than a man who stood his ground amongst well-educated townspeople. Such critics should read Gill's introduction to the Song. It combines a high standard of devotion with a high standard of learning. His church must have been thoroughly grounded in the Word and not unfamiliar with the names of the various expositors who had gone before Gill. They must have also been able to follow a long stream of logical argument. Rather than being material for supposed country yokels, it may be said without exaggeration that few town churches today would be able to tackle such strong meat with sound theological teeth. Gill, however, had an amazing gift of making the 'divine mysteries' of the gospel understandable. Comparing Gill with John Owen in his review of Gill's commentary on the Song, J. C. Philpot admits that Owen is the greater expositor but adds that Owen is often not as clear as Gill and his expository work is too massive, too learned and too long drawn out for the average Christian. Gill's expositions, he finds, 'shine with peculiar and unrivalled lustre' and are 'more readable, more concise and pregnant, more lively and animated than Owen'.[4]

William Whiston probably never read Gill's refutation of his findings. It did come to his ear, however, that Gill thought highly of the Song. In 1748 Whiston wrote a massive tome which he entitled *Memoirs of his own Life and Writings, published by himself* in which he wrote these words:

About August this year I was informed of one Dr Gill, a particular or Calvinistic baptist, of whose skill in the oriental languages I had heard a great character: so I had a mind to hear him preach: but being informed that he had written a folio book on the Canticles, I declined to go and hear him.

Whiston did not realize what a treat he had missed! As Gill's flock listened week after week to Gill's declaration of love to his Redeemer, one can imagine how the devoted hearers must have been thrilled with the sheer poetry of his message. Modern critics who delight in portraying Gill as a stiff and starchy legalistic proclaimer of God's sovereignty, to the exclusion of God's love for sinners, cannot possibly have read his exposition of the Song of Songs — or much else from his pen, either! James Hervey, who was called 'the poet of prose' because of the beauty of his writings, drank deep at the wells of Gill's language and doctrine. Writing of the inspiration he received from this ever bubbling spring and commenting on Song of Solomon 2:14 in his book *Theron and Aspasio*, he says:

> Should the reader have an inclination to see this sacred, but mysterious book explained, I would refer him to Dr Gill's Exposition of the Canticles: which has such a copious vein of sanctified invention running through it, and is interspersed with such a variety of delicate and brilliant images, as cannot but highly entertain a curious mind; which presents us also with such rich and charming displays of the glory of Christ's person, the freeness of his grace to sinners, and the tenderness of his love to the church, as cannot but administer the most exquisite delight to the believing soul. Considered in both these views, I think the work resembles the paradisaical garden described by Milton, in which

Blossoms and fruits at once of golden hue,
Appear'd with gay enamell'd colours mix'd.[5]

J. A. Jones, writing in old age, testified that he wanted to close his life by recommending something most precious to him. He thus recommended Gill's beautiful exposition of true love with the words:

> I know not a work containing more experimental savour, written by man. I have, during more than forty-five years spent in the Christian Ministry, repeatedly obtained *marrow and fatness* from a perusal of its pages. Nothing from Gill's pen has perhaps been made so useful to *devotional* Christians as *this*; so that I can well recommend it to all those who would cry out with the Spouse, 'Let Him kiss me with the kisses of his mouth: for thy love is better than wine.'[6]

Outlining the longing for affectionate displays of Christ's love in the Old Testament church, Gill expounds the opening words of the Song saying that they are a request:

> For the manifestation of Christ in the flesh; than which nothing was more passionately longed for, and earnestly desired; many kings and prophets greatly desired it; yea, all the Old Testament saints did more or less pray, as David did, 'O that the salvation of Israel were come out of Zion,' Psalm 14: 7, and this they were so vehemently desirous of, because they knew hereby redemption from all evil would be obtained, the curse removed, and all spiritual blessings procured for them; Christ's incarnation being, like kisses, a pledge and indication of his love, was very desirable to the church, and as appears by her expressions, would be exceeding grateful to all those who were 'waiting for the consolation of Israel'. He had sent his prophets, and by them had spoken unto her 'at sundry times and in diverse places'; yet she is not easy and contented herewith, but would have greater displays of his grace, by his appearing in his own person to kiss her with the kisses of his mouth.

Gill goes on to show the uniqueness of Christ's love to his Bride. His love for her was stronger than death itself. He shows also the fulness of Christ's love for her in that 'all the blessings of grace flow from it, such as vocation, sanctification, justification, adoption, and glorification'. Christ's is a veritable baptism of love which, 'as the waters in Ezekiel's vision, increase and rise from the knees to the loins, and from thence become waters to swim in, a river, an ocean of love which cannot be passed over'. This ocean of love is one into which a sinner is baptized but out of which the believer can never step as '"having loved his own, which were in the world, he loved them unto the end," John 13: 1; his love is invariable, unalterable, and unchangeable: it is like himself, "the same yesterday, to-day, and for ever;" all the waters of sin and corruption cannot extinguish it; nor can any creature in heaven, earth or hell, separate his people from it.'

The church at Goat Yard had been influenced by the Arminian and Socinian teaching of John Gale (1680-1722) and his dubious thoughts on Adamic sin and the extent of the Fall.[7] Speaking of Canticles 2:5: 'Stay me with flagons, comfort me with apples, for I am sick of love', Gill outlines the difference between being sick in sin and being sick of love. Stressing the total depravity of man, Gill argues:

> There is a sickness of sin, which, if mighty grace prevent it not, is a sickness unto death; it is in its own nature mortal, and can only

be cured by Christ, the great Physician, who heals diseases by forgiving iniquity: this is what is natural and hereditary to us; we bring it into the world with us; for we are all 'shapen in iniquity, and in sin did our mothers conceive us': it is an epidemical distemper, which has infected all human nature; all are diseased with it, though all are not sensible of it; and it has overspread all the powers and faculties of the soul of men, as well as all the members of the body; so that there is no part, no place exempted from it; for the whole head is sick, and the whole heart faint.

This is good old-fashioned Calvinism which puts man's need and God's grace in their correct places. It is a far cry from the teaching of the self-styled 'moderate Calvinists' who maintain that man still manages to stand upright after a limited Fall. Mr Dan Taylor, the Arminian Baptist leader who strove to put the General Baptists back on a biblical footing, presumed logically that Andrew Fuller, as a professing Calvinist, must teach that fallen man had 'no will nor power to believe in Christ, nor any concern in the matter' prior to the Spirit's work. Fuller surprised him by replying:

> That is what I have never affirmed. On the contrary, I maintain that men have the same power, strictly speaking, before they are wrought upon by the Holy Spirit, as after; and before conversion as after; that the work of the Spirit endows us with no new rational powers, nor any powers that are necessary to moral agency.[8]

Gill's is certainly not the duty-faith teaching that a sinner is capable of using all the natural faculties that God gave unfallen Adam to defy or condescend to believe his Creator as he wills. Guarding the truth against those who maintained that fallen man had still enough spirituality to harbour a secret longing for Christ, Gill made it his priority from the beginning of his ministry to show man his correct, deplorable, loveless state so that he could preach the gospel of the sinner's acceptance into the covenant love of Christ. Gill's message was always that a lost lamb could only love Christ after being sought out and found and loved by the Good Shepherd.

After describing what sin-sickness is, Gill goes on to describe what love-sickness means to an awakened sinner, saying:

> There is a sickness which souls are incident to, that arises from a sense of sin, want of the fresh manifestation of pardoning grace, absence of Christ Jesus, and a longing after the enjoyment of his person, and the discoveries of his love; which though it is not a

sickness unto death, yet it is very painful and afflicting, and can only be cured by the enjoyment of the object loved; this discovers itself by a violent panting after Christ; a carefulness and activity in the use of means, to enjoy his presence and company; a resolution to go through all difficulties for the sake of him, and an uneasiness until it receives some instances of favour from him: with such souls, Christ is the subject of all their discourse; they love to hear his name mentioned, especially with commendation, their thoughts are continually upon him, and their minds are not easy till they enjoy him.

Although the Song of Solomon is strictly the love story of Christ and his church, Gill also saw it as being the history of how Christ came to woo and to win his Bride. Preaching on 4:16: 'Awake, O north wind, and come thou south, blow upon my garden that the spices thereof may flow out,' Gill deals with the work of the Holy Spirit in convicting and converting the sinner. 'When ye see the south wind blow,' says Christ (Luke 12: 55), 'ye say there will be heat, and it cometh to pass:' so the Spirit of God brings heat along with him to the cold heart of a sinner 'dead in trespasses and sins'; and by the mighty influence of his grace, thaws and melts his hard and frozen soul; and with his soul-warming gales, and comfortable discoveries of love, warms, enlivens, comforts, and refreshes the saint, when in a cold, lifeless, and uncomfortable frame.

Here Gill is at the very heart of the gospel of grace. He does not tell his readers to consider man's supposed, inherent, known duty to believe with all the onus of salvation resting in man's will. Rather we see that, in his fallen state, the law has condemned man in unbelief and only a heavenly pardon can save him. This pardon, Gill teaches, comes when the wind of the Spirit blows with all his cleansing power in the lives of sinners loved by the Son. Just as the spring winds cause the sap to flow, so new life is instilled in Christ's chosen ones leading them on to grow in grace and a knowledge of their Lord and Saviour. That such knowledge is entirely absent from the lives of the unsaved is shown by Paul's words in 1 Corinthians 2:7-9: 'But we speak the wisdom of God in a mystery, even the hidden wisdom, which God ordained before the world unto his glory: which none of the princes of this world knew: for had they known it, they would not have crucified the Lord of glory. But as it is written, Eye hath not seen, nor ear heard, neither hath entered into the heart of man, the things which God hath prepared for them that love him.' The inherent wisdom of man makes him merely 'wise in his own conceit' and such wisdom knows nothing of duties to Christ. True, heavenly wisdom is that which God prepared as a dowry for his Son's Bride before the foundations of the world. Sadly, this true-love story which is written down by the pen of inspiration in the Best of Books is rejected as a 'cheap penny-dreadful' by the self-styled 'evangelical Calvinists' who emphasize in true Tillotson manner their high view of natural man.

Such 'moderates' reject the doctrine of God's everlasting love to his elect, and their eternal covenant union with Christ, thus disregarding the very foundation of the gospel and opening the doors to modernistic teaching which will save no man.[9] They seem to believe that there is an Esau and a Jacob in every man until either his Jacob or Esau side takes over in willing to follow his inert sense of duty or not. Against such teaching Gill expounds Song of Solomon 8:7: 'Many waters cannot quench love,' arguing that the whole of mankind is drowned in the deluge of sin which, 'like a mighty torrent, or rather inundation, has entered this world, and brought death along with it, upon all the posterity of Adam; it has drowned them in destruction and perdition, as all hurtful and foolish lusts do. Now the elect of God themselves are not exempted from the universal deluge; but though these waters of sin have come into their souls and overrun all the powers and faculties thereof; yet they have not extinguished Christ's love towards them; nor in the least alienated his affection for them.'

For Gill the north and south winds of the Spirit show the two sides of God's work in the sinner's heart. Just as the north wind comes sharp and nipping, killing that life may come of it and wounding that healing may be applied, so the south wind promotes healing, growth and expansion. The north wind humbles a man in his own eyes but the south wind exalts him in Christ. Thus, 'Christ's garden stands in need of both winds: that the saints sometimes need the Spirit as a reprover, to bring them to a sense of themselves; as well as a comforter, to relieve them under their distress.'

Commenting on Song of Solomon 7:10-11, Gill argues that though Christ has loved his church from eternity, she must first reach ripeness for marriage through being reared on the Word. Then, but not until then, is it time for the Bridegroom to come to take the Bride prepared for him. 'It is true,' Gill explains, 'he loved her before, even from eternity, with an everlasting love; but that was hidden and secret both to herself and others: but now her "breasts are fashioned"; he looked upon her, and "her time is the time of love": he openly espouses her to himself, and lets all the world know, as well as herself, what favour she found in his sight.'

Gill expounds chapter 8, the culminating chapter in the Song of Songs, as referring to 'the success of the Gospel, the planting of churches, and establishment of Christ's interest in the Gentile world'. Here the London pastor sees the worldwide task of 'Christ's multitudes' in promoting the fruitfulness of the vineyard, watering and pruning the vines, propping them up when necessary, and fencing them off against the wild boars of the world. God's keepers of the vineyard are the ministers of the gospel. Their task is to see that 'doctrine drops as the rain, and their speech distils as the dew, as the small rain upon the tender herb, and as the showers upon the grass,'[10] so that they become fruitful. The gifts of ministry are varied, argues Gill, teaching that some are more useful for the edification of the church, whereas others are more able to preach conversion to the unsaved. Some are planters, some are more able to water and others are called to reap. Some are sought out by God as pruners. These are able to reprove and admonish others without breaking their bonds in Christ. Others are at their best when supporting and strengthening weak believers, whereas others are employed by the Spirit to protect and defend the church from the foxes in the vineyard. As soon as Gill wrote down these thoughts, however, he warned the Christian minister against thinking that he should be fully taken up with but one of these gifts and exhorts his brethren to seek to be more or less useful in all, though excelling in at least one. 'I have chosen you, and ordained you,' he quotes Christ's words, 'that you should go and bring forth fruit.'[11]

Gill did not have the high 'priestly' view of the pastorate of his predecessors and, when outlining the duties of pastors, he did not neglect to show that all believers have a corner of the vineyard under their care, even if it is only the vineyard of their own heart. Every dweller in Christ's vineyard has 'a mutual interest in each other's persons, gifts, graces, prayers, etc. and being all members of the one and the same body, should, as the apostle says, 1 Cor. 12: 25, "have the same care one for another"'.

A good deal of the work in the Lord's vineyard is the conversion of sinners. This Gill finds expressed in the words, 'Thou, O Solomon, must have a thousand, and those that keep the fruit thereof two hundred.' The hope, joy and crown of rejoicing for a Christian, Gill maintains, is to make sure that when the Lord returns in glory with his own, there shall be those among them who have come to a knowledge of the truth through our witness. 'We live' he says, quoting 1 Thessalonians 3:8: 'if ye stand fast in the Lord.' It is obvious here that Gill is arguing that one's own calling as God's under-gardener is verified in that one calls others to serve the same Lord. Here is a conundrum indeed! Scores of writers, who say they cannot swallow Gill's doctrine as he allegedly rejects gospel invitations and applications must accept that here, at least,[12] that very man is arguing that ministers should harvest their 'thousands' and the so-called laity their 'hundreds'.

Whatever one's doctrines, no Christian who earnestly seeks to follow his Lord can fail to profit from this great work of Gill which outlines all the beauties of Christ and all that the church and the world owes to him. It also puts the ideal, sin-free church into a light hardly surpassed in the New Testament and on reading it, one would like to conclude with Solomon in saying to the divine Bridegroom: 'Make haste, my beloved, and be thou like a roe or a young hart upon the mountains of spices.' To that, we can only say with John, 'Amen. Even so, come, Lord Jesus.'[13]

7.
The defender of the faith

When John Fellows heard of Gill's death, he penned a lengthy elegy, highlighting what he thought had been Gill's major contributions to the life of the church. Fellows looked upon Gill first and foremost as a defender of the faith, writing of him:

> The cause of God and truth employ'd his thoughts;
> And his whole strength to its defence he brought.
> Say, all ye sons of Zion! how he rose
> With potent arm against your num'rous foes;
> How bright his helmet, and how broad his shield,
> And with what mighty force he swept the field.[1]

The modern Baptist historian Raymond Brown, reacting against Robert Hall Junior's unwarranted statement that Gill's books were 'a sea of mud' says:

> Gill's work as a commentator on the whole of the Bible was prized and used by hundreds of preachers in the eighteenth century, while his three-volumed *Body of Divinity* provided ministers, students and others with an exposition of Calvinistic theology which gave them confidence at a time when, in a rationalistic age, biblical doctrine was under attack. Under the influence of writers like James Foster, ministers and churches could easily pass from doctrinal freedom to theological indifference, and then to Unitarianism. Gill and Brine helped to keep many a reader in the way of truth when others were hopelessly confused.

Throughout his entire Christian life, Gill was called upon from within and without his denomination to break a lance for the evangelical faith and combat heresy wherever it raised its ugly head. Gill was, of course, singularly fitted out for such a task because of his dedication in working for the Lord and because of his scholarly attributes. Such a man as Gill was a real necessity for his day. The biblical truth concerning the narrow way which few tread was very apparent during his ministry, especially in the earlier years before the Evangelical Awakening had gained in momentum. Arianism and Socinianism were most prevalent throughout the denominations and these heresies were fused together in the teachings of the Deists who, though professing to be Christians, not only denied the deity of Christ but denied that God was active in the world in any sense. Though most of these Deists were brilliant academics, their naive view of God was of a deity who had created the world to run according to its own internal clockwork and thereafter sat back to relax from the effort with no further thought for the toy he had created. Of such 'great thinkers' Cowper says:

> Learning itself, received into a mind
> By nature weak, or viciously inclined,
> Serves but to lead philosophers astray,
> Where children would with ease discern the way.

In 1713 the Deist Antony Collins published his *Discourse on Free-thinking* which was followed by *A Discourse of the Grounds of the Christian Religion* (1724), and *The Scheme of Literal Prophecy considered* (1727). Collins strove to rid Christianity of any idea of the supernatural. He felt that the religion was built on a faulty interpretation of the Old Testament prophesies concerning the Messiah. These, he argued, were not literally but merely allegorically fulfilled in Christ. Christ was thus not the literal Messiah but merely a product of what he called a perfected 'priestcraft' and the early church's fantasy. Friends of Collins, realizing what a foe to Christianity he was, asked him why he allowed his servants to go to church if he believed that the church taught untruths. Collins replied that he sent his servants to church so that they would learn not to rob and murder their master!

Collins' works moved a large number of writers to argue either for or against his arguments but it was widely reported that Calvinists had no arguments to bring forth which would clarify the confusion. This reached Gill's ears and as Collins' influence was spreading amongst many church-goers, Gill decided to preach a series of sermons on the Messiah. These were published under the title *The Prophecies of the Old Testament, respecting the Messiah, considered and proved to be literally fulfilled in Jesus. Containing an answer to the objections of the author of the Scheme of Literal Prophecy*.

Gill had worked hard at the Hebrew language before taking over Goat Yard. When he settled down in his pastorate, he was delighted to find that he had a skilled Hebraist close at hand in his fellow pastor, John Skepp, pastor of Currier's Hall, Cripplegate. Skepp was formerly an Independent and member of Joseph Hussey's church but left Cambridge for London on becoming a Baptist. Gill and Skepp became great friends and, for some two or three years, studied the Targums, Talmud, Rabboth and Zohar together, believing that they would find linguistic gems there which would enable them to understand the Old Testament language better. Skepp died, however, just when his friendship with Gill had deepened but Gill was able to purchase Skepp's large collection of Rabbinical literature and carry on their scholarly work.

Charles Haddon Spurgeon was always rather critical of the energies Gill put into his Hebrew studies. He was appreciative of the jewels that Gill dug out of the linguistic mines of the prophets but obviously felt he could have used much of his time spent with his dictionaries for better things. Though Spurgeon himself criticized the 'moderate Calvinists' often, he obviously allowed much of their criticism of Gill to stick. Of his predecessor's linguistic abilities he says:

> Beyond all controversy, Gill was one of the most able Hebraists of his day, and in other matters no mean proficient. When an opponent in controversy had ventured to call him 'a botcher in divinity', the good doctor, being compelled to become a fool in glorying, gave such a list of his attainments as must have covered his accuser with confusion. His great work on the Holy Scriptures is greatly prized at the present day by the best authorities, which is conclusive evidence of its value, since the set of the current of theological thought is quite contrary to that of Dr. Gill. No one in these days is likely to be censured for his Arminianism, but most modern divines affect to sneer at anything a little too highly Calvinistic. However, amid the decadence of his own rigid system, and the disrepute of even more moderate Calvinism, Gill's laurels as an expositor are still green. His ultraism is discarded, but his learning is respected: the world and the church take leave to question his dogmatism, but they both bow before his erudition. Probably no man since Gill's days has at all equalled him in the matter of Rabbinical learning. Say what you will about that teaching, it has its value. Of course, a man has to rake among perfect dunghills and dustheaps, but there are a few jewels which the world could not afford to miss. Gill was a master cinder-sifter among the Targums, the Talmuds, the Mishna, and the Gemara.

Perhaps Spurgeon was not familiar with Gill's defence of the Messiahship of Christ, a doctrine which had, to a large extent, dropped out of the teaching of the churches because of the strong emphasis being placed on the remoteness of God to the neglect of teaching based on God's immanence and plan of reconciliation in Christ. Gill's intensive knowledge of ancient Hebrew literature was most useful in debunking the theories of Deists such as Collins. For decades such men had been blinding the eyes of the church with their own learning, using later, extra-biblical Jewish literature to tell Christians what their ancient Bible meant. Invariably the Deists used their learning to show how the doctrinal interpretations of the Old Testament understood by the Reformers and the Puritans had little to do with the life and times of the judges, kings and prophets of Israel and Judah. They particularly attacked the Reformed teaching of the Messiah as being a novel theory, unknown to the ancient Jews.

In his preface, Gill shows that the Jewish conception of a Messiah was not a product of the early Middle Ages, as Collins argued, but had always been a central doctrine of the Jewish religion and was even held by the Sadducees, Samaritans and Josephus, which Collins denied. Against Collins' argument that the Jewish idea of a Messiah was merely allegorical, Gill points out that the scribes always emphasized a literal interpretation of the Scriptures and stressed that the Messiah was to be a literal Son of David. Collins' arguments, Gill shows, can only be valid if one takes references in Jewish literature which stress a belief in the Messiah to be mere later glosses and interpolations. The 'interpolation' theory became the supporting pillar of much of the Higher Critical school. Gill rejected the theory on internal scriptural and external historical evidence. This all might appear to be 'cinder-raking' to some critics but it was certainly helpful in enflaming the churches with a new sense of the authority and reliability of the Word of God.

Gill's main point in his first chapter is that argument from prophesy is only one proof amongst many and not the major proof of the validity of Christianity. The main issue is salvation by Jesus Christ. Nonetheless, salvation in Christ cannot be separated from fulfilment of prophecy as Peter points out when he says, 'Of which salvation the prophets have enquired, and searched diligently, who prophesied of the grace that should come unto you: searching what, or what manner of time the Spirit of Christ, which was in them, did signify, when it testified, before hand, the sufferings of Christ, and the glory that should follow.'[2] Gill shows how Christ admonished his hearers to search the Scriptures which testify of him and read what 'Moses and all the prophets' say about him.[3] Here there is no indication whatsoever of any interpretation other than a literal one.

After chiefly considering Genesis 3:15 and its New Testament applications, Gill concludes his first chapter by affirming: 'From this prophecy, we learn, that the Messiah was to be incarnate, born of a woman, and not begotten by man; that he was to suffer and die; as also, that he was to destroy satan and his works, which Jesus has done: And it may be observed, that salvation was proclaimed, as soon as sin was committed, and a prophecy of a Messiah given forth as soon as there was need of one.' So much for the 'later interpolation' theory!

In the following chapters Gill shows how Messianic prophesies move from a general reference to the seed of a woman to the seed of Abraham, going on to describe Christ's exact human lineage up to his miraculous conception in a place named by prophecy. He shows, too, how even the major scenes in Christ's life up to his atoning death on the cross and his resurrection are foretold in the writings of the prophets. The Messiah they write of was seen first and foremost as a Redeemer and Justifier who is to remove ungodliness from Jacob and redeem Israel from all her iniquities, but also to be a light to the Gentiles and extend his salvation unto the ends of the earth and 'speak peace unto the heathen'. All this was fulfilled in Christ.

Gill's critics, who always affirm that his evangelistic horizon never extended beyond the back pews in his own chapel, ought to read this missionary account of Messianic work which is to infuse mankind with an awareness of the Lord from the least to the greatest until the earth is full of the knowledge of the Lord, as the waters cover the sea. Gill's vision is that of the prophet Jeremiah who saw a time when no one will need to teach anyone as all will one day know the Messiah who is called Christ. All in all, in these thirteen, at times exhilarating, chapters, Gill expounds some 244 Old Testament texts which are supposed to point to a mere 'allegorical' Messiah and shows how they are literally fulfilled in Christ.

It is strange to relate that Gill's strong testimony against Collins' rationalism is hardly mentioned by modern church historians of both free-church and Anglican persuasions.[4] They emphasize that 'giants' such as Clarke, Conybeare, Bentley, Berkeley, Butler, Hoadly, Law, Swift, Warburton and Whiston all took up their pens against Collins but none of these men, with perhaps the exception of Bishop Butler, were able to lay the axe to the roots of Collins' fallacies as Gill did, and none of them had his skill in giving Scripture its rightful meaning. Some of Collins' critics such as Swift and Whiston were even more imaginative than Collins in their pseudo-rational criticisms of the faith once delivered to the saints.

Gill's expertise in putting Old Testament study to use in expository preaching was shown in one of his very earliest sermon publications, on Deuteronomy 33:8: 'And of Levi he said, Let thy Thummim and thy Urim be with thy Holy One, whom thou didst prove at Massah, and with whom thou didst strive at the waters of Meribah.' After studying the meaning of the words Urim and Thummim carefully in Hebrew literature and setting his findings against the light of Scripture, Gill argues that the words mean and typify 'light of knowledge and integrity of life in relation to God's true

Israel'. Such knowledge and light, he explains, are to be found fully and complete in Christ. He then goes on to use this imagery to show the superiority of Christ's priesthood to that of Aaron, how the Levitical ceremonial law was but a shadow of things to come and how Christ is the substance of that shadow. He then points his hearers to the glory of Christ in the gospel dispensation 'in which the day is broke, and the shadows are fled and gone; and we all with open face beholding, as in a glass, the glory of the Lord, are changed into the same image, from glory to glory, even by the Spirit of the Lord'.

Not all the heresies Gill combated were outside of his fold. On rare occasions, he had to take up his pen to warn his own flock of the dangers within them. There are occasional references in Gill's church book to disciplinary action taken against members who visited Anglican, Methodist and Moravian meetings,[5] or because of non-attendance or even drunkenness. It was always stressed in the church meetings that inter-church activities should be within churches of the same 'faith and order' and that a godly testimony was expected of all members, shown by good works and regular attendance at the home church. Grave heresy, however, seldom troubled Goat Yard or Carter Lane, though when it did occur, its influence always lingered for a number of years. This was chiefly because of the church's patient and loving care in matters of discipline which gave the unrepentant a long time in which to spread their ideas. The minutes of a church meeting held on 24 July 1768, for instance, report a serious matter which touched the very heart of the Christian faith. A member named Isaac Harman, who had been in fellowship since May 1757, suddenly declared that 'He had long been at Enmity with the doctrine of the Eternal Sonship of Christ by the Generation of the Father.' Harman was not excommunicated on the spot but visited several times by 'messengers' and eventually banned from the Lord's Table by a unanimous vote until he repented. This was the usual procedure of the church. If members resigned orally, or sent letters of resignation, these resignations were accepted without further ado. If the members did not request their dismissal, a process of counselling ensued which could last months before a final decision was taken. Repentant excommunicants were speedily taken back into fellowship. One such person was none other than John Gill's son of the same name who was excluded from membership in 1755 but soon came back expressing his sorrow and was reaccepted into membership.

A special church meeting was called on 7 August 1768 to discuss methods of dealing with the denial of Christ's eternal Sonship which was troubling members. It was very well attended and those present agreed to add clauses to the 1729 Declaration of Faith, denouncing the error.[6] The heresy prevailed, however, and in September 1769 another member, Brother Blunt, professed to deny the doctrine. At least four church meetings between September 1769 and January 1770 were called to discuss what was to be done with Blunt and he was visited and warned with expulsion three times. Finally Blunt confessed that he could not remain in communion with a church who believed that Christ was the eternal Son of God and was thus struck off the membership list.

Gill had already published *The Doctrine of the Trinity Stated and Vindicated* in 1752 but now he wrote particularly about the controversy that was troubling his congregation and published *A Dissertation concerning the Eternal Sonship of Christ* soon after the 1768 church meeting on the topic. His earlier work was more expositional but in this more specific work Gill tackled the problem from a historical point of view. Gill was moved to do so by the numerous Sabellians, Arians and Modalist factions in the various denominations and churches who were arguing that the doctrine of the eternal Sonship was a novel, post-Reformation teaching.

Gill argues from the start that the eternal generation of the Son is written 'as with a sun-beam' both in the Old and New Testaments and what was denied by his contemporary Socinians was known by David, Micah and Daniel. He shows how in the first century that father of heretics, Simon Magus, taught that there was only one person in the Godhead and the apostle John's arch-enemy Cerinthus, followed by Ebion, believed that Jesus was a mere man. Gill shows how John dealt with these heresies in his Gospel and how Clement of Rome and Ignatius stressed the truths found there, i.e. that Christ was true God and true Man but the true Son of God by his divine nature and not because of his human birth. Turning to the second century, Gill deals with the heresy of Valentinus who taught the second variation of a heresy prevalent in Gill's day. This was the belief that Christ was eternally the human Son of God and was born *by* a virgin but not *of* a virgin, as he merely passed through Mary 'like water through a pipe'. Gill shows how Policarp, Justin Martyr and Irenæus dealt with such teaching, demonstrating how the Son of God *became* man. Thus Gill works through the centuries dealing with, for instance, Arius who was refuted by Gregory, Basil, Ambrose and the great Athanasius himself. In the fifth century, we find Augustine bringing the Arian's gaze back to the Bible; in the sixth, the synod of Gothic bishops condemning the Sabellianism of Chilpericus; in the seventh century, we read how the Christian councils combated Mahomet's views, and so on until the Reformation with its threats from Servetus and Faustus Socinus who gave his name to the Socinian heresy and who looked upon the doctrine of the eternal Sonship of Christ as his main target for destruction.

Gill demonstrates how 'all sound divines and evangelical churches, from the Reformation to the present time' teach the eternal Sonship of Christ. Gill then deals with two later theologians, the Dutchman Roell and Dr Thomas Ridgeley of London, a Professor of Divinity, who though

Trinitarians, still were unorthodox on the question of Christ's Sonship. Gill
then speaks of 'a third person of great fame among us' who was none other
than Dr Isaac Watts, whom Gill cannot link with the Trinitarians who do
not believe in the eternal Sonship of Christ because he finds Watts a rank
Sabellian as his Dissertations published in 1725 indicate. Gill refers to
Lampe's work *Theological Disputations* for arguments against Watts'
heretical views. Watts' position has once again become very strong
amongst evangelicals in recent years, in spite of his highly liberal views
concerning the Word of God and the doctrine of the Trinity. His contemporary evangelicals such as Gill and Cotton Mather viewed the hymn-
writer with far more critical and discerning eyes. As hymn singing now
plays such an important part in modern evangelical worship, 'Watts'
whims', as contemporaries called his lyrics, have been up-valued, although
they were written because of Watts' strong dissatisfaction with using the
exact words of Scripture as a basis for church worship and his strong
interest in making worship more jolly.[7]

After listing the relatively few protagonists who either denied Christ's
eternal Sonship or affirmed his eternal human nature and flanking them
with a very large number of orthodox defenders of the faith, Gill concludes:

> Now since it appears that all the sound and orthodox writers
> have unanimously declared for the eternal generation and Sonship
> of Christ in all ages, and that those only of an unsound mind and
> judgement, and corrupt in other things as well as this, and many of
> them men of impure lives and vile principles, have declared against
> it, such must be guilty of great temerity and rashness to join in an
> opposition with the one against the other; and to oppose a doctrine
> the Church of God has always held, and especially being what the
> Scriptures abundantly bear testimony unto, and is a matter of such
> moment and importance, being a fundamental doctrine of the
> Christian religion, and indeed what distinguishes it from all other
> religions, from those of Pagans, Jews and Mahometans, who all
> believe in God, and generally in *one* God, but none of them believe
> in the Son of God: that is peculiar to the Christian religion.[8]

A year after publishing the above historical survey, Gill turned to more
expository work in his *Of the Distinct Personality and Deity of the Son*
which was part of a longer thesis on the Trinity in Book One of his *Body
of Divinity*. Gill proves Christ's personality by showing that he is the
express image of God's person, so must be a person himself. He is,
however, distinct from the Father and Spirit as he is begotten, whereas the
two other persons are not. The fact that Christ was with God as the Word
shows that he is distinct from God as also does the fact that he is set up from

eternity to be a Mediator, a Saviour and a Sacrifice for his people, after which he sits at God's right hand and is coming to judge the world, thus proving his distinct personality.

Next Gill shows Christ's deity by proving from Scripture that he was not created but is the Creator, he bears the biblical names of God such as the Lord our Righteousness and Immanuel, and even doubting Thomas finally saw him as his Lord and God. Christ is also displayed in the Scriptures as sharing divine perfections because 'in him dwells all the fullness of the Godhead'. Thus Christ is all-perfect, all-eternal and all-omnipotent, the First and the Last. He is also shown to be true God because his works are the same as his Father's. Christ forgives sin, resurrects the dead and judges them because he is God in person. Gill concludes fourthly that Christ is divine in his person because both angels and men worship him and all men are called upon to honour him as they honour the Father and pray to him as God.

Gill was often called upon to break a lance for the Baptist churches on the question of adult baptism, usually because of wild and exaggerated claims made against them by defenders of pædobaptism. Perhaps Gill was called upon to exercise his skills in such work too often as his antagonists were rarely the best of apologists and the massive amount of work Gill put into refuting them lacks the skill and polish of his more scholarly and less controversial works. Often we find Gill in his thoroughness bogged down in the mire of non-essentials in his effort to give a thorough refutation of anti-Baptist criticism. Toplady's and Hervey's brotherly criticism of John Ryland Senior may apply here: 'If he had done less, he might have done more.' Though Gill does not always shine because of the *content* of his arguments in this field, he certainly shines in his *conduct* as he preserves a dignity of manner and style throughout, allowing himself rarely to be pulled down into the brawlings of his opponents.

Before going on to discuss Gill's views of baptism and Dissent it would be helpful to see why the established church was so suspicious of the Baptists that in spite of the religious freedom brought by William of Orange, the Baptists still experienced persecution and ostracization in various degrees. After the formal rejection of papal supremacy in 1534, the Church of England began to draw up a confession of faith which would consolidate and affirm the principal doctrines of the Reformation. The double purpose of such a move was to guard against the erroneous claims of the papal system but also to protect the church against heresies which even the Church of Rome had not tolerated and which had been condemned by the councils of Nicea, Constantinople, Ephesus and Chalcedon. These heresies, such as Sabellianism, Socinianism, Arianism and the teaching that Christ's human nature preceded his human birth were pouring in to Britain from the Continent through the preaching of the Anabaptists,[9] an umbrella term used to describe a multitude of different sects, most of whom stressed that those who joined their ranks must undergo a new form of baptism. Thus in 1536 ten basic articles of faith were agreed upon 'to stablyshe christen quietnes and unitie amongst us, and to avoyde contentious opinions'. These articles were so ambiguous on Reformed doctrine and so bound by Medieval tradition that leading churchmen such as Cranmer and Hooper soon pressed for a more Reformed set of articles demanding 'an entire purification of the Church from the very foundation'. A letter is preserved from Hooper to Baucer dated 25 June 1549 in which the Reformer complains that the Anabaptists are flocking to his lectures yet denying the Incarnation, affirming sinless perfection and teaching that those who fall into sin after partaking of the Holy Ghost will be lost for ever. In the same letter Hooper complains that 'a great portion of the kingdom so adheres to the popish faction as altogether to set at naught God and the lawful authority of the magistrates'.[10] Thus the Ten Articles were quickly revised and added to until they had reached forty-two in number by 1553. The number was reduced to thirty-nine in 1571 when most of the papists had separated themselves from the English church as the result of a papal bull.

The more the Thirty-Nine Articles developed, the more they gained an anti-Anabaptist form in combating Continental anti-Lutheran and anti-Reformed movements until the anti-Anabaptist articles were almost as numerous as the articles against Rome. Articles I, II and III were especially aimed at Anabaptist errors concerning the Trinity whereas Article IV defended the doctrines of the Incarnation and manhood of Christ. The main heretic in mind here was Casper Schwenkenfeld (1489-1561) who, in 1528, contended that Christ's flesh was never that of a created human and, after the resurrection, Christ dropped all resemblance of humanity.[11] Article VI defends the canonical status of the Old Testament which was rejected by many Anabaptists. Articles VIII to X dealing with original sin, free will and grace were aimed at the Pelagian Anabaptist doctrine which taught that Adam's curse did not apply to his offspring and that man, of his own will, was able to co-operate with God in salvation. Article X attacks the Anabaptist teaching that man's sin was a fiat of God. Articles XV and XVI oppose the Anabaptist heresy that sins committed after baptism cannot be repented of and thus redeemed. Article XVIII is against the Anabaptist error that sincere followers of pagan religions will be saved even if they wilfully reject Christ. Article XXIII stresses that ministers of the gospel must be called to preach through their church, thus attacking the Anabaptist doctrine that all believers are seen as exercising a teaching and pastoral function. Article XXXVIII is a direct refutation of the view of many Anabaptists that Christians should have all their goods in common.

In the early eighteenth century it was still the dominating opinion amongst Anglicans that Anabaptists were the main threat to the Church of

England and the Crown. It was also widely considered that the British
Baptists were guilty of carrying on the political extremes of Münzer and the
exegetical fantasies of Schwenkenfeld. Proof that Baptists were in fact
Anabaptists under a shortened name was found in the fact that they
rebaptized former members of the Church of England. Nor, until Gill
broke a lance for the Baptists, were Baptist efforts at defending themselves
against such accusations at all successful. This was mostly the Baptists'
own fault. Matthew Caffyn and John Gale had been viewed as the greatest
apologists of the Baptists but both these men succumbed to heresy. This
was also true of Gill's contemporary Robert Robinson whose work on the
history of baptism could hardly be taken seriously by orthodox Christians
as Robinson followed Caffyn and Gale in their Arian pursuits. Nor did
Thomas Crosby help matters in his *History of the English Baptists*, based
on Stinton's notes. Crosby directly identified the British Baptists with the
Continental Anabaptists, made wild claims that Anglicans such as John
Wycliffe were Baptists and criticized the strict way they handled Arians.
Benjamin Keach, another of Gill's predecessors, had angered both Baptists
and Evangelicals with his High Church, sacerdotal view of baptism
accompanied by the laying on of hands and promise of the Spirit. Many
Anglicans and Independents looked upon him as being little better than a
common fraud, indeed, a forger of evidence, to support his baptismal
theories. Richard Baxter had written a pamphlet on confirmation, arguing
that without faith such a ceremony was in vain. Keach saw that many of
Baxter's arguments dealing with confirmation were very similar to his own
when dealing with baptism. Instead of pointing this out to Baxter and using
this as a basis for joint discussion and even fellowship, Keach did a most
dishonourable thing. He cut out all the parts of Baxter's pamphlet which
could, in Keach's opinion, be equally used for adult baptism and fitted
them together on a single sheet and had them published under the
purposefully misleading title of *Mr Baxter's arguments for believers'
baptism*. Mr Baxter was not let into the secret until he heard hawkers crying
out in the streets that he had become a Baptist. Ivimey, the Baptist historian,
says that this was Keach's 'first work published on the subject of baptism'.
The historian gives this as an example of Keach's 'zeal', saying he had
'good grounds' for the deception, yet when Anglicans or Presbyterians
were guilty of similar dubious actions, Ivimey terms their deeds 'infa-
mous' or 'vile'.

John Gill can be claimed to be the first and greatest Baptist who stood
in the traditions of the Reformers and Puritans to work out a definite
systematic theology for his own church and the Baptist movement as a
whole. His works were written at a time when the Evangelical Awakening
was gaining momentum in the Anglican Church and Evangelicals were
asking themselves why Dissenters were so slow to work side by side with

their Anglican brethren in bringing the gospel to the man in the street and in the market-places. By the beginning of the eighteenth century Evangelicals and even the not-so-evangelical in the Established Church were planning foreign missions and weekly prayer-meetings at set times all over the country, looking to Dissenting churches to follow their example.

The truth was that up to Gill's age the Baptists were a movement shaking off persecution and undergoing formation. They were now more or less legally 'free churches', that is they were in a position to freely choose and define what they believed from the grass roots upwards and not have their beliefs thrust upon them by church hierarchies and governments. This formation into a united body with a united doctrine was no easy task as those who came to be known as Baptists actually traced their roots back to very different pasts, both politically and doctrinally. Few of these roots had anything to do with the Continental Anabaptist extremists. This did not prevent them from being looked upon as rebels to law and order, even by many of their Evangelical brethren who were growing in power in the Church of England after the Restoration in spite of much inner-church difficulties. The Evangelicals felt strongly that 'to serve God and honour the King' was the priority of every Christian who took his faith seriously. The Baptists, in the eyes of their Anglican brethren, politicized their religion by denouncing any form of church government 'from above', denying any responsibility of the State for the well-being of the church and relying on principles of Greek democracy in church government in the form of one man one vote to determine what they ought to believe.

The Evangelicals also looked upon the Baptists' treatment of their children with horror, especially at the doctrine that children stood outside of God's covenant with their believing parents. They also recoiled at the common belief held amongst Baptists[12] in Gill's day that the curse which original sin brought with it either did not apply to children, who were in a regenerate state by nature anyway, or was removed by Christ's death, leaving only post-infant sins to be repented of.[13] The belief was rife amongst Evangelicals that the Baptists postponed baptism for their children because they equated baptism with the washing away of sin and reception of the Holy Spirit and thus believed that their children, being regenerate, had no sins to be washed away. Thus baptism was unnecessary for them. The fact, too, that Baptists so often stressed that they became members of the local body of Christ through 'the gateway of Baptism' reminded them of the High Church movement in their own church whom they felt were papists at heart.

Evangelicals of the Establishment were also quick to point out that whenever Arians and Sabellians found the going too hot in the Anglican church, as in the case of Whiston, they had themselves rebaptized[14] and became members of Baptist churches. This was a two-way process, however, as when Particular Baptist Sayer Rudd, pastor of Turners' Hall, turned Arian, he was expelled from his association and eventually became Vicar of Walmar in 1757. Apparently the Anglicans did not think it was necessary to 'rebaptize' Rudd.

Many Evangelicals, following a number of the British Reformers, were sympathetic with the Baptists concerning immersion, practising such themselves, and would have accepted discussion with the Baptists who were developing their views on the subject. They felt, however, that the Baptists' dogmatic insistence that a sufficient amount of water to cover a person entirely was absolutely necessary to make it ritually effective was a sacramental belief in modes rather than meaning.[15] They were also very suspicious of the fact that Baptists seemed to differ so obviously in all points of doctrine amongst themselves but looked upon all those who were baptized in a certain way as 'brethren'. This led them to consider Pædobaptists who might believe with them on all other points of doctrine as mere seekers who still had not come to a full experimental knowledge of the gospel. To the Evangelicals the Baptists were not yet fully Reformed as they did not appreciate the federal, covenantal aspect of baptism and aimed for union via an inauguration ceremony rather than doctrine. In their eyes, the Baptists had turned the ordinance into a sacerdotal ritual.[16]

Evangelicals felt that the Presbyterians had kept a Reformed balance between the ritual and the spiritual but believed that as, to use Milton's words, 'presbyter' was but 'priest writ large' they had no true ecclesiastical reason for separation, only a political one. With the Baptists and the Quakers it was different. They felt that these two separatist movements had gone to two radical extremes: the Baptists stressed the ritual side of true worship, whereas the Quakers stressed the spiritual. They also felt strongly that the Baptists' placing of a font where the Lord's Table had been, took the emphasis away from experimental church fellowship and placed emphasis on the ritualism of church entrance. This mistrust was strengthened with the new form of evangelicalism fostered by Fuller which they felt placed the whole of gospel preaching on the conversion of people outside of the church to the neglect of 'the communion of the saints' and the nurture of Christian families.[17] The Baptist faith, to Evangelicals, was an adult religion in which education and instruction played the vital part and not social church life and witness.

Another bone of contention, closely allied to ritualism, was the Baptist insistence that there had been a continuous 'apostolic succession' of Baptists from New Testament times on. Thus, since the days of the early church, those who were baptized in the Baptist way (though the Baptists were far from united concerning how this was traditionally performed and what ceremonial forms were used on the occasion) had always been baptized by a person who had been baptized in the same way back to John the Baptist.[18] This was why the British Baptists, on the whole, refused to accept such pioneers of their movement as John Smyth because he had either baptized himself, as many early British Baptists had done, or been baptized by an unbaptized person.[19] This also explains why American Baptists still stress that they had not originally baptized themselves but arranged for a baptized brother from Wales (Thomas Griffiths) to come over and baptize them. Such teaching was all High Church hocus-pocus to the Evangelicals.

Perhaps the greatest hindrance to a common understanding amongst Gill's Evangelical contemporaries and the Baptists was the 'I am holier than thou' attitude that the latter showed their brethren of the Establishment and their Independent doctrinal allies. Anglicans, for instance, were banned from joining in fellowship at the Lord's Table at Baptist gatherings, though they made provisions in their own churches for non-Anglicans such as Lutherans, Reformed, Episcopalians and Baptists to share such fellowship with them. Though a Presbyterian was allowed to preach before a Baptist gathering, no Anglican would be asked to do so as Toplady experienced to his dismay when he offered to preach at Gill's funeral. If a Baptist believer married a believing Anglican, the couple were pronounced as living in adultery by many Baptist churches. Only when the non-Baptist was baptized in the Baptist way was the marriage pronounced valid, thus adding to the belief in the ritual powers of baptism.[20]

When debates between Anglicans, Independents and Baptists were organized, Baptists invariably accused their Anglican and Independent fellow-debaters of holding popish views and thus invalidating them as equal partners. In reality, it was, at times, highly difficult to see which side was being more popish. What really angered the Evangelicals was that the Baptists insisted that no Anglican could be a true believer as he neglected his obedience to Matthew 28:19-20 and thus could have no fellowship at a church level with Baptists. Bunyan's ideal of a church composed of the dipped and sprinkled was an impossibility in most Baptists' way of thinking. A sad example of this view which tears brother away from brother is seen in the church founded by the Serampore Trio (Carey, Ward and Marshman) and their multi-national and multi-denominational friends in India.[21] The newly converted there shared sweet communion with former members of Baptist, Anglican, Presbyterian and Lutheran churches and all gathered around the Lord's Table together as the Bride of Christ. When this news reached Andrew Fuller, a 'closed' Baptist, he objected to the church's right to determine its own practice, arguing that it should come under his jurisdiction as secretary of the Baptist Missionary Society and that certain communicants were not full Christians as they had not been baptized according to exclusive Baptist rites and so must be banned from the Lord's Table. Fuller had in mind men of God such as David Brown who, though an Anglican chaplain, was one of the most enthusiastic supporters of the Baptist mission's work and deserves to be regarded as one of its earliest supporting pillars. This moved Anglicans — who were providing almost the entire political lobby to keep the mission open and helping to finance it — to argue that when it came to the pinch, the Baptists neither believed in a 'free' church nor in the sovereignty of the local church.

Dr John Ryland was horrified when he heard the news of Fuller's unbrotherly, unilateral action and it seemed as if there would be a break in fellowship between him and Fuller, and the Serampore Trio and the British support group. Ryland and the Serampore church, however, decided to accept Fuller's dictate for the sake of peace.[22] It was, however, enforced administrative peace from outside and not that peace which comes from the inner harmony of brethren worshipping their Lord together. Many see this step as the beginning of the down-grading movement and the modern interest in para-church organizations rather than local church-based evangelism which Gill practised. This gave rise to Spurgeon's refusal to work with the BMS unless they returned to church-based missionary work.[23]

As criticism from Anglicans, Presbyterians and Independents grew, those who knew Gill throughout the country begged him to use his scholarship to work out a Baptist apology for the faith. Gill did not meet all the criticisms levelled against Baptists, nor was he successful in presenting a water-tight case for the points he raised, but his was a fair start to a reasonable dialogue between brethren. He outlined fairly and squarely the reasons for his not being a Pædobaptist on the one hand and sought to put Baptist policies and doctrines on a sound biblical footing on the other.

On the matter of political allegiance Gill, unlike his fiery friend John Ryland Senior, was a staunch Royalist and felt that the monarchy was a far more stable means of government than a republic. Rippon stresses that no one was a heartier friend of the Hanoverian Royal Family than Gill who often looked to King George as a bulwark against Rome and Continental Roman Catholic influence on Britain.[24] Writing on 2 December 1745, 'Let them be ashamed which act treaterously without cause', when the Stuarts were planning to put the clock back and once again subject Britain to a pro-French and pro-Roman Catholic rule, Gill exclaims:

> Such are those who are now risen up against our rightful Sovereign King George; a parcel of perfidious, treacherous wretches; some of them who were in the last rebellion, and obtained his father's pardon; others that partook yearly of his royal bounty, for the instruction of their children, and all have enjoyed the blessing of his mild and gentle Government; and therefore are without cause his enemies.[25]

Unlike the non-jurors and the numerous Jacobite-minded Dissenters —
not forgetting the many followers of Atterbury still in the Anglican Church
— Gill's brand of Christianity in its political outworking was thus above
suspicion in the eyes of Evangelicals who had welcomed the Glorious
Revolution and were now faithful subjects of King George. Not only Gill's
politics but more especially his doctrines caused the Evangelicals to have
reconciliatory views concerning the Baptists as they realized that he was
quite free from the bulk of denominational idiosyncrasies and bigotry that
separated them both from former and contemporary Baptist apologists.
Influenced by Gill's sermons and works on systematic theology Toplady,
Hervey, Middleton and later Venn, followed by a substantial number of
Oxford and Cambridge Evangelicals and Irish Churchmen, all played their
part in offering the right hand of fellowship to those Baptists who agreed
with them on Reformed doctrine other than denominational baptism. This
is in stark contrast to the Methodists under Wesley's leadership who
remained highly critical of any Baptist whether Arminian or Calvinist.

Gill's Dissenting hackles were raised in 1751 when a Welsh Anglican
strove to use his influence to have all Dissenting children in Wales
catechized according to the Thirty-Nine Articles to rid them of 'Anabaptist
influence'. Gill came to the assistance of his Welsh Dissenting brethren in
his *The Dissenter's Reasons for Separating from the Church of England*
complaining that the clergyman was 'not content highly to commend the
Church of England, as the purest church under heaven, but reflects greatly
on dissenters, and particularly on such whom he calls rebaptizers; and
repeats the old stale theory of the German Anabaptists and their errors,
madnesses and distractions; and most maliciously insinuates, that the
people who now go by this name are tinctured with erroneous principles;
for he says, they spread their errors in adjacent countries, which are not
fully extinguished to this day; whereas they are a people that scarce agree
with us in any thing; neither in their civil nor in their religious principles,
nor even in baptism itself; for they were for the repetition of adult baptism
in some cases, which we are not, and used sprinkling in baptism, which we
do not; the difference between them and us, is much greater than between
the papists and the Church of England'.[26]

Gill's reaction was translated into Welsh and quickly ran into many
editions in both languages. Much of what Gill says in the booklet is aimed
at the weaknesses in Anglican church order and the fact that many
Anglicans do not live according to their doctrines. Obviously disagreeing
with the whole concept of Anglicanism, Gill nevertheless strives to be
objective and inoffensive, explaining what he 'disliked' rather than
thought was heresy. Actually Gill had a high opinion of the Thirty-Nine
Articles and was constantly holding them up before heretical Anglicans to
show them what they believed. In his controversy with Wesley, he was

quick to show him that the Thirty-Nine Articles taught the doctrines of grace. Gill believed that if Anglicans only knew just why Dissenters did not feel happy having fellowship within the framework of the Book of Common Prayer, they would be less aggressive in their criticism. He thus argues:

> Whereas Dissenters from the Church of England are frequently charged with schism, and their separation is represented as unreasonable, and they are accounted an obstinate and contentious people; it may be proper to give some reasons why they depart from the Established church; by which it will appear that their separation does not arise from a spirit of singularity and contention, but is really a matter of conscience with them; and that they have that to say for themselves, which will sufficiently justify them, and remove the calumnies that are cast upon them.[27]

Although Gill lists eleven points of disagreement which he applies to the special Welsh situation in general and the Church of England in particular, they are mostly points which may be raised against any professing church body, including the Baptist churches, which has swerved from the doctrines and practices once committed to the saints and replaces gospel practices with an institutionalized view of the church and its ministry.[28]

First Gill argues that he dislikes the constitution of the Anglican Church because it is established by the law of men rather than the law of God. Churches, he argues, ought to be constituted by the Acts of the Apostles not by acts of Parliament. Secondly, Gill cannot accept the Anglican Church as a true church as he argues that the only visible churches referred to in the New Testament are local churches not national churches. Gill feels that Anglicans thus contradict their own doctrine in Article XIX which states that 'The visible church of Christ is a congregation of faithful men.' Gill interprets 'congregation' locally, arguing that if the Anglican Church was a congregation, it would always meet in one place, which is impossible in a national church.

Thirdly Gill argued that all born in England (presumably he included the Welsh here) are automatically members of the Church of England. It is a church composed of fallen men and thus not a true church, so a true Christian cannot have fellowship with it. Gill is aware that Anglicans would deny this and say they believe in baptism and confirmation and covenantal promises to believing families but he argues that Anglican teaching on baptism was not according to the Word of God and confirmation has nothing to do with the Word of God at all. In fact Gill denies that the Anglican ordinances are practised in accordance with biblical patterns.

Gill's fourth argument is against incomplete Anglican doctrines. He argues that they are mostly biblical as far as they go, but are not generally observed in the denomination and are incomplete. He misses an article on the covenants of grace and works, on creation and providence and the Fall. There is no article on the nature of sin and its punishment, adoption, effectual calling, sanctification, faith, repentance, and the final perseverance of the saints. He would also like to see statements on the law of God, Christian liberty, church government and discipline, the communion of the saints, the resurrection of the dead, and the last judgement. A pure church, Gill argues, ought to preach and practise the full gospel.[29]

Gill takes up what he calls the ordinances of baptism and the Lord's Supper in his fifth argument, declaring that Anglicans wrongly profess to administer the ordinances according to Christ's command. Christ did not appoint the sign of the cross to be used in baptism ceremonies, nor the introduction of sponsors and sureties, godfathers and godmothers, nor prayers that the baptized 'may receive remission of sins by spiritual regeneration'. Most Evangelicals would have agreed with Gill concerning the sign of the cross and other rituals but disagreed with Gill on the church's duty to support the baptized in the faith. Gill's Anglican friends were only too aware of the linguistic and theological difficulties in the Prayer Book and constantly urged for reform. Hervey, Gill's friend and admirer, wrote, 'In an affair of the highest consequences, how negligent is the community, I mean in the long expected reformation of the liturgy, in which, excellent as it is upon the whole, there are some passages so justly exceptionable, that every bishop in the kingdom will tell you he wishes to have them expunged; and yet, I know not for what political or timid reasons, it continues just as it did. Had our first reformers been thus indolent, we still had been Papists.'[30] Hervey blamed Parliament for this state of affairs, which would have been wind in Gill's sails. Sadly modern amendments and radical alterations to the Prayer Book have left its theological testimony more dubious than ever and would have reaped great criticism from such Evangelical stalwarts as Romaine, Hervey, Toplady, Newton, Venn and Whitefield.

Lastly in this section, Gill argues that as there is no biblical proof that infants are to be baptized, they ought not to be. He strengthens this argument by saying that infants cannot be sensible of sin and therefore repent, nor can arguments concerning the covenant with Abraham, circumcision and the baptism of households be used to prove infant baptism. Gill could argue in this way as he rejected the Reformed two-covenant doctrine i.e. of a covenant of works as laid down by Moses and a covenant of grace or promise laid down with Abraham, believing that the covenant with Abraham was part of the covenant of works.

For Gill, baptism must be by immersion, in the sense of being plunged[31] totally in water and then taken out, and is to be administered to those who already have a saving faith in the triune God.[32] The problem of identifying baptism symbolically at least with regeneration so obviously prevalent in the Prayer Book does not leave Gill unaffected, one could even say — untainted. In the chapter 'On Baptism' in his *Of the Public Ordinance of Divine Worship*, Gill allows himself two references from history and a third in a footnote to back up his insistence that believers' baptism was the original form of baptism and it was always by immersion. In these passages he comes very near to claiming for the Baptists what he finds wrong amongst Anglicans. He quotes first-century Barnabas who says, 'We descend into the water, full of sin and filth; and we ascend, bringing forth fruit in the heart, having fear and hope in Jesus, through the Spirit.' This, of course, is not believers' baptism but the teaching that faith and the indwelling of the Spirit is available through baptism. Gill, of course, completely denied this in his scriptural exegesis and it is very ill-chosen as 'proof' that the infant church practised total immersion if one does not believe in baptismal regeneration. His other examples of being 'dipped quite under water' concern whole peoples, troops etc. who were baptized by the twenty thousand on order of their princes under the influence of Roman Catholic 'missionaries'. This reminds one of the story in school history books that the Saxons all allowed themselves to be baptized to show their allegiance to Charles the Great. The ceremony was to be by immersion in the local river. Whilst being dipped, however, the wily Saxons kept their weapon hands above the waters in order to retain some of their independence! Again, such stories hardly seem convincing evidence to prove 'believers' baptism' by total immersion. Nor is Gill more discerning in his quote concerning second-century Tertullian's scepticism of infant baptism as 'proof' that it was a novelty at the time. Tertullian's words are also a 'first' in distinguishing between adult baptism and infant baptism which would equally suggest that the distinction itself was a novelty. Tertullian is, however, not arguing that infant baptism is a novelty but, in the particular case of first generation Christians only, it should be postponed. This would indicate that infant baptism was practised in established Christian families. One can only postpone what is already a practice at an earlier time, otherwise there would be nothing to postpone.

Indeed the insistence that baptism could only refer to immersion or dipping was still a novel idea to older Baptists who had practised adult baptism by sprinkling. A generation or two before Gill moved to Southwark, Baptists there were quite split as to whether believers should be dipped or sprinkled.[33] Nevertheless, Gill argued that believers' baptism by immersion was an ordinance of Christ along with the Lord's Supper but, unlike the Supper it was not an ordinance of the church but performed outside of the church, before membership was sought. Gill saw no covenantal relationship between circumcision and baptism and maintained that both the covenant of works (in Adam) and the covenant of grace (in Christ) were between God and adults only and these were the only covenants God made with man. This is rather daring reasoning as Deuteronomy 29:10-12 and Numbers 3:28 clearly teach that infants ('your little ones') were not only members of the covenants of promise and law but were also regarded as co-responsible in taking oaths to enter into these covenants i.e. the covenants with Abraham and Moses. It is also clear from Scripture and the words of our Lord that the covenant with Abraham was one of gracious promise and had fellowship with Christ as its goal.[34] The Bible also shows that Samuel was a believer as a child as also was David. Paul, when addressing Christian families in Ephesians 6:1-4, has a special word for the children 'in the Lord' and explains their duties as 'saints and faithful'. Colossians 3:20 finds Paul again addressing Christian children as well as their parents. These are obviously regarded by Paul as being part of the 'one body' in Christ that he refers to. It would be a speculative theologian indeed who would argue from these New Testament texts that these young members of the body of Christ were not baptized as they did not come under the covenant of grace. Who would argue that Samuel was not within the covenant of grace or Samson, for that matter, who was a 'Nazarite' from the womb on?

In Gill's *Reply to Mr Clark's Defence of the Divine Right of Infant Baptism*, published in 1754, he apparently modifies his view of the covenant by arguing that 'a little child' may be baptized if obviously 'called by grace and converted, and gives reasons of the hope that's in it'.[35] Nevertheless, though Gill's daughter became a believer in her early teens, her father did not baptize her, which was a source of anxiety for the girl at her early death.

Gill's view that baptism is not a church ordinance, but merely a preparatory rite before entrance into a church, would not appeal to most present-day Baptists who teach that a person wishing to be baptized must be first accepted by a church and recommended for baptism with their pastor performing the ordinance.[36] The *Standard Confession* of 1660[37] clearly accepts that Matthew 19:14 ('Suffer little children, and forbid them not, to come unto me: for of such is the kingdom of heaven') refers to infant salvation, though the authors refuse to believe that infants ought to be baptized. It is interesting to note that the Arminian Baptists of the *Standard Confession* do not seem to be criticizing the fact that believers' children are baptized but rather that in baptizing certain children only, i.e. the children of believers, they feel that Anglicans are saying that Christ died for a select number and are thus shutting out other children from salvation which do not have the opportunity of being brought up in a Christian family. They also seem to be arguing that children dying in infancy are not under the law, therefore they are not under condemnation.[38] Benjamin Keach complicated the issue by declaring that though dead infants are members of the Kingdom of Glory, they were never members of the visible church. This statement was partly the cause of Keach's trouble with the Church of England who had him sentenced to two weeks' imprisonment for heresy.[39]

It must have been quite a surprise for Gill's Anglican and Independent friends to find that he did not accept baptism as being an ordinance of the church,[40] though it was a covenantal ordinance. Devout Anglicans usually refer critically to a baptism performed without the gathered congregation as a 'hole in a corner affair' which smacks of Romanism. The Prayer Book refers to such a baptism only in extreme cases, for instance, when a child is certain to die soon. Otherwise baptism is not 'duly ministered' when it is not ministered within the visible Body of Christ. It was thus as foreign to an Anglican to think of preaching not being an ordinance of the church as it was to think that baptism and the Lord's Supper were not part and parcel of his inner-church worship and fellowship. Gill opens his essay 'Of Baptism' in his *Body of Divinity* Book III also with the strong claim that baptism is an ordinance of God but not an ordinance of the church. The fact that Anglicans spell the word 'Church' with a capital and Gill with a small 'c' when referring to baptism as an ordinance shows where part of the mystery lies. The Anglican tends to think of baptism in relation to a universal, or at least nationwide Church. Gill thinks of it in terms of eligibility for membership in the local church only. Explaining what he means, Gill argues:

> When I say it is not a church ordinance, I mean it is not an ordinance ministered in the church, but out of it, and in order to admission into it, and communion with it; it is preparatory to it, and a qualification for it; it does not make a person a member of a church, or admit him into a visible church; persons must first be baptized, and then added to the church, as the three thousand converts were; a church has nothing to do with the baptism of any, but to be satisfied that they are baptized before they are admitted into communion with it. Admission to baptism lies solely in the breast of the administrator, who is the only judge of qualifications for it, and has the sole power of receiving to it, and of rejecting from it; if not satisfied he may reject a person thought fit by a church, and admit a person to baptism not thought fit by a church.[41]

Gill's scriptural backing for this radical statement would also come as a surprise to Anglicans. Gill quotes Acts 9 concerning Saul who was converted on the road to Damascus and then baptized by Ananias 'without any previous knowledge and consent of the church and it was many days after this that he proposed to join himself to the disciples, and was received'.

This quote shows that, in reality, it is not so much the teaching on baptism which divides Anglicans from Gill, but it is the doctrine of the visible Church. All Anglicans are at home spiritually in all local branches of their Church. They do not see themselves as belonging *solely* to a specific, local church with a closed membership. Wherever they meet when the Word is preached and the ordinances practised, they are the Church. When an Ananias meets up with a Paul they constitute a Church as they are one in Christ and it is obvious that Ananias preached the Word to Paul and the ordinance of baptism was carried out. Gill is virtually arguing that Paul was not yet a Church member as he did not belong to a locally organized Christian church.

Whilst defending believers' baptism from Pædobaptist criticism, Gill does not forget to defend it from the peculiar views of the Socinians and Arians in his own denomination who had virtually given up requiring baptism of all their members as they argued that baptism was only for first generation Christians, their believing offspring not needing the ordinance. Gill wastes no time in showing that repentance and baptism are demanded of all who follow Christ in all ages and that each must be baptized for himself.

When dealing with the Lord's Supper, most of Gill's objections display a love for an exact correspondence between the symbol and the truth signified which borders on the very ritualism which he accuses Anglicans of practising and which goes quite contrary to his usual methods of biblical exegesis. Thus he cannot accept the Anglican Communion Service as it is supposed to be the Lord's *Supper* but, as it does not always take place at supper-time, it cannot be a true celebration. To be effectual, it seems for Gill, the Lord's Supper must take place in the evening and is invalid at any other time. Gill also objects to the bread being cut with a knife and not broken with the hands and he is shocked that communion is sometimes celebrated outside of the church building. Church ordinances, Gill stresses, must take place in the necessary church building. At times, one must ask oneself if these are truly the words of a Dissenter and are not rather the words of an officiating sacramentalist. Gill's criticism of the Anglican for cutting rather than breaking the bread seems unconvincing when one learns that the wine in the Carter Lane communion service was taken from a large number of small silver cups rather than from one large chalice. Subsequent critics of Gill have pointed out that the Goat Yard/Carter Lane church never sat at the Lord's Table in an upper room!

Gill objects to Anglicans kneeling when given the bread and wine as he thinks this indicates a form of worship of the elements. This is hardly a valid argument when used against the Church of England as the communion service is a service of repentance and prayer directed to Christ for those 'with a full trust in God's mercy' and one kneels in prayerful adoration of the Saviour and not the elements. Furthermore, Gill feels that no discipline is shown when admitting believers to the Supper. Any familiarity with the communion service reveals that the most solemn and strict warnings concerning the destruction of body and soul are given to those who misuse the occasion. Such warnings are rarely given in Dissenting churches. In addition, the Prayer Book service goes into the finest, intricate detail as to what the Supper represents, banning any room for the papist interpretations Gill places on it. Perhaps this moved Gill, in all fairness, to conclude that, 'since kneeling at most is but an indifferent rite, it ought not to be imposed as necessary, but should be left to the liberty of persons to use it or not'.

Gill is on firmer ground when criticizing the Test Act. This allowed Dissenters to take up government posts if they showed that they were still in fellowship with the Established Church by what was termed 'occasional conformity', which meant taking the Lord's Supper with Anglicans now and then. It must be stressed that such liberality was not reciprocal and Anglicans were banned from Baptist celebrations of the Lord's Supper. Almost from the start, however, this act was abused by those, chiefly from a nominal position within the Anglican Church, who took communion with a seared conscience so that they could step into a lucrative, often sinecure, post. Of this misuse, Cowper the Anglican, quite in agreement with Gill the Baptist, wrote in his *Expostulation*:

> Hast thou by statute shov'd from its design
> The Savior's feast, his own blest bread and wine,
> And made the symbols of atoning grace
> An office-key, a pick-lock to a place,
> That infidels may prove their title good
> By an oath dipp'd in sacramental blood?
> A blot that will be still a blot, in spite
> Of all that grave apologists may write,
> And though a Bishop toil to cleanse the stain,
> He wipes and scours the silver cup in vain.

Though nominal Anglicans such as Lord Chancellor Thurlow (1731-1806) climbed up the highest ladders in society through abusing the act, it was also abused by a number of office-bearing Dissenters, including Baptists though the latter's churches usually, but, according to Ivimey, not always,[42] put such abusers under church discipline. Gill was, however, also condemning those Baptists who could join in fellowship with their Anglican brethren with a clear conscience.

In practice, Gill tended to be lenient in admitting brethren to communion. His church allowed for 'transient members' to have fellowship with them at the table and also 'occasional members'. Apparently, few questions were asked of those who practised this kind of 'occasional conformity' but if the 'transient' or 'occasional' friends decided to stay within the church fellowship, they were more closely examined and contact was made with their home churches should such exist. Otherwise they came under the full discipline of the church which held believers' baptism to be a stipulation for access to the table. The temptation to speculate on whether Toplady, who often worshipped with Gill's flock, also shared the Lord's Supper with them, is great but no evidence either way is forthcoming. Evangelicals had usually no scruples in sharing the Lord's Table with Dissenters and even Hannah More who was as Anglican as they come, though an Evangelical, attended Jay's church at Argyle Chapel 'frequently and commonly' and certainly took communion there on at least one occasion, which caused the *Anti-Jacobin Review* to protest loudly.[43]

Gill's sixth complaint against the Church of England is that it has offices which are not mentioned in Scripture such as archbishops, deans, vicars, curates, chantors and the like. He argues that the New Testament knows only bishops and deacons. The former takes care of the spiritual side of the church and the latter temporal affairs. This is a valid argument and shows that the Church of England is organized in a way quite different to the New Testament pattern. One would think, however, that the criticism, coming from a Baptist, is far from just, or again shows that Gill is arguing from the point of view of his own Particular Baptist church which had a singular elder and a plurality of deacons and not from that of Baptists in general. During the eighteenth century the Baptists had apostles(!), administrators (for purposes of baptism), overseers,[44] moderators, travelling ministers, bishops, pastors, co-pastors, elders, messengers (whom Goadby calls 'an episcopy, a presbytery, and an inquisition all in one'),[45] deacons and deaconesses, not to mention all the office-bearers in the many parachurch organizations such as coffee-house clubs, associations, assemblies, unions, societies, committees and boards. Even the Particular Baptists, however, had, as is seen through the Goat Yard correspondence with the Hanover Coffee House, elders who exercised jurisdiction over a church without being in membership with it. It is also worth noting that it is easy to criticize the offices of other churches when they are not available to one's own denomination. During Commonwealth days, however, Anglican titles were taken over with no scruples and Henry Jessey, for instance, who could be called the founder of the Southwark Baptists,[46] was Vicar of St George's, Southwark. One of the earliest pastors of the Barbican Particular Baptist Church was John Gosnold, friend of Tillotson and formerly chaplain to Lord Grey, who left the Established Church when the Act of Uniformity was passed. Neal points out in his *History of the Puritans* how Baptists had nothing against taking over Anglican patronages, livings and titles when this was legally and church-wise possible.[47] Spurgeon did not hesitate to call Gill an archbishop[48] — jokingly, of course!

In Gill's seventh point, he criticizes the Established Church for having a king, indeed for once having a woman (Elizabeth I), as its head, rather than Christ. This is rather over-polemic but the point is worth making as the ambiguous position of the sovereign in the Anglican hierarchy suggests the messianic idea of a king-priest which can hardly be fulfilled in an earthly king, particularly when one thinks of the worldly nature of many a merry monarch! Strictly speaking, the Anglican Church looks on the monarchy as a reflection of the true theocracy. The king is set by God over the people as his steward contrary to the theory that the people elect the king. Anyone familiar with Rutherford's *Lex Rex* in which he argues for the voice of the people being the voice of God, or Hobbes' *Leviathan* in which he argues that the king is God's appointed one and the people have a duty to keep their covenant with the monarch, know how easily one can go to extremes on either side. It all goes back to the appointment of Saul as King of the Jews. Was Saul merely proclaimed king by a people rebellious against the theocracy or was he appointed by God as a symbol of the theocracy which the people were in danger of leaving? It is interesting to note that there is a very large anti-European Union lobby amongst present-day British evangelicals of all denominations who argue that the British Monarchy and Constitution are bulwarks of Protestantism against a Roman Catholic Europe which will fall if Britain becomes a member of a United States of Europe.

Gill's eighth point is that there is a want of discipline in the Anglican Church which shows it is not a true church of Christ. Again, Gill is obviously thinking of his own little flock at the time of writing, where discipline was tight but performed with loving care. There were those who thought otherwise. Crosby, once Gill's deacon, complained in his *History* that the Anglican Church was far more strict in upholding her doctrines and in her conception of orthodoxy than the Independents and Baptists and criticized her strongly for being so hard on Arians Clarke and Whiston.[49]

Crosby, who put being a Baptist before the need for doctrinal ortho-doxy, declared that the Established Church's attitude to Whiston, who became a Baptist but did not change his Arian views, was 'scandalous'. He also, however, criticized his own churches for the 'unbecoming heat' in disciplining heretics Caffyn (General Baptist) and Rudd[50] (Particular Baptist). Neal, following the Stinton/Crosby notes which he had borrowed for his *History of the Puritans*, emphasizes the harsh, strict discipline of the Anglicans such as when Cranmer had Joan of Kent[51] burnt at the stake for denying the true incarnation of Christ. Looking from an Anglican point of view Pamela Russel, a descendent of Gill's family, gave her opinions concerning a stricter discipline in the Anglican Church in her *BQ* article *Mr Russel of White Street*.[52] After carefully scrutinizing the eighteenth-century disciplinary measures of the White Street, Eagle Street, Maze Pond and Unicorn Yard churches (Goat Yard and Carter Lane are not mentioned!), which reveal that two pastors in her family had been guilty of 'defect in moral character' and 'drunkardness' respectively, Pamela Russel concludes that Baptist discipline was more merciful, less cruel and less stringent than Anglican discipline.[53] The strict Church of England's disciplinary measures she cites are against unchastity, non-payment of tithes and failure to take communion. She also points out that whereas Baptists came voluntarily under their churches' discipline, Anglican church authorities could exercise compulsory powers and had the secular authorities to back them up.[54] This kind of secular intervention in church matters was, of course, unscriptural in Gill's eyes. The nationwide aspect of the Church of England had enormous consequences in the matter of excommunication. Once excommunicated, former Anglicans were barred from Anglican fellowship wherever they went. Excommunication really hurt! When Crosby was excommunicated from the Goat Yard church, he merely joined another Particular Baptist church just up the road. When that church also excommunicated him, a few years later, it readmitted him apparently because the relations Crosby had wronged had left the church to join Gill's and thus no opposition was present. It is no wonder that Crosby claimed that Anglicans were more strict in their discipline! These actions, of course, were fully against the normal Particular Baptist procedure as a letter of dismissal and recommendation was usually required of those moving from other churches.

The ninth criticism which Gill levels against the Church of England is that he finds her ceremonies and rites either pagan, Jewish or popish. He mentions bowing to the east, bowing whenever the name of Jesus is mentioned, bowing to the altar, kneeling at the communion table, performing the sign of the cross and wearing a surplice. Most Evangelicals, indeed, most Anglicans whatever their doctrines, would have agreed with Gill here, barring kneeling at communion, and did not practice what Gill criticized. Gill himself however, to the chagrin of many a Baptist, insisted on wearing a gown adorned with very large bibs as a symbol of his office and was most particular that the correct rituals were performed in the baptism service and when celebrating the Lord's Supper.

Gill's tenth objection is aimed at the Prayer Book. He finds the use of set prayers against the practice of the primitive church, objects to the Scriptures being read 'piecemeal' (his word) during services and protests against passages from Isaiah and Jeremiah being called 'epistles'. He alleges that the version of the Psalms the church uses is a papist translation and objects to the fasts and festivals that the Prayer Book proscribes. Again he condemns the baptismal and communion services and argues that marriage and the burial of the dead have no place in a service book as they are civil ceremonies and not church ceremonies. It is truly surprising that coming to belief, being baptized in the Lord, being married in the Lord, and being buried by loved ones in the Lord are all seen by Gill as activities outside of church fellowship and, one could just as well say, thus outside of the covenant. His objections to the Anglican burial service reflect his own uncomfortable feeling at being present at such ceremonies but also clearly his inability to examine what the Prayer Book says with a fully opened mind. How else can one explain that Gill regards the prayer, 'beseeching — that we with all those that are departed in the true faith of thy holy name, may have our perfect consummation and bliss, both in body and soul' (Gill's quote), as indicating prayers for the dead? Gill's bias here is excellently documented in his *Essay on the Original of Funeral Sermons, Orations and Odes* 1729, where he argues that such practices are developments from pre- and non-Christian times.

Gill's last point is a rejection of the Church of England because he finds it a persecuting church, referring to times that had passed, rather than to his own day and age. Gill maintains that it was not the Anabaptists who started church strife but the Pædobaptist papists before the Reformation and the Lutherans (and presumably the Anglicans) who were Pædobaptists during and after the Reformation. Here Gill is obviously saying that had the Pædobaptists been more tolerant, they would never have had trouble with the Anabaptists. Gill is now sawing off the branch he is sitting on. In spite of his protests that he is not an Anabaptist, he nevertheless allies with them and indicates that their sufferings were those of the Baptists. This endeavour to reap the benefits of the martyrs' sufferings has become typical of Baptist apologists who either forget what enormous doctrinal differences separated them or do not take these differences seriously enough. This is seen clearly in Crosby's *History* but is also very much a feature of Charles Haddon Spurgeon's claims concerning Baptist witness against persecuting odds. In his *The Metropolitan Tabernacle: Its History and Work*, when speaking of the way Anabaptist teaching has been fought, he suddenly says, 'The afflicted Anabaptists, in their past history, have had such fellowship with their suffering Lord, and have borne so pure a testimony, both to truth and freedom, that they need in nothing be ashamed. Their very existence under the calumnies and persecutions which they have endured is a standing marvel, while their unflinching fidelity to the Scripture as the sole rule of faith, and their adherence to the simplicity of gospel ordinances is a sure index of their Lord's presence among them.'[55] It is a pity that Spurgeon did not name names so that one could test the veracity of his statement!

No matter from what angle Gill's 'defence' is seen, it only shows that there is room for criticism on both the Pædobaptist and adult-baptist sides and that if Gill achieved any result whatsoever with his pamphlet, it could only be that of a basis for further joint study of the Word and joint tolerance.

It is obvious from the history of the Church of England and what has already been said that the black sheep have often been the more numerous in the fold and the tares have threatened to smother the wheat. Nevertheless the eighteenth-century Evangelical wing produced such sound men as Walker, Hervey, Romaine, Whitefield, Toplady, Conyers, Cowper, Newton, Scott, Cecil and Venn. Baptists have also little room for thinking that their overall testimony is more representative of true Christianity. The General Baptists, before Dan Taylor's reforming influence, leave a sad record behind them. If one regards, say, the Barbican Baptist Church, made notorious through generations of heretical pastors, or the teaching of Gill's Particular Baptist contemporaries Dr Sayer Rudd and Robert Robinson, or the leap back into Latitudinarianism and Grotianism that the Particular Baptists suffered from after Gill's influence had waned, or, for that matter, the Downgrade Controversy of Spurgeon's days, they all show the wisdom of the biblical maxim concerning who should throw the first stone and emphasize that those who live in glasshouses should not throw stones at all. Nevertheless, the truth is that the comparatively tiny group of Baptists under the name of 'Particular' has produced a grand display of faithful men of God such as Kiffin, Knollys, Gill, Brine, the Wallins, Ryland Senior, Skepp, Button, Beddome, Booth, Kinghorn and Martin,[56] men who are only less known today than their Anglican counterparts because church historians have yet to make their stories available to the general Christian public.

Gill's views were taken well by Evangelicals in general as they revered Gill's doctrine as a whole. They were not averse to hearing his views on baptism though they had refused to listen to such teaching from the pens and mouths of the denominations' former apologists Gale and Foster. Anglican Erasmus Middleton, following Toplady, praises Gill's tolerance and openness on baptism,[57] arguing that his publications on the topic were not produced in bigotry but as a compulsory reaction and defence when he or his followers were attacked by Pædobaptists. Middleton adds that he wished Gill's overall attitude was shared by all denominations. Seymour stresses Gill's toleration of non-Baptists saying, 'John Gill was unquestionably an uncompromising Dissenter and a convinced Baptist. Yet, in all the bulk of his writings, it is surprising to discover how little he has to say about the relationship of the Dissenter to the Established Church, and it is even more surprising to discover how seldom he spoke about Baptists as such.'[58] Indeed, the Evangelicals were forced to respect Gill as it was easy to say that believers' baptism must be wrong when it was obviously practised by those who were quite anti-scriptural in their overall doctrines. It was not so easy at all when faced with Gill's orthodoxy and learning. The Evangelicals were the first to argue that all the churches' articles and homilies were useless unless accompanied by a new-born heart. Hervey,

Gill's friend, respected the Baptist position highly, although he did not share it, and often defended his Baptist brethren when they came under attack. Baptists and Pædobaptists often sat at his table and Hervey always made sure that no unbrotherly friction arose between the dipped and the sprinkled. Writing to his Baptist friend John Ryland Senior, Hervey could say, 'I am just come up from dinner, and who should be there but Rev. Mr H. who was so unseasonably zealous, as to attack Mr S. on the principles of anti-pædobaptism. I thought it a breach of delicacy and propriety of conduct, especially to do this to my guest, and at my table; therefore I took up the cudgels, and impersonated a baptist.'[59]

William Cowper, an Anglican, nevertheless shared sweet fellowship with many a Baptist, being particularly impressed by the work and testimony of Abraham Booth. The pain he experienced when he saw the brethren at war with one another caused him to write his long poem 'Charity' in which he says:

Were love in these the world's last doting years
As frequent, as the want of it appears,
The churches warm'd, they would no longer hold
Such frozen figures, stiff as they are cold;
Relenting forms would lose their pow'r or cease,
And ev'n the dipt and sprinkled, live in peace;
Each heart would quit its prison in the breast,
And flow in free communion with the rest.[60]

Gill's scholarly expertise and wide reading came to the Baptists' assistance in the matter of Jewish proselytes. It had become the fashion of Pædobaptists, led by the scholars Kidder, Broughton, Ainsworth, Selden, Hammond, Wall and Lightfoot to argue that the practice throughout the history of the Jews had been not only to circumcise male converts to Judaism but baptize by dipping whole families of both males and females, whatever their age. They then deduced that this custom was taken over by John and Christ thus 'proving' that infants ought to be baptized. Gill looked upon this as a declaration of exegetical bankruptcy on the part of the Pædobaptists, arguing that it was their 'last refuge and dernier resort'. He refutes the theory soundly in *A Dissertation Concerning the Baptism of Jewish Proselytes*. Using all his skill in Hebrew, he examined the various names for proselytes in the Old Testament, such as 'the stranger that is in thy gates', (literally 'the proselyte of the gate' גר שַעַר and the 'proselyte of righteousness' גר צדק). He examines minutely what they were expected to believe and what ceremonies they had to go through in the light of the Old Testament, the Apocrypha, Middle East and Ethiopian works of history, ancient Hebrew writings such as the Misnah, Bahir, Zohar and the Targums of Onkelos and Jonathan Ben Uzziel, the works of Jewish secular writers such as Josephus, Eleazer and Philo and those of the early church fathers. Gill goes to the sources quoted as providing evidence for proselyte baptism and finds not only that the supposed evidence is not there but 'scholars' have passed on these alleged sources from hand to hand as proof texts without either looking them up themselves or having the linguistic ability to do so. Thus Dr Wall quotes Selden who finds a reference in the Gamara referring back to the Mishna concerning a child who was baptized on becoming a proselyte. Gill finds the passages which he quotes at length. The child is there and the fact that she is 'redeemed' and become a proselyte is there, but there is no reference whatsoever to baptism.

Gill seems to have read all that can be read on the subject and quotes from a breathtaking number of works from many countries. In minute detective work he traces the origin of the mistakes and the exact way in which they have been reproduced and handed down. After spanning the whole of Hebrew literature from the earliest times to several centuries after Christ, Gill discovers the first references to proselyte baptism in the Talmuds which, as a conservative estimate, date from the end of the fifth century A.D. onwards, possibly as late as the eighth century. Even then Gill finds only one reference to a minor being baptized, the word used being of children up to thirteen years of age.

Gill argues that even if Lightfoot, Selden and others could find proof of proselyte baptism in pre-Christian documents, it would not help their case. Such proof showed that only the first generation of converts were baptized. Gill says that such a view will only please the Socinians who argue that first converts to their cut-down version of Christianity in a nation are to be baptized but not their offspring. He also points out that the late sources Lightfoot etc. quote to show that proselyte baptism was taken over by the Christians say that when pregnant women are baptized, the offspring in their wombs are also baptized. Again, hardly a practice in keeping with Scripture.

Gill ends his treatise on a most triumphant note, showing that all the Pædobaptist arguments mentioned refer to the baptism of proselytes by immersion. If this is so, asks Gill, whence comes their unbiblical and untraditional belief in sprinkling?

By far the most popular, though scholarly, work done by Gill was his mammoth Bible commentary. It is an immense one-man effort probably unique in the history of the church. The 1810 edition, used for modern facsimile reprints, has some 7,350 pages of multi-columned, tiny print which in terms of modern page layouts for encyclopedias etc. would easily fill 12,000 pages. Writing in praise of the work, J. M. Cramp the Baptist historian says: 'The peculiar excellence of this work lies in its plain, strong sense, its perspicuous style, the care with which every sentence and almost every word is explained, and, especially, the light thrown upon many passages by extracts from Jewish authors.'[61]

Reviewing the 1854 reprint of Gill's commentary, J. C. Philpot did not hesitate to say:

> For a sound, consistent, scriptural exposition of the word of God, no commentary, we believe, in any language can be compared with Dr. Gill's. There may be commentaries on individual books of Scripture, such as Vitringa on Isaiah, Venema on the Psalms, Alting on Jeremiah, Caryll on Job, Lampe on John, Luther on the Galatians, Owen on the Hebrews, Mede on the Revelation, which may surpass Dr. Gill's in depth of research and fullness of exposition; and the great work from which Poole compiled his Synopsis may be more suitable to scholars and divines, as bringing together into one focus all the learning of those eminent men who in the 16th century devoted days and nights to the study and interpretation of the word of God. But for English readers there is no commentary equal to Dr. Gill's. His alone of all we have seen is based upon consistent, harmonious views of divine truth, without turning aside to the right hand or the left. It is said of the late Mr Simeon, of Cambridge, that his plan of preaching was, if he had what is called an Arminian text, to preach from it Arminianism, and if he took a Calvinistic text, to preach from it Calvinism. Not so Dr. Gill. He knew nothing about Arminian texts, or Arminian interpretations. He believed that the Scriptures, as an inspired revelation from God, must be harmonious and consistent with itself, and that no two passages could so contradict each other as the doctrines of free-will contradict the doctrines of grace. The exhortation of the Apostle is, 'Having then gifts differing according to the grace that is given to us whether prophecy, let us prophesy according to the proportion of faith' (Rom. 12:6). This apostolic rule was followed closely by Dr. Gill. 'The proportion,' or as the word literally means, 'analogy of faith', was his rule and guide in interpreting the Scripture; and therefore, as all his explanations were modeled according to the beautiful proportions of divine truth as received by faith, so every view disproportionate to the same harmonious plan was rejected by him as God-dishonouring, inconsistent, and contradictory. It is this sound, consistent, harmonious interpretation of divine truth which has stamped a peculiar weight and value on Dr. Gill's Commentary, such as no other exposition of the whole Scripture possesses.[62]

Gill's own sense of calling in undertaking his task is expressed humbly in a letter to a Mr Yeoman[63] of Northampton in 1744, in which Gill outlines why he started out on the work and what he intended to accomplish by it:

Dear Brother

I need not tell you that I have been some years past engaged in writing an exposition of ye New Testament, which is now just finishing and through the solicitations of my friends I have printed proposals for ye publication of it, some of which I have sent you by which you will see yt (that) ye work is large and heavy, and will require all ye assistance my friend, can give me and the whole strength of our interest to get it out into ye world but inso much as nothing of this kind has been done by any of our denomination, and such a work seems necessary both for ministers and private Christians, that they may have something to have recourse to in their own way; it may be hoped, that our friends will exert themselves in giving cheerful assistance and encouragement to it; I send these proposals to you because I dont know ye brother, nor his name who ministers to our friends at Northampton, I doubt not but you will do all ye service you can, if you think fitt you may send one of ye specimens to Dr Doddridge, and spread some of the proposals among the pupils. What Subscription may be obtained, in either way of subscribing proposed, be pleased to send me with ye names of ye Subscribers, in convenient time, as soon as you can. I hope you are in health both in Soul and body I wish you much of ye divine presence and ye discoveries of ye love of God to you: you will excuse brevity in writing, having much of this work upon my hands, who am your

affectionate friend and
Brother in X
John Gill

London Jan, 28th 1744-5.[64]

Spurgeon had a love-hate relationship to Gill's commentary, ever praising it, yet ever showing his suspicion of it. It was as if the Prince of Preachers was always conscious that Gill was behind him, testing his orthodoxy, and Spurgeon, ever willing to try out new ideas, did not know whether he should comply or rebel. When commenting on Gill's method of exegesis in his sermons-cum-commentaries, Spurgeon confessed that the general state of doctrine in his denomination was far lower than in Gill's day. He also laments that Arminianism had the upper hand in contemporary evangelical exposition. Yet he was mercilessly critical of Gill's scholarly but practical method in preaching of first destroying the false hopes and ideas of his hearers before giving them the comforting truth which is in Christ Jesus. Spurgeon, though acknowledging the high value of Gill's research, nevertheless pokes fun at this didactic way of instructing hearers in his *Commenting and Commentaries*, saying:

> He delivered his comments to his people from Sabbath to Sabbath, hence their peculiar mannerism. His frequent method of criticizing is, 'This text does not mean this,' nobody ever thought it did; 'It does not mean that,' only two or three heretics ever imagined it did; and again it does not mean a third thing, or a fourth, or a fifth, or a sixth absurdity — but at last he thinks it does mean so-and-so, and tells you so in a methodical, sermon-like manner. This is an easy method, gentlemen of filling up the time, if you are ever short on titles for a sermon. Show your people firstly, secondly, and thirdly, what the text does not mean, and then afterwards you can go back and show them what it does mean. It may be thought, however, that one such a teacher is enough, and that what was tolerated from a learned doctor would be scouted in a student fresh from college. For good, sound, massive, sober sense in commenting, who can excel Gill? Very seldom does he allow himself to be run away with by imagination, except now and then when he tries to open up a parable, and finds a meaning in every circumstance and minute detail; or when he falls upon a text which is not congenial with his creed, and hacks and hews terribly to bring the Word of God into a more systematic shape. Gill is the Coryphaeus of hyper-Calvinism, but if his followers never went beyond their master, they would not go very far astray.

Obviously Gill's method was highly successful in teaching his flock to beware of hirelings and false prophets. Spurgeon's remark that 'nobody thought it did', when Gill pointed out what a text did not imply, is soon seen to be unfounded when one examines Gill's sermons. When the preacher refers to sanctification, for instance, he is careful to inform his hearers that he is not talking about do-gooders who stand high in their own praise, nor about those evangelically self-righteous people who believe by sincere obedience to the gospel to inherit heaven, but about those who believe in the outworking of a new nature infused into the heart by the Holy Spirit. Such a refutation of false ideas was highly relevant in Gill's church as a small group of members were denying 'the internal sanctification of the Spirit, as a principle of grace and holiness wrought in the heart' and causing unrest in the church by criticizing the need for Christ's righteousness and emphasizing the meritorious effects of good works. Heresies such as Deism, Arianism, popery and Arminianism were not held by 'two or three heretics' but by thousands upon thousands in the various denominations of Gill's day and the general teaching on sanctification and holiness was very low because of these heresies. Rippon gives quite an alarming picture of the number of errors prevailing in the Baptist churches and stresses how Gill 'adorned the pulpit' by taking a firm stand against them, though 'with a meek, humble and sympathizing spirit'. It is strange that Spurgeon rejected, and even ridiculed, Gill's sound method of preaching in order to enliven his own with a touch of ill-founded humour though, at the same time, confessing that the errors Gill successfully debunked were very much prevalent in his own day which had seen a departure from Gill's doctrines and methods. Strange, too, is the way Spurgeon links Gill's teaching with Hyper-Calvinism and his statement that if his followers never went beyond their master, they would not go very far astray. Is this an argument to show that Gill was not the Hyper-Calvinist the so-called Moderate Calvinists thought him to be or is Spurgeon saying Hyper-Calvinism is not very far wrong?

To Augustus Toplady at least, Gill's life of study was always accompanied by a life of sound doctrine and exemplary living. A rather critical man himself, he found only praise for the way in which his friend honoured God in the pulpit. This moved him to write shortly after Gill's death:

> The Doctor considered not any subject superficially, or by halves. As deeply as human sagacity, enlightened by grace, could penetrate, he went to the bottom of every thing he engaged in. With a solidity of judgement, and with an acuteness of discernment, peculiar to few, he exhausted, as it were, the very soul and substance of most arguments he undertook. His style, too, resembles himself; it is manly, nervous, plain: conscious, if I may so speak, of the unutterable dignity, value, and importance of the freight it conveys; it drives, directly and perspicuously to the point in view, regardless of affected cadence, and superior to the little niceties of professed refinement.
>
> Perhaps, no man, since the days of St. Austin, has written so largely, in defence of the system of Grace; and, certainly, no man has treated that momentous subject, in all its branches, more closely, judiciously, and successfully.
>
> His learning and labours, if exceedable, were exceeded only by the invariable sanctity of his life and conversation. From his childhood, to his entrance on the ministry; and, from his entrance on the ministry to the moment of his dissolution; not one of his most inveterate opposers was ever able to charge him with the least shadow of immorality. Himself, no less than his writings, demonstrated, that the Doctrine of Grace does not lead to Licentiousness.
>
> Those who had the honour and happiness of being admitted into the number of his friends can go still further in their testimony. They know, that his moral demeanour was more than blameless: it was,

from first to last, consistently exemplary. And, indeed, an undeviating consistency, both in his views of evangelical truths, and in his obedience, as a servant of God, was one of those qualities, by which his cast of character was eminently marked. He was, in every respect, a burning and a shining light —Burning with love to God, to Truth, and to Souls —Shining, as 'an ensample to believers, in word, in faith, in purity'; a pattern of good works, and a model of all holy conversation and godliness.

The running phrase 'as sure as John Gill is at the bookseller's' which became common parlance in Kettering in the days of Gill's youth, was soon changed to 'as sure as Gill is in his study', once Gill became a pastor. Spurgeon says, 'He was always at work; it is difficult to say when he slept.' This must have been a common talking point amongst Gill's flock as contemporary writers were always wondering how Gill found the time and the effort to do all he did. Later writers have thought that Gill must have been something of a hermit, never leaving his study both day and night. Spurgeon tended towards this interpretation. Gill, however, as contemporary records show, was a very social man, often to be seen at inter-denominational ministers' fraternals, church anniversary meetings, annual dinners, public lectures and the like. He spent at least one lunch-time a week dining with pastors from a number of different denominations and was very active in inter-denominational activities besides fund-raising projects for needy students, pastors and retired ministers. He took particular care that his members were regularly visited and obviously knew his congregation individually. The records show, as in the case of John Russel of White Street, that Gill found time to visit other pastors. It is often rumoured nowadays that Gill found visiting his flock a burden but no testimony to this effect ever came from his lips, and his references to the family life of his members are many showing that he knew what was going on in their homes and loved them dearly. Furthermore, the facts show that Gill was a most affectionate father, husband and son and he often had visitors to stay in his house, particularly from Kettering, a town which Gill frequently visited to spend days at a time there with his mother.

It is strange that Gill has reaped most criticism here from a free church background emphasizing that Gill did not do all the visiting and all the counselling that went on in his church. Gill was a Dissenting pastor and not an Anglican bishop or vicar who bore all the responsibility for witness on his own shoulders. Surely if the free churches have anything to be proud of at all, it is the fact that they believe every member is an evangelist and every member has a duty to witness to those both within and without the fold? Gill was a firm believer in this praiseworthy method of running a church. After Rippon took over Gill's flock, he never suggested that Gill had neglected them but rather quotes those who knew Gill well as saying that he watched over his people 'with great affection, fidelity, and love'.

This pastoral care was not confined to Gill's members as abundant evidence shows that Gill added to his visiting list those in his district, especially the sick and dying, who had nothing whatsoever to do with his church. On one occasion Gill heard that a young country curate had been brought to London to be cared for by his brother in nearby Miles Lane and was now at death's door. Gill did not hesitate to visit the fever-stricken patient, although he was of a different denomination, and continued to care for him regularly. He soon discovered that the Anglican possessed a true experience of the righteousness of Christ in his life and formed a great friendship with him. The young man confessed that every visit of Gill made him wiser and helped him to grow in grace. He also grew in strength and was able to return home after spending two years in London. During this time James Hervey, for that was the young man's name, laid the foundations for the books which were to make him famous. It was no wonder that Hervey always referred to Gill as a giver of wisdom and a 'Father in Israel'.

John Ryland once asked Gill how he managed to be so active, and presumed, as Spurgeon did later, that it was through long hours of intense labour. Gill surprised his friend by informing him that he was not in favour of rising very early and going to bed late and found such a life most injurious to study. He started his day as soon as it was light in the winter and shortly before six in the morning during the summer. He drank chocolate in lieu of breakfast and first took solid food in the early afternoon having worked constantly through that period. The stories of his perpetual sojourn in his study is really a myth. In point of fact, Gill loved to sit with his family whenever he could and, though he did sermon preparation in the evenings when he was not preaching, he rarely entered his study after tea-time but sat in the living-room doing his reading and preparing his notes amongst his dear ones.

The fact that Gill did not use his study quite as much as was imagined, under the grace of God, saved his life. On the morning of 15 March 1752 a violent hurricane blasted through London bringing death and destruction with it. Gill had just closed his study door and was off to take a morning service when the storm attacked his house. A stack of chimneys was blown over in no time and crashed through the roof of his upstairs study, smashing his writing desk to pieces. If Gill had been there, he would have been crushed to death in a moment. A friend of Gill had quoted to him a saying of Dr Halley, the famous astronomer, shortly before the storm. Halley had said, 'Close study prolonged a man's life, by keeping him out of harm's way.' When Gill met his friend again, he told him, 'What becomes of Dr Halley's words now, since a man may come to danger and harm in his closet, as well as on the highway, if not protected by the special care of God's providence?'

The faculty of Marischal College, University of Aberdeen, had long been interested in Gill's publications and followed the development of his scholarly progress with great interest. This led the Principal, Professor Osborn, encouraged by Prof. Pollock, the Professor of Divinity, to award Gill the degree of Doctor of Divinity in the year 1748. When his deacons congratulated him on the award, Gill commented, 'I never thought it, nor bought it, nor sought it.' Nevertheless he accepted it. This caused some considerable criticism amongst those Baptists who believed that academic honours should be despised by Christians. Baptist historian Joseph Ivimey was strongly against taking on 'religious distinctions', believing that Christians should live according to the command 'Be ye not called Rabbi.' He thus argued that Gill was offered, and accepted, the degree purely on literary grounds. Ivimey cannot help but point out here that Andrew Fuller was awarded a doctorate from an American university, but refused to acknowledge it, adding, 'These remarks are not intended to convey any censure upon the conduct of Dr Gill.' Ivimey's own interpretation is quite contrary to the very letter he quotes (following Rippon) from Prof. Osborn who stressed that the doctorate was given Gill 'on account of the honest and learned defence of the true sense of the Holy Scriptures, against the profane attacks of deists and infidels, and the reputation his other works had procured him in the learned world'. It is salutary indeed to find a secular university wishing to honour the truth in this way.

8.
The good news of God's everlasting love

By 1729 Gill's fame as a preacher and writer of note had spread throughout all Bible-loving churches in all denominations and was even being noted in publications abroad.[1] This caused a number of non-Baptists to argue that Gill's ministry was too good to be restricted to one group of believers and seekers alone. They thus asked Gill if he would be willing to preach weekly at inter-denominational gatherings in a hall financed by sponsors. Gill agreed to the proposal and a lecture hall large enough for the purpose was found in Great Eastcheap. Here Gill commenced a ministry to the 'other sheep' that was to continue uninterrupted for over twenty-six years. He opened the lectures by expounding Psalm 71:16: 'I will go in the strength of the Lord God; I will make mention of thy righteousness,' explaining that he stood there not in his own strength but in the strength of his Lord, assisted by the Holy Spirit and the grace of God. His main concern, he argued, was to preach the free justification of sinners by the righteousness of Christ imputed to them. This he believed was the central theme of the Bible as it had been the central theme of the Reformation and was the doctrine by which the church either stood or fell. This doctrine, to Gill, was the main arch of the bridge over which a burdened sinner must go in his pilgrim's progress from sin to salvation.

In stressing that he was going forth in the name of the Lord, mentioning his righteousness and his only, Gill was shaking off the misty cobwebs of Restoration theology with its emphasis on 'playing the man', fine manners and moral duties. This teaching, ethically sound as it may have been theoretically, nevertheless left out the essential truth that without the righteousness of Christ man was but a worm and all his righteousness was merely filthy rags. In the face of the exaggerated elevation of man in such theology, Gill stressed that, 'Man is become, through sin, a weak and impotent creature; though he is very hard to be brought to a sense and acknowledgement of his weakness; true believers are sensible of it, and own it; and such, knowing that there is sufficiency of strength in Christ for them, look and go to him for it; to do otherwise, to attempt to do anything in our own strength, betrays our weakness, folly, and vanity, and is dangerous, attended with bad consequences.' Quoting Matthew 26:33 ff., Gill showed how even Peter, a chosen apostle, was compelled to realize that when he boasted in his own strength, his boasting could only end in shame and remorse. After denying Christ three times, 'He went out, and wept bitterly.'

Gill's words of exhortation in expounding Psalm 71 are a passionate plea to 'look unto Jesus, the author and finisher of our Faith'. Only when one sees the pure, perfect and spotless righteousness of Christ can one see one's own state and be moved to 'put on Christ' and his 'robes of righteousness' which is 'better than the best of man's, better than Adam's innocence, or than the angels' in heaven'. Such a righteousness, he maintains, is 'the only law-honouring, justice-satisfying, everlasting one', and is the only righteousness that a child of God can plead before the judgement throne.

As more and more people became convinced that Gill had a message to the nation, efforts were made to organize lectures in the London area and beyond so that a wider circle could learn of this new emphasis of the old biblical truth that those who have Christ dwelling in them are accounted righteous because of that fact and none other. Gill had little time to concede to all the demands placed upon him as he felt called to a pastoral ministry and not that of an itinerant preacher. Nevertheless, he promised to give a series of lectures at various places on a regular basis, either once a month, twice a year or annually. Most of these lectures provided material for his numerous publications.

Just as the demand for Gill's teaching was growing, the Deists and Arians were also very much at work and Dissenters were flocking to them in alarmingly large numbers. The 'light of reason' and an inner awareness of 'the fitness of things' was being proclaimed as man's source of revelation, seeing Christ as a mere man who used 'the senses that God gave him' to their fullest capacity. Natural religion was deemed sufficient enough to bring man to a saving knowledge. These Deists and Arians, supported by the Anglican Latitudinarians, tended to disbelieve the doctrine of man's depravity and rejected the biblical teaching of the need for Christ's righteousness, believing that through education and 'moral influence' salvation was only a matter of course. In Europe Hermann Samuel Reimarus (1694-1768) came under the influence of British duty-faith Deists and, assisted later by Gotthold Ephraim Lessing (1729-1781), taught that the Holy Spirit promised by Christ was human reason and this indwelt all men, preparing them eventually to become as the gods.[2]

Early in 1730, Gill was approached by Christians of various denominations to use his voice and pen to combat this false gospel. Other ministers were also approached and it was soon decided that over a period of six months, seven Independent ministers, including Abraham Taylor and two Baptists, Samuel Wilson and John Gill, would give weekly open lectures as a defence of true biblical doctrine. It was decided to make the ministers' findings available to a wider public by publishing the lectures. To this end, Gill, Abraham Taylor and a few others joined forces to read their lectures to one another for mutual appraisal and criticism in order to make them more acceptable for publication.

Gill was glad of this chance to hear Mr (later Dr) Taylor's lecture on the 'Insufficiency of Natural Religion' again as, given from the pulpit, it had contained elements which he found were historically incorrect, offensive and unscriptural. When Mr Taylor came to read his lecture, Gill had decided on the advice he felt he must give him on the matter. Great was his surprise and pleasure, however, when he found that his Independent colleague had obviously seen the inappropriate nature of those very passages which had offended Gill, and removed them. Thus Gill held his peace, rejoicing in his heart.

This joy was of short duration. When Mr Taylor's sermons were eventually printed, Gill found to his dismay that the offending passages had not only been replaced but also embroidered upon in a way most offensive to the memory and teaching of the Calvinistic ministers of the Commonwealth and Restoration ages. Here was a minister who was supposed to be defending revealed religion against natural religion yet maintaining that those ministers who had 'preached up but faith in Christ' in those troubled times had not insisted on moral duties. These men, Taylor insisted, who had preached God's everlasting love to the church and 'insisted much' on the elect's eternal union with Christ, were 'ignorant enthusiastic preachers' who must have believed that 'sin could do a believer no harm', their whole teaching being an 'immoral conceit'.

Gill wasted no time in writing to Taylor and publishing his views on the matter in *The Doctrines of God's Everlasting Love To His Elect, and Their Eternal Union with Christ* (1732). Deftly and accurately, he argued how those who faithfully preached Christ during the civil commotions did not preach him to the exclusion of moral duties but that the need for goodness and godliness was stressed, observance of the Lord's Day and collective worship were insisted upon, and morality in all its branches flourished where faith in Christ was the theme.

Next, Gill pointed out that the main preachers of this period who had by some come under suspicion of Antinomianism, such as Eaton, Saltmarsh, Simpson, Town, Richardson and Crisp, far from making much of the eternal union between Christ and his Bride, did not 'insist much' at all on the doctrine but emphasized union with Christ at the point of experiencing faith in Christ. Quoting briefly from these men's works, Gill shows how the important doctrine had almost disappeared from view in their teaching. Richardson and Crisp touch gently on the subject, but only in a most indirect way. Gill confessed his disappointment when reading these works to find that 'Eternal union was so far from being a subject much insisted on in those times, as you say, that I do not find it was insisted on at all.'

Taking up the alleged point that these theologians taught that sin could not harm the believer, Gill argues that Saltmarsh, Simpson and Town show plainly their abhorrence and detestation of sin. In the whole of Richardson's works, there is only one sentence which may be interpreted as thinking lightly of sin where the writer quotes Romans 8:28 and says 'If all things work together for our good, then, all falls, pains, diseases, crosses, afflictions, &c. do us no hurt, but work for our good.' This, says Gill, is no more than many sound divines have said without them being accused of Antinomianism. He goes on to outline Richardson's doctrine of sin which shows he took sin very seriously indeed.

Next Gill considers Tobias Crisp's doctrines, and it is this considera-tion which all subsequent writers, antagonistic to Gill's theology, have used to condemn Gill as an Antinomian. It is explained by them *ad nauseam* that Crisp was an Antinomian — which he was not; and that Gill defended this — which he did not. It is also argued that Gill dealt more with Crisp than anything else in this letter.[3] The truth is that Gill dealt very briefly though very critically with Crisp, especially in comparison with Richardson. Crisp, in Gill's eyes, says hardly anything about eternal union and is the only writer mentioned above who is unguarded in his statements concerning sin. Quoting Hoornbek, Witsius and Chauncy, with whom he agrees, Gill shows that when Crisp says that believers must not be afraid of their sins or that sin does not 'hurt' a believer, he is merely referring to the fact that believers will not experience the penal wages of sin. Gill adds, nevertheless, 'I must confess, I do not like the expressions, but am of opinion they ought to be disused.'[4]

In spite of having a number of able defenders of his orthodoxy, including John Brown of Haddington, James Hervey, Augustus Toplady, John Rippon and Charles Haddon Spurgeon, the modern trend in certain circles is once more to accuse Crisp of at least aiding and abetting Antinomianism. This view can be traced back to the assembly of Baptist churches called to meet at Lorimer's Hall on 17 April 1704 which condemned Crisp and with him the Reformed doctrine of the imputation of Christ's righteousness. The pretence was that the doctrine made the work of the Holy Spirit unnecessary and 'tends to overthrow natural as well as revealed religion'. It had thus made its holder, Crisp, an Antinomian. It is quite obvious from the anti-Crisp statements recorded, that Crisp was condemned for not holding Neonomian views.[5] Now if Crisp was thought to err, it was purely because of the difficulty Neonomians had in interpreting certain phrases taken out of their context concerning fallen man's inability to perform righteous acts. The Neonomian view of the gospel departs, however, from the Reformed or Calvinistic view all along the line! Thus the 1704 assembly, in criticizing Crisp, were leaving themselves wide open to criticism by succeeding Reformed Baptists. These Reformed Baptists seem, however, to be few and far between at the present time. On the contrary, Crisp's words, in spite of his books *Free Grace the Teacher of Good Works* and *The Use of the Law*, are strangled by modern inquisitors until a confession of lawlessness is forced out of them. Commenting on a statement of Crisp that even our supposed righteous acts are clothed in sin, Naylor says, 'The Antinomian implication for the unwary was clear: it was better to avoid righteous acts than to perform them.'[6] This conclusion is so far-fetched that one must ask in amazement what Naylor is trying to achieve by such innuendoes. Rather than pointing to Hyper-Calvinism and Antinomianism, Crisp's words reflect strongly both the teaching of Scripture and Calvin's understanding of it. Does not Isaiah say that 'all our righteousness is filthy rags'? How then can Crisp be an Antinomian when he says the same? Calvin always argued that it is easier to obtain oil out of a stone than good works from any man and that all man's virtues were vices. He even went so far as to say, 'The thought is ever and anon recurring to me, that I am in danger of insulting the mercy of God by labouring with so much anxiety to maintain it, as if it were doubtful or obscure.' If Crisp had said this, his critics would have cried out 'Hyper-Calvinist and Antinomian in one!' There is much more of a similar nature to be found in Calvin, never a one for praising works of supererogation. Nor does Calvin merely refer to the unregenerate when he lowers their righteousness to the dust. Of the saved elect he says, 'No believer ever performed one work which, if tested by the strict judgement of God, could escape condemnation; and, moreover, that were this granted to be possible (though it is not), yet the act being vitiated and polluted by the sins of which it is certain that the author of it is guilty, it is deprived of its merit.'[7]

It was this insight which, through the working of the Holy Spirit, brought Calvin to his senses concerning salvation. Calvin was still blinded by popery when his cousin Olivetan helped to give him sight. 'There are only two religions in this world,' Olivetan said. 'In the one class invented by men, man saves himself (or supposes he can) by ceremonies and good works; the other is that one religion which is revealed in the Bible, and which teaches men to look for salvation arising solely from the free grace of God.'[8] Gill and Crisp, like Calvin, built their faith on this truth.

Writing in Letter 84 to Lady F. Shirley, a member of a large family of Evangelicals, Hervey praises Crisp's stand for the truth and argues:

Dr Crisp proceeds upon that important, but too much disregarded principle, that we should work from life, but not for life. Our works should proceed from the Spirit of the Lord Jesus dwelling in our hearts, and then they will be truly good. They should aim, not at obtaining salvation, but at glorifying him who hath obtained salvation for us.

Referring to these words, John Brown of Haddington said, 'I look on Dr. Crisp, as by no means an Antinomian, but as a deeply convinced and holy divine, pressing after gospel light.'[9]

After commenting briefly on Crisp, Gill mentions at length writers such as Dr Goodwin and Witsius, who taught Christ's eternal love for his church in the period referred to. Rather than being 'ignorant, enthusiastic preachers', they displayed great learning. Gill's trump card was Abraham Taylor's own father, Richard Taylor, who had defended eternal union in a book entitled *The Scripture Doctrine of Justification,* showing deep theological insight and understanding. Moreover, Abraham Taylor's name was on the title page of that very book as its editor![10] Lastly Gill confesses that he, himself, believes in God's everlasting love to his elect though he would not like to classify himself as 'ignorant and enthusiastic'.

After this preamble, Gill opens up to Taylor the biblical doctrine of Christ's eternal love for his Bride. He argues that Taylor will probably see eye to eye with him as to whom is united to Christ. The point of difference is regarding when this union takes place and what is the bond of union with Christ. Most modern exponents, Gill continues, teach that the believer is united to Christ when he actually believes and the bond is established by the work of the Holy Spirit on God's part and faith on ours. A critical observer must then ask what Christ has to do with such a union?

Gill confesses that he cannot accept such a teaching as it reflects the adage, 'God helps those who help themselves' or at least suggests that each side believes, 'If you do your bit, I will do mine.' The bond of union, Gill maintains, is neither the mission of the Spirit in the heart of a sinner, nor an exercise of faith. The Spirit's quickening, sanctifying and sealing work and the bestowing of his gifts and graces is a consequence of, and comes by virtue of, the union of Christ with his Bride. The work of the Spirit has its antecedents and it is in these antecedents that one finds the reasons for union with Christ. The elect are 'first chosen in him, adopted through him, made one with him, become heirs of God, and joint-heirs with Christ', and then, as the apostle says, 'Because ye are my sons, God hath sent forth the Spirit of his Son into your hearts, crying, Abba, Father.'[11] The Spirit of God in the lives of the saints is thus evidence of union with Christ but it is not the cause and not the bond of such a union.

Nor is faith the cause or bond of union with Christ. Here the Calvinists separate themselves from the Arminians who lay great store by the compelling nature of faith to move a merciful God to accept a willing subject. Gill thinks differently. 'Faith', he explains, 'looks to Christ, lays hold on him, embraces him, and cleaves unto him; it expects and receives all from Christ, and gives him all the glory; but then hereby a soul can no more be said to be united to Christ, than a beggar may be said to be united to a person to whom he applies, of whom he expects alms, to whom he keeps close, from whom he receives, and to whom he is thankful.' Faith, he maintains, cannot be the uniting factor as faith is a gift of God. If we believe that it is our faith which unites us to Christ, we make faith a work. If we believe that God grants us faith, it cannot be the faith which unites us as there must have been a cause for God to grant us that faith. True faith, seen as the gift it is, cannot possibly have a uniting nature as it is merely having one's hand opened as a father opens the hand of his child and places a sweet or a toy in it. Such an act is motivated by love on the part of the father.[12]

Love as a bond of union is, however, as misunderstood as faith. Gill quotes those who believe that faith is the uniting factor between Christ and his Bride as it demonstrates an exercise of mutual love. Gill is not satisfied with this teaching either. Union with Christ must not only be before faith but also before any love shown by man to Christ as the Bible teaches that just as faith is a gift of God, man can only love God when he finds out what true love is when God in love grants him faith.

Now Gill has the reader where he wants him. Faith and love are demonstrated as expressions of a believer's trust in God but they are not the reason for that trust. The reason is to be found in God's love for his elect and nowhere else. Now the question is, 'When did God start loving his elect if it was not when the faith and love of the believer was first exercised?' Gill answers this question under five points.

First he argues that there has been an election-union with Christ since before time and from eternity as stated in Ephesians 1:4: 'He hath chosen us in him before the foundation of the world, that we should be holy and without blame before him in love.' Though by our fallen nature we were not fit to be loved by Christ, God 'to the praise of the glory of his grace' has made us 'acceptable to the beloved'. Arminians teach that this text refers to man's faith foreseen by God, accepted and rewarded. It does, however, say nothing of the kind, but emphasizes that God planned to make his elect acceptable before ever they were born. Thus there must have been some kind of union between Christ and his Bride from all time.

Gill's second point is that there must have been a legal union between Christ and the elect from eternity. It was then that Christ worked out his suretyship for his elect. Before the world began, Christ was determined to become a ransom for his church and pay the debts they had fallen into. In the eyes of the law, Christ and his church were one so that if one paid the debt, it was the same as if the other had done so. This doctrine is the foundation of the doctrine of Christ's imputed righteousness. Our sins became his and his righteousness ours.[13]

The third point which Gill makes is that there is a federal union between Christ and the elect from everlasting. Christ is the Mediator of a better covenant and has pledged himself to keep it for ever. This covenant was not thought out in time but before time, which led Paul to say that God 'hath saved us, and called us with an holy calling, not according to our works, but according to his own purpose and grace, which was given us in Christ Jesus before the world began'.[14] This has resulted in the elect being blessed with all spiritual blessings in heavenly places in Christ, because they were reserved there since the foundation of the world for Christ's covenant Bride.[15]

Fourthly, there is a natural union between Christ and his Bride. 'He that sanctifieth, and they who are sanctified, are one.'[16] This became a union in time when Christ took upon himself our flesh and blood but it was part of the divine will before the Incarnation, before Abraham, before Adam and before time.

Finally Gill argues that there is a representative union between Christ and his Bride. Christ represented his church in election, in the covenant of grace, on the cross and in the grave. He also represented us in his resurrection and in taking his everlasting place with God. All this, and more, was wrought out because Christ loved his church and gave himself for her, promising her that he would never leave her nor forsake her and would make her calling and election sure.[17]

Here Gill had planned to end his letter but turning to Taylor's work again, he saw good cause to develop the consequences of being in God's eternal covenant of love. Taylor had written: 'There have been some, who, by their life and conversation, have shewed, that they were far from being enemies to holiness, who have amused themselves with fancies about God's loving and delighting in his elect, while they were in a state of nature; of his seeing no sin in his people, and good works not being necessary to salvation.'

Of course, here, Taylor's Arminianism[18] was running away with him. He could not believe for a minute, though Scripture stared him in the face, that Christ could love the loveless and die for the undeserving. He could not understand that 'greater love' which caused the sinless One to die for sinners. If this is all fancy, Gill argued, then it is a very scriptural one and a truth which is written in the sacred writings as if by sunbeams. Now Gill brought out the Scriptures' heaviest guns and aimed them all at Taylor's Doubting Castle.

God did not just decide to love us yesterday, argued God's Valiant-for-the-Truth. We love him, because he loved us long before we were rescued from the powers of darkness: 'I have loved thee with an everlasting love;

therefore with lovingkindness have I drawn thee.'[19] God drew us with the cords of love of his eternal decree into our effectual vocation.

This God-shown love is as unchangeable as it is unalterable because God is love himself and 'He that dwelleth in love, dwelleth in God and God in him'[20] This makes all the promises and blessings of God irreversible and the 'sons of Jacob are not consumed' because 'He is the lord, who changes not.' 'Though love produces a mighty change in man, there is no variableness in God nor shadow of turning.'[21] God sometimes hides his face but even this is within his providential care of his people and for their benefit. As it is thus obvious that God's love is from everlasting, asks Gill, why should it be called a fancy by Taylor?

Gill next argues that proof of God's love for his elect in their pre-conversion state is not difficult to find. The Scriptures make it clear that 'When we were yet without strength, in due time Christ died for the ungodly.'[22] He died for them because he loved them and reconciled them to himself whilst they were still enemies. For Gill, this is evidence enough of God's love to his people but he provides two more pages of quotes from the Bible to drive his point home.

Now Gill takes up the valid point that, humanly speaking, God can have no delight in viewing his people in their fallen state. Arminians teach that God loves the elect because he foresaw that they would love him. This would reverse Scripture and make it say, 'God loves us because we first loved him.' This would also mean that God loves the elect merely with a view to their new-born state. Gill rejects this by stressing that God loved his elect not only in their pre-converted state but before their very birth in time when they were elected *to* God's love, not *because of* their future love. Gill argues from Scripture that God loves the Son from eternity but the Son compares the eternal love of the Father to him with his eternal love for his people. Christ's high-priestly prayer was that he 'should give eternal life to as many as thou [God] hast given him', and 'the world may know that thou hast sent me, and hast loved them, as thou loved me'.[23] Arguing from Scripture that God's love for his Son is shown by his continual delight in him from all eternity, Gill concludes that God also continually delights in the elect. He had a delight in the fathers of Israel and their offspring[24] and he rejoices over his people to do them good.[25] Using Wisdom as a synonym for Christ and quoting Proverbs 8, Gill shows how Christ's delights were with the 'sons of men' before ever the earth was created.

Gill now takes up the Arminian argument that as it is impossible to please God without faith,[26] God cannot take delight in the unconverted elect. He shows how they argue that because it is impossible to please God without faith, it is impossible that God would choose anyone to salvation without faith. Gill shows that although what is not of faith is sin and sin cannot please God, he nevertheless sees his people in eternity as being the

Bride of his Son and in this capacity he delights in them. True love loves though the loved one is by nature unlovable. This is the heart of divine love and was illustrated in God's dealings with the elect of Israel of whom he said, 'For this is my covenant unto them, when I shall take away their sins. As concerning the gospel, they are enemies for your sakes: but as touching the election, they are beloved for the fathers' sakes.'[27]

The taunt that, according to the Calvinist, God sees no sin in his people, is now dealt with. Gill confesses to believing this doctrine absolutely and claims that it is one of the most comforting of his beliefs and is what makes the gospel good news to him. This, however, does not mean that there is no sin to be seen in believers. Dividing his argument into four points, he argues first that sin is in all believers and if a man says he has no sin, he deceives himself.[28] Secondly, sin is not only in the saints but is sadly actively committed by them as 'There is not a just man upon earth, that doeth good and sinneth not.'[29] In conjunction with this second point Gill admits that the Bible also says that 'Whosoever is born of God doth not commit sin, because he is born of God.'[30] Gill outlines the biblical teaching of the new creature in Christ, the new Adam who does not commit sin, indwelling the old creature in Adam who cannot but commit sin. This doctrine of the two Adams is at the heart of Pauline teaching, but it is rejected by the bulk of Gill's critics as is also his doctrine of Christ's imputed righteousness which is so closely allied to it.[31] For Gill, no holiness was possible without Christ indwelling the new creature, imputing his own righteousness in his otherwise unrighteous Bride.

Thirdly Gill argues that though believers are justified from all sin by Christ's righteousness imputed to them, sin is still in their old nature and will remain there until death and the putting on of the resurrection body. Fourthly, Gill explains that the work of sanctification will thus never be complete in this life, which is a life of grace. This would not be so if the old man had become perfect.

Next Gill challenges the idea of God behind any human statement that God *could not* see the sin of his people. Quoting Job 34:21-22: 'His eyes are upon the ways of man, and he seeth all his goings; there is no darkness nor shadow of death, where the workers of iniquity may hide themselves', he shows that God's 'not seeing' is with the eye of justice, as he no longer has cause to punish his people. This does not mean that God deals with his children like an over-indulgent Father with spoilt brats. Whom he loves, he chastens and makes it quite clear that, 'If his children forsake my law, and walk not in my judgements; if they break my statutes, and keep not my commandments; then will I visit their transgressions with the rod, and their iniquity with stripes. Nevertheless my lovingkindness will I not utterly take from him, nor suffer my faithfulness to fail.'[32] Thus no one, not even God himself, can lay anything to the charge of God's elect as God himself has justified them in Christ. Their trespasses have been laid to Christ's charge and he has made satisfaction for them, sinners as they still are. This does not mean that God is not angry when his children sin and closes his eyes to rid himself of the responsibility. There will always be a need for his chastening rod until the elect are gathered in at the end of time. Thus when Christ views his Bride, due to what he has done for her, he can say, 'Thou art all fair, my love; and there is no spot in thee.'[33] Gill concludes by saying:

> If this is a fancy, it is the glory of the Bible, and the marrow of the gospel; what most displays the riches of God's grace, the efficacy of Christ's blood, the completeness of his righteousness, and the fullness of his satisfaction; it is the foundation of all solid hopes of future happiness, what supports the life of faith, and is the ground of a believer's triumph. One would have thought, Sir, you might have forbore so severe a reflection on this truth, of God's seeing no sin in his people, since it is the το ρητον, the express words of the sacred oracles: He hath not beheld iniquity in Jacob, neither hath he seen perverseness in Israel.[34]

In defending the doctrine of God's eternal love for his church, Gill was drawing a line of demarcation between Calvinistic and Arminian Baptists and thus correcting the blurring of doctrinal issues during Stinton's term of service. However one twists and turns the Arminian doctrine of election, it still declares that God loves only the loveable and the deserving. It also rejects the doctrine of a Christ who so loved his Bride that he gave his life for her and atoned for her sins. Arminians teach that Christ died for both the sheep and the goats. Furthermore, the sheep can become goats and the goats can become sheep at any time irrespective of God's will. This takes away the saving and loving initiative of God and gives it to whomsoever can make up his mind to follow Christ for today but not necessarily tomorrow. This doctrine is certainly 'another gospel' as it insults God's love, Christ's work and the decrees of the Divine Council. It is quite plain, when reading Stinton's view of the matter, that he was influenced in arguing for a merger of Calvinistic and Arminian Baptists by sheer pecuniary motives. Writing in 1717 of the fund the Particular Baptists managed for budding ministers, Stinton protested at the use of the name 'Particular' (i.e. referring to particular atonement) and argued that the name should be dropped and the fund opened to all 'Antipædobaptists' irrespective of their doctrines. One of the reasons given was: 'Because this article gives great offence, to several wealthy and generous gentlemen, whose assistance in this design would be of great service to the public, and is like to keep several rich and numerous churches from enjoining with us; who if they were engaged herein, would very much increase the fund, and help to preserve it to futurity.'[35] Crosby adds that Stinton was outvoted but shows his agreement with his former pastor by writing, 'We do not always find in such cases, wisdom to be on the major side.'

Thinking that Gill was of the same businesslike calibre as Stinton probably motivated influential friends of Taylor, who also helped finance Gill's work, to pay the Goat Yard pastor a visit. They gave him due notice of their financial power and made it quite plain that if Gill published against Taylor, some of his wealthy supporters would withdraw their financial aid and he would thus lose much of his maintenance fees. 'Don't tell me of losing,' Gill is recorded as saying; 'I value nothing, in comparison of gospel truths. I am not afraid to be poor.'[36]

9.
A saint is slandered

Though John Gill was second to none in the kingdom for scholarly learning, evangelical unction and prowess as a preacher, his works have sadly faded from the reading of many present-day evangelicals. This is because his successors held to a radically different view of the Fall, the law and the gospel and their views won the day. Now Gill is being rediscovered as the number of publications dealing with him over the last few years show. Something, however, is going seriously wrong. Though modern American works such as Thomas Nettles' *By His Grace and for His Glory* and Timothy George's essay on Gill's life and works in *Baptist Theologians* reveal Gill as the great evangelical eighteenth-century pioneer he was, he is being displayed by a number of British critics as a Hyper-Calvinist with no commitment whatsoever to taking the gospel to the unsaved. Jack Hoad in his book *The Baptist* maintains that 'Dr John Gill was the prince of the hypercalvinistic preachers'[1] calling those Hyper-Calvinists whom he believes adopt 'a supralapsarian view that God's decree of election preceded his decree to permit the Fall of man'.[2] Hoad is convinced that it was Gill's influence 'which was a major factor in the retention of a High Calvinist theology' in the Baptist churches.

Peter Naylor, in his history of the Particular Baptist churches entitled *Picking Up a Pin For the Lord*,[3] equates Hyper-Calvinism with High-Calvinism which he defines as being 'more Calvinistic than Calvin himself'. Of this teaching he says:

> 'High Calvinism' was a theological system which would appear to have co-ordinated two denials. First, there was the denial that God calls all who hear about Christ to believe in him; no man is obliged as a matter of duty to trust in Christ as a condition of salvation. This denial applied to both the reprobate and to the elect.

The 'reprobate' are all those who were not originally chosen in Christ before the world began, for whom Christ did not die, who will be left in their sinful state by God, and who therefore will never repent and believe. The 'elect' are all those who were originally chosen by the Father to form the church of God, for whom Christ did die, and who will certainly come to a living faith in the Saviour. The reasoning was that if God alone can, and sometimes does, give repentance and faith, such should be demanded of no man, whoever he might be; sovereign grace is irresistible. Second, high Calvinism denied that it is the responsibility of the churches to call upon all men indiscriminately to repent and to believe in Christ for the salvation of their souls.[4]

Naylor further maintains, 'High Calvinism denied that a person insensitive to his sinfulness should ever be summoned to conversion' and affirms that, 'This approach rested firmly upon the dogma that fallen humanity is beset by an inability to turn from sin and turn to God. So what men cannot do in their own strength, they need not do.'[5]

Naylor's words concerning Gill in relation to High/Hyper-Calvinism are worthy of note. Although he considers a statement by John Ryland Junior which would indicate that Brine, Toplady and Gill did not meet Naylor's definition of a Hyper-Calvinist and although he quotes the Baptist historian Ivimey who believed that Gill's 'correct statements'[6] were misunderstood by some of his followers, he still holds that, 'Among the Baptists of the period, John Gill was *without doubt*[7] the most prominent exponent of high Calvinism.' He then goes on to quote Lewis Wayman and John Brine to prove *their* Hyper-Calvinism, leaving the reader with the impression that Naylor need not produce evidence for *Gill's* Hyper-Calvinism as no one could possibly doubt it. Naylor, however, deals in some detail with Gill's doctrines of the eternal love of God for his people and justification from eternity which is so closely allied to it as if these doctrines point to Hyper-Calvinism and unorthodoxy though they were held by orthodox Calvinists through the ages such as Witsius and Goodwin. Naylor tries hard, but does not succeed in bringing forward proof from Gill's works that he is indeed heretical nor from Calvin's works to prove that the Reformer thought otherwise than Gill. A glance at Calvin's *Institutes*, *The Eternal Predestination of God* and *The Secret Providence of God* would have assisted Naylor greatly in coming to a more positive appraisal of Gill's Calvinism.

This method of associating Gill with the belief of others and then condemning him is shown at its weakest in Naylor's reference to a quote from Wayland, followed by remarks on Brine, claiming: 'Adam had not the faith of God's elect before the fall, and did not lose it for his posterity; therefore they (the elect) are not debtors to God for it while in unregeneracy.' Naylor argues that this shows that Hyper-Calvinists do not believe that faith is the duty of the non-elect because they argue that inability to believe does not depend on the result of the Fall but in the manner Adam was originally created. This quote from Wayman's writings is used to draw quite unwarranted conclusions concerning Gill and it will be shown that it is completely erroneous to equate Gill with any view of pre-lapsus Adam that ruled out faith in Christ, which is 'the faith of God's elect'.

Robert Oliver, writing in *Foundations*[8] is, on the whole, in agreement with Naylor's view, saying of Hyper-Calvinism: 'The term, Hyper-Calvinism, has come to be used as a description of the system of theology, which couples a belief in the Five Points of Calvinism with a denial of the doctrine of the free offer of the Gospel. The Hyper-Calvinist does not believe that indiscriminate exhortations to faith and repentance should be addressed to the unregenerate.' After tracing what he feels is the history of Hyper-Calvinism from the teaching of Joseph Hussey to John Skepp he introduces Gill as a contender for 'strong Hyper-Calvinism' which he feels developed through Gill's opposition to John Wesley's Arminianism on the subject of predestination. Gill's doctrine of election was, however, developed a quarter of a century before he crossed swords with Wesley and was formed during his earliest days amongst the Kettering Baptists. It is strange too, after Oliver's often repeated reproach that Hyper-Calvinists do not believe in evangelism amongst the unsaved, that he lists William Huntington as the pioneer of the resurgence of Hyper-Calvinism. Oliver, however, admits that Huntington preached regularly to a congregation of 2,000, itinerated throughout the country, converting men and stimulating Christians to seek a deeper and more personal knowledge of God. If this were true, and the facts speak for themselves, then Oliver's interpretation of his own definition of Hyper-Calvinism needs to be radically revised. What Oliver calls Hyper-Calvinism is seen by other writers, even those not in sympathy with Gill, as being straightforward Calvinism.[9]

With Oliver's anti-Gill background, one can imagine with what interest he tackled Thomas J. Nettles' positive assessment of Gill in his book *By His Grace and for His Glory*. On reading the book, Oliver was moved to write a three-page review article on it for the *Banner of Truth* magazine which appeared in May 1987. Oliver opens by acknowledging the eloquent style of Nettles' book and outlines the author's aims and comments on his warm and masterly handling of doctrine. Nettles allots a mere part of one chapter to Gill's alleged Hyper-Calvinism in a work of sixteen chapters. Yet Oliver devotes a good half of his review to this topic exclaiming 'Perhaps Dr Nettles' most surprising conclusion is that John Gill was not a Hyper-Calvinist.' Oliver remains unconvinced by Nettles' weighty arguments, or rather does not give them due regard, and reiterates the traditional arguments against Gill which Nettles has taken such care to reveal as the soap bubbles they are. Oliver's conclusion is thus the same as if he had never read the book i.e. 'Nevertheless when Gill's writings are considered, the weight of the evidence supports the traditional view that he was a Hyper-Calvinist.'

Faced with Nettles' apparently strong evidence that Gill is no Hyper-Calvinist but one who felt a calling to preach the gospel to all men, Oliver must be very sure of his counter-arguments to be so dogmatic. Indeed he feels he can produce a trump card to prove his own views correct. Nettles, he argues, is guilty of misquoting Gill when he represents him as saying that those who hear the gospel 'are obliged to love the Lord on account of redemption by Christ; since all who see their need of it, and are desirous of an interest in it, have no reason to conclude otherwise, than that Christ died for them, and has redeemed them by his blood'.[10] Though anyone checking Nettles' source would agree that this is actually Gill's point and Gill is clearly for preaching the gospel to all, Oliver contradicts this by maintaining: 'Gill does not, in fact, make this statement of "those who hear the gospel", but of "all to whom the gospel revelation comes". Of unbelievers he has just declared that, "such cannot be obliged to love the Lord for that revelation, which was never intended for them, nor for that grace which will not be vouchsafed to them". In Gill's thinking, those "to whom the gospel revelation comes" are those who "have no reason to conclude otherwise than that Christ died for them, and has redeemed them by his blood",[11] in a word, Christians.' Oliver here apparently means the already saved. He thus leaves us with the picture that Gill was a preacher who always brought coals to Newcastle and owls to Athens. He preached the need of salvation to those whose need had already been met and left the unsaved, who needed salvation, without it. It is thus then a real wonder that Gill's Church Book reveals so many conversions and baptisms in his congregation!

Nettles says that Gill preached to the saved and the unsaved alike and Oliver says he preached only to the already converted. Who is correct? The context shows clearly that Oliver's criticism is quite invalid and that, through his selective interest in what Nettles actually wrote, he has grasped neither Nettles', nor Gill's point. In the context from which Oliver has taken his 'Christians only' quote, Nettles actually paraphrased and quoted Gill as saying: 'Indeed, some might ask, is it the duty of all men to love the Lord? Absolutely! Because they are the creatures of his making, enjoy the care of his providence, and are supplied by him with the blessings of life; therefore all men must joyfully love the Lord.'[12] But even beyond creation and providence, Gill affirms that those who hear the gospel 'are obliged to love the Lord on account of redemption by Christ; since all who see their need of it, and are desirous of interest in it, have no reason to conclude otherwise, than that Christ died for them, and has redeemed them by his blood'.[13]

Oliver seems to be so intent on sticking to the myth that Gill only addressed believers with the gospel and not unsaved sinners, that he has quite overlooked Gill's emphasis that even the unsaved have a duty to love Christ for the very reasons Nettles gives. In fact, Gill refers several times in the context alternatively to the unsaved and the saved in his emphasis that all men have a duty to love Christ, explaining why. Oliver has grouped all these explanations under one heading 'For Christians Only' whereas Gill is arguing concerning 'all men' whether they be Jews or Gentiles. Gill's actual words are:

> It is said, that 'the great duty required from the Jew and Gentile is, to love the Lord with all our hearts; but if he intended no such kindness to the greatest part of mankind (as the sending of his Son to be their Saviour), what motive can they have to love him, who never had any love to their souls? Surely they cannot be obliged to love him for that redemption which never was intended for them, or for that grace which will not be vouchsafed to them.' To which may be replied; that it is the duty of all men to love the Lord, as they are the creatures of his make, the care of his providence, and supplied by him with the blessings of life; and, so long as they are, the obligation to love him continues, and would have continued, had there been no redemption at all by Christ. It is true, redemption by Christ lays a fresh obligation on those who are interested in it, to love the Lord; and, indeed, those who have no interest in that special blessing of grace, have reason to love the Lord upon the account of it; since it is owing to Christ's engagement to redeem his own people, that the rest are continued in their being, and supplied with the blessings of providence, which were forfeited by sin. Besides, though such cannot be obliged to love the Lord for that redemption[14] which never was intended for them, nor for that grace which will not be vouchsafed to them; yet, all to whom the gospel revelation comes, are obliged to love the Lord on the account of redemption by Christ, since all who see their need of it, and are desirous of interest in it, have no reason to conclude otherwise, than that Christ died for them, and has redeemed them by his blood.

Thus even non-Christians, according to Gill, have an obligation to love Christ irrespective of the outworking of salvation. When Oliver says, 'Of unbelievers he has just declared that, "such cannot be obliged to love the Lord for that **revelation**,[15] which was never intended for them, nor for that grace which will not be vouchsafed to them,"' he has not grasped the point

Gill is making. Gill is arguing *against* the supposition that this rules out any duties on sinful man's part and not *for* such a view. The argument Gill places in inverted commas is the argument that he is refuting, not Gill's own argument as Oliver wrongly concludes. Besides, Gill is not arguing that there is a 'revelation' which was never intended for the non-elect, but that there is a 'redemption' which the non-elect will never experience. This is a view quite in keeping with orthodox Calvinism. Oliver, however, reads 'revelation' where Gill has 'redemption'. The source Nettles gives also clearly refers to 'redemption'. If Oliver feels that 'redemption' must be a faulty reading, he ought to have explained this, giving his reasons. It is also clear from the syntax of Gill's passage that 'such' who 'cannot be obliged to love the Lord on the account of redemption by Christ' are nevertheless included in 'all to whom the revelation comes'. As so often, Gill is emphasizing the need to preach the gospel to all men because only the response to the gospel determines the future lives of those who accept it, yet this is denied by his critics for unbelievable reasons.

Robert J. Sheehan argues that Hyper-Calvinism comes in various forms but dwells in his writings on a form which bears little resemblance to Gill's theology. Nevertheless, in two articles written in *Foundations*,[16] he refers to Gill as 'a prominent hyper-calvinist'. Sheehan maintains that Hyper-Calvinists teach that:

1. The unregenerate cannot be commanded to repent and believe.
2. All scriptural commands, exhortations and invitations to repent and believe must either be made to the regenerate or made in a context unconnected with spiritual salvation.
3. Only those conscious of the Spirit's work within can heed the commands to repent and believe and only these should be directed to do so.

Here we see that there is a shift from Oliver's view that Hyper-Calvinists do not believe in a 'free offer' of salvation and in 'exhorting' sinners to repent to the idea that Hyper-Calvinists do not even believe in 'commanding' sinners to repent and believe. There is, of course, theologically speaking, all the difference in the world between indiscriminately offering someone repentance and belief and commanding someone specifically to repent and believe. Sheehan also adds that Hyper-Calvinists deny that 'man is responsible to repent and believe'. Gill is quoted vaguely, three times in the article, leaving the reader wondering what the supposed 'prominent Hyper-Calvinist' has to do with Sheehan's definitions and why he bothers to quote Gill in relation to Hyper-Calvinism at all. The first reference to Gill is to his interpretation of Isaiah 55:1: 'Ho, every one that thirsteth, come ye to the waters.' Gill takes this to refer to all those who hunger and thirst after righteousness and not, as Fuller argued, anybody seeking after 'a natural desire of happiness'.[17] The task of an evangelist, according to Gill, is to bring in the sheep and not to entertain the goats. Sheehan's second reference is to Gill's belief that all men should pray though only spiritual men can pray spiritually.[18] His third reference is to Gill's declaration that preachers are ambassadors for Christ who have come to proclaim terms of peace not to haggle about them.[19] There may be room for a difference of opinion regarding these points of interpretation, but Sheehan's claim that Gill is a Hyper-Calvinist needs more substantial and relevant evidence than this if it is to be backed up at all.

Peter Toon is another modern exponent of the view that Gill was a Hyper-Calvinist. In his book *The Emergence of Hyper-Calvinism in English Nonconformity 1689-1765*,[20] he devotes a whole chapter to a definition of the term arguing that Hyper-Calvinists place excessive emphasis on the eternal decrees of God and thus obscure the central message of the gospel, this being 'Christ and Him crucified' — as if this were not one of the central eternal decrees of God! Toon does not quote Gill here as an example but elsewhere in the book refers to Gill time and time again as a Hyper-Calvinist. In his chapter defining Hyper-Calvinism and Hyper-Calvinists, he does, however, deal with Saltmarsh, Eaton and Tobias Crisp as being 'doctrinal antinomians' and he then brings Gill into association with them by saying, 'John Gill defended the doctrines of Saltmarsh, Crisp and Eaton in his *Doctrines of God's Everlasting Love to His Elect*.' Toon's words are tantamount to saying that Gill defended doctrinal Antinomianism. As shown in the chapter on that topic in this biography, Gill did no such thing. In his chapter entitled 'The Factors Involved in the Change from High to Hyper-Calvinism', Toon argues that Hyper-Calvinists *'were sincere men of average intelligence,*[21] but they lacked a prophetic and discerning spirit'. This would hardly apply to Gill, nor to most of the other writers Toon brands as Hyper-Calvinists.[22]

Such approaches are symptomatic of much modern criticism of Gill. Though they see Gill as one of the leading exponents of Hyper-Calvinism, they are very sparing in the evidence they produce against him, preferring rather to bundle him with other alleged Hyper-Calvinistic pastors such as John Stevens and W. J. Styles whom they quote at great length. Nettles, too, has seen this tendency in a number of critics, and thus concludes, 'Gill becomes guilty by association and silence rather than from direct violation of principles.'[23]

Most authors, like Toon, who link Gill with Hyper-Calvinism, also link Hyper-Calvinism with Antinomianism. Naylor suspects those whom he takes to be Hyper-Calvinists-cum-High-Calvinists of being Antinomians because he believes they incline 'to the view that repentance is not necessary for salvation; sin does not have to be given up'.[24] He holds that they see man's incapacity to repent as a natural limitation rather than as 'a culpable evil arising from a perverted and sinful heart'.[25] Naylor admits that there is no strong proof of his inkling that High-Calvinists were Antinomians but says, 'It is all very suspicious', obviously believing that, when all is said and done, the cap fits. This is obviously the opinion of the Baptist historian Thomas Armitage who says, for instance, that Gill 'was so high a supralapsarian, that it is hard to distinguish him from an Antinomian'.[26]

The terms Hyper-Calvinism and High-Calvinism as used by such critics cover a host of ideas, which, if all are true, might substantiate the conclusion of another writer, that Gill's teaching was 'a deviation from biblical Christianity'.[27] If all that they associate with Hyper-Calvinism is taken into account, the subject of this biography John Gill was a supralapsarian, who taught that God does not call all who hear about Christ to believe in him, nor command them to repent. He also must have taught that one should only preach the gospel to those whom God has justified from eternity irrespective of their faith. Furthermore he believed that no man, whether elect or reprobate, is obliged as a matter of duty to trust in Christ as a condition of salvation. Moreover, he denied that a person insensitive to his sinfulness should ever be summoned to conversion because fallen humanity is beset by an inability to turn from sin to God. Gill must have believed that Adam before his fall had no faith in Christ nor sense of duty towards him. He is also suspected of being an Antinomian denying that repentance is necessary for salvation and refusing to believe that sin must be given up. All this alleged heresy forced Gill and his flock, it is argued, to lose their evangelistic impulse resulting in declining vigour in the churches under his influence. All these serious accusations must now be looked at in detail and the evidence carefully sifted. Was Gill guilty of unbiblical or, indeed, unchristian teaching or was he God's clarion-caller to his age as this writer believes?

All these accusations are used against Gill to show that he was 'more Calvinistic than Calvin'. Serious students of Calvin will, however, have noticed that these accusations almost exactly fit those which were brought forward against Calvin himself. In his defence Calvin said of his accusers, 'Just like an unclean hog, therefore, you root up with your foul snout all doctrine that is of sweet odour, hoping to find in it something filthy and offensive.'[28] This is exactly how 'illegitimate Calvinists' tackle Gill. They delight in taking his 'one-off' statements, or lifting odd words quite out of context and embroidering them with a background and content that are quite foreign to Gill but very much reflect the theological weakness of his opponents' theology. They see Gill through a glass darkly and thus see only a shadow of the real man. Nevertheless, anyone comparing Gill's defence of his theology with the way Calvin defends himself from the calumnies of his accusers under similar circumstances will marvel at the gracious and balanced words of the Southwark pastor in comparison to the very spicy, if not downright peppery, protests of the Reformer. It is now necessary to analyse the arguments of Gill's critics in detail.

Supralapsarianism

Anyone striving to accuse anybody of being Hyper-Calvinistic on the grounds of supralapsarianism is treading on thin ice and leaving solid biblical and even rational reasoning for metaphysical abstractions. The term supralapsarianism and its supposed opposite sublapsarianism (also called infralapsarianism) were coined by Dutch academics during the Arminian Controversy in an attempt to understand the relationship between God's eternal decrees and their outworking in history. The pivoting point appears to be whether the elect and reprobate were ordained as such before the idea of a lapsus, i.e. Fall, entered God's mind or whether God ordained the reprobate and elect after taking the Fall into consideration. Supralapsarians, it is alleged, are those who place election as first and foremost in rank and time in God's mind before creation and the Fall. The sublapsarians are supposed to believe that God adjusted his ideas of reprobation and election to tie in with the outcome of the Fall. Critics of these schemes say that the supralapsarians teach that God thus willed the Fall in order to display his grace in election and his wrath against sin in reprobation, whereas sublapsarians are accused of teaching that God permitted man to fall, though he could have stopped it. Both the supralapsarian and sublapsarian schemes have no place for the idea that God ordained sin and is thus its author though especially supralapsarians are accused of believing so.

It must be stressed that such speculative theology was not intended by the Dutch divines as a yardstick for orthodoxy and certainly not to distinguish Hyper-Calvinism from Calvinism. The Dutchmen simply strove to define what plain, ordinary Calvinism was. If they had stuck to Calvin's *Institutes*, they would have been better served and made better use of their time. Philip Schaff in his eight-volumed *History of the Christian Church* perhaps makes a most sensible comment when he says, 'The difference between the two schools is practically worthless, and only exposes the folly of man's daring to search the secrets of God's eternal counsel.'[29] Apart from the folly of analysing God's pre-creation thoughts, there is the even greater folly of trying to sort them out in a chronological or pre-historical order before time and history began! Thus whether a person is presumed a supralapsarian or a sublapsarian has nothing to do with his orthodoxy as a Christian.

Hoad links Hyper-Calvinism closely with supralapsarianism and seems to suggest that the one is a definition of the other. Whether Gill was a supralapsarian or not, however, is irrelevant to the question of whether he was a Hyper-Calvinist or not. This is especially the case as many writers look upon Calvin as a supralapsarian himself! Schaff dismisses the relevancy of such theory-building, although he argues guardedly that, because Calvin taught that the Fall cannot be excluded from God's decrees and that it is futile to distinguish between what God wills and what God permits, Calvin 'must be classed rather with the supralapsarians'.[30] Louis Berkof, in his standard work *Systematic Theology*, agrees fully with Schaff about the speculative nature of both terms. Berkof, however, is prepared to state dogmatically that 'Calvin was clearly a Supralapsarian',[31] again because of his teaching that the Fall was included in the divine decrees.

Calvin's teaching on the matter has always been a ground for speculation for those who wish to force Reformed doctrine into either the supralapsarian or the sublapsarian camp. Wesley was certain that Calvin was a supralapsarian who held that God decreed to create the elect and reprobate irrespective of subsequent history regarding the Fall. In fairness to Calvin it must be said that Wesley trimmed his quotes to make them suit his argument in a way that caused Calvinists such as Toplady to accuse him of blatant deceit and forgery. Some of Calvin's writings, taken in isolation, could be interpreted as indicating an election to salvation or reprobation irrespective of whether Adam fell or not. In Book III, Chapter 21 of the *Institutes*, for instance, the Reformer writes: 'All are not created on equal terms, but some are preordained to eternal life, others to eternal damnation; and, accordingly, as each has been created for one or other of these ends, we say that he has been predestined to life or to death.'[32]

Though Calvin usually argues that God elected from the 'sinful mass', i.e. he elected by grace taking into account man's fall, this is nowhere referred to here in the wider context. Thus rather than being 'more Calvinistic than Calvin', to use Naylor's definition culled from Fuller, even if Gill showed signs of being a supralapsarian he would be quite 'as Calvinistic as Calvin' and because of this could hardly be called a Hyper-Calvinist or even High-Calvinist. This point is made clear by David Engelsma, an ardent Calvinist, in his book *Hyper-Calvinism & the Call of the Gospel* where he argues, with tongue in cheek, that, 'We have now found for the defenders of the well-meant offer of the gospel the original hyper-Calvinist — John Calvin himself.'

Gill was too experienced a theologian to adopt speculative theories of the supralapsarian and sublapsarian kind and would certainly never have entered into the debate were he not pulled into it by writers who preferred to speculate about such matters rather than learn God's will through the Scriptures. In 1736 a man called Job Burt attacked Gill with an anonymous pamphlet entitled *Some Doctrines in the Supralapsarian Scheme Examined*. It is clear in Burt's booklet that he views Gill as a supralapsarian but it is also very clear that Burt had not the foggiest idea what supralapsarianism was, confusing it constantly with what was traditionally seen as sublapsarianism. The main accusation against Gill appears to be that he allegedly refused to pray for the pardon of sin,[33] thus displaying himself as a supralapsarian Antinomian.

Gill regarded Burt as a sciolist, but people were reading his book and as he was spreading unscriptural ideas concerning God's everlasting love for his elect and his plan of justification for man, Gill felt he must reply with a tract called *Truth Defended*. In it he denies Burt's allegations that his denomination has supralapsarianism as its fundamental article of faith but shows, nevertheless, how both sublapsarians and supralapsarians hold to the doctrine of election as 'an eternal act of God: that it is unconditional, irrespective of faith, holiness, and good works, as causes and conditions of it; and that it entirely springs from the good-will and pleasure of God'. Gill then explains, quoting original sources, that the Dutch Contra-Remonstrants were not all of one mind concerning how supralapsarianism and sublapsarianism were to be defined, nor did they think it of any importance concerning church unity. He argues that we are not to consider God's plan of salvation, formed in eternity, as a this-happens-before-that event, each event being chronologically and logically subordinate to the preceding event, and decreed so in a cause and effect sequence. God's plan of salvation is a co-ordinate complete plan made before the foundation of the world, Gill argues, putting his finger on the weaknesses of both systems under dispute.

On reading Gill's meticulous criticism of Burt and his outline of the agreements and disagreements between the supralapsarian and sublapsarian schemes, it becomes obvious that Gill accepts that in both schemes there are some points which are scriptural and some which are not. Contrary to those writers who believe Gill is a supralapsarian and therefore a Hyper-Calvinist, Gill at times comes down soundly in the sublapsarian corner. Burt is obviously under the impression that supralapsarianism teaches that 'We were not elected as holy and obedient beings, but to the end we might be such.' Gill, however, accepts this teaching but says of it, 'I am much mistaken if this is not the settled opinion of all Sublapsarians, except such as are in the Arminian scheme.' Burt had criticized Gill for believing in justification from eternity as if this were a supralapsarian heresy. To this Gill says, 'I must confess, I never considered justification from eternity, any other than a sublapsarian doctrine, proceeding upon the suretyship engagements of Christ, and his future satisfaction and right-eousness; upon which foot the Old Testament saints were openly justified, and went to heaven long before the satisfaction was really made, or the justifying righteousness brought in; and indeed, if the objects of justification are the ungodly, as the scripture represents them to be, they must be considered as fallen creatures.'

The above summary of Gill's very lengthy exposition of his relationship to supralapsarian and sublapsarian beliefs shows how wary one must be of putting tags and titles on one's supposed opponents and expect them to behave in a certain conditioned way. Gill was certainly no man's man and reserved the right to be independent from all cliché attachments whilst being fully dependent on God's Word. It is interesting to note that Augustus Toplady, a close friend of Gill, was convinced that his friend was a thorough sublapsarian and this is obviously the conclusion of Gill's only biographer of note, Dr John Rippon. It is also noteworthy that John Bunyan was widely reputed to be a thoroughgoing supralapsarian but no one as yet has thought it worthwhile to brand this great evangelist and pastor with the name of Hyper-Calvinist. Be that as it may, the facts show that it is obviously as futile to brand Gill as being a supralapsarian as it is to consider supralapsarians as being by their very nature Hyper-Calvinists.

Eternal justification

Though Gill argues that his doctrine of eternal justification is sublapsarian, Peter Naylor believes it is the very backbone of Hyper-Calvinism. He examines Gill's arguments (mentioned in the previous section) for justification on the grounds that Christ's sacrifice in time atoned for the elect before that time and calls it 'an even more glaring weakness' than the other weaknesses he believes he has found in Gill's system.[34] Naylor attempts to refute Gill by stating that the Old Testament saints were justified because of their faith and not because of God's justifying decree before time. He interprets Gill as teaching that what justified the Old Testament elect was 'a notional doctrine of eternal justification', apparently implying that Gill sees this doctrine as a substitute for faith. Needless to say, Gill taught no such thing and saw no contradiction in his belief that the just shall live by faith and the fact that this faith is a gift of God according to God's eternal decree.

Naylor, choosing his words — and his dots — carefully, makes Gill say:

Justification is not only before faith, but it is from eternity, being an immanent act in the divine mind and so an internal and eternal one: as may be concluded . . . if they bore this character of elect from eternity, or were chosen in Christ before the world began; then they must be acquitted, discharged, and justified so early . . . for there is no condemnation to them which are in Christ, Rom. viii. 1; and therefore must be considered as righteous, and so justified.[35]

Referring to Gill's use of Romans 8:1, Naylor says, 'The point here is that it is just possible that Gill, an acute scholar who seldom missed much, misquoted Paul to suit his own exposition.' He emphasizes that Gill has left out the 'now' in 'There is therefore now no condemnation'. Naylor argues that the word 'now' indicates 'since faith was born'. He thus concludes that Gill did not let the word 'slip accidentally' but 'His omission would seem to have served an interest.'

Believing as Naylor that 'Gill seldom missed much', it must also be pointed out that Naylor has missed very much. In fact he has missed out no less than 109 words (replaced by dots) in a very self-explanatory passage which would have thrown light on his problem if he had not exercised criticism with a pair of scissors. Naylor's additional information that 'now' refers to the time when faith is born can hardly be claimed to fit Romans 8:1 as nowhere is faith referred to. The emphasis is on being in Christ, walking after the Spirit and being made free from the law of sin. Paul is talking about what God does, not what man exercises. Naylor has, however, truncated Gill's words to the point of removing the Romans quote from its syntactic embedding and sense context. After 'concluded' before the first row of dots, Gill gives reasons for his argument which are omitted by Naylor who has also linked 'justified so early' with Romans 8:1 giving the impression that Gill merely relates the verse back to pre-history. After 'so early' Gill continues, 'so as nothing could be laid to their charge: besides, by electing grace men were put into Christ, and were considered as in him before the foundation of the world; and if they were considered as in him, they must be considered as righteous or unrighteous; not surely as unrighteous, unjustified, and in a state of condemnation; for there is no condemnation to them which are in Christ.' It is obvious here that Gill is referring, as he explains in detail in the wider context, not merely to a pre-historical date in the pre-past but to the eternal outcome of that decision of God to place his elect in Christ in whom they find no condemnation now nor ever. Thus, as Gill says, where Naylor silences him by placing dots, no one can lay anything to the charge of God's elect because it is God that justifieth. In this context Gill refers to Ephesians 1:6 which states unmistakably that through election God has made us 'accepted in the beloved'. This 'acceptability', as Gill shows, is not only past but present and future — it is eternal.

Thus we have Naylor accusing Gill of misquoting Paul on purpose when he is himself — we trust inadvertently — sifting Gill's words to make them appear to say what they do not say. If leaving out the word 'now' which Gill legitimately takes up in the logical term 'therefore',[36] and which nevertheless Gill implies emphatically even in its temporal meaning, is a misdemeanour in Naylor's opinion, how are we to judge the many truncated quotes and part-quotes of scriptural texts which Naylor himself

uses in his arguments against Gill? Surely this is a legitimate practice
providing it is done carefully and without changing any meaning either
unintentionally or otherwise. Gill's full quote shows he is keeping to an
exact interpretation of the texts, whereas Naylor's truncated re-rendering
and the interpretation he puts on it smacks of 'special pleading'.

     Naylor pays little attention to Gill's doctrine of faith which is essential
to an understanding of his doctrine of justification. Though he entitles one
very short chapter *John Gill and Faith*, the subject 'faith' is conspicuous
by its nigh absence. Any reader of Naylor's book must receive the
impression that Gill has next to nothing to say about it. He even accuses Gill
of Sandemanianism by defining Gill's doctrine of faith as merely 'assent
to the facts of the Gospel',[37] and where he should be concentrating on Gill's
very detailed and thorough teaching on the subject, he discusses Gill's
doctrine of law and repentance. This is a pity as Gill, immediately before
and after the words quoted by Naylor concerning the justification of the
Old Testament saints,[38] outlines in detail his doctrine of faith as centred in
Christ, the object of faith. This is repeated, at times almost verbatim, in
Gill's sermon on *The Doctrine of Justification Stated and Maintained*. For
Gill faith is 'the recipient of it (Christ as the object of faith); it is the grace
by which the soul lays hold on, apprehends, and embraces Christ's
righteousness, as its justifying righteousness before God.'[39] This is a far cry
from the view that faith is a bare assent to the work of Christ as propagated
by John Glas and Robert Sandeman. Further, Gill argues that:

> Faith is the sense, perception, and evidence of our justification.
> Christ's righteousness, as justifying, is revealed from faith to faith.
> It is that grace whereby the soul, in the light of the divine Spirit,
> beholds a complete righteousness in Christ, having seen its guilt,
> pollution, and misery; when it is enabled to renounce its own
> righteousness, and submit to the righteousness of Christ; which it
> puts on by faith, as its garment of justification: which it rejoices in,
> and gives him the glory of; the Spirit of God bearing witness with
> his Spirit, that he is a justified Person.[40]

Here it is clear that Gill is not saying that faith is dispensable in the
matter of justification in the way Naylor seeks to prove. Faith, according
to Gill, does not procure justification, it is not the *causa sine qua non* of
justification but it is God's gift enabling the sinner to apprehend and
appropriate it.[41] Without faith no one is 'evidently and declaratively
justified in the name of the Lord Jesus, and by the Spirit of our God'. To
those whom God justifies, he gives the faith to believe in the Justifier. This
is entirely within Calvin's teaching on the relationship between justification and faith. The Reformer argued:

The order of justification which it (God's mercy) sets before us is this: first, God of his mere gratuitous goodness is pleased to embrace the sinner, in whom he sees nothing that can move him to mercy but wretchedness, because he sees him altogether naked and destitute of good works. He, therefore, seeks the cause of kindness in himself, that thus he may affect the sinner by a sense of his goodness, and induce him, in distrust of his own works, to cast himself entirely upon his mercy for salvation.[42]

Calvin, as Gill, thus maintained that faith was the manifestation and ratification of justification. No man was drawn to Christ because he was willing but the elect are drawn to Christ so that they might be made willing. No one can approach the Father unless he is drawn to the Father by the Father.[43]

Though Naylor questions Gill's distinction between 'active' and 'passive' justification, it is the very distinction which Calvin makes. Active justification in Calvin's eyes is the decreeing of the elect to justification and the exercising of faith is 'only the instrument for receiving justification'.[44] He can thus conclude, 'For, in regard to justification, faith is merely passive, bringing nothing of our own to procure the favour of God, but receiving from Christ everything that we want.'[45] 'In Calvin's eyes this active justification is eternal as it is the status of those eternally elected by God.'[46] He can thus argue that when Paul speaks of predestining the elect to the adoption of children by Jesus Christ, making them accepted in the Beloved, he is talking about being justified freely by his grace.[47]

Naylor sees a conflict of ideas between Gill's perfectly orthodox Calvinistic belief that faith is not the active instrument or means of justification and the scriptural truth that a sinner is justified by faith. This is no problem at all to Gill who argues:

That those places of scripture, which speak of justification, by, or through faith, do not militate against, nor disprove justification before faith: for though justification before, and by faith differ, yet they are not opposite and contradictory: yea, justification by, or through faith, supposes justification before faith. For if there was no justification before faith, there can be none by it, without making faith the cause or condition of it.[48]

In his *Institutes*, Book II, Chapters XI-XVI Calvin expounds at great length his doctrine of justification confessing that 'We simply interpret justification, as the acceptance with which God receives us into his favour as if we were righteous; and we say that this justification consists in the forgiveness of sins and the imputation of the righteousness of Christ.'[49]

This is no more and no less than Gill asserts and, as both theologians see this justification as being arranged before the beginning of time, one wonders how Gill can possibly be labelled a Hyper-Calvinist.

As so often, Gill's theology can be closely compared with that of John Bunyan. In *The Pharisee and the Publican* Bunyan argues that justification goes hand in hand with being chosen in Christ before the foundation of the world. As the gift of justifying imputed righteousness goes before faith and produces faith, obviously, in Bunyan's view, justification preceeds faith. A man is justified whilst he is ungodly that he might become godly and walk by faith. Thus Bunyan can say, 'He then that is justified by God's imputation, shall believe by the power of the Holy Ghost; for that must come and work faith, and strengthen the soul to act it, because imputed righteousness has gone before.' Moreover, Bunyan can also argue, 'A man may be justified before God, even then when himself knoweth nothing thereof, Isai. 40:2, Matth. 9:2, and so when, and while he hath not Faith about it, but is ungodly.' Bunyan distinguishes between being justified in the divine decree, which he calls 'justification before God', and to which he is referring in my quote, and 'Justification to the Understanding and Conscience', referring to the approbation of faith.[50] This tallies with Gill's and Calvin's view of active and passive justification and also with the views of Owen, Hervey, Toplady, Whitefield, Huntington etc. that the formal cause of justification is Christ's righteousness. In fact this was the established view of the eighteenth-century Evangelical Revival marred only by the denial of this teaching by Baxter at its beginning and Fuller's metaphorical reinterpretation towards its end.

Combating the more or less Arian Samuel Chandler (1693-1766) who believed that the moral law was rationally inherent in man so that he only had to see the 'fittness of things' to find supreme happiness, Gill saw this as a denial of the Mosaic law of God that reflected his true holiness that man had lost at the Fall.[51] This was true Antinomianism to Gill as Chandler taught that God had no law of his own and expected of man only what man himself knew from creation. Many Christians, however, were viewing Chandler as something of a prophet yet were calling Gill an Antinomian because he believed in justification before the foundation of the world. To this Gill says:

> Now, to set aside, and disregard the law of God, as a rule of life
> and conversation or action, is strictly and properly Antinomianism.
> For my part, I have been traduced as an Antinomian, for innocently
> asserting, that the essence of justification lies in the eternal will of
> God; my meaning is, that God in all his all-perfect and comprehen-
> sive mind, had from all eternity, at once, a full view of all his elect;
> of all their sins and transgressions; of his holy and righteous law, as

broken by them, and of the complete and perfect righteousness of his Son, who had engaged to be a surety for them; and in this view of things he willed them to be righteous, through the suretiship-righteousness of his Son, and accordingly esteemed, and accounted them so in him; in which will, esteem, and account their justification lies, as an immanent act of God. By this way of thinking and speaking I no ways set aside, nor in the least oppose the doctrine of justification by faith; I assert, that there is no knowledge of justification, no comfort from it, nor any claim of interest in it, until a man believes. I abhor the thought of setting the law of God aside as the rule of walk and conversation; and constantly affirm, that all that believe in Christ for righteousness, should be careful to maintain good works, for necessary uses. But here is a Gentleman that talks of something prior to, and independent of the will of God, and antecedent to any law of his as the supreme, original, universal and most perfect rule of action to reasonable beings; as the immutable and eternal obligation of moral virtue, or from whence moral obligation is derived; whereby all authority on God's part, and all obedience on ours, are at once entirely destroyed. One should think, for the future, that not John Gill, but Samuel Chandler, must be reckoned the Antinomian.[52]

Naylor quotes Toplady approvingly and obviously does not think he is a Hyper-Calvinist nor an Antinomian, yet Toplady entered into his diary on Saturday 26 December 1767:

Gave Dr. Gill's tract on Justification another reading; not without much edification and comfort. I do think that this great man's arguments for the proper eternity of this blessing, *ex parte Dei*, are unanswerable. Glory be to thee, O Lord, for my sense of special interest in thy everlasting love! Were all the treasures of ten thousand worlds displayed to my view, the sight of them, the mere sight, would not make me the richer nor the happier; it is the knowledge of peculiar property in any blessing, that felicitates the soul. In this the comfort lies. And, thanks to divine grace, I can look upon all the unsearchable riches of Christ, as my own. Lord, increase my faith, and add to my thankfulness more and more.[53]

Naylor, in assessing Gill's doctrine of justification, always stresses one side of Gill's teaching i.e. active justification in eternity. He leaves out most of Gill's teaching on the relation between the gift of faith and justification in time. He also presents Gill as a cold analyst whereas the passages from which he takes his quotes are often exuberant in emphasizing the love of God and the experimental outcome of this love. Gill has indeed a great deal to say about justification being worked out in faith through and after conversion. Though he insisted that justification is eternal because it is eternally in the divine will, he also argues that faith is 'a pre-requisite to the knowledge and comfort of it, and to a claim of interest in it; and this is readily allowed, that no man is evidently and declaratively justified until he believes'.[54]

Graham Harrison in his Evangelical Library Lecture *Dr Gill and his Teaching* shows how radically different was Fuller's doctrine of justification to that of Gill and how he reacted to the 'almost oracular quality'[55] with which Gill's teaching was regarded. He points out that Fuller looked upon what he called 'the sentence of justification' as being merely 'the voice of God in the Gospel, declaring that whosoever believeth shall be saved'. Justification has thus nothing to do with 'a purpose in the Divine mind'[56] as Gill argued. This teaching falls short of even Wesley's Arminianism and is the doctrine taught by the more radical New Divinity schoolmen, especially Bellamy. These philosophers-cum-divines were strongly influenced by Grotius and motivated Fuller to emphasize that a table of justification is spread before the sinner who only needs to sit down and eat,[57] there being no mention in Scripture of a gift required to fit one out to do so. Fuller's questionable doctrine obviously moves Harrison to warn critics against dismissing Gill's doctrine with 'a contemptuous wave of the theological hand'. He points out that Gill was following in the steps of many an orthodox expositor and stresses that Gill's doctrine of justification was because of a desire 'to give to the Lord all the glory and the credit that was due to his most holy name'.[58] Timothy George gives Gill a very fair hearing here and confesses that in hands such as Gill's the doctrine of eternal justification is quite safe. He does feel, however, that there are those who might find the doctrine 'perilous' in that they will be tempted to believe they are justified irrespective of their personal response to Christ.[59] This is indeed so, and Gill, in his sermons, is constantly warning against this danger. However, any gospel truth which can be both a savour of death and a savour of life is 'perilous' in the wrong hands. This applies equally to all the Five Points.

The gospel call and duty faith

A Hyper-Calvinist, Gill's critics say, does not believe that God calls indiscriminately all who hear about Christ to believe in him. They say this because they believe that man is obliged as a matter of duty to trust in Christ as a condition of salvation, or, as they put it, to trust savingly in Christ. It is odd that this opinion is often so closely associated with Gill for several reasons. First, this view applied to Gill is an anachronism as the idea of saving faith being the known duty and within the natural ability of all men reached its fullest expression in 1785 with the publication of Andrew Fuller's notorious book *The Gospel Worthy of All Acceptation*. Gill, however, died in 1771 thus obviously having nothing to do with the debate that tore the Baptist churches apart after the book was published. The second reason is that during the earlier part of the eighteenth century the view of what came to be called duty-faith, formerly propagated by the Anglican Latitudinarians, was gaining ground amongst the Independents. However Gill, a Baptist, maintained he did not take part in this debate.[60] This is confirmed by Andrew Fuller himself and Dr John Ryland not only argues that Gill did not take part in the debate, he exonerates him from the major extremes associated on that count with Hyper-Calvinism.[61] John Rippon acknowledges that Gill says he took no part in the earlier debate but nevertheless assumes that he did so in later life because of certain 'corrections' he made to his book *The Cause of God and Truth*. Rippon, however, does not state what these 'corrections' are and how they might have applied to the debate in question.[62]

Whether Gill took part in the debate or not, his own position is one of biblical balance between the two absolute extremes of those who will not take the gospel to sinners and those who stress the ability and therefore duty of the unconverted to believe savingly. In *The Cause of God* Gill clearly stresses the Christian duty, under the guidance of the Holy Spirit, to call and command sinners to repent.[63] He argues that all men are naturally bound to repent because they have naturally broken the law. Commanding them to repent is putting them under the curse of the law which they have broken in their natural state and thus brought on that curse for themselves. For Gill, this means that all men are under a legal obligation to repent. What man has broken, he has a duty to mend. This does not mean that man has the ability to do so but he is still a debtor to the law for having broken it. The law forces its demands on every one because all have sinned and fallen short of the glory of God.

Abraham Taylor had criticized men such as Gill, maintaining that they were 'forward to condemn pressing men to duty, as legal preaching; and to speak of exhorting to repentance, mortification, and self-denial as low and mean stuff'.[64]

Gill's answer must have surprised Taylor as he argued:

> I cannot but wonder that you should esteem such culpable or blame-worthy, who condemn pressing men to duty, as legal preaching; for pressing men to duty, can be no other than legal preaching, or preaching of the law; since duty can be referred to nothing else but the law, which obliges to it. Should they condemn pressing men to duty, as criminal, or deny that there ought to be any preaching,

or that there is any use of the law, you might justly have blamed them. The duties which the law requires, ought to be in their place insisted on in the ministry of the word; they should be opened and explained; men should be taught their duty to God and one another; they should be pressed: that is, if I understand it, be exhorted unto it, with gospel-motives and arguments, such as the apostles frequently make use of in their epistles. They should, at the same time be told where grace and strength lie, and are to be had to assist them in it. The preaching of the law is of use both to saints and sinners; it is made useful by the Spirit of God to convince of sin; By the law is the knowledge of sin; though by it is no knowledge of a Saviour from sin; it shews the exceeding sinfulness of sin, the deformity of nature, the imperfection of man's obedience, and what is requisite to his justification before God; though it leaves him ignorant of that righteousness which can only answer its demands, and render him acceptable in the sight of God.[65]

In other words, rather than condemn preaching duties, Gill insisted that this was the first aim in preaching so that fallen man can see that he stands guilty before a broken law which he has failed in his God-given duty to keep.

All duty belongs to law in Gill's eyes and the law demands that every man should do his duty. Grace and promises of grace, however, belong to the gospel. 'Preaching duty, is preaching the law; preaching the free grace of God, and salvation by Christ, is preaching the gospel; to say otherwise, is to turn the gospel into law and to blend and confound both together.'[66] Thus, in Gill's eyes, if the gospel was merely seen as preaching duties it would turn biblical preaching into nothing less than Neonomianism which provides a watered-down gospel-law for sinner and saint alike, thus completely doing away with the need for putting a man first under the curse of the Mosaic Law until the sinner by grace is given Christ's imputed righteousness to put on. The Latitudinarian duty preachers were therefore at best only doing half of their duty as evangelists and at worst completely confusing law with gospel. This is why Cotton Mather (1663-1727) complained of the activities of the first British missionary society 'The Society for the Propagation of the Gospel in Foreign Parts' as it stressed duties rather than the gospel of grace. This led him to call the organization 'The Society for the Molestation of the Gospel in Foreign Parts'.[67] This is also why Mather, rather than support the English society, gave his expertise and prayers to the missionary endeavours of Franke and Ziegenbalg concerning India which he felt were on a more balanced biblical basis. One American sufferer from this English duty-gospel was David Brainerd who, accepting the teaching of the 'missionary' clergy, actually became convinced that Christianity was a mere system of duties. His glorious conversion through grace put an end to this false gospel which only brought self-centred pride when duties were kept and great depression when duties were neglected.[68]

Dealing with the second major part of preaching, to balance the issue, Gill argues that evangelical repentance, rather than legal repentance, belongs to the gospel of grace. Evangelical repentance is a turning from sin to receive pardon in Christ. This can only come about by a sovereign act of God's goodness carried out by the work of the Holy Spirit in man. The sinner is not required to exercise this faith as a feeling of duty but he is drawn to the Saviour by the Saviour's love who gives the sinner faith to accept him. Naylor believes the distinction between 'legal repentance' and Gill's term 'evangelical repentance' is merely a 'high-Calvinist distinction' but the phrase 'evangelical repentance' was common to all evangelicals in the seventeenth and eighteenth centuries. The General Baptists in their Orthodox Creed, Article XXII 'Of evangelical repentance' freely use the term as referring to turning to God.[69] More interesting still, to those moderns who pronounce a fellow-Christian as a 'Hyper' as soon as he talks of legal and evangelical repentance, is the fact that Andrew Fuller, the doyen of Anti-Hypers, used the very same terms. Preaching at Ipswich in 1798 on the text 'Renew a right spirit within me' (Psalm 51:10), he says: 'Here we may distinguish between legal and evangelical repentance; while the first leads to rebellious despair, the latter leads to a holy submission to God.'

Nevertheless, Gill's consistent teaching was gravely misunderstood by Andrew Fuller who drew consequences from it which certainly did not reflect Gill's thoughts when referring to the Christian's duty to evangelize.[70] If there is no such thing as duty-faith, a natural, general awareness of one's duty to accept Christ when the gospel is preached, Fuller argued, then what purpose can evangelism have? This is why Fullerites deduce that Gill was against evangelism because he was against levelling the gospel down to preaching to a feeling of supposed duties in man. Such a gospel may be worthy of all acceptance but it is far from being the full gospel.[71] In Gill's eyes, however, no sinner can become alive to Christ before he is condemned to death by the law. This is preaching the full gospel. This is doing the work of an evangelist. This was the teaching of the Calvinist revivalists of the eighteenth century as Cowper explains concerning the true heaven-sent preacher:

By him the violated law speaks out,
It thunders; and by him, in strains as sweet
As angels use, the gospel whispers peace.

It is interesting to note that modern critics of Gill invariably follow
Fuller's faulty interpretation of Gill's theology of evangelism. This is
nowhere so well illustrated as in Robert Oliver's recent heavy criticism of
Gill where he states: 'Gill made his own position quite clear in 1752, when
he wrote: " ... that there are universal offers of grace and salvation made to
all men, I utterly deny".'[72]

This short quote, removed from its contextual and syntactical position,
is passed on from critic to critic and used as the major, if not only, proof that
Gill was a Hyper-Calvinist with a false view of evangelism, causing him
not to exhort sinners to repentance and faith. Erroll Hulse, for instance,
quotes this mutilated sentence to 'prove' that Gill's works 'are destitute of
pleadings with sinners to repent, earnestly and personally', believing that
this caused Gill's church to shrink, to which he comments ' ... and we are
not surprised'.[73] Apart from the fact that Gill's church, when at its lowest
ebb, contained more members than those of the leading 'free-offer' men of
the day, it will be obvious to readers of this book by now that Gill was most
urgent in preaching repentance and individual responsibility before God.
If there are still doubts concerning this, the next chapter will produce more
conclusive evidence.

The few words quoted by such as Oliver and Hulse, removed from their
context, are so often laboured upon that any reader must gain the impression that Gill did little else than condemn 'offers' though such words are
a rarity in Gill's works and are never used without a detailed explanation
of what is meant by the term. Often Gill's critics use the term 'offer' in a
most ambiguous way and they thrust their unclear meaning of the term on
to Gill's usage.[74] The words are invariably used to suggest that Gill left
possible reprobates out of his general offers of grace as if he knew who was
marked out as such when preaching. In the context Gill is not arguing in this
direction at all but he is claiming that sinners are never called universally
and indiscriminately, *en bloc*, to salvation or judgement as the case may be.
They are always called particularly and in God's good time. Thus Gill's
words can hardly be used as evidence that he has left the realms of
orthodoxy. Furthermore, in the context, Gill is actually emphasizing
evangelism's importance and scope within the worldwide strategy of the
Holy Spirit, not denying it. The pastor-scholar thus says in the passage
from which the words in question are carefully selected:

The gospel is indeed ordered to be preached to every creature to
whom it is sent and comes; but as yet, it has never been brought to
all the individuals of human nature; there have been multitudes in
all ages that have not heard it. And that there are universal offers of
grace and salvation made to all men, I utterly deny; nay, I deny that
they are made to any; no, not to God's elect; grace and salvation are

provided for them in the everlasting covenant, procured for them by Christ, published and revealed in the gospel, and applied by the Spirit.[75]

The particular context here is very important. Gill is defending the doctrine of Christ's effectual call of his sheep and writing specifically against Whitby's and Wesley's teaching concerning a universal atonement and their theory that all have been atoned for and thus all are in a position to respond to the gospel whenever this is indiscriminately offered on a take it or leave it basis. Gill rejects this kind of evangelism, saying that though we are ordered to preach the gospel to every creature, the Spirit always speaks to particular sinners, at particular times and in particular places, either making them 'sensible' to their lost situation and drawing them to himself, or passing them by.[76] The Spirit, however, moves where *he* will at the time *he* determines according to *his* invincible plan. This means that even the elect must await their turn before being effectually called. Though there must be universal evangelism, there is no such thing as indiscriminate evangelism. The Holy Spirit is not the Spirit of Higgledy-Piggledy.

This is clearly not the teaching of Gill's modern critics but is it the sign of a Hyper-Calvinist that they make it appear to be? What did Calvin say on the matter? His opening words on the subject in his *Institutes*, Book III chapter 21 are clearly and distinctly a refutation of the idea that there must be a general and universal indiscriminate offer of salvation to all who come within hearing distance of the gospel. Calvin's exact words are: 'The covenant of life is not preached equally to all, and among those to whom it is preached, does not always meet with the same reception. This diversity displays the unsearchable depth of the divine judgement, and is without doubt subordinate to God's purpose of eternal election.' Calvin goes on to say that it is 'plainly owing to the mere pleasure of God that salvation is spontaneously offered to some, while others have no access to it'. He continues by stating that he 'does not adopt promiscuously to the hope of salvation, but gives to some what he denies to others. It is plain how greatly *ignorance of this principle detracts from the glory of God, and impairs true humility.*'[77]

In *The Cause of God*, Gill makes it quite plain that the gospel is to be preached to all, as the Spirit leads, but it is not preached 'equally to all'. It comes as 'a savour of death unto death' for some and 'a savour of life unto life' for Christ's Bride.[78] Gill specifically emphasizes that he is not denying the use of 'calls, invitations, and messages of God to men by his ministers'[79] but maintaining that such calls, etc. are 'not sufficient in themselves, without powerful grace, to produce true faith in Christ, evangelical repentance towards God, and new spiritual obedience, in life and conversation'. Gill can argue in this way because he believes that there is a two-fold call in evangelism. First there is the internal effectual call which is the 'powerful operation of the Spirit of God on the soul' which cannot be resisted, then there is the external call by the ministry of the Word which 'may be resisted, rejected, and despised, and become useless'. Such teaching, when compared with Calvin's exposition of God's call in Book II, Chapter XXIV of his *Institutes,* reflects fully the heart of Calvinism. How then can Gill possibly be called a Hyper-Calvinist? Even Andrew Fuller acknowledged Gill's evangelistic outreach at times. In fact, modern Fullerites tend to be far more critical of Gill than Fuller himself.[80]

The insensitivity and inability of man

Next, the suspicion that Gill denied that a person insensitive to his sinfulness should ever be summoned to conversion as fallen humanity is beset by an inability to turn from sin and turn to God, must be dealt with, particularly as it is assumed that such a denial reveals a Hyper-Calvinist behind it. This emphasis on the natural impossibility of pleasing God is contrasted with the optimistic view of man as taught by Fuller which proclaims 'No natural impossibilities!'[81]

In Article Four of the *Declaration of the Faith and Practice of the Church of Christ in Carter Lane, Southwark,* Gill sees the Fall as permeating the very being and nature of man and not merely his will to believe. Man is physically, spiritually and morally fallen. He cannot serve God of himself either in body, soul, or spirit.[82] Much later in his ministry, Gill had still not moved an inch from this position. Expounding John 5:40: 'And ye will not come to me, that ye might have life,' he says: 'These words are so far from being expressive of the power and liberty of the will of man to come to Christ,[83] that they rather declare the perverseness and stubbornness of it; that man has no desire, inclination, or will, to go to Christ for life, but rather go anywhere else, than to him. Man is *stout-hearted,* and *far from the righteousness of Christ,* and submission to it; is not *subject to the law of God,* nor the gospel of Christ; nor *can he be,* till God works in him both *to will and to do of his good pleasure*; or until he is made *willing in the day of his power.* No one *can come to Christ, except the Father draw him*; nor has he a will to it, unless it is wrought in him.'[84]

Those who take umbrage at Gill's low view of man usually argue that man is merely fallen in his moral abilities (which they sometimes equate with his spiritual or godly abilities) but his natural abilities remain intact. Calvin thought otherwise and found a worthy champion in Gill. Writing in Book II, Chapter II of his *Institutes* Calvin confesses: 'I feel pleased with the well-known saying which has been borrowed from the writings of Augustine, that man's natural gifts were corrupted by sin, and his supernatural gifts withdrawn; meaning by supernatural gifts the light of faith and righteousness, which would have been sufficient for the attainment of heavenly life and everlasting felicity.'

Calvin emphasizes that not only abilities which were 'above nature', such as love to God, were abolished (Calvin's word) in man but also man's 'very mind and being' were corrupted leaving him with but a residue of intelligence and judgement. Man's reason is now a mere 'shapeless ruin' so that when the divine reason, *Logos*, comes, 'The light shineth in darkness and the darkness comprehended it not.' It takes reason to understand reason and man has forfeited his. All this was a bone of contention to Fuller who argued that man's reason, in fact all his 'natural powers' were left intact at the Fall.[85]

Perhaps the strongest biblical argument for the insensitivity and inability of fallen man to understand the gospel is I Corinthians 2:14 which Gill expounded in his *Cause of God and Truth*: 'But the natural man receiveth not the things of the Spirit of God: for they are foolishness unto him, neither can he know them, because they are spiritually discerned.'[86] It is clear to Gill that this proves conclusively that the gospel of Christ can only be a stumbling block and foolishness to the unconverted unless it is accompanied by a demonstration of the Spirit and power of God.

Gill's critics are never tired of complaining that if man is fully depraved he cannot be held responsible for his own depravity. He is at worst a sick man, with a natural chance of getting better. He is not a dead man because dead men are neither addressable or responsive. This is Andrew Fuller's argument throughout his dubiously titled book *The Gospel Worthy of All Acceptation*. Fuller appears to feel that the full Fall only occurs once man has heard the gospel and wilfully rejected it. Until this time, he has the natural ability to exercise duty-faith savingly. Thus Fuller says: 'If sinners were naturally and absolutely unable to believe in Christ, they would be unequally unable to disbelieve; for it requires the same powers to reject as to embrace.'[87]

Here Fuller is again forgetting the total nature of the Fall, not thinking that man had the ability to believe but fully forfeited it. Paul's words in Romans 11:32 are timely here: 'For God hath concluded them all in unbelief', as also are those in Ephesians 2:1: 'And you hath he quickened who were dead in trespasses and sins.' A sense of man's killing, blind-making sins never seem to penetrate Fuller's logic. He takes up the case of the naturally dead man and the naturally blind man as 'proof' that man is not totally fallen. He says, 'A dead body is equally unable to do evil as to do good; and a man naturally and absolutely blind could not be guilty of shutting his eyes against the light.' He concludes that if fallen man were either dead or totally blind to spiritual truths, he could not be held responsible for rejecting Christ. As man is held responsible, he must have spiritual insight in the form of a knowledge of his duty to believe savingly.

Fuller forgets that though man is dead in trespasses and sins, God can quicken him and give him faith. He also does not recognize that man's spiritual blindness is the result of sin irrespective of whether he has heard the gospel or not. He is thus voluntarily blind and thus fully responsible for his blindness. Fuller's parallels drawn with both the dead man and the man who is physically blind are therefore non-applicable and quite unscriptural. The Scriptures make it plain that naturally dead men are judged according to their acceptance or rejection of Christ and that the man who was truly born physically blind in John 9 was not blind because of his personal sin or the sins of his parents but because of God's purpose in the matter. Spiritually blind men are 'concluded in unbelief' and cannot discern spiritual things.

Paul argues in 2 Corinthians 4:3: 'But if our gospel be hid, it is hid to them that are lost. In whom the god of this world hath blinded the minds of them which believe not, lest the light of the glorious gospel of Christ, who is the image of God, should shine unto them.' If all man's natural powers given him at creation were intact, as Fuller so vociferously argues, then man would have an inbuilt means of communication with his Creator. In withholding his image, Christ, from the lost, they are left completely blind and helpless of themselves and have no means whatsoever in themselves of discerning anything of Christ's light. To argue against this is to accept the Quaker maxim which speaks of 'that of God in every man' and to believe that there is a spark of spiritual life in man that only needs to be fanned into a blaze by 'free offer' preaching. This is completely contrary to the Scriptures and it was a view Gill could not tolerate for a moment. If man is to see, according to Gill, he must receive the gift of sight. Gill argues in Part One, Section XXX, point 3, of *The Cause of God*, following Scripture which teaches that man has got himself into his own mess:

> Though man lies under such a disability, and has neither power nor will of himself to come to Christ for life, yet his not coming to Christ, when revealed in the external ministry of the gospel, as God's way of salvation, is criminal and blame-worthy; since the disability and perverseness of his will are not owing to any decree of God, but to the corruption and virtiosity of his nature, through sin; and therefore, since this virtiosity of nature is blame-worthy; for God made man upright, though they have sought out many inventions, which have corrupted their nature; that which follows upon it, and is the effect of it, must be so too.[88]

As it is maintained that a Hyper-Calvinist is one who views man's incapacity to repent as a natural limitation rather than as 'a culpable evil arising from a perverted and sinful heart', there are no grounds here for calling Gill a Hyper-Calvinist as the Baptist scholar was fully biblical on this point, arguing both for a natural (fallen) limitation and for the truth that fallen man has a perverted and sinful heart. Referring to Gill's statement of faith concerning man's sin, helplessness and responsibility, Timothy George writes, 'Bunyan and Keach before him, and Fuller and Spurgeon after him, could have embraced without reservation Gill's congregational confession which, in reality, was merely an abstract of the 1689 Second London Confession.'[89] Though one may reserve judgement in Fuller's case, this quote shows how orthodox Gill appears to George in every respect.

The faith of Adam before the Fall

John Ryland Junior, writing in his *Memoirs of Mr Fuller*, criticizes a group of writers, including Wayman and Brine, for teaching that 'Adam, as they then thought, had not power (that is, he had no occasion, or opportunity) to believe in Christ.' This was, Ryland believes, the reason for protests against the contemporary stress laid on preaching duty-faith in the evangelism of his day. Naylor, after claiming that Gill was 'without doubt' the most prominent exponent of High/Hyper-Calvinism, sees this lack of power in Adam to believe in Christ as their typical badge. Ryland, however, on the very same page as the above quote adds:

> Yet Dr Gill, in his *Cause of God and Truth*, Part III, p. 31, gives up this chief argument of Mr Brine, and says: 'That Adam, in a state of innocence, had a power of believing in Christ, and did believe in him, as the second person in the Trinity, as the Son of God, cannot well be denied; since, with the other two persons, he was his Creator and Preserver, the knowledge of which cannot well be thought to be withheld from him. And his not believing in him as the Mediator, Saviour, and Redeemer, did not arise from any defect of power in him; but from the state, condition, and situation in which he was, and from the nature of the revelation made to him.'

The argument Gill had with duty-faith enthusiasts was not that they demanded full powers to believe of pre-lapsus Adam, but that they demanded the same unfallen Adamic powers of fallen man. It is obvious, as Gill points out, that fallen sinners are in a different 'state, condition, and situation' to Adam in his innocence, so the gospel's demands on them must be different. It also must be argued, as Huntington argues so conclusively in his book *The Loss and Restoration of the Image of God in Man*,[90] that Christ's imputed righteousness is a better righteousness than Adam's

natural righteousness as Adam's ended with the Fall but Christ's is
everlasting. This righteousness, however, has nothing to do with natural
powers or abilities. It is a gift of God.

Antinomianism

Most of Gill's critics have difficulty in demonstrating that Gill was an
Antinomian but they nevertheless link him closely with that faction. Daniel
believes that Crisp taught 'Antinomianism proper', and argues that what
Crisp 'had in common with Gill can also be considered a form of
Antinomianism'.[91] Hulse, with Gill in mind, maintains that 'The essence
of hyper-Calvinism is to minimize the moral and spiritual responsibility of
sinners.'[92] Naylor maintains that Hyper-Calvinism is a 'benign form of
Antinomianism' and quotes Augustus Montague Toplady in his definition
of what an Antinomian believes, i.e. 'That believers are released from all
obligation to observe the moral law as a rule of external obedience: That,
in consequence of Christ's having wrought out a justifying righteousness
for us, we have nothing to do, but to sit down, eat, drink, and be merry; that
the Messiah's merits supersede the necessity of personal inherent sanctification.'[93]

Naylor stresses that Toplady was not an Antinomian himself, probably
thinking of the numerous times John Wesley had accused him of being
such a heretic. Nevertheless, Naylor's choice of Toplady in defining
Antinomianism is most odd. Toplady was one of John Gill's most intimate
friends and regarded Gill as a pastor, scholar and brother in Christ *par
excellence*. Furthermore Toplady stressed that Gill was the one person
who, in face of the perpetual Arminian accusation of being an Antinomian
had shown that 'the Doctrine of Grace does not lead to Licentiousness'[94]
and that 'his moral demeanour was more than blameless'.[95] Hoad, too,
links Antinomianism with the Particular Baptists and Hyper-Calvinism
and says that it was Gill's 'influence which was a major factor in the
retention of a "High Calvinist theology" of a substantial part of those
churches'.[96]

Gill was often maliciously accused of Antinomianism, especially by
Arminians, throughout his Christian life. One of his most prolific antagonists in this matter was Dr Abraham Taylor, whose works so influenced
Fuller against Gill. Taylor had continually accused Gill of being against
good works and thus an Antinomian and Gill had written a long letter to him
explaining that he was nothing of the kind. Taylor never replied to this letter
and Gill certainly gave neither Taylor nor anyone else cause to accuse him
of Antinomianism in his succeeding works. Six years later a work was
published which Taylor thought showed severe signs of Antinomianism.
Though the work bore the name of the author, which was not Gill, Taylor
immediately associated Gill with the work, claiming that he was the author

under an assumed name. Without checking his suspicions, Taylor produced a pamphlet which he named *An Address to young Students in Divinity, by way of Caution against some Paradoxes, which lead to Doctrinal Antinomianism.*

The work was a monstrous display of abuse in which no vulgarism was considered too low to be levelled, obviously at Gill and like-minded believers. The scholar-pastor, faced with such pseudo-learned attacks, could only say, 'When these ill names and hard words are taken out, there is very little left for me to reply to.' Nevertheless Gill replied as Taylor's message in his pamphlet made true holiness an impossibility and attributed to man what only God can provide.

In his answer entitled *The Necessity of Good Works Unto Salvation Considered*, Gill opens by disclaiming any connection whatsoever with the work Taylor assumed was his, stating that there is not a line in it from his pen and that he did not know of the book until it appeared in print. As Taylor is obviously calling Gill an Antinomian because he does not believe that good works move God to save the good worker, Gill, in his reply, first defines Antinomianism and then goes on to discuss the meaning and usefulness of good works:

> This man ought to have informed his students what doctrinal Antinomianism is. Since he has not, I will. Doctrinal Antinomianism, properly speaking, is a denying, or setting aside the law of God, as a rule of life, action or conversation. Now what tendency has the above proposition to such a notion? Or how does it appear, that the very quintessence of doctrinal Antinomianism is cauched in it, as is suggested? Though we say, that works are not necessary to salvation; do we say, that they are not necessary to anything else? Do we say, that they are not necessary to be done in obedience to the law of God? Do we say, that the commands of the law are not to be regarded by men? That they are things indifferent, that may be done, or not done? No; we say none of these things, but all the reverse. Do we make void the law through this doctrine? God forbid: Yea, we establish the law, as it is in the hands of Christ our Lawgiver; to which we desire to yield a cheerful obedience; to show our subjection to him as King of saints, and to testify our gratitude for the many blessings of every kind we receive from him.[97]

Regarding good works, Gill tells Taylor:

> That they are necessary to be done, or ought to be done, by all that hope to be saved by the grace of our Lord Jesus Christ, is readily granted; but not in point of salvation, in order to that, or with a view

to obtain it. Good works are necessary to be done, on account of the divine ordination and appointment; for such as are the *workman-ship* of God are *created in Christ Jesus unto good works, which God hath before ordained, that they should walk in them*. They are necessary, *necessitate precepti & debiti*, on account of the will and command of God, and of that obedience we owe to God, both as creatures, and as new creatures. They are necessary upon the score of obligation we lie under to him, and in point of gratitude for the numerous mercies we receive from him, and that by them both we and others may glorify him our father which is in heaven. They are necessary to adorn the doctrine of God our Saviour, to recommend religion to others, to testify the truth of our faith, and give evidence of the reality of internal holiness. They are necessary for the good of our neighbours, and for the stopping of the mouths of our enemies.[98]

When defending Warren Hastings, Governor General of Bengal, against accusations concerning his supposed misuse of authority to enrich himself, his old school-friend William Cowper noted that the accusers, in reality, were blaming Hastings for the very evils that they themselves practised. He suspected that those who were crying 'Thief!' were doing so to create a distraction whilst their own hands were in the Indians' pockets. Parallels can be drawn here with those who accused Gill of Antinomianism. It is also interesting to note that those who were loudest in associating Gill with Antinomianism amongst 'Moderate Calvinists' were the very same people who accused William Huntington, a strict adherent to the law of God, of the same heresy. It can be clearly demon-strated that both Gill and Huntington held to the eternal purpose of the Holy Law in its spiritual and moral function far more literally than did their accusers who tended to spiritualize away the commandments of God and the need to teach the law to prepare men's hearts for the gospel. Their Neonomian accusers tended to deny the validity of the law in convincing, convicting and condemning men and used it merely as a modified moral guide for the already-converted to produce 'evangelical righteousness' through 'sincere obedience'. Gill's critics who are influenced by the Grotian and New Divinity Moral Government Theory are true doctrinal Antinomians as they do not believe that the moral law is a true reflection of God's eternal character, but that its demands on man are purely transient and abitrary, and that there is no true penal satisfaction in Christ's vicarious death for his Bride. In other words, there is more evidence to suggest that Gill's accusers are Antinomians than the reverse. According to modern scholarship,[99] it seems that Fuller and the so-called 'Evangelical Calvin-ists' were highly influenced by Hugo Grotius. This humanist, however,

clearly taught that the law was not eternally binding and that God relaxed
it or enforced it according to his temporary will. In fact Grotius taught that
God could and did reject his own law at times as it was only a demonstration
of moral necessity and never an absolute legal necessity.

Calvin warns against any misuse of the law, especially concerning its
legal nature, and speaks of the 'antithesis between Legal and gospel
righteousness'. Quoting Romans 10:5-9, he argues that there is a righteousness which is according to the law described by Moses, 'that the man who
doeth those things shall live by them'. This is quite different to the
righteousness of faith which says, 'If thou shalt confess with thy mouth the
Lord Jesus, and shalt believe in thine heart that God hath raised him from
the dead, thou shalt be saved.' Calvin then adds,

> Do you see how he makes the distinction between the Law and
> the gospel to be, that the former gives justification to works,
> whereas the latter bestows it freely without any help from works?
> This is a notable passage, and may free us from many difficulties if
> we understand that the justification which is given to us by the
> gospel is free from any terms of Law. It is for this reason he more
> than once places the promise in diametrical opposition to the Law.
> 'If the inheritance be of the law, it is no more of promise' (Gal. iii.
> 18).[100]

In Book I, Chapter 6 of Gill's *Body of Divinity*, Gill sweeps all
accusations of Antinomianism aside, arguing: 'The moral law, which lies
chiefly in the Decalogue, or Ten Commandments, Exod. xx. 3-17. and
which our Lord has reduced, even both tables of the law, to two capital
ones, love to God, and love to our neighbour, Matt. xxii. 36-40. as the
apostle has reduced the commandments of the second table to one, that is,
love, which he calls the fulfilling of the law, Rom. xiii. 9-10. And this law,
to love God and our neighbour, is binding on every man, and is eternal, and
remains invariable and unalterable.'

In *The Character and End of the Wicked, considered*, Gill drives away
any idea that he might have a low view of the law. In this sermon he tells
his hearers:

> This law is of such a nature, that every man is obliged by it; for the
> sum and substance of this law is, to love the Lord our God with all
> our heart and with all our soul; and to love our neighbour as
> ourselves.

> A good man, a man that has the grace of God implanted in him, is
> very desirous to be under this yoke; for though those who believe
> in Christ are delivered from the law, in which they were held, as it

is a covenant of works (for they are not under the law, but under grace, and are delivered also from the curse and bondage of it); yet they are under it as a rule of walk and conversation, in the hands of Christ, delight in the law of God after the inner man, and serve it with all their hearts; though with the flesh they serve the law of sin. But as for wicked, carnal, and unregenerate men, children of Belial, they are without this yoke; they cast it off, and do not chuse to have any thing to do with it. As for the wicked, says the Psalmist, *they are far from thy law*: far from it indeed! they do not care to come nigh, or be under it; they despise it, and cast it away from them. Instead of its being before them, to read it, and meditate on it; instead of having it before them as the rule of their lives and actions, they cast it behind their backs, determined to have nothing to do with it. God has wrote unto them the great things of his law, but they are reckoned by them as strange things. Such is the enmity of the carnal mind against God and his law, that it is not subject unto it, neither indeed can be; there is such a contradiction between the law of God and a wicked man. The law is holy, just, and good; but he is carnal, and sold under sin, in the worst sense of this expression: it is, I say, quite contrary to him, and therefore the natural man disapproves of it, despises it, casts it away from him; and every thing he does, thwarts and contradicts this law. The thoughts and the imaginations of the thoughts of his heart, are evil, and that continually, which this law condemns. His words and actions, as they are against the will, so they are against the law of God; every sin whatever, in thought, word, and deed, is a transgression of this law: no carnal man is subject unto it; however he may be externally, yet not internally, from the heart. He cannot be so, unless his heart is changed; unless the stoney heart is taken away, and an heart of flesh is given: unless a new and right spirit is renewed within him, and the Spirit of God enable him to walk in the statutes and judgments of the Lord, to do them. A man must have this law written in his heart, by the Spirit of God, or he will never be willing to obey it: he must be made willing in the day of the Lord's power, or he will never be contented to bear the yoke of the law, but will be a son of Belial, one that is without a yoke.[101]

Now it perhaps could be carnally imagined by one keen on maintaining his own 'evangelical righteousness' that Gill is being rather hard on the poor sinner here and rather exaggerates the place and purpose of the law in both believer and unbeliever alike. It must, however, be a sheer impossibility to label the man that wrote these words an 'Antinomian'.

It would thus seem quite contrary to the facts to accuse Gill of being an Antinomian as if he saw no need for good works and a commitment to moral righteousness. Actually this was admitted by Dr John Ryland, one of the original 'Fullerites'. In his *Memoir of Mr Fuller*, written 1816, forty-five years after Gill's death, he takes up the matter of Antinomianism and says: 'Dr Gill, Mr Brine, and Mr Toplady utterly reprobated that pernicious sentiment, into which so many have eagerly run within these last thirty years.' Obviously, then, any growth in the spread of Antinomianism had nothing, in Ryland's opinion, to do with Gill. This is also Timothy George's conclusion when he says, 'Anyone who has examined Gill's *Body of Practical Divinity* or looked at his sermons on *The Law Established by the Gospel* (1756) and *The Law in the Hand of Christ* (1761) will know how spurious is the charge of antinomianism against him.'[102] Thomas J. Nettles also clearly sees that Gill stood above all such mean charges and argues, 'If Gill were antinomian, may God grant the church a deeper holiness produced by this kind of "antinomianism".'[103]

One might add that if Gill's teaching were Hyper-Calvinism then we must completely alter our negative conception of the word and see that it is being used merely as a means to depreciate the gospel of God's love to his people. This is the stance David Engelsma takes when he argues, 'In most cases the charge "hyper-Calvinist" is nothing but a deceptive attack upon Calvinism itself. Someone hates Calvinism, or the uncompromising, consistent defence of Calvinism; yet he hesitates to attack Calvinism openly and forthrightly, and therefore he disguises his attack as an attack on "hyper-Calvinism" and "hyper-Calvinists".'[104] The truth of Engelsma's statement becomes obvious when it is found that the great bulk of Gill's critics profess to be Calvinists but deny from one to three of Calvinism's 'Five Points'. It is thus Calvinism and the Reformed Faith as a whole that they are attacking, not merely Gill.

The conclusions of Gill's traducers always add up to a denial of Gill's evangelistic fervour and a stubborn, dogmatic refusal to believe that he accepted any kind of preaching of the gospel to the unsaved. This is such topsy-turvy thinking that it will be necessary to devote a chapter to the gospel preaching of this godly man who stressed the need to go into the highways and bye-ways to draw men to Christ. This was long before para-church organizations were founded, taking this responsibility from the churches themselves and which have been accredited with pioneering the missionary spirit as if the Church Triumphant had slept until then.

10.
The pastor in the pulpit

Gill was a prolific author and it is commonly assumed that he spent most of his time writing with a view to publication, thus spending far less time on sermon preparation and pastoral work. The fact is that most of the over 10,000 pages of his works started life as sermon notes or grew out of conversations with his church members and fellow ministers.

As Gill preached at least five sermons weekly at his own chapel, besides preaching regularly outside of his flock and lecturing in aid of charity schools and various societies, he soon found that he needed to be continually engaged in sermon and lecture preparation. As soon as one sermon was delivered, he would start praying and thinking about the next. He would meditate on a word throughout the day, consulting his books from time to time. His family were quite used to seeing him walking about the house or working in the garden, seemingly talking to himself. He was sorting out a word from the Lord for his next service. Writing time for Gill was in the evenings when he would commit to paper the thoughts given him throughout the day. In this way, Gill was hardly ever surprised by a request for a sermon as he received new ideas day by day. On most occasions when Gill preached, his hearers felt he finished on the most moving and edifying part of his sermon, leaving his congregation wishing he had not stopped and longing for more.

Systematic as he was in his times of preparation, Gill rarely made it his routine to preach through a whole book sermon by sermon. He varied his subject as he was led. Even his exposition of the Song of Solomon, which took 122 sermons to finish, was not dealt with in consecutive sermons as Gill always preached on a different book during the Sunday afternoons, Sunday evenings and mid-week services to the ones he expounded on Sunday mornings. Usually Gill based a sermon on between six to eight verses. One-verse sermons were a rarity with him, though he was known at times to paraphrase a large portion of Scripture and then draw out the implications of a single verse under several headings. Whilst preaching, Gill never read from a manuscript. He would outline his thoughts on paper and take this outline into the pulpit with him. His hearers thus never had the impression that they were receiving a message learnt off by heart but were usually given good tidings straight from the heart.

It is very difficult to conceive that anyone familiar with the ministry of John Gill could accuse him of being without vigour in preaching the gospel to sinful man. Thomas Wright called Gill 'the profoundest preacher', claiming that 'Dr Gill's voice rose clear and distinct above the babblement of the day.' Wright ranked fellow-Anglicans Berridge and Hervey, and Baptists Gill and Brine as preachers of the pure gospel and men who 'were baptised with the Holy Ghost and with fire, setting their faces as a flint — men with whom religion was a transporting passion'. Wright's portrait of young theology student Toplady is very moving. He describes how, in an effort to receive the very best, Toplady would hear Gill preach in Southwark and then dash off to hear Whitefield at Tottenham Court Chapel. Toplady's friends could not understand how one training for Holy Orders could spend so much time listening to a Baptist but Toplady knew that he was receiving the pure Word of God.[1]

Gill's chapel was renowned throughout the country for the power of gospel preaching which was maintained in it and John Rippon, who succeeded Gill in the pastorate, and William Button, who published his sermons, tell of the influence of his message of joyful Christian experience which spread far and wide amongst the Baptists and influenced 'all the evangelical denominations at home and abroad'. Furthermore Gill was one of the very few Baptist preachers who took a very active part in working with Anglican Calvinists who were pioneering the Great Awakening in the middle eighteenth century. James Hervey, Augustus Toplady, Erasmus Middleton and Henry Venn[2] were only a few of the many members of the establishment who received ever new impulses from Gill's sermons and theological works, and they snatched up his books with the print fresh on them whenever they could. Toplady was not too proud as an Anglican to sit under Gill's ministry, always taking the opportunity to make copious notes. The great many quotes in Toplady's works from Gill's sermons are testimony enough of the power he found in them. Toplady also quoted extensively from the East Cripplegate and Lime Street lectures. Wesleyan critics were quick to spot the unity of heart that there was between Gill and Hervey. They poked fun at Gill for making Anglicans (thinking of Toplady) and criticized Hervey for supporting Baptists (thinking of Gill and Brine). Venn distributed Gill's printed works amongst his friends. Hervey highlights time and time again the beauty of Gill's language in spreading the good news of Christ's love for sinners.

Augustus Toplady has left us with one of the earliest eye-witness accounts of Gill as a preacher. Of his mentor he wrote:

> As a minister, his deportment in the pulpit was grave and solemn. His language plain and expressive: His method natural and easy: His reasoning strong and nervous: His addresses affectionate: His matter substantial, clear and consistent, well digested, and delivered with great fluency and accuracy, which failed not to command and fix the attention of his hearers. In prayer, he poured out his soul with great freedom and fervency, with much importunity, familiarity and liberty; and, like another Apollos, was mighty in the Scriptures, and had the tongue of the learned to speak a word in season.

Toplady goes on to discuss all the truths that Gill preached, concluding that:

> He did not shun to declare the whole counsel of God, and kept back nothing that might be profitable to the people; constantly affirming, that those who believe should be careful to maintain good works. His ministry, by the blessing of God, was very much owned, and greatly succeeded to the awakening, conversion, comfort, instruction, edification and establishment of many, who enjoyed the opportunity of attending upon it.[3]

The fact that such a devoted and constant hearer as Toplady testified that Gill 'kept back nothing' of the gospel in his pulpit ministry must be stressed in days when his numerous modern critics ridicule such a testimony. Though Gill's contemporaries stressed that sinners were awakened, converted and established in the faith by his ministry, these modern critics prefer to believe the myth that Gill never preached to sinners and certainly never preached repentance and faith. One wonders whatever their motives could be. In his book *The Forgotten Spurgeon*, Iain Murray paints a bleak picture of the Hyper-Calvinism of 1855 and then uses a quote of Spurgeon to imply that it was all Gill's fault, though Spurgeon was obviously pointing at a misuse of Gill's works. Spurgeon, we are told, believed that whenever a Hyper-Calvinist heard the full gospel, he would automatically think, 'This cannot mean what it says; I must trim it down and make it fit into Gill's commentary,'[4] indicating that Gill had a cut-down gospel. Though such a quote might be used to criticize Hyper-Calvinists, it cannot be used as a valid criticism of Gill's teaching as Spurgeon's own notes in his copy of Gill's commentaries testify. Spurgeon wrote, for instance, in his copy of Gill's *Song of Solomon*, 'This priceless work of my learned predecessor has always been helpful to me.' In his *Commenting and Commentaries*, he says of Gill's work, 'Those who despise it, have never read it, or are incapable of elevated spiritual feelings.' This sums up much of present-day second-hand criticism of Gill which is based on other people's reading and other people's feelings. Mr Murray wrote of the year 1855 but in 1886 Spurgeon jotted in his copy of vol. VI (Ezekiel to Malachi) of Gill's commentaries the words, 'Many sneer at Gill, but he is not to be dispensed with. In some respects, he has no superior. He is always well worth consulting.' If Spurgeon's words quoted by Iain Murray really were a criticism of Gill and not would-be imitators, of whom there were many, it seems that by 1886, at least, the great preacher had changed his mind! One might add that all Gill's commentaries were marked with three stars by Spurgeon, which was his highest award and indicated 'most heartily recommended'. It must also be pointed out that Mr Murray quotes a letter of Spurgeon, dated February 1855, some eleven pages after linking Hyper-Calvinism with Gill, in which the Prince of Preachers says: 'My position, as Pastor of one of the most influential churches, enables me to make myself heard and my daily labour is to revive the old doctrines of Gill, Owen, Calvin, Augustine and Christ.' Why Spurgeon put Gill first and Christ last is not explained, but this could hardly mean that Spurgeon thought Gill's doctrine was, to use Mr Murray's words, 'more than a mere theoretical deviation from the gospel'.

Gill was valued as a preacher because those under his ministry knew that he was a man who practised what he preached. His hearers trusted him with full and thankful hearts, knowing that his great aim was to lead his flock into green pastures and protect them from the snares and wolves of the world. Referring to the fact that all who knew him from his childhood on were deeply impressed by the sanctity of Gill's life, Rippon says,

> Those who had the honour and happiness of being admitted into the number of his friends can go still further in their testimony. They know, that his moral demeanour was more than blameless: it was, from first to last, consistently exemplary. And, indeed, an undeviating consistency, both in his views of evangelical truths, and in his obedience, as a servant of God, was one of those qualities, by which his cast of character was eminently marked. He was, in every respect, a burning and a shining light — burning with love to God, to Truth, and to Souls — Shining, as 'an ensample to believers, in word, in faith, in purity'; a pattern of good works, and a model of all holy conversation and godliness.[5]

Rippon points out that Gill was extremely skilled in judging the needs of his hearers and could often provide them with spiritual comfort and solve their doubts in a single sentence or so. When he preached many were converted, others were awakened from their lethargy, established in the faith or comforted and edified. Gill's demeanour was always meek and humble, showing great sympathy with his hearers and those who came to him for assistance.

At a church meeting on 20 December 1756 the Goat Yard church declared that it was 'Absolutely Necessary that a new Meeting House be Erected for religious Worship'. This step was found necessary as the aged wooden building was in such a poor condition that either radical costly repairs were necessary or the chapel would have to be rebuilt. It was not considered practical to do either because the old forty-year lease had almost run its course and the enclosed site of Goat Yard made necessary extensions impossible. By the autumn of the following year the Goat Yard congregation had moved into their newly-built, tall utility-type chapel in Carter Lane, St Olave's Street, not far from the old place of worship. This time, the site had been obtained on a 99¼ year lease basis. The new premises contained not only a hall with extensive galleries for the worshippers but also a separate vestry for the minister and meeting rooms (former out-houses) which had been lacking in the former chapel. There were also a number of rooms under the chapel which could be let out to help finance church affairs. Finding burial facilities for Dissenters was always an embarrassing and expensive business as few Anglican ministers were prepared to open their churchyards to those of other denominational persuasions. Thus an important feature of the chapel construction was special and extensive vault facilities below ground-level where members could be buried.[6]

On the opening day, 9 October, Gill preached on Exodus 20:24: 'In all places, where I record my name, I will come unto thee, and I will bless thee', outlining the main points of the gospel and his calling as pastor. He told his flock:[7]

> As we have now opened a new place of worship, we enter upon it, recording the name of the Lord, by preaching the doctrines of the grace of God, and of free and full salvation by Jesus Christ; and by the administration of gospel ordinances, as they have been deliv-ered to us. What doctrines may be taught in this place, after I am gone, is not for me to know; but, as for my own part, I am at a point; I am determined, and have been long ago, what to make the subject of my ministry. It is now upwards of forty years since I entered into the arduous work, and the first sermon I ever preached was from the words of the apostle: 'For I am determined not to know anything among you, save Jesus Christ, and him crucified.' Through the grace of God, I have been enabled, in some good measure, to abide

by the same resolution hitherto, as many of you here are my witnesses; and I hope, through Divine assistance, I ever shall, as long as I am in this tabernacle, and engaged in such work.[8]

After preaching the terrors of the law in the sermon, Gill goes on to display 'The Lord, the Lord God, merciful and gracious, long-suffering, and abundant in goodness and truth; keeping mercy for thousands, forgiving iniquity and transgression and sin.'[9] He then goes on to point his hearers' gaze to Jesus and exclaims, 'What a glorious display of thy perfections is made in the earth, through the preaching of the gospel! whereby, in the first times of it, to which this passage belongs, was given the light of the knowledge of the glory of God, in the face, or person of Jesus Christ? that is, of the glorious perfections of God, as they are set forth in the person of Christ, and in the work of redemption: and so in the latter day, by the same means, will the earth be filled with the knowledge of the glory of the Lord, as the waters cover the sea.'[10] Gill could rarely preach without emphasizing the worldwide scope of the gospel.

Forty years in the same occupation and not tired of it one bit! Yet Gill was to serve the church for another fourteen years and when he then told his flock that he must retire and they should find a new pastor, the church became quite alarmed and asked Gill how a loving father could possibly think of giving up his children and how could loving children possibly wish to give up their father.

Far from being 'grim' and 'high and dry'[11] when preaching, Gill was very emotional and pleading in his urgent delivery and gave himself to the utmost, often descending the pulpit stairs in exhaustion after his sermon was over. His kind hearers in the pews nearest the pulpit always took a supply of large handkerchiefs with them to the services. As their pastor warmed to the subject, he would sweat profusely and then his hearers would pass handkerchief after handkerchief up to the pulpit so that Gill could wipe his brow and face. A 'normal' sermon would be accompanied by three or four handkerchiefs being put to this use. Funeral services tried Gill the most and these were occasions for much laundering after the service!

This kind of preaching did not suit everybody, however. One old man proved a veritable thorn in the flesh for his pastor. He decided that Gill was not sound and resolved to 'correct' him in his own cynical way. He used to sit opposite Gill up in the gallery, grinning at his pastor in a contemptuous way, trying to put him off his preaching. When Gill descended the pulpit steps, this old man would rush to meet him, repeating the question for all to hear, 'Is this preaching? Is this preaching?' Such behaviour is enough to make any pastor feel that he needs a holiday, but Gill withstood this terrible display of bad manners for some time. Such rudeness cannot be tolerated for long, however, and one day Gill found himself confronted by the old man again at the bottom of the pulpit stairs. In a loud voice, heard by all, the blameworthy man cried out, 'Is this the great Doctor Gill? Is this the great Doctor Gill?' This time Gill had an answer. Looking the man straight in the face and pointing to the pulpit, he said in a strong loud voice, 'Go up, and do better. Go up, and do better.' The man did not go up, nor did he do better, but he left his pastor in peace from then on.

At times a number of ladies became very critical of Gill. Sometimes it was Gill's attention to his wife, at other times it was their pastor's old-fashioned appearance in the pulpit and the fact that he kept to the tradition of wearing a wig and adorning his neck with very long bibs as a sign of his office. These bibs really angered one lady member who decided to turn her anger into action. Armed with a pair of scissors, she asked her pastor if she could do him a good turn. Receiving an affirmative answer, the determined lady took hold of Gill's bibs and with a snip of her scissors shortened them by a good length. Now it was Gill's turn. He asked the lady if he could do her a reciprocal favour. The lady agreed and Gill asked for her scissors. On taking them in his hand, he told his sister that the length of something in her possession had been a cause of concern for some time. Would the lady kindly stretch out her tongue!

Gill watched his own pulpit with the eye of an eagle. If he needed a supply preacher, or as in the last two years of his life, someone to take over the task of preaching on account of his failing health, he would scrutinize candidates almost ruthlessly. He would sound them out on the Trinity, especially on their doctrine of Christ. Even if preachers did not pray in the name of the Father, Son and Holy Ghost, Gill would become suspicious. There were a number of Sabellians, Arians and Socinians who regularly preached in Baptist churches but they soon learnt that Goat Yard, and later Carter Lane, were closed to them. This specific care on Gill's part often made him feel as lonely as Elijah after God's revelation to him on Carmel and before the prophet heard God's 'still small voice'. Writing in 1750 when church growth seemed to have stagnated amongst the Baptists and gospel preachers were comparatively rare, Gill says:

> The harvest is great, and faithful and painful ministers are few. There are scarcely any that naturally care for the estate and souls of men, and who are heartily concerned for their spiritual welfare: all comparatively seek their own things, their honour and applause from men, their ease, reputation, and riches; and none or few the things that are Jesus Christ's, or, which relate to his honour, glory, kingdom, and interest in the world. And what adds to the sorrow is, that there are so few rising to fill the places of those that are removed; few that come forth with the same spirit, and are zealously

attached to the truths of the everlasting gospel. Blessed be God, there is here and there one that promises usefulness, or otherwise the sorrow and grief at the loss of gospel ministers would be insupportable.[12]

These words, expressing a longing for labourers to take part in the heavenly harvest, were preached at a funeral service commemorating the life of Samuel Wilson who had represented the Baptists with Gill at the Lime Street lectures. Though these words are often quoted by Gill's critics, their relevance for an understanding of his preaching fervour are not seen and correct conclusions are not drawn. Thus we find Naylor cavilling at Gill's supposed weakness as a preacher borrowing sentiments from Ivimey and saying:

A *good example of Gill's preaching*[13] is contained in a funeral address for one of his deacons and messenger from his church to the Baptist fund, John Davenport, when Gill was fifty-seven years of age. In addressing the bereaved family and others, Gill exhorted: 'Attend the means of grace, and may the Lord call you by it, in due time, that you may fear and serve your father's God, and fill up his place in the world and the church.'[14]

Again echoing Ivimey, Naylor poses the question 'Is this preaching Christ *the hope of glory*,[15] as Paul did?' Apart from the fact that there is nothing anti-evangelical in Gill's statement in its context, it is quite unfair of Naylor to present this single sentence as if it summed up the whole of Gill's message and teaching and is thus a *good* example of Gill's preaching. Such behaviour merely testifies to the bad example Naylor sets in unbalanced criticism. The sentence was not even part of the body of the sermon preached but words addressed, as Ivimey clearly states, personally to the family of the deceased at the end of the sermon. Naylor's act in using such a dubious example of Gill's lack of preaching prowess is all the more blameworthy considering Gill's open aversion, which Ivimey stresses, to preaching funeral sermons. Gill hated preaching such sermons especially in the case of deceased good friends as in the example chosen by Naylor. This is why Gill begged his successors not to preach a sermon at his own funeral, not wishing to place anyone under the same pressure that he had been under on such occasions. This wish is also recorded by Ivimey but not taken into account by Naylor. Ivimey quotes a whole page from the actual sermon which was preached on Job 30:24 concerning the man who was ill (here Davenport) who had found his ransom (Christ). There is certainly much in the sermon which points to a 'hope of glory' and if one turns to Gill's exposition of Job 30 in his commentary, one will find a feast of good things which would delight Paul's heart.

Ivimey also tells us that far from being a nondescript preacher at funeral services, Gill was greatly in demand for such occasions[16] as he was also as a preacher at ordination services.[17] This kind of preaching alone shows how immensely popular Gill was amongst a wide range of churches. Ivimey also quotes at length from Gill's sermon at the death of Samuel Wilson on Acts 20:28, showing the broad coverage of Gill's doctrinal teaching concerning repentance and faith — the very two ingredients that generations of critics say they cannot find in Gill's preaching. Ivimey quotes Gill as saying:

> The doctrines the apostle chiefly insisted upon, during the whole of his ministry, were reducible to these two heads — repentance towards God, and faith towards our Lord Jesus Christ. God, against whom man has sinned, is the object of the one; and Christ, who is the Redeemer and Saviour, is the object of the other. Repentance must be towards God; it lies in a true sense of sin, and godly sorrow for it; in shame and blushing at it; and in owning and forsaking it; flowing from a view of the love of God, and of pardoning grace and mercy through Christ; attended with faith in him, and expecting grace and life, and salvation, by him. Faith has Christ for its object; and it is a believing in his person, blood, righteousness and sacrifice; a looking to him, leaning on him, trusting in him, and expecting life and salvation from him. These two doctrines went together in Christ's ministry, and are what he ordered his disciples to teach, and which they did; endeavouring first to bring men to a sense of sin, and then encouraging them to believe in Christ. And this is the usual order of the Spirit's work upon the soul, through the ministry of the word; first to convince men of sin; then to work faith in their hearts, and take of the things of Christ, and show and apply them to their souls for their peace and comfort. And these doctrines were taught by the apostle, without respect to persons; he testified them both to the Jews and the Greeks.[18]

It would be impossible for an unbiased critic to understand these words as indicating that the Christian has no message for the sinner and only comfort for the saints. Here Gill is stressing as few of his contemporaries — or modern critics for that matter — stressed, that first the sinner must be confronted with his sin and have that dealt with and then, when he has come to a true knowledge of his plight, present to him faith in Christ as the only way of salvation. Gill shows conclusively that this was the method of the Master and the Master's servant Paul and thus ought to be the method of every law and gospel-abiding Christian.[19]

Another funeral sermon of hope was Gill's preaching on the death of Mrs Ann Button. His text was Psalm 42:5-6: 'Why art thou cast down, O my soul? and why art thou disquieted within me? Hope thou in God, for I shall yet praise him, who is the health of my countenance, and my God.' Anyone reading this stirring sermon, to be found in volume II of Gill's *Sermons and Tracts*, pp. 415-435 entitled 'The Dejected Believer's Soliloquy', will soon be struck by the fact that Gill was a master at proclaiming the gladness that God is able to put into a distressed heart.

Naylor is often guilty of criticizing Gill's preaching and teaching from behind Ivimey's back rather than referring directly to primary sources, but he is far more one-sided, or rather lop-sided, than Ivimey of whom he nevertheless says: 'It might be that John Gill, great scholar and divine that he was, has been the target of more harsh and even malicious criticism than any other English Baptist of similar attainments. Joseph Ivimey, indeed, seems to have taken every possible opportunity to attack the Southwark pastor.'

Naylor, here, is being as unfair to Ivimey as he is to Gill and criticizes the Baptist historian for doing what he does himself to a far greater degree. Though Ivimey is free with his criticism of Gill, he does strive to be balanced. Naylor, however, simply reiterates and highlights the negative points that Ivimey brings against Gill and leaves out the number of positive things he says.[20] For instance, on the subject of preaching Ivimey records Rippon as saying that Gill 'came into the pulpit, at times, with an heavenly lustre on his countenance, in the fullness of the blessing of the gospel of Christ; enriched, and generally enriching'. Ivimey also stresses that in funeral services, Gill was careful to comment on whether the deceased brother or sister had been industrious in witnessing even during their employment hours.[21] This latter reference comes immediately before the quote which Naylor has taken out of its more positive context and commented on so negatively. One looks in vain for Ivimey's positive references to Gill in Naylor's comments on his preaching.[22] We thus have the odd case of Ivimey being heavily criticized for faults which are less than those of his critic. This is the old story of the mote and the beam!

Gill's works abound in examples of preaching the gospel in power and Naylor obviously knows these works as he quotes from them on other topics. This makes his parody on Gill's preaching the more questionable especially as he goes on to compare this hand-picked 'good example' of Gill's preaching at Davenport's funeral with the best of Whitefield when evangelizing the masses! It would be equally easy to compare a more nondescript utterance of Whitefield with a warm appealing word from Gill but what could be the aim of such a futile comparison apart from wishing to discredit the preacher? Naylor comes near to admitting that he has overstepped the bounds of fairness when he quotes John Martin who preferred Gill to Whitefield. He takes back this admission, however, by arguing that Martin was 'something of an odd man out'. Words of wisdom on this topic come from John Ryland Senior. His relation and chronicler, William Newman, says, 'In conversation, Feb. 8, [1792] he told me Mr. Brine assured him that sometimes he could not think at all; that Doddridge acknowledged he sometimes could not speak sense; and that he has heard even George Whitefield speak nonsense and rubbish!'[23]

Though Gill was always uncomfortable preaching funeral sermons, at times they were full of eloquence and evangelistic fervour and his flock urged him to have them printed for a wider circulation. Gill did not allow the bulk of them to be published, but a number of fine funeral sermons were, and many samples have been preserved in lengthy quotes found in Toplady's writings such as his *Excellent Passages from Eminent Persons*. Toplady regarded the messages Gill preached at the death of his members both 'refreshing and comforting', obviously because of the 'hope of glory' so evident in them.

It is a common saying that there is no such thing as a good dying and a bad mother. Gill begged to differ, at least regarding the former case. Like the Huntingtonians after him, on his deathbed visits he received many opportunities to quote Psalm 37:37: 'Mark the perfect man, and behold the upright: for the end of that man is peace.' Preaching comforting words to all who must go through the valley of the shadow of death, Toplady records Gill as saying, 'Though a believer may have his darkness, doubts, and fears, and many conflicts of soul while on his dying-bed; yet usually these are all over and gone before his last moments come, and death does its work and office upon him. From the gracious promises of God, to be with his people even unto death; and from the scriptural accounts of dying saints; and from the observations I have made through the course of my life; I am of opinion, that generally speaking, the people of God die comfortably; their spiritual enemies being made to be as still as a stone, while they pass through Jordan, or the stream of death.' To believers sorrowing for a lost one he felt moved to say, 'The consideration of the state of the dead as of persons asleep, should moderate our Sorrow for the loss of departed friends. What master of a family can be uneasy at finding his family, his wife, his children, his servants, in a sound fast sleep at midnight? May he not expect that they will rise in the morning well and healthful, and ready to go about any service that may be proper for them? When Christ said, concerning Lazarus, "Our friend Lazarus sleepeth"; "Lord," said the disciples, "if he sleep he shall do well." The saints, who are fallen asleep, must needs do well. They cannot do otherwise than well, who not only sleep but sleep in Jesus.'

Though Gill was quick to mention that the Christian should not allow himself to be cast down in sorrow over the loss of a saint, he did not agree with the opinion that maintained a Christian should never be sad. For him, there is a time for joy but also a time for grief in every life. He thus could preach, 'Abraham came to mourn for Sarah and to weep for her. Joseph made a mourning for his father seven days. The children of Israel wept for Moses, in the plains of Moab, thirty days. David lamented the deaths of Saul, Jonathan, and Abner. Christ wept over the grave of Lazarus. Devout men, who carried Stephen to his burial, made great lamentation over him. And the apostle Paul signifies concerning his friend Epaphroditus, who had been sick nigh unto death, that if the Lord had not had mercy on him he should have had sorrow upon sorrow.'

Gill's words in his funeral sermons nearly always centred around the blessings which death brings. The words 'grace and glory' will be forever associated with Gill, who used them as often as he spoke of 'the cause of God and truth'. Again, giving comfort to the bereaved, he says, 'If it should be said, "How shall we know that this is the case of our departed friends?" let the following question be put: "Is there any reason to believe that the grace of God was bestowed on them?" If this is a clear point, their safety is beyond all doubt; for nothing is more certain than that to whom God gives grace he also gives glory. We may be assured of the happiness of our friends in the next world, from their having tasted that the Lord was gracious to them in this.'

One of Gill's most moving funeral sermons was that preached at the burial of his own daughter Elizabeth[24] who died on 30 May 1738. Gill explains how Matthew 7:7 ('Ask and it shall be given you ...') had helped his daughter to come to a knowledge of the truth. After being spoken to by this verse and being praised as if she were a great saint by her school-mistress, Elizabeth received a deep conviction of her own sin and lost state followed by an experience of sealing and pardoning grace so that she could cry out concerning Christ, 'I love him; methinks, I could hug him in my arms.' On her deathbed Elizabeth assured her father that Christ had died for her and, shortly before she died, she said that she could see Christ waiting for her. Nevertheless one thought troubled her in her last hours. She thought of how she had never been baptized and joined the saints at the Lord's Table. Her father assured her that she was safe in the Lord's arms as salvation comes by faith through the grace of Christ and is thus not dependent on the ordinances, though they have their proper place for those who are able to submit themselves to them. After that Elizabeth spent some time talking in prayer to her 'dear Lord' before she sweetly fell asleep in Jesus aged twelve years, two months and sixteen days.[25]

Another example of a most moving presentation of the hope of glory in Gill's funeral preaching can be found in the words occasioned by the death of Joshua Hayes, a member of Gill's church and a personal friend. In this sermon, Gill expounds 2 Timothy 1:12: 'I know in whom I have

believed, and am persuaded that he is able to keep that which I have
committed unto him against that day.' In this sermon Gill had every excuse
to refer the gospel merely to the 'gathered church' in front of him,
especially as Hayes had loved this verse and had often quoted it, referring
to his own life as a believer. In spite of this, Gill looks at the text from all
angles and though he starts by examining it in relation to the life of the
deceased, he goes on to apply it to all those who are within the fold, after
which he deals with the worldwide scope of the gospel — and this at a
funeral service of a devoted 'Gillite'! A large piece must be taken from this
sermon and quoted as it shows up the shallowness of all the piece-meal,
mini-quotes of Gill's traducers who insist that they have found evidence
that Gill limits the gospel designed for sinners to the already saved or that
Gill was frightened to preach hope lest he should preach against God's
sovereign purpose in individuals. Hear Gill opening up his text!

> In the 9th and 10th verses of this chapter, we have the sum and
> substance of the everlasting gospel; which lies in salvation by the
> free grace of God (in distinction from the works of men), according
> to the eternal purpose of God, and the wise scheme of things formed
> in the divine mind from everlasting: where it was a secret and
> hidden thing, but now made manifest by the appearance of our Lord
> Jesus Christ in our nature; who by his obedience, sufferings, and
> death, hath abolished death, and brought life and immortality to
> light through the gospel. All this you will see in the verses I have
> referred to, which run thus: Who hath saved us, and called us with
> an holy calling, not according to our works, but according to his
> own purpose and grace, which was given us in Christ Jesus, before
> the world began: but is now made manifest by the appearing of our
> Saviour Jesus Christ, who hath brought life and immortality to light,
> through the gospel. Which exactly agrees with what the apostle
> elsewhere affirms, that we are saved by grace not by works, lest any
> man should boast.[26] And that those, who are the chosen of God are
> blessed with all spiritual blessings in heavenly things in Christ
> Jesus; according as he hath chosen us in him, before the foundation
> of the world.[27] Christ incarnate is become the High Priest of these
> great things laid up in the everlasting purpose, covenant, and
> promise of God: and has abolished death, even corporal death, as a
> penal evil, and destroyed the second death, so that it shall have no
> power over those whom he has redeemed by his precious blood: and
> by his obedience, sufferings and death, hath opened a way for them
> to enjoy eternal life. He came that we might have life, and that we
> might have it more abundantly.[28] This is a compendium of the grace
> of the gospel; of that gospel, of which the apostle says he was

appointed a preacher. And a gospel preacher indeed he was. Never was the gospel more freely, fully, faithfully, and powerfully or constantly preached, than it was by him. He was appointed to this work from all eternity. He was a chosen vessel of salvation (as the Lord himself says) to bear his name among the Gentiles.[29] He was also appointed by a gospel church at Antioch: for, said the Spirit of God in the prophets there, Separate me Barnabas and Saul for the work whereunto I have called them.[30] He was an apostle of Jesus Christ, and had all the signs of apostleship in him. An apostle, not of men, neither by man, but by Jesus Christ:[31] sent forth, commissioned and qualified by him for the important work of preaching the everlasting gospel. And particularly he was, as he said, a teacher of the Gentiles: for though all the apostles and ministers of the word were included in the same commission, and commanded to go into all nations, teaching and baptising them in the name of the Father, and of the Son, and of the Holy Ghost; yet our apostle had a special and particular commission to preach the gospel among the Gentiles. As the gospel of the circumcision was committed to Peter (for he was the person more particularly pitched upon to preach the gospel to the circumcised Jews), so Paul was particularly pitched upon to preach among the Gentiles the unsearchable riches of Christ. And it is not easy to say, to how many nations he was sent, and among whom he preached the gospel, and among whom he was made successful in founding and raising churches for the honour and glory of God.

Naylor writes that 'Gill insisted that faith understood as assent to the facts of the gospel, is an exercise demanded by God from all who hear; we ought to believe what we are told.'[32] This reveals that his understanding of Gill is quite different to that of Oliver who will not admit that Gill has anything to say about faith to sinners. It also reveals, however, that Naylor looks upon Gill's view of faith as being merely notional, rational or even intellectual. Faith is summing up the facts and believing them when they make sense. He goes so far as to say that Gill redefines faith and thus departs from Scripture, believing that 'people convicted of their sinfulness were not to be summoned to trust in Christ'.[33] This is hardly a fitting description of Gill's view of faith whether in its reference to believers or unbelievers. This is what comes of writing a chapter on 'John Gill and Faith' and leaving out all the essential elements of his doctrine. For such critics, Gill's exposition of 2 Timothy 1:12 will come as a refreshing eye-opener!

Gill explains in the sermon that faith must centre in its object which is not a rational appreciation of propositions and axioms but the person of the Lord Jesus Christ. When a trembling soul says, 'Sirs, what shall I do to be saved?' The answer must be, 'Believe on the Lord Jesus Christ, and thou shalt be saved.' He thus goes on to preach:

Christ is the object of a sensible sinner's trust: the object of a true believer's faith in the business of salvation. But then let us enquire a little into the nature of this faith he exercises upon him. It is not to be considered as a mere historical faith: a bare assent to a set of propositions concerning Christ, his person, offices, and the like; no, the devils have a faith; they have a creed, and in many respects a more orthodox one too than some that call themselves Christians. The devils believe that there is a God, and that there is one God; though they tremble at it. They know and believe, that Jesus Christ is the Holy One of God; yea, that he is the Son of God, and that he is the Christ, the Anointed of the Lord, sent into the world to be the Saviour of men. All this they believe, and a great deal more that they are obliged to believe, and cannot help it, concerning the Son of God; but this is not the faith of God's Elect. There are some weak people in our days that talk of a bare belief of the simple truth, and call this, faith in Christ Jesus, but it falls greatly short of it. For a man may have all faith of this kind, may believe every thing that is proposed and revealed in the word of God, and yet not have that faith which is of the operation of God.

Special faith is a spiritual thing. It is a spiritual sight of Christ. Yea, faith is the eye of the soul, the enlightened eye of the soul, opened by the Spirit of God, to see the glory, the excellency, there is in our Lord Jesus Christ: to see his glory as the glory of the only begotten of the Father full of grace and truth: to see him as the able, willing, all-sufficient, and most suitable Saviour. Faith is said to be the evidence of things not seen. It has a sight of unseen things, as of the unseen Saviour; and in its continual and constant actings is a looking unto Jesus. Looking off from every other object (a man's own righteousness, and everything else) unto Jesus Christ the Lord our righteousness, as the living Redeemer, the only and all-sufficient Saviour. It is no other than a soul's going out of itself to Christ, to lay hold upon him, and trust in him for everlasting life and happiness. Expressed often by a coming to him, influenced by his Spirit and grace, and the declarations of grace he makes, saying, Come unto me all ye that labour and are heavy laden, and I will give you rest.[34] And all that the Father giveth me shall come to me; And him that cometh to me I will in no wise cast out.[35] A poor sinner, sensible of his wretched lost state by nature, and of what he deserves, is encouraged to go out of himself to lay hold on Christ, who is the tree of life to them that lay hold upon him. It is, I say, a

going forth and laying hold of Christ, under a sight of sin and a sense
of danger, of ruin and destruction without him.

The myth, however, that Gill never warned sinners to flee from the
wrath to come persists and most modern critics build their proofs on the few
words culled from Ivimey concerning attending the means of grace. Curt
Daniel uses this passage to argue that 'There is no direct invitation to
Christ, no offer of salvation, no warning of damnation'[36] in Gill's preaching. Graham Harrison also refers to the quote, taking it as proof that Gill
did not exhort sinners to consider their danger, or warn them of their
impending doom and that they must flee from the wrath to come.[37]
Harrison, seeing no applications tagged on to the end of Gill's sermons,
concludes that Gill believed in a non-application, non-invitation ministry.
Though it is true that Gill did not tag on a general exhortation and
application at the end of a sermon every time he preached, such a method
is far from a rarity in his sermons. Gill was very versatile in his methods
of expounding the Word to meet the needs of his hearers. His strategy was
often to apply the word continually to the hearers' hearts, sometimes
dwelling on the needs of the saints, at others, on the needs of the unsaved.
In 'The Knowledge of Christ: The Support of a Believer' based on 2
Timothy 1:12, Gill applies his message to those 'who have made a
profession' but ends his sermon with a general exhortation to 'sensible
sinners', to 'commit their souls into the hands of Christ, who is able to save
to the uttermost; and who hath assured us, that whosoever believeth in him
shall not perish, but have eternal life.'[38] Sometimes Gill applied his
message continually throughout the sermon but at the end summed up the
gospel's message to the unsaved. This is seen in his sermon on 'Jehovah's
Declaration, Man is Become One of Us'. Here Gill never relents in
showing what sin has done to the sinner and how provision has been made
for the lost. He tells his hearers, 'Learn hence the vile nature of sin ... See
the vanity of seeking life by our own performance ... Observe the grace of
God ... Let us look to Christ alone; for he is a tree of life, to them that lay
hold of him; and happy is every one that retaineth him' (Prov. 3:18).[39]

In his sermon 'The Mutual Duty of Pastor and People', preached at the
ordination of George Braithwaite on 28 March 1734 at the Devonshire
Square Meeting House, Gill took 1 Timothy 4:16 as his text: 'Take heed
unto thyself, and unto thy doctrine; for in doing this, thou shalt both save
thyself, and them that hear thee.' To Braithwaite, he said, 'Ministers are
Instruments by whom Souls believe, and so are saved; the Word preached
by them being by the Grace of the Spirit, an engrafted Word is able to save
them; and the Gospel being attended with the Demonstration of the Spirit,
is the Power of God unto Salvation. What can, or does, more strongly
engage ministers to take heed to themselves, to their Doctrine, and abide

therein, than this? That they may be useful in the Conversion, and so the Salvation of precious and immortal Souls. He that converteth a Sinner from the Error of his ways, shall save a soul from Death, and shall hide a Multitude of Sins (James 5:20).'

Gill, contrary to the beliefs of a host of critics, often ended a sermon with a rousing plea to sinners to flee from their danger. In his sermon on 'The Character and End of the Wicked, Considered', based on 2 Samuel 23:6-7, Gill ends his sermon by saying to his congregation, 'If any of you are seeking to flee from the wrath to come, which is revealed from heaven against all unrighteousness and ungodliness of men; and should be asking, "Whither shall we flee?"... There is no other way of escaping the wrath to come, due to the sons of Belial, but by fleeing for refuge to lay hold on the hope set before you in the everlasting gospel; by fleeing to Christ, turning to him, the strong hold, as prisoners of hope; and, being justified by his blood, you shall be saved from wrath, through him. It is he, and he only, who delivers from wrath to come.'[40]

One of the most controversial texts in evangelistic work is Revelation 3:20: 'Behold I stand at the door and knock: if any man hear my voice, and open the door, I will come in to him, and will sup with him, and he with me.' Generations of Christians have taken sides concerning the interpretation of this verse, some taking it to be a challenge to go knocking at the 'hearts' doors' of the unconverted, whereas others maintain staunchly that the verse has to do with the internal problems of a backsliding church and has nothing to do with evangelism. It would surprise Gill's critics very much to find that the so-called Hyper-Calvinist, who allegedly did not believe in addressing sinners, should nevertheless belong to that section of the Christian church who believe in knocking at the hearts' doors of the unconverted, bidding them let Christ in. But this is indeed the case.

The picture of Christ knocking is, of course, an Old Testament picture used in the Song of Solomon 5:2, where the inspired king writes: 'I sleep, but my heart waketh: it is the voice of my beloved that knocketh, saying, Open to me, my sister, my love, my dove, my undefiled: for my head is filled with dew, and my locks with the drops of the night.'

On expounding this text from his Goat Yard pulpit, Gill acknowledges the relationship it has to Revelation 3:20, but nevertheless divides it into four points arguing first that Christ's voice which bids the sleeping soul awake is the voice of the gospel which quickens dead sinners and awakes sleepy saints. Secondly, the knocking mentioned is the knocking at the heart's door of the sinner, bringing conversion with it. Here, as in Revelation 3:20, not all would be happy to ascribe such a knocking to the unbeliever but Gill has no such inhibitions. Thirdly, Gill argues that the gospel should be a knocking at 'the hearts of particular believers' or the Church, breaking down the middle wall of partition, convincing them of their state of need and chastising them in love. Lastly, Gill expounds the text as referring to the work of a minister expostulating with his flock, building them up in the faith, teaching them all the blessings which are to be had in Christ, but also turning their gaze on all that the Saviour has suffered in his redeeming sacrifice of love for the loveless that they might love him who gave himself for them. It is here, however, in view of the base criticism of Gill's opponents that we must underline and emphasize what the scholar-pastor has to say about Christ's standing at the door of the unbeliever's heart, leaving aside his heartening words to the Church. On this subject, Gill says with the true heart of an evangelist:

> There is a knocking at sinners' hearts at first conversion. The heart of an unconverted sinner is bolted and barred against Christ, with the strong bolts and bars of sin and unbelief: elect sinners, whilst in a state of nature, are stout-hearted, and far from righteousness; they are unwilling to submit to Christ and his righteousness, nor to open the doors of their hearts, and let the king of glory in: he stands and knocks there, by the preaching of the gospel; and, having the key of David in his hands, 'he openeth and no man shutteth, and shutteth, and no man openeth'; with this key of almighty and efficacious grace, he openeth their hearts, as he did Lydia's; and, with the hammer of his word, breaks them in pieces, and causes all bolts and bars to fly before him; plucks down the strongholds which Satan had made; dispossesses the strong man of his armour, wherein he trusted, to keep his palace in peace and safety; and reduces all in obedience to himself; where entering with his glorious train of graces, and having dethroned sin, sets up grace to reign in his stead; and takes possession of the heart as his palace, from whence sin and Satan will never be able to eject him. Now in this mighty work of grace, in thus conquering and subduing a sinner's heart, we are not to suppose that here is a force upon the will; for though before they were unwilling, as well as unable to open and let him in, yet are now made willing in the day of his power, to submit unto him; they become voluntary subjects to him; and Christ meets with a kind reception and hearty welcome from them; so that they are as desirous of having him there, as he is of entering in, when this day of his power has passed upon them.

It would appear that those writers who emphasize that Gill never preached to the unconverted are thinking in terms of modern evangelism with its 'campaigns' and 'crusades' where sinners are invited to 'love Jesus' as if they were not fallen creatures and they are assured that all that the gospel offers them is guaranteed theirs, should they but grasp out and take it. They also obviously believe that Gill, as a Baptist pastor, had a congregation of saints with no unbelievers amongst them. This is far from the truth. Apart from the fact that Gill also preached for years outside of his own church membership, it would be wrong to imagine that his congregation always tallied with an ideal 'church state'. Gill drew many unbelievers to his meetings and all his earlier biographers stress that many were converted under his ministry. Rippon, especially, is very clear in his statements that all kinds of people attended Goat Yard and Carter Lane, including some 'very wicked people'.

For those willing to spend a few profitable hours reading Gill's sermons to saints and sinners alike, it will soon become clear how wrong critics are in their failure to see their gospel and evangelistic nature. Preaching on Matthew 11:28: 'Come unto me, all ye that labour and are heavy laden, and I will give you rest', Gill puts to flight all criticism that he taught the importance of 'bare ordinances' and that the gospel should only be preached to the converted. The saint proclaims freely the gospel exhortation to come to Christ:

> Christ having signified, that the knowledge of God, and the mysteries of grace, are only to be come at through him, and that he has all things relating to the peace, comfort, happiness, and salvation of men in his hands, kindly invites and encourages souls to come unto him for the same: by which is meant, not a local coming, or a coming to hear him preach; for so his hearers, to whom he more immediately directed his speech, were come already: and many of them did, as multitudes may, and do, in this sense, come to Christ, who never knew him, nor receive any spiritual benefit by him: nor is it a bare coming under the ordinances of Christ, submission to baptism, or an attendance at the Lord's supper, the latter of which was not yet instituted; and both may be performed by men, who are not yet come to Christ: but it is to be understood of believing in Christ, the going of the soul to him, in the exercise of grace on him, of desire after him, love to him, faith and hope in him: believing in Christ, and coming to him, are terms synonymous, John vi. 35. Those who come to Christ aright, come as sinners, to a full, suitable, and able, and willing Saviour; venture their souls upon him, and trust in him for righteousness, life, and salvation, which they are encouraged to do, by this kind invitation; which shows his willingness to save, and his readiness to give relief to distressed minds.

In this exposition of the gospel call, Gill goes on and on in the same vein, preaching from the heart to the hearts of men. Nor is this an isolated instance as such passages are to be found in very many of Gill's Old

Testament and New Testament sermons. Gill's language is indeed often a warm, even poetic, appeal to the sin-burdened soul, pointing him to the Saviour in whom he finds his eternal rest. Reading his exposition of the Song of Solomon alone is a transportation into the heavenly language of Christ's true love for sinners, full of vigour and commitment.

In view of the vast evidence which is easily produced to show that Gill preached the whole counsel of God to sinners and saints alike, it must be asked why Gill's preaching has such a bad reputation amongst many present-day evangelicals. It is not difficult to find a reason. Gill was so successful as a preacher in his day that the bulk of preachers in his denomination, and a good many outside, looked upon Gill as the Prince of Preachers and worthy to be copied. And copy him they did! Time and time again one reads of preachers being criticized because they preached as if Gill were preaching through them, though they lacked his dynamic and his flexibility. Sermon upon sermon was preached throughout the country and in North America straight out of Gill's commentaries. Many who had his commentaries at home and knew them off by heart could have preached in chorus with the preacher who had also learnt Gill by rote. True lovers of Gill such as Huntington and Philpot were constantly warning their fellow ministers that to ape Gill was not a sign of being called to the ministry but rather the experimental outworking of the Spirit through the voice and character of the preacher. Writing of this problem within his own denomination of Strict Baptists, J. C. Philpot confessed:

Unless a man comes nowadays with a Shibboleth, he is almost set aside as a man of truth. He must use certain words, whether Scripture or not, must preach in a prescribed manner, as well as with prescribed matter. He must not vary from a certain mould, and if he dares to use his own way of setting forth truth, in his own simple language, and as he simply feels and has felt, many can hardly tell whether he is right or wrong, and the majority perhaps set him down as wrong altogether. I dislike, amazingly, the artificial mode of setting forth truth by which, when you hear a text given out, you know all the divisions and mode of handling it before they are mentioned, and can tell the end of every sentence nearly as soon as you hear the beginning. It smells too strongly of Dr. Gill and premeditation to suit me, but some cannot eat the dish unless served up every day in a plate of the same pattern; and, like children, when a different shaped or different painted cup comes on the table, cannot drink, as being so occupied with the novelty. But God will bless His own truth and His own servants, and when He thrusts forth His own stewards, will not send them forth as apes and imitators either of Huntington, Gadsby, or Warburton. They shall have their

John Gill and the Cause of God and Truth

own line of truth and their own method of setting it forth, and they shall be commended, sooner or later, to spiritual consciences as men taught of Him.[41]

Philpot too, as Gill, had his 'apes' and a far from small number of admirers vainly believed that in reproducing Philpot in themselves, they were furthering the gospel. Gill however, like Philpot, was God's own individual. He aped nobody and nobody could, in the cause of God and truth, ape him successfully. Nowadays when Gill is so little known that few would ever think of imitating him, it is high time that we turn to the testimony of the original man of God. Gill had a powerful message for the eighteenth century, but James Hervey was convinced that Gill's teaching, under God, would also be especially relevant to the generations to come. It is the conviction of this writer that John Gill is, indeed, a worthy messenger of God to the times we are now in. Gill used to labour in prayer with God in barren times, pleading that he would 'bow the Heavens and come down and return to this place'. Through reading the works of Gill, the gospel seeker can still experience this 'coming down' of the Lord into his own life.

11.
Laying the axe to popery's roots

One Sunday Gill preached on the kingly office of Christ and extolled his Saviour as the Righteous One whose standards of holiness must become those of his people. On that same day, a member of Gill's congregation had brought along a friend from the country to hear the urban pastor preach. After the rousing sermon which had moved most hearers to a deeper longing to be filled with the Spirit, the countryman was asked what he thought of the message. His critical reply was surprising considering the witness to gospel truths which Gill had just made. 'Please do not be offended,' the man said, 'but if you had not told me that he was the great Dr Gill, I would have thought he was an Arminian.'

John Rippon has some very interesting comments to make about this critic's observation. He says:

> Probably this incompetent judge formed his opinion, as many other mistaken persons still do; who, when they hear anything *practical* recommended, or even the term *duty* mentioned, violently exclaim in some opprobrious terms or other; yet, in the superabundance of their wisdom, *not knowing what they say, nor whereof they affirm*. However the plenitude of their folly is no more conspicuous, than the mistake or malevolence of others, who, running to the contrary extreme, whenever they hear the doctrine of *sovereign* and distinguishing grace, *eternal* election even to *holiness*, and the perseverance of the saints, though it be in *grace* to glory, fully and scripturally preached, immediately cry, Antinomianism! — horrid Antinomianism! — Thus exhibiting the very spirit of those ancient heretics, who *slanderously* affirmed, concerning the apostolic preachers themselves, that they said *Let us do evil that good may come*. But Paul repelled the charge, demolished the accusation, and

magnified his office, that their guilt is on their own foreheads, and of such uncommon atrocity, that their *damnation* is just. The Doctor had, doubtless, consistency enough not fairly to incur the charge of espousing contrary and totally opposite schemes. He *could* not be an Arminian, for he *maintained* the five distinguishing and Scriptural points which they *deny*. Nor could he be an Antinomian, as he for ever *denied* what they *affirm*, viz. the destructive and damning text, which is the very soul of their system, that believers are not under the moral law, as the rule of their conduct.[1] Yet he was charged with these glaring inconsistencies.[2]

Here we have the dilemma of the conscientious pastor who is prepared to preach the whole truth and nothing but the truth. Man's delight seems always to be in half-truths and thus many find Gill's comprehensive preaching to be a stone of stumbling. It is a sad fact that the great bulk of Gill's critics either detest him for the emphasis he places on God's sovereignty or for the equal emphasis he places on that same Sovereign's demand that his subjects be holy.

Of all these one-sided critics within the ranks of professing Christians, Gill was particularly opposed to the Arminians. For him, they represented a counter-movement within Christianity to rationalize and humanize theology, thus robbing it of its spiritual content and presenting a broad-path way to heaven which was at its best only an argument for self-righteousness and at its worst sheer scepticism. The anecdotes concerning Gill's clashes with Arminians and his treatment of them are legend. Many of them are no doubt exaggerated, such as the story of why Gill looks so snooty, austere and flustered in the well-known portrait of him painted in later years. It is said that Gill sat for the picture immediately after an interview with a particularly tenacious Arminian free-willer. As the gentleman outlined his humanistic theology which magnified man and attempted to de-sovereignize God, Gill in horror screwed up his nose at the stench of the perverse doctrine. Whilst sitting for his portrait Gill could not rid himself of the smell in his nostrils and turned over the unpleasant conversation in his mind throughout the sitting. Thus Gill's anti-Arminian feelings were immortalized in the portrait![3]

The following is a true story, recorded by Toplady who relates how Gill was once preaching on the total depravity and spiritual inability of man when a gentleman in his congregation became deeply offended. The man decided to call on Gill and give him a piece of his Arminian mind. 'You have degraded man and laid him much too low,' he told Gill. 'Pray, sir, how much do you think men can contribute towards their own conversion and salvation?' This was the cue the man had been waiting for and he promptly gave Gill a long list of all that man could do to vouchsafe God's eternal favour. 'Have you done all these things for yourself?' Gill asked. 'No, I cannot say that I have,' replied the man. Gill looked at him with some surprise and said, 'If you really have all these things in your power and have not done them for yourself, you deserve to be doubly damned, and are but ill qualified to stand up for that imaginary free will which, according to your own confession, has done you so little good. However, after you have made yourself spiritually whole (if ever you find yourself able to do it), be kind enough to come and let me know how you went about it; for at present I know but of one remedy for human depravation, namely, the efficacious grace of him who worketh in men both to will and do of his own good pleasure.'[4]

Gill never aimed, as is said of many a 'moderate Calvinist' preacher, to be Calvinistic in his doctrine and Arminian in his preaching. He felt that the two systems were direct opposites and two different gospels, whereas a man's preaching should be his doctrine put into practice. This was rather embarrassing to a number of his hearers as Gill was often asked to preach to mixed congregations and was then very forthright in telling Arminians that they were mixed up in their theology. He was preaching a charity sermon before such a mixed assembly one day after which a collection was to be made for some good cause. When appealing for money Gill addressed the congregation in his usual blunt way mixed with a fine touch of humour saying, 'Here are present, I doubt not, persons of divided sentiments, some believing in free will, and some in free grace. Those of you who are free-willers and merit-mongers, will give to this collection of course, for the sake of what you suppose you will get by it. Those of you on the other hand, who expect salvation by grace alone, will contribute to the present charity out of love and gratitude to God. So between free will and free grace I hope we shall have a good collection.'[5]

During the early 1730s the Arminians started up a new campaign against the Reformed faith by republishing a book called *Dr. Whitby's Discourse on the Five Points*, which was supposed to sound the death-knoll of Calvinism. Dr Daniel Whitby (1638-1726) was an Oxford graduate, fellow of Trinity College and an Anglican scholar of note who had become well known for his attacks on Roman Catholicism and Calvinism and his popularizing of post-millenialism. He was particularly open to Dissenters and had campaigned strongly for Anglican policy to be changed, making it easier for Nonconformists to return to the Established Church. Whitby has gone down in history 'best remembered for his striking theological changes'[6] moving from Arminianism to Arianism. In 1733 Gill was approached by a number of people requesting him to take up his pen against Whitby's arguments which his followers were boasting were unanswerable. Even Arminians urged Gill to write against Whitby's findings, taunting him that he would have a very difficult task indeed. Gill was already dealing with anti-Calvinistic complaints in his Wednesday lectures and though he was familiar with Whitby's book, which was reprinted in 1734, he decided to go through it again with a view to refuting it. His main reason for doing this was not so much the taunts of his enemies but the way Gill had come to view the growing problem of popery in Britain. In his foreword to a new edition of *The Cause of God and Truth*, which was the title Gill gave to his defence of orthodoxy against Arminianism, Gill tells his readers:

> This work was published at a time when the nation was greatly alarmed with the growth of Popery, and several learned gentlemen were employed in preaching against some particular points of it; but the author of this work was of opinion, that the increase of Popery was greatly owing to Pelagianism, Arminianism, and other supposed rational schemes men run into, contrary to divine revelation. This was the sense of our fathers in the last century, and therefore joined these and Popery together in their religious grievances they were desirous of having redressed; and indeed, instead of lopping off the branches of Popery, the axe should be laid to the root of the tree, Arminianism and Pelagianism, the very life and soul of Popery.

The view that Arminianism gave rise to popery had not only been shared by the Reformers and the Puritans but also by men of the Evangelical Awakening such as Toplady and Hervey.[7] Of course this view was not shared by the arch-Arminian Wesley whose statements often show how close he really was to Romanish views. Wesley denounced the Calvinist reformer John Knox as 'fierce, sour and bitter of spirits' and said that he used the work of the devil to forward God's work.[8] On reading Dr Stuart's *History of Scotland*, Wesley proclaimed enthusiastically, 'He proves beyond all possibility of doubt, that the charges against Queen Mary were totally groundless; that she was betrayed basely by her own servants, from the beginning to the end; and that she was not only one of the best Princesses then in Europe, but one of the most blameless, yea, and the most pious woman!'[9] It is no wonder that Wesley was called both a papist and a Jacobite by his opponents for these and many similar remarks!

Gill divided his work against popery and Arminianism into four parts, publishing each part separately from 1735 to 1738. The first part deals with the texts Whitby uses to back up his free-willism, adding several others that had been put forward as pro-Arminian proof since the Council of Dort. Part two is concerned with texts that deal with God's special and distinguishing grace and Arminian arguments against the doctrine. The third part is concerned with the rationalistic arguments Arminians use to back up their system. In this part Gill argues that the doctrines of grace are no more disagreeable to right reason than they are to divine revelation. He emphasizes, however, that Arminians should not put their trust in the use of reason but rather pay attention 'to the law and to the testimony, if they speak not according to this word, it is because there is no light in them'. The fourth part takes up all the quotes Whitby gives from the early church fathers and explains them in the light of their own context and Scripture.

It is impossible to deal with the great bulk of Gill's arguments in a work of this kind though *The Cause of God and Truth* must be dealt with in some detail as it is a clear testimony of Gill's outstandingly Reformed theology. Most of Whitby's arguments against Calvinism were either based on texts taken out of context, texts which presume a mere hypothetical condition to emphasize the very opposite; texts used to denote a general application where a particular one is stressed; texts irrelevant to the problem at hand; texts which are used to 'prove' a universal justification of sinners on a take-it-or-leave-it basis or texts based on a general meaning of the Greek term for 'all' which the Arminians invariably take to mean 'every man jack', whereas Calvinists allow the context to determine the meaning. This is nowhere made more clear than in 1 Corinthians 15:22: 'For as in Adam all (παντεσ) die, even so in Christ shall all (παντεσ) be made alive.' Gill usually makes short work of such universalist ideas by showing that all mankind is 'in Adam' but only the elect are 'in Christ'.

Typical of the arguments out of context and from hypothetical conditions which Whitby used was his exposition of Psalm 125:3: 'For the rod of the wicked shall not rest upon the lot of the righteous, lest the righteous put forth their hands unto iniquity.' Here, he believed, was proof that the once-saved always-saved slogan of the Calvinists was at fault. Gill replies: 'These words are made use of to prove, that "saints, or true believers, or men once truly good, may cease to be so: for it is said, that they seem plainly to insinuate, that great and long impressions might have this effect upon them, and surely that which God is thus careful to prevent, might possibly befall the righteous: there being no need of care to prevent that which he hath absolutely engaged to preserve them from." Strange! seeing,

I. The doctrine of the saints' final perseverance is so plainly intimated in the two preceding verses of this psalm: *They that trust in the Lord shall be as mount Zion, which cannot be removed, but abideth for ever. As the mountains are round about Jerusalem, so the Lord is round about his people, from henceforth even for ever.* If they that trust in the Lord, who are saints, true believers, men truly good, are as mount Zion, then they cannot be removed neither from the heart of God, nor out of the hands of Christ; but will abide there for ever, and consequently cannot cease to be what they are. If, as

the mountains are round about Jerusalem, so the Lord is round about
the same persons before described, who are his people, and that
even forever; how is it possible that they should ever perish?

II. These words are strictly connected with the former, and express
a certain effect that should surely follow from the safe state and
happy situation of such who trust in the Lord, כי *for*, or *because* it
is so and so with them; *therefore the rod of the wicked*, the
tyrannical government, oppressions and persecutions of wicked
men, to which the saints are often subject, *shall not rest*, always
continue and abide, *upon the lot*, not the *back*, as Dr. Whitby cites
the words, *of the righteous*; meaning either their persons or their
goods, lest the righteous, who are made so by the righteousness of
Christ, put forth their hands unto iniquity; that is, lest through the
oppressions of wicked men, the instigation of Satan and their own
hearts, they should be moved to that which would dishonour God,
bring a reproach on his ways, and wound their own souls; all which
they may do, and yet not cease to be saints, true believers, truly good
men; as the instances of David, Peter, and others, fully make appear.
The righteous may put forth their hands unto iniquity, and fall into
great sins, and yet not totally fall away, or so fall as to be lost and
perish: total apostasy is not intended by putting forth their hands
unto iniquity.

III. It is stranger still, that the care of God to prevent the righteous
putting forth their hands unto iniquity, should be improved into an
argument against their perseverance, and in favour of their apostasy. It will be readily allowed, that what God is thus careful to
prevent, even suppose a total apostasy was meant, might possibly
befall the righteous, should they be left to themselves, destitute of
the powerful protection of God, nor would there be a possibility of
its being otherwise; but since the care and power of God are so
greatly employed about their preservation, it is impossible that it
should befall them.

IV. It is an egregious mistake to say, that 'there is no need of care
to prevent that which he (God) absolutely hath engaged to preserve
them from'; since God's engagement to preserve his people, is the
true reason of the employment of his care about them; which is
necessary to prevent their doing the iniquity, which otherwise
would be done by them: God having absolutely resolved, determined, and engaged, that those that trust in him should not be
removed, but abide for ever; therefore he will be round about them

for ever, and take care of them, that nothing hurt or destroy them; he will keep them by his power through faith unto salvation.

Typical of the Arminians' predilection to apply a text dealing with a particular operation of grace to a chosen group to mankind in general is their constant use of Isaiah 55:1, a text also favoured by Andrew Fuller and his followers as evidence of a universal atonement. The words so often chosen to sound the death-knoll of Calvinism are, 'Ho, every one that thirsteth, come ye to the waters, and he that hath no money; come ye, buy, and eat, yea, come buy wine and milk without money and without price.' Gill is quick to point the Arminian to the true context of the passage, arguing:

> These words are no call, invitation, or offer of grace to dead sinners, since they are spoken to such who were *thirsty*, that is, who, in a spiritual sense, were thirsting after pardon of sin, a justifying righteousness, and salvation by Christ; after a greater knowledge of him, communion with him, conformity to him, and enjoyment of him in his ordinances, which supposes them to be spiritually alive; for such who are dead in sin, thirst not after the grace of God, but the lusts of the flesh, they mind and savour the things of the flesh, and not the things of the Spirit; only new-born babes, or such who are born again, are quickened and made alive, desire Christ, his grace, and the sincere milk of the word, that their souls may grow thereby; besides, the persons called unto, are represented as having no money; which, though true of unconverted persons, who have nothing to pay off their debts, or purchase any thing for themselves; yet they fancy themselves to be rich, and increased in goods, and stand in need of nothing; whereas the persons here encouraged are such, who not only have no money, but know they have none; who are poor in spirit, and sensible of their spiritual poverty; which sense arises from the quickening influences of the Spirit of God upon their souls, nor are Isa. i. 18,19, Luke xiii. 3, John iii. 16, and viii. 24, any offers of grace, as they are with this represented to be.

Gill continues by arguing that no power or natural ability to come to Christ in fallen man is presumed in the text nor any self-sufficiency in man to procure anything of himself by good works. He limits his refutation to the chapter under debate but the entire context shows how correct his exposition is. The preceding chapter shows how God is speaking of Christ's Bride, the elect, and not of the world in general, when he says, 'For thy Maker is thine husband; the Lord of hosts is his name: and thy Redeemer the Holy One of Israel; The God of the whole earth shall he be called' (54:5). This Bride is promised everlasting kindness and mercy (v.8) from the hand of the Lord which will never fail, 'For as I have sworn that the waters of Noah should no more go over the earth; so have I sworn that I would not be wrath with thee, nor rebuke thee. For the mountains shall depart, and the hills be removed; but my kindness shall not depart from thee, neither shall the covenant of my peace be removed, saith the Lord that hath mercy on thee' (vv. 9-10). As if not to allow any doubt on the matter, the prophet stresses that, 'This is the heritage of the servants of the Lord, and their righteousness is of me, saith the Lord' (v. 17).

How different to Gill's exposition are the words of Andrew Fuller concerning the text. His rationalization goes far beyond the Arminian interpretation. He argues of those the prophet addresses, 'The thirst which they are supposed to possess *does not mean a holy desire after spiritual blessings, but the natural desire of happiness which God has implanted in every bosom,*[10] and which, in wicked men, is directed not, to the sure mercies of David, but to that which is "not bread" or which has no solid satisfaction in it.' This exposition would make the passage meaningless as a gospel encouragement as, according to Fuller, a spiritual response is not required but merely a 'natural' response. The whole context, however, has to do with the spiritual relationship between Christ and his people — a relationship of grace. What belongs to grace and the gospel in the passage is allotted to natural abilities, duties and the law by Fuller who, after arguing that the thirsty ones are not initially spiritually motivated, goes on to say, 'The duty to a compliance with which they are so pathetically urged, is a relinquishment of every false way, and a returning to God in His name who was given for "a witness, a leader, and a commander to the people"; which is the same thing as "repentance towards God, and faith towards our Lord Jesus Christ".'[11] Fuller can argue in this way as he believes that man has natural abilities to interpret natural revelation as pointing to spiritual things. Whatever Fuller's views, however, it is obvious from the context that the text has to do with Christ and the people he chooses and not to the masses seeking 'a natural desire of happiness'.

Gill could never accept the Arminian teaching that Christ's redemption is conditionally sufficient for all men should they wish to avail themselves of it. This to him left the onus of salvation to man and gave the impression that Christ's atonement was completely in vain should no one wish to accept it. The text the Arminians produced to back up their claim was Ezekiel 24:13: 'Because I have purged thee, and thou wast not purged, thou shalt not be purged from thy filthiness any more till I have caused my fury to rest upon thee.' In other words, God has purged all sin and this only needs to be acknowledged in order to benefit from it. Gill notes:

These words are represented as irreconcilable with God's decrees of election and reprobation as inconsistent with the doctrine of particular redemption, and in favour of sufficient grace given to all men. But,

1. The words are not spoken to all men, nor do they declare what God hath done for, or what he would have done by all men; but are directed only to Jerusalem, or the house of Israel, whose destruction is here represented under the parable of a boiling pot; and do not discover any design of God, or steps that he has taken towards the purgation of all mankind, and therefore no ways militate against the decrees of election and reprobation.

2. This purgation of Jerusalem, and the inhabitants thereof, is to be understood either of ceremonial purifications, or of an external reformation of life and manners, and not of an internal cleansing of them, much less of all men, from sin, by the blood of Jesus; and so is no ways inconsistent with the doctrine of particular redemption.

3. These words do not express what God had done, and was not done, which is a contradiction in terms; nor what he had done sufficient for their purgation, but was obstructed by their obstinacy; or that he would have purged them, and they would not be purged, for *our God is in the heavens; he hath done whatsoever he pleased*, but what he commanded to be done, and was not done; for so the words should be rendered; as they are by Pagnine, *Jussi ut mundares te, et non mundasti te — I commanded that thou shouldest purge thyself, and thou hast not purged thyself*, to which agrees the note of Junius on the text. *Verbo præcepi te mundari et toties et tamdiaper prophetas imperari — I have in my word, and by my prophets, so often and so long commanded them to be purged.* The sense of them is that God had commanded either ceremonial ablutions and purifications, or a moral, external reformation, and they had not obeyed; and therefore threatens to leave them in their filthiness, and pour out all his fury on them; and so are no proof of God's giving sufficient grace, or sufficient means of grace to all men.

In Part One, Gill takes up John 1:7 which is of great importance in the development of the duty-faith controversy which arose in the 1780s. Commenting on the words 'The same came for a witness to bear witness of the light, that all men through him might believe,' Gill says:

A considerable argument in favour of the extent of Christ's death to all men is thought to arise from the obligation which is, and always was, upon all persons to whom the Gospel is or was revealed, to believe in Christ, that he came to save them, and died for them for if he died not for them, they are bound to believe a lie; and if condemned for not believing, they are condemned for not believing an untruth. I observe

1. That the argument is most miserably lame and deficient. The thing to be proved is that Christ died for every individual man and woman that have been, are, or shall be in the world. The medium by which this is attempted to be proved is, the obligation that lies on such to whom the Gospel is revealed, to believe that Christ died for them, and the conclusion is, that therefore Christ died for all men. Now the Gospel has not been nor is it revealed to all men, only to some, wherefore was there any truth in the medium, the conclusion would not follow. The argument stands thus: all men to whom the Gospel is revealed are bound to believe that Christ died for them; some men have the Gospel revealed to them, therefore Christ died for all men. The weakness and fallacy of such an argument must be seen by every one, a most miserable argument this, which proceeds upon a partial revelation of the Gospel to an universal redemption. I observe,

2. That the obligation to believe in Christ and so the faith to which men are obliged, are in proportion, and according to the nature of the revelation of the Gospel, which obliges them. Now the Gospel revelation is either external or internal: the external revelation is by the word, and the ministry of it, which respecting Christ, lies in these things, that he is really and properly God, and truly man, that he is the Son of God, and the Mediator between God and men; that he is the Messiah, who is actually come in the flesh; that he died and rose again the third day, is ascended into heaven, and sits at the right hand of God, and will come a second time to judge the world in righteousness; and that by his obedience, sufferings, and death, he is become the Saviour of sinners, and that none can be saved but by him. Now let it be observed, that this revelation is general, and not particular, and does not necessarily oblige persons to whom it comes to believe that Christ is their Redeemer and Saviour, and that he died for them particularly, though the Spirit of God may and does bless it to many for the begetting special faith; and it may and does lay a general foundation for special and appropriating acts of that grace, yet it only requires an historical faith, or bare assent to the truth of the said propositions. Now such a faith is not saving; men may have this, and yet be damned; yea, the devils themselves have it. It follows that men may be obliged to believe, and yet not to the saving of their souls, or that Christ died for them. Besides, this revelation is not made to all men; and therefore all men, such as

Indians, and others, are not obliged to believe in Christ, nor even to give bare assent to the truth of the above said things, much less to believe that Christ died for them, and indeed, *How shall they believe in him of whom they have not heard? and how shall they hear without a preacher?* And perhaps all are not obliged to believe who live in a land where this revelation does come; as those who have not their natural reason and hearing, or the due and proper use and exercise of the same, such as infants, idiots, madmen, and those who are entirely deaf, only such to whom this revelation is made, and are capable of hearing and understanding it, are obliged to have faith in Christ by it, as were the Jews of old, who were condemned for their unbelief, not because they did not believe that Christ died for them, to which they were not obliged, but because they did not believe him to be God, the Son of God, the true Messiah, and Saviour of sinners. The internal revelation of the Gospel, and of Christ through it, is by *the Spirit of wisdom and revelation in the knowledge of him*; whereby a soul is made sensible of its lost state and condition, and of its need of a Saviour; is made acquainted with Christ as the alone Saviour, both able and willing to save to the uttermost all that come to God by him; whence it is encouraged to venture on him, rely upon him, and believe in him to the saving of it: now such a one ought to believe, and none but such, that Christ died for them. This faith all men have not; it is the faith of God's elect, the gift of God, the operation of his Spirit, and the produce of almighty power.

Now, according to the revelation is the faith men are obliged to, and what is produced by it: if the revelation is external, or the Gospel comes in word only, the faith men are obliged to is only an historical one, nor can any other follow upon it; and that Christ died for every individual man is no part of the revelation. If the revelation is internal, a special spiritual appropriating faith is the result of it, but then this revelation is not made to all men, nor are God's elect themselves, before conversion, bound to believe that Christ died for them, and when they are converted, to believe that Christ died for them is not the first act of special faith; it is the πλεροπηορψ, the full assurance of faith, to say, *he hath loved me and hath given himself for me*.

Gill then goes on to argue that Arminians always stress that sinners will be condemned for rejecting Christ, which quite overlooks the fact that sinners are condemned already because they have sinned against the light God has given them by breaking the laws of nature and the Mosaic Law before ever they had a chance to deny the gospel — a gospel which they may never hear. All men are potentially doomed because of their sin, yet

God opens the hearts of his elect which were formerly shut up in unbelief and grants them the gift of faith.

Then Gill tackles several texts in which the word 'all' occurs in relation to Christ's atonement such as John 12:32, Romans 5:18 and Hebrews 2:9. Whitby is particularly firm in stressing that the latter verse has 'no restraint at all, nor any seeming limitation of the comprehensive phrase, he tasted death for every man, distributively taken'. Whitby says this believing that 'How sure the grace of God will be more magnified by this general extent of our Saviour's death, than by contracting the intentment of it to a few; for, if the grace of God be great in sending his Son to die for a few chosen people, it must be greater in sending him to die for many, and greater still in giving him up to die for us all.'

Gill dampens this speculation by arguing that the phrase translated 'for every man' (υπερ παντοσ) (genitive singular masculine and neuter) means 'for the whole', 'for every one' and is not the same as υπερ παντων (genitive plural masculine and neuter) which could mean 'for all men' wherever they may be. He points out that the text is talking about Christ dying for his Church 'bringing many sons unto glory' of whom he declares, 'Behold I and the children which God hath given me.' These 'children' are also called 'the seed of Abraham' whom Scripture denotes as the elect who receive imputed righteousness. They are also referred to in the context as Christ's 'brethren' all of which, says Gill, 'does not help the cause of general redemption'.

As to Whitby's idea that the greater the extent of the atonement, the greater the grace, Gill argues that it is just what Arminians do not believe. They have no doctrine of triumphant grace leading to certain salvation whatsoever. They believe that Christians can fall away and perish at any time, thus rejecting not only God's preserving grace but also Christ's atonement for their sins. Man's free will, to them, is stronger than God's electing will.

Part Two of *The Cause of God and Truth* starts with an eye-opener for many an Arminian and many a modern critic. Gill takes up what Whitby had said about reprobation and claims that he is unfair in its presentation and misrepresents Calvinism. Whitby had allowed his polemics to run away with him and started his book by painting a horrible picture of how the Calvinists' God elects the bulk of mankind to hell-fire, ignoring the biblical teaching regarding the Fall.[12] This view is still held by a number of Gill's modern critics who insist that Gill taught a double predestination, the sheep being predestined to heaven and the goats being predestined to hell, as if sin and belief had nothing to do with the matter. Seymour, for instance, writes that according to Gill, 'Whether God considered man as fallen or unfallen when He made this choice is unimportant', and argues that in Gill's eyes, 'The decree of reprobation also originated in eternity.

By this act, God sentenced certain persons to damnation and forever rejected them as possible candidates for salvation.'[13] This is not Gill's teaching at all as he confesses both in his *Cause of God* and writings against Wesley that reprobation is referred to sparingly in the Scriptures and left to be concluded from the doctrine of election but the subject cannot be dealt with unless the Fall is taken into consideration.

Gill's teaching concerning reprobation is most important as all Calvinists are invariably caricatured by Arminians, as they were by Whitby, as accepting an extreme form of supralapsarianism. Such a doctrine, the Arminians argue, makes God the author of sin as he decreed the Fall, though man was innocent, merely so that he could display his mercy. They also go to great stretches of imagination to work out how few will be saved according to alleged Calvinist claims. Gill thought and taught quite differently. He claims that the Bible teaches that the total number of saved sinners will be countless and he disclaims any connection with Whitby's idea of a Calvinist regarding reprobation, saying:

> The true state of the question before us, and what ought to be attended to, is this, that as God, of his sovereign good will and pleasure, has, from all eternity, chosen some men unto salvation by Jesus Christ, through sanctification of the Spirit, and belief of the truth, so he has, of his sovereign will and pleasure, from all eternity passed by others, and determined to leave them to themselves, and deny them that grace which he gives to others, and damn them only for their sin. This author [Whitby] observes, 'That the word, αδοκιμοσ, which we render *reprobate*, hath no relation, in Scripture, to any decree concerning the damnation of men, or withholding from them the means by which they may escape it, but only denotes such actions which will certainly be disapproved by God and man.' But then it should also be observed, that in all those places, 2 Tim. iii. 8, Rom. i. 28, Tit. i. 16, Heb. vi. 8, 1 Cor. ix. 27, excepting the last, referred to by this author, the word relates not to the evil actions, but to the persons and internal dispositions of the most profligate and wicked among mankind; so that though there is no express mention of any decree of reprobation concerning them, yet there is a great deal of reason to conclude, from the account given of them, that they were such whom God had never chosen in Christ, but had passed them by and had determined to leave them to their own heart's lusts, to deny them his grace and justly damn them for their iniquities.

Here Gill is on common ground with the Arminians who argue that some will be saved and some perish rather than all shall be saved in the end.

Gill argues that the Arminians are correct when they attribute damnation to unbelievers but goes on in Chapter Two, Part Two, to argue that Arminians are wrong in claiming that God elects according to acceptability rather than grace alone. He does this by showing that God absolutely elects individuals savingly and not, as Whitby argued, mere nations and churches to work out God's general purpose in history, as they are composed of believers and unbelievers alike. Whitby argued that these nations and churches etc. are elected 'to the enjoyment of the means of Grace but not to a certainty of being saved by those means'. Gill counters these theories with such scriptural texts as John 6:37: 'All that the Father giveth me shall come to me; and him that cometh to me I will in no wise cast out', and Acts 13:48: 'And as many as were ordained unto eternal life believed.'

In Chapter Three entitled 'Of Redemption', Gill examines Whitby's claim that Christ died *sufficiently* for all, but *intentionally* only for those who will believe. He sees that Whitby is really arguing that Christ did not purchase actual pardon or reconciliation by his death but merely put people in a situation whereby they could be justified and pardoned if they exercised conversion and faith. To this Gill says, 'I firmly believe that Christ died for all the elect of God, and them only; that in consequence of the absolute and unconditional covenant of grace being ratified and confirmed by his blood, faith and repentance are bestowed upon and wrought in these persons, not as conditions but blessings of that covenant; in which way they are brought to the full enjoyment of that salvation Christ has obtained for them.' Here Gill quotes Matthew 20:28 concerning Christ dying as 'a ransom for many' and John 10:15 concerning his dying for his sheep. Whitby, playing havoc with Scripture, insists that although Christ says he lays down his life for his sheep, he does not say he lays down his life for his sheep only! Whitby can thus conclude that the text is not proof against a general redemption.

Gill now goes on to argue that 'The work of grace or conversion, is an internal one, wholly owing to the efficacious grace of God, and wrought in the soul by a supernatural, irresistible, and insuperable power, in the production of which man is purely passive.' Whitby had argued against such a position as it was contrary to 'rational choice'. How can a soul who delights in abominations and is blind in his understanding make a 'rational choice', Gill argues, showing that if God did not make such a choice for his elect, they would never make such a choice for themselves.

This thought moves Gill to argue that both man's corrupt human nature and impotency make him totally unable to discern what is spiritually good. Whitby had argued that 'The doctrine which teacheth that man, by the fall, hath contracted such a disability to what is good, that without the special grace of God he can do nothing that is truly good, and is fallen under such a servitude to sin, as renders it necessary for him to be still doing evil, has no foundations in the holy Scripture.' To this, Gill asks with Job, 'Who can bring a clean thing out of an unclean?' (14:4) and states with David and Isaiah, 'Behold, I was shapen in iniquity, and in sin did my mother conceive me'[14] and affirms with born-again Paul in Romans 7:18: 'For I know that in me (that is, in my flesh) dwelleth no good thing.'

Gill closes Part Two with a chapter on the perseverance of the saints. Whitby had utterly denied that God has promised his people he would keep them from making a shipwreck of their faith but Gill argues that this is just what God has indeed promised. Ever one to stress the love of Christ for his Bride, Gill quotes those beautiful words in John 13:1: 'Having loved his own which were in the world, he loved them to the end.' This is because the gifts and calling of God are without repentance, he argues, quoting Romans 11:29.

It is strange how Arminians are so keen on denying the very hope that they ought to possess as Christians. They look upon the words of the Scriptures with such scepticism, yet stubbornly affirm that they are the true gospel-believing Christians and that Calvinists come a very far-off second in attaining to the truth. Paul's great and comforting words in Romans 8, affirming that nothing can separate a child of God from the love of his father, leave Whitby cold as he argues that in reality they do not prove that nothing can eternally separate a converted man from the love of God but show merely the apostle's personal persuasion and assurance at the time of writing. He further argues that the reason why the scriptures so often stress that a Christian cannot fall away is because he can very easily do so. In spite of Whitby's protests, Gill remained sure of the Scriptural truth of John 10:28, where Christ says, 'And I give unto them eternal life, and they shall never perish; neither shall any pluck them out of my hand.'

Part Three merely takes up the doctrines discussed in Part Two and deals with Whitby's rational arguments against them. Whitby's main point seems to be that the doctrine of a general atonement is more comforting to sinners than a limited atonement. Gill asks how this can be as, when taken to its logical conclusion, the Arminian theory works on a take-it-or-leave it basis with the taker never sure whether he has truly received salvation or not until it is too late to do anything about it. Death alone, to the Arminian, can seal his being accepted or not in the Beloved.

Part Four takes up Whitby's far-fetched statement that Calvinism was a novelty, unheard of by the Church Fathers until the time of Augustine. Gill retorts by saying that the so-called Church Fathers were often but very young men in the faith and no special importance ought to be attached to them merely because they were born in a previous generation. It is obvious that Gill is comparing them with the men of the Reformation and the Puritans who had great linguistic and exegetical powers coupled with their staunch faith in the Lord. Gill also explains that the early Christian fathers directed their apologetics against Jews and pagans and the main point of debate was the doctrine of the Trinity. Nevertheless, Gill believes that the early church held to the doctrines of the Fall and election to grace, Arminian doctrines first making themselves widespread through the teaching of Pelagius, a Briton who taught in Rome around 383-410. This can be seen, Gill argues, by the fact that when Pelagius outlined his views concerning grace and free will, the churches rose up, almost *en bloc*, to condemn him.

After beginning in this cautious way, Gill nevertheless finds evidence to show that Clement of Rome in the first century, Ignatius, Justin Martyr, Minutius Felix, Irenæus and Clement of Alexandria in the second and Tertullian, Origen, Cyprian and Novatian in the third, followed by Athanasius, Hilary, Basil, Cyril, Gregory, Ambrose, John of Antioch and a host more in the fourth century, all believed in the doctrines of predestination, election and the perseverance of the saints.

As soon as *The Cause of God and Truth* was published the Arminians, this time led by a Mr Henry Heywood, took up their pens to refute the scholar-pastor. Their reply shows how little was their learning and zeal for the truth compared with Gill's, yet they argued that he had wrongly translated the Church Fathers and showed impertinence at pretending to be more learned than he was. One sample of their greater 'learning' will suffice. Gill had translated Irenæus' *antiqua serpentis plaga* as 'the old plague of the serpent' referring it to the natural corruption and sin of man after the Fall. Gill's critics protested that this was a faulty translation and what Irenæus was talking about was a 'pestilential disorder' which is to be understood merely physically. It did not take Gill long to show that whether one calls sin a plague or a pestilential disorder, it has rendered man incapable of saving himself and thus he can only be saved by grace.

Given Gill's strong antagonism against Arminianism, it was inevitable that he would clash with John Wesley, who was very proficient in publishing works that Gill found popish to the core. Wesley's pamphlet *Serious Thoughts upon the Perseverance of the Saints* [15] soon caught Gill's attention as it left the task of keeping in the faith completely to man's arbitrary will. Wesley states, claiming scriptural authority, 'I believe a Saint may fall away; that one who is holy or righteous in the judgement of God himself, may nevertheless so fall from God, as to perish everlastingly.' He further argues that 'He who is a child of God today, may be a child of the devil tomorrow.' His 'evidence' is found in such chapters as Ezekiel 18 and 33. In these passages the righteous man is threatened with death if he commits iniquity.

Wesley admits that generalizing on the basis of Ezekiel 18 etc. is problematic as other passages of Scripture, such as Psalm 89, clearly teach that the believer who turns to iniquity will experience God's rod but God will not break his covenant and allow his loving-kindness to be utterly removed from the righteous should they fall into sin. The Arminian leader surmounts this difficulty by arguing that whereas Ezekiel is referring to ordinary believers wherever they are, Psalm 89 refers merely to David and his immediate family and is thus not a general promise to believers. Wesley further argues that all God's promises of perseverance are to institutions and peoples and not to individuals. The fact that God's church will persevere to the end merely means that though individual believers will drop out and be lost, the church as such will remain. This was no new argument amongst the Arminians as it had already been fully expounded by Whitby.

For Wesley, it is obvious that salvation is not so much an intervention of God in the life of a sinner as a realization on man's part of his need to depend on God and exercise a willingness to remain in such a relationship. As long as he believes, he experiences God's love and thus is in reception of that which makes life eternal. As soon as man disbelieves i.e. falls into sin, that love is forfeited and with it eternal life. This is tantamount to saying that God saves only saints and never sinners, thus denying Scripture which teaches that Christ came to seek and to save that which was lost. Wesley's thoughts are developed through an appeal to Christ's teaching concerning the olive tree and the vine. He seems to envisage a continual grafting in and cutting off of believers who alternate between being saved and lost according to whether they momentarily believe or disbelieve. It is plain to see from Wesley's exposition that had Peter died when he denied Christ, he would have gone to hell, and had Thomas died at the moment he doubted Jesus, he would have followed him. Election, for Wesley, is merely determined by the believing state of a person.

This means that God would be perpetually changing his mind about his children's future state, in proportion to the rate at which they change their minds about him. The Arminian admits that this is contradicted by Romans 11:29, which plainly states that 'the gifts and calling of God are without repentance', but Wesley was too experienced a debater to let such a text worry him. He argues that this text does not mean that those whom God saves will be kept in salvation as he never changes his mind. It means that God will keep his promise to the Jewish nation in general. Wesley thus believes in a specific election of David and his offspring and a general election of the Jews as also the church, but there is no guarantee of election from God's side, whether specific or general, for the bulk of believers in Christ who still have the man of sin within them.

In a similar way Wesley goes through text after text which assures the believer of his safety in God's hands and tells him that the text applies to others and not to himself or has some other restricted meaning. Thus Christ's words of assurance in John 10:27-29 merely imply that Christ's sheep belong to him merely as long as they are willing to hear his voice; and John 13:1: 'Having loved His own which were in the world, he loved them unto the end', merely refers to the fact that Christ loved the apostles until the end of his own life. The fact that the apostles, with the exception of Judas the son of perdition, remained true to Christ does not mean, according to Wesley, that Christ remained true to them. On the contrary Wesley maintains that the fact that Judas fell by the wayside proves that one cannot speak of certain election to salvation even when referring to the Apostles. It does not seem to have entered Wesley's head that Jesus' reference to Judas as 'the son of perdition' could indicate that he was not of the elect as Wesley does not believe in particular and personal election or reprobation. Wesley sums up his total denial of the sovereign action of God in salvation and the vicarious suffering of Christ for the sake of his known and chosen elect by saying,

> The sum of all is this. If the Scriptures are true, those who are holy or righteous in the judgement of God himself: those who are endued with the faith that purifies the heart, that produces a good conscience: those who are grafted into the good Olive tree, the spiritual, invisible church: those who are branches of the true Vine, of whom Christ says, I am the Vine, ye are the branches: those who so effectually know Christ, as by that knowledge to have escaped the pollutions of the world: those who see the light of the glory of God, in the face of Jesus Christ, and who have been made partakers of the Holy Ghost, of the witness and of the fruits of the Spirit: those who live by faith in the Son of God: those who are sanctified by the blood of the covenant; *may nevertheless so fall from God, as to perish everlastingly.*[16]

In 1752 Gill, shocked by such an attitude to the sure promises of God in the Scriptures, took up his pen against Wesley in a work entitled *The Doctrine Of The Saints' Final Perseverance, Asserted And Vindicated*, with the subtitle 'In Answer to a late Pamphlet, called serious thoughts on that subject'.[17] In this essay Gill lists all Wesley's arguments, deals with them, at times rather heatedly, and then puts forward what he feels is biblical proof for the doctrine of the perseverance of the saints. This was followed by a more systematic and devotional essay entitled 'Of the Perseverance of the Saints',[18] which shows less signs of being written in the heat of controversy and begins with the positive statements of Scripture on the subject before going on to deal with Wesley's objections without mentioning him by name. In the introduction to this work, Gill points out that the heresies so soundly combated by the Reformers are once more raising their heads and Sabellian, Photian, Socinian, Pelagian and Arminian errors are 'drawing a veil over the glory of the Reformation, and the doctrines of it'. In combating Wesley, Gill makes it clear that Arminianism is no respectable branch of Christianity but belongs to pre-Reformation popery and as such is part of the Counter-Reformation. Gill opens his *Saints' Final Perseverance* by saying,

> The doctrine of the saints' final perseverance in grace to glory, being a doctrine so fully expressed in the sacred scriptures, so clearly wrote there as with a sun-beam, having so large a compass of proof, as scarce any other doctrine has; a doctrine so agreeable to the perfections of God, and the contrary so manifestly reflecting dishonour upon them, particularly the immutability of God, his wisdom, power, goodness, justice, truth, and faithfulness; a doctrine so well established upon his purposes and decrees, his counsel and covenant, and which so well accords with all his acts of grace towards, and upon his people; a doctrine so well calculated for their spiritual peace and comfort, and to promote holiness of life and conversation; doctrine one would think, that every good man must *wish* at least to be true; it may seem strange, that any man believing divine revelation, and professing godliness, should set himself to oppose it, and call such an opposition *Serious Thoughts* upon it, as a late writer has done;[19] who has published a pamphlet under such a title, and which now lies before me, and which I have undertook to answer, and shall attempt to do it in the following manner. And, it is to be hoped, he will think again, and more seriously, and that his latter thoughts will be better than his former.

Gill's stand is plain, namely 'Those who are truly regenerated, effectually called, and really converted, and internally sanctified by the Spirit and grace of God, shall persevere in grace to the end, and shall be everlastingly saved; or shall never finally and totally fall, so as to perish everlastingly.'[20] In arguing for this position, Gill takes up all eight of Wesley's arguments, turning them completely around; but he also introduces a wealth of biblical material not mentioned by Wesley. He shows Wesley the main fault in his method of arguing, that a man may turn from his own righteousness and perish. No Christian would deny this, Gill argues, but it is not the point. The topic under discussion is whether or not a converted man may fall from the righteousness which Christ imputes to his own as their saving warrant, guarantee and security. The difference in doctrine between Gill and Wesley is thus centred on their interpretations of what is meant by a 'righteous man'. Quoting Job 17:9: 'The righteous also shall hold on his way; and he that hath clean hands shall be stronger and stronger!' in his *Body of Divinity*, Gill says of such a person, 'By the righteous man is meant one that is made truly righteous, by the righteousness of Christ imputed to him, and which he receives by faith; in consequence of which he lives soberly and righteously: and by *his way* is meant, Christ the way; in which he walks as he has received him, as the Lord his Righteousness.'[21] Gill argues that as it is Christ who makes a man righteous by imputing his own righteousness to him, so it is Christ who keeps the righteous one in that righteousness, so that even if he slips and falls and stumbles he cannot slip or fall or stumble out of fellowship with Christ as it is Christ who maintains that fellowship not the man himself.

After quoting Job 17:9 in *Sermons and Tracts*, Gill argues that after adopting the elect as his children, God gives them a justifying righteousness which is not their own, nor even theirs to accept or reject at will. Of these 'children of God', in contra-distinction to Wesley's argument that one can be a child of God today and a child of the devil tomorrow, Gill says,

> Such who are justified, can never be unjustified, or be removed from the state of justification, in which they are, into a state of condemnation, but always remain righteous persons through the righteousness of Christ, imputed to them; the righteousness by which they are justified is an *everlasting* one; the sentence of justification passed upon them, can never be reversed by man or devil; if God justifies who can bring a charge of any avail? who or what can condemn? there is no condemnation to them that are in Christ, and are clothed with his righteousness; they are passed into justification of life, and shall never enter into condemnation; they have a right to eternal glory, through the justifying righteousness of Christ, and shall enjoy it; between their justification and glorification there is an inseparable connection: Whom he justified, them he also glorified, Rom. 8:30, 33, 34. Wherefore, those that are righteous in the judgement of God himself, as all such are whom he justifies by the righteousness of Christ, cannot possibly so fall, as to perish everlastingly.[22]

Now Wesley had quite a different idea of righteousness and it is thus no mere coincidence that he appended to his essay rejecting the doctrine of the perseverance of the saints an essay entitled 'Thoughts on the Imputed Righteousness of Christ'. In this essay Wesley argues that though the Scriptures speak of God's righteousness, they nowhere speak of the righteousness of Christ. He admits that Christ is called the Lord our Righteousness. However, he does not relate this to the believer but to the fact that Christ is 'the sole purchaser, the sole meritorious cause, both of our justification and sanctification'. Wesley seems to baulk at the idea that the Lord our Righteousness is not only the cause of our sanctification but also the effect of it, namely Christ's righteousness being imputed to us. This is shown by his interpretation of 1 Corinthians 1:30: 'Jesus Christ is made of God unto us wisdom, and righteousness, and sanctification, and redemption.' This means, according to Wesley, nothing more than that Jesus is the author of our whole salvation. He cannot interpret the text in the sense that the sinner is saved because he becomes partaker of Christ's wisdom, righteousness, sanctification and redemption, in fact he becomes partaker of the divine nature. In dealing with Genesis 15:6 and Romans 4:5, referring to Abraham's imputed righteousness, he denies that this is Christ's righteousness but merely 'the righteousness which is by faith'. Wesley remains silent as to the source of Abraham's righteousness but implies that it is the product of his faith rather than the source of his faith. However, in Wesley's correspondence on the subject with his former pupil James Hervey, he states clearly that Abraham's righteousness arose from his exercise of faith and not from any imputation of Christ's righteousness. Wesley seems to forget that the Bible teaches that Abraham's faith was directed at Christ his Righteousness and without the righteousness of Christ there is no such thing as righteousness.[23]

Finally Wesley rejects the doctrine of the imputed righteousness of Christ as, in his opinion, it leads to Antinomianism and makes Christ the author of sin. He ends his refutation by completely misquoting Hervey out of context, making him say that the doctrine is quite unnecessary.[24] Hervey actually wrote the work to which Wesley refers in order to expound this very doctrine i.e. 'the imputation of our sins to Christ and the imputation of Christ's righteousness to us'. Furthermore, Hervey claimed that 'On these two doctrines hang all the privileges and the whole glory of the gospel.'[25] This statement won for him the lasting animosity of Wesley who allowed himself in anger to spread the evil rumour that Hervey died cursing him. Hervey was too busy contemplating the righteousness of Christ at death, as eyewitnesses testify, than to be bothered with Wesley's unrighteous animosity.[26]

Saintly James Hervey read both Wesley's attack on perseverance and Gill's defence of it. He must have been in something of a quandary as Wesley had been one of his mentors and he looked upon Gill as one of his masters in Israel. The master in Israel won over the university mentor. He found Gill's arguments 'full of weight, rich with consolation, and worthy of a place in our memory and in our hearts', and adds, 'May our own meditation fix them in the one, and the Spirit of our God implant them in the other!'[27]

Gill's *The Doctrine of the Saints' Final Perseverance* had not been in print long before Wesley brought out a much lengthier work than his *Serious Thoughts* which he subtitled 'A full answer to Dr Gill's pamphlet on perseverance'. Both this subtitle and the title of the work brought surprises to the readers. Wesley entitled his work *Predestination calmly considered* and thus moved the debate from the perseverance of the saints to their predestination. He gave no reason for this change but caused readers to look in vain for the full refutation of Gill's arguments on perseverance which he had promised in the subtitle. An attempt is, however, made by Wesley to defend his own eight original arguments against perseverance at the very end of his lengthy work. This perhaps explains why Wesley dropped the word 'full' from his 'full answer to Dr Gill' in the subtitle of subsequent editions and eventually dropped any reference to Gill whatsoever on his title page.

Wesley's work on predestination is far less specific than Whitby's (Gill calls it a *harangue* rather than an *argument*) though it is prefixed by numerous statements taken from various Calvinistic writings and creeds such as the *Institutes*, the 1559 Protestant Confession of Paris, the Synod of Dort of 1618 and the Westminster Confession of 1646. The quotes and part quotes used, however, centre wholly around the doctrine of reprobation as if this were the sole interest of Calvinists in forming creeds. Calvinism, in Wesley's opinion, is the belief in 'broad, barefaced reprobation'. This he strives to hammer home in very numerous arguments in which Scripture is conspicuous by its absence apart from a reference to 'Jacob have I loved and Esau have I hated.' This has nothing to do with the patriarchs' eternal state, Wesley argues, nor does God's destruction of Pharaoh have anything to do with that tyrant's eternal salvation, either. In keeping with his belief that God never elected individuals but always nations, communities etc., Wesley argues that 'Jacob have I loved and Esau have I hated' refers to their posterities, not to their persons.[28]

In Argument XVI, Wesley turns to the problem of election rather than reprobation and argues that there is a limited kind of personal election to do specific tasks as when Cyrus was elected to rebuild the Temple, though this had nothing to do with Cyrus' eternal state. Again, Wesley uses Judas as an example, arguing that Jesus says 'Have I not chosen [elected[29]] you twelve, yet one of you is a devil?' (John 6:70), obviously teaching that election brings, at best, merely conditional salvation with it but no fixed decree of God. This thought is proof enough for Wesley that election to salvation and reprobation from salvation are entirely conditional states summed up in the phrase, 'He that believeth shall be saved: he that believeth not shall be damned.'

Wesley now goes on to argue that as God saves souls 'through belief of the truth', there is no actual election until actual belief takes place. One is not elected to belief but elected on believing. Only in this way is the phrase 'elect from the foundations of the world' to be understood. Wesley uses Christ as an example. Christ is the Lamb slain from the foundation of the world, he argues. He was slain, however, some thousands of years later, just as the elect were not really elected before the foundations of the world but when they were converted. The reference to pre-history merely refers to God's prescience of events to come. The Arminian loses himself in his own argument here. Just as God knew Christ would be slain thousands of years ahead, so he knew that certain people would believe. Wesley seems to be saying that Christ was no more predestined to die and become the Saviour of his church than Paul was predestined to believe and become the Apostle to the Gentiles. God merely looked into the future and saw it was all going to happen, and let it happen. Wesley's God is therefore one who does not manage his own creation and govern everything according to his own good will. He did not even decree what his Son was going to do before the foundations of the world. He was only prescient of salvation and did not predestine it. This view also seriously challenges the doctrine of the unity of the Godhead and the eternal Sonship of Christ.

After this brief pause Wesley turns again to reprobation in Argument XIX claiming that it is contrary to Scripture. A very large number of references are produced but as the Arminian leader neither comments on them exegetically nor explains how they back up his opinion, their purpose is unclear. In Argument XXIII Wesley takes up the Calvinistic belief that God could have passed by all men with his salvation as all have sinned. He denies that there is such teaching in Scripture as the God of justice is never separate from the God of mercy. This brings Wesley to Romans 9 and the imagery of the potter who has power over his own clay. Again, Wesley sees no predestination here but argues that the verse really means that it would be 'unjust of God to show that mercy to the Gentiles, which he withheld from His own people' and 'that accordingly, "he hath mercy on whom he will have mercy", namely, those that truly believe; *and whom he will*, namely, obstinate unbelievers, he suffers to be *hardened*'.

The first signs that Wesley has read Gill's defence of perseverance are to be found in Argument LXIX. Here *The Doctrine of the Saints' Final Perseverance, Asserted and Vindicated*, is mentioned in a footnote without the author's name being appended. Nor does Wesley mention Gill though he quotes from him verbatim on several occasions. Wesley does not deal with Gill's original contribution to the discussion but merely deals with some of Gill's observations on his own eight arguments against the perseverance of the saints, reiterating the arguments once more.

On reading Wesley's new work, Gill penned *The Doctrine of Predestination Stated and Set in the Light of Scripture*. After expressing surprise that Wesley had shifted his emphasis from a denial of perseverance to a denial of predestination,[30] Gill argues for predestination under the two major headings of General and Special Predestination. Quoting from such passages as Acts 15:18, Acts 17:26, Job 14:5, Ephesians 1:11 etc., Gill states that history past, present and future is in the hands of God who directs everything according to his own good will. Everything is ruled by his providence, and predestination in this sense is merely a synonym for such action on God's part. This is general predestination. God's electing and decreeing powers make sure that nothing happens by chance whether it be a man carrying a pitcher of water in such a place at such a time, or the exact moment of the birth of the Messiah. Thus all things temporal and civil relating to all creatures are part of this kind of predestination.

There is also a predestination which is special, relating to particular persons and to things spiritual and eternal. Quoting such verses as Romans 3:25, 1 Peter 1:20, Luke 22:29, Acts 2:23, Gill shows how Christ was preordained to be the Mediator between God and man and the Head of the Church and is thus called God's elect and his Chosen One. In the same way angels are objects of predestination as also are men.

Special predestination with reference to man is two-fold. There is election and reprobation. Election is a predestination to life as an act of God's free grace. Those chosen were not picked out of the common mass of men for any particular abilities or merit, but God chose them to partake of spiritual blessing and happiness for the glory of his grace alone. Those elected to salvation — in spite of their sin — are few in comparison with the majority of mankind who turns its back on God, yet the Bible says that they are great multitudes which no man can number (Revelation 7:9). Arguing against Wesley who taught only a special predestination of nations and types, Gill stresses that he is talking about individuals. It is for these specially elected people that Christ died to redeem them from their sins and give them a new righteousness. God's predestination leads to their effectual calling which leads to their justification, which leads to their glorification. This is God's plan with his chosen ones and nothing can thwart it.

Gill confesses himself baffled with Wesley's view of election as it is entirely conditional and he believes that Wesley has not come up with a shred of proof for such a view. He points out that Wesley always claims that Mark 16:16 is proof enough: 'He that believeth shall be saved; but he that believeth not shall be damned' (Wesley usually left out the reference to baptism within the quote), but Gill insisted that this is not an expression of a conditional decree but a declaration of the revealed will of God. Gill objects to Wesley's teaching that election is for already-believers only because it was whilst we were yet sinners that Christ died for his Church. This is an important point in understanding Gill's theology as Arminians and Fullerites always stress that Gill's gospel is for saints only. This is the Arminian gospel in full but also the Fullerite gospel in part as they stress that the gospel comes to those who are in a position to understand it, i.e. those who already have spiritual awareness. Thus when Gill's theology is compared with that of Wesley and Fuller, he must be seen as the only one who really teaches the biblical doctrine that the good news recreates sinners who are totally unable to reform themselves savingly.

This moves Gill to criticise Wesley for rejecting the clear teaching of Scripture. He also reminds the Arminian that though he has quoted a number of Calvinistic creeds to show how they allegedly understand predestination merely as reprobation, he had left out the Calvinistic creeds of his own church which are clearly scriptural. Gill thus quotes Article XVII[31] of the Church of England to him:

> Predestination to life is the everlasting purpose of God, whereby (before the foundations of the world were laid) he hath constantly decreed by his counsel, secret to us, to deliver from curse and damnation those whom he hath chosen in Christ out of mankind, and to bring them by Christ to everlasting salvation, as vessels made to honour. Wherefore they which be endued with so excellent a benefit of God, be called according to God's purpose by his Spirit working in due season: they through grace obey the calling: they be justified freely: they be made sons of God by adoption: they be made like the image of his only begotten Son Jesus Christ: they walk religiously in good works, and at length by God's mercy, they attain to everlasting felicity.

Gill reminds Wesley that he has *subscribed* and *sworn* to this Article, which 'will stare him in the face as long as subscriptions and oaths stand for any thing with him'. It is a creed which shows that it is impossible to believe in election without reprobation as if only some are taken, the remainder must be left. The difference between Wesley and Gill is that the latter sees the taking or leaving as God's initiative, whereas Wesley leaves this to man.

Now Gill deals with reprobation under two headings: *preterition*, which he also calls a passing-by, and *pre-damnation*. The former refers to the fact that there are those who do not have their names in the Lamb's Book of Life, the latter to the decree that the ungodly must perish for their ungodliness. Wesley challenged this on the grounds that it left no room for mercy. Gill thought it left more room for mercy than Wesley's doctrine. The elect, according to Gill, are solely elected for reasons of mercy, whereas Wesley would only elect them if they showed a constant exercise of meritorious faith. Both Gill and Wesley believed that unbelievers would suffer condemnation so Gill's view of Scripture defended the mercy, the justice and, above all, the sovereignty of God in his creation far more than Wesley, whose ideas could only lead to spiritual pessimism as the onus for salvation is left in men's hands.

Gill now turns to Wesley's Argument LXIX where the Arminian

defends his use of eight Scriptures which, he believes, prove that there is
no such thing as a total perseverance of the elect in the faith. His first quote
is from Ezekiel 18:24: 'But when the righteous turneth away from his
righteousness, and committeth iniquity, and doeth according to all the
abominations that the wicked man doeth, shall he live? All his righteousness that he hath done shall not be mentioned: in his trespass that he hath
trespassed, and in his sin that he hath sinned, in them shall he die.' Gill had
outlined that this chapter referred to the state of Israel and to the law of God
which demanded, 'Do this and live, break this and die.' Every man was thus
responsible for his own righteousness and his own sin in respect to God's
standards. A son would thus not be made responsible for the sins of his
father. The righteousness shown referred to the strivings of wicked men to
keep the law and thus natural righteousness was indicated, not Christ's
law-fulfilling righteousness given to God's elect. He had shown, too, how
the entire text referred to what would happen if Israel became a lawless
nation. 'The soul that sinneth, it shall die' (v. 20). For Gill the text
nevertheless shows that repentance is possible and restores a sinner to God.
The text is thus a warning of what happens when a nation turns from God,
but it does not indicate that individual elect souls may finally perish.
Wesley agrees to differ, arguing that, in this passage, truly righteous people
are being referred to, who truly fall and perish. There is no condition here
'supposed' but merely facts 'asserted'. Wesley had argued against reprobation on the grounds that it left no room for God's mercy but here he is
quite merciless, leaving no room for repentance. He can thus conclude
dogmatically: 'It remains then, that one who is righteous in the judgement
of God himself, may finally fall from grace.'

Next Wesley takes up 1 Timothy 1:19-20: 'Holding faith and a good
conscience; which some having put away, concerning faith have made
shipwreck, of whom is Hymenæus and Alexander'. Gill had argued
contrary to Wesley that Hymenæus and Alexander were never true
believers as they had 'put away' the faith which brings a good conscience
with it, the word in the Greek απωθεισθε being the same as Paul and
Barnabas use to show that the Jews *rejected* the gospel in Acts 13:46. It is
impossible, however, to argue like this with Wesley, who in his reply
merely says that the Jews must have had the Word of God spoken by Paul
and Barnabas or they would not have been able to reject it. You can only
'put away' what you have. This is strange reasoning indeed as the context
says that the Jews 'were filled with envy, and spake against these things
which were spoken by Paul, contradicting and blaspheming'. Obviously
the Good Seed was rejected because it fell on stony ground — as it did in
the case of Hymenæus and Alexander. Wesley, however, concludes that he
has won his point and thus still maintains 'that one who has the faith which
produces a good conscience, may yet finally fall'.

Taking up Romans 11:17-24 concerning the grafting in and cutting off of the vine branches, Wesley argues that here is proof that the universal invisible Church of Christ contains members who may be cut off eternally. Gill relates this passage to the history of the Jewish race and their rejection of Christ and of the Gentile Church. He also sees the passage as referring to the outward visible gospel church-state. Thus dead branches may be cut off from church fellowship as they are not truly part of it. This is quite revealing in Gill's case as Baptists generally refer to the visible church-state as a true church composed solely of baptized believers. Gill could never accept this ideal vision. Although the Jews as a nation were cut off, there is nothing to indicate in the text that the children of the New Covenant would go the same way as their 'ideal' forerunners as there is a biblical difference between those who had the law written on tablets of stone and those who have the law written on their hearts and have the Spirit working in them. Gill takes this passage, therefore, as a warning to Christians to keep them spiritually awake. Wesley takes it as proof that believers can depart from the faith.

Turning to John 15:1-5 Wesley again contradicts Gill's assertion that the dead branches are only professing Jews or Christians with no true faith. Wesley argues that the passage teaches that true branches may become dead and thus be burnt. Jesus, however, plainly states that those to whom he is talking did not choose him but he chose them to bring forth much fruit and that their fruit should remain. It is also evident from the context that those who do not bear fruit are those whom the Father did not elect and are those who hate the Son.

2 Peter 2:20-21, concerning the dog that returns to its vomit, is Wesley's fifth proof against perseverance. He argues that this text shows that after conversion one can be de-converted. Again Gill sees no such thing here, believing that dogs can become sheep but not that sheep can be turned into dogs. Gill would rather see such texts in the light of John 17:2-3 which stresses that Christ has been given all power over all flesh to give eternal life to as many as God has given him. Obviously the dogs that return to their vomit have never had eternal life given them, otherwise it would be endless and they would still be saved. His use of John 17, however, makes no impression on Wesley who affirms that Jesus is merely referring to the fact that he has not lost eleven of his chosen Apostles during his lifetime and the very fact that Judas was lost speaks against Gill's belief in the perseverance of the saints.

Wesley's sixth and seventh 'proofs' against perseverance can hardly be taken seriously as they entail a most questionable retranslation of Hebrews 6:4-6 and Hebrews 10:38 in which Wesley finds the A.V. translators have translated the texts wrongly in the direction of Gill's interpretation. He would have the words 'If they shall fall away', concerning those who have 'once tasted the good word of God', changed to 'and have fallen away', thus turning a conditional warning into an accomplished fact. Gill points out that it is quite impossible to give an aorist participle the meaning of a present perfect verb. Wesley was very sensitive of having his Greek corrected by anybody and here was a person who had never been to university correcting a former Fellow of Oxford and a former lecturer in Greek. This caused him to lose his temper and cry out, 'Shall a man lie for God? Either you or I do', implying most rigorously ('flatly averring') that Gill was the liar, not he.

Hebrews 10:38 reads, 'Now the just shall live by faith: but if any man draw back, my soul shall have no pleasure in him.' Gill points out that the author is quoting the Greek version of Habakkuk 2:4 which compares the man who lives by faith with the man that lives by his own conceits. Wesley denies this firmly, asserting that one and the same person is being referred to. The man who draws back is the very same person as the man who had lived by faith but changed his mind. In order to strengthen his argument, Wesley makes his own translation which is, 'If the just man that lives by faith draws back, my soul shall have no pleasure in him.' Gill is quick to point out that Wesley has moved the word 'if' from its syntactical place in one sentence (we would say 'clause' in today's English) to another, where it certainly does not belong; he has inserted the word 'that' where there is no grammatical or syntactical necessity for it; he has left out a conjunction which distinguishes between two propositions in the Greek which now have been merged, and he has changed the tense of the verb to the present, whereas it is future. He has also made one subject out of two.

Wesley did not really need Gill to tell him all this as the context clearly shows him that his interpretation is wrong. The next verse (39) says, 'But we are not of them who draw back unto perdition; but of them that believe to the saving of the soul.' The author himself is quite certain that he is referring to two different people or groups of people.

Finally Gill looks at Wesley's eighth argument for his scepticism concerning perseverance, Hebrews 10:29: 'Of how much sorer punishment, suppose ye, shall he be thought worthy, who hath trodden under foot the Son of God, and hath counted the blood of the covenant, wherewith he was sanctified, an unholy thing, and hath done despite unto the Spirit of grace?' Here the two scholars are at loggerheads again concerning the Greek. Wesley maintains that the person who is sanctified by the blood of the covenant is the same as he that trod underfoot the Son of God. In other words, here we have a clear case of a believer becoming a castaway and despising the Spirit. Gill, however, argues that the antecedent of the relative 'he' is the Son of God so that it is Christ who is sanctified by the blood of the covenant and not the apostate. He quotes Gomarus, Lightfoot, Owen and Ridgley to back his opinion. Gill, however, admits that the relative 'he' is unclear and could refer to the apostate and gives both possibilities in his commentary on Hebrews, though he obviously prefers relating the relative pronoun to Christ's being consecrated and set apart. The commentator of Hebrews, in the work bearing Matthew Henry's name, gives both possibilities, though he obviously prefers the same interpretation as Gill. Whoever the 'he' refers to, the whole context is suppositional, being used to spur the Christian on to keep close to his Lord, the last verse showing that the strong warning is given to keep the flock within the fold, without this meaning that some, indeed, have left the fold.[32] Calvinist commentators usually recognize that such warnings are absolutely necessary for the faint-hearted Christian as, though he has been given faith as a gift, there is a vital necessity to exercise that faith.

Gill refused to comment on the final part of Wesley's *Predestination Calmly Considered*. This was not because he was unwilling to combat Wesley's whims further but because he believed that the Scriptures Wesley quoted were quite foreign to the subject and Wesley had not explained their relevance in any way at all. For instance, in order to prove that 'the true believer may finally fall', Wesley quotes Matthew 12:43: 'When the unclean spirit goeth out of a man [as he doth out of every true believer[33]], he walketh through dry places, seeking rest, and findeth none. Then he saith, I will return ... and he taketh with him seven other spirits ... and they enter in, and dwell there. And the last state of that man is worse than the first.' The Arminian says this of the saints, yet in the context Christ uses this picture to illustrate the condemnation of 'an evil and adulterous generation'. If Wesley feels this is the fate of true believers, as he, indeed, stresses, then his religion must be nothing but blank scepticism with no hope for the elect and thus no mercy. Obviously Gill thought that the best way to cope with such a far-fetched heresy was to ignore it.

There are two sequels to this story. The first is that Wesley gave up hoping to gain the advantage of Gill and did not challenge him in print again. Failing to confute Gill, he rounded off his works against the doctrine of grace by viciously attacking Gill's young disciple Augustus Toplady. In a libellous pamphlet entitled *The Consequence Proved*[34] Wesley leaves all honest debate to the four winds and quotes profusely concerning the presumed number of the elect which he assures his readers stems from Toplady's pen. To smear his reputation further, Wesley likens Toplady's case to a loathsome story with which God's name and Toplady's moral integrity are associated. It is a low-down story, told in a dirty-minded way to emphasize a point that must turn the stomach of any Christian. The fact that the leader of the Arminian Methodists stooped to conquer in this way brings disrepute to the whole movement. Needless to say, Wesley's allegations of what Toplady had written and how he sought to ruin Toplady's reputation was all sheer evil fantasy from beginning to end, although Wesley affirmed that he had seen Toplady's signature under the supposed article. All who knew Toplady and had read his works were aware of the false witness that Wesley was guilty of but Wesley's story spread amongst his people like wildfire and, although Toplady denied the slanderous allegations in print, and Wesley was unable to produce the supposed documents he referred to, Toplady's name was smeared for ever amongst the gullible Arminians.[35]

The second sequel is to be found in the entry for Sunday 19 February 1786 in Wesley's *Journal*. The old itinerant preacher had long wished to enter Gill's territory and preach in an area that had been so greatly influenced by Gill for over fifty years and in which his memory was still treasured and where Nonconformity was still strong. At last the opportunity came and Wesley paid his first visit to Horselydown though Gill had now been dead for fifteen years. Wesley felt he would cut quite a figure and all would be either awed by him or pleased to see him. His entry shows what a comedown his visit was. After the service at the Anglican Church Wesley returned to his lodgings to pen the following, terminated with a large exclamation mark: 'I preached in Horselydown church, where (to my no small surprise) no man, woman, or child, seemed to know me either by face or by name!'

12.
The work accomplished

A verse of Scripture which was constantly with Gill in his later years was Matthew 24:44: 'Therefore be ye also ready, for in such an hour as ye think not, the Son of man cometh.' Gill understood this to refer not only to Christ's coming in judgement but also to his coming to take his chosen ones home at their death. The gospel ministry to Gill was preparing a people for the Lord from the time of their coming under the gospel to their being called home. Every believer, he urged, should utilize this all too short a time of preparation so that he would be ready when his Master called.

Though Gill was never at ease preaching funeral sermons as he found his emotions difficult to control, he often preached on the subject of death and felt that a major part of his pastoral work was to comfort the sick and dying. One of his typical sermons on death was 'The Quiet and Easy Passage of Christ's Purchased People Through Death to Glory'. This was an exposition of Exodus 15:16: 'Fear and dread shall fall upon them; by the greatness of thine arm, they shall be as still as a stone; till thy people pass over, O Lord; till the people pass over which thou hast purchased.' Gill divides his sermon into four parts:

1. That Christ has a people, and these are a purchased people.
2. That this purchased people must pass through death to glory, and will pass through it safely.
3. That this their passage, as it is always safe from their spiritual enemies, it is, generally speaking, quiet and easy for them: they are not suffered to disturb them.
4. That this is owing to the greatness of the arm of the Lord, or to his almighty power.

The whole sermon is a mighty exposition of that hope of glory that critics such as Naylor profess was never part of Gill's message. Death, to

Gill, is going home, which must be the yearning of every true Christian heart. It is the crossing of the threshold of Jordan to be for ever in the tearless zones of God's Canaan where Christ, who has gone before his Bride, will be to give her a well-prepared reception. Triumphantly Gill declares:

> This their passage is attended with the utmost safety; there is no danger in it; no evil is to be feared from it: as all the people of Israel passed clean over Jordan, perfectly, completely; not one was lost or missing in the passage over it; so all Christ's purchased people pass safely through death to eternal glory; none ever were lost in it; nor will any be missing at the great day, when Christ makes up his jewels, and takes the account of them, to see that all are safe.

Here is the true biblical hope of glory that cannot be equalled by the moderate Calvinist and Arminian doctrine of a universal atonement with a limited efficacy and arbitrary application. Here is the true biblical teaching that God ransoms us, Man for man, from the power of the grave and redeems us, Blood for blood, from eternal death so that we can defiantly cry, 'Death; where is thy sting?' and 'Grave; where is thy victory?'[1]

Elizabeth Gill crossed over Jordan in 1764 in her sixty-eighth year, seven years before her husband and after a very lengthy, painful illness. She had proved a faithful wife for forty-six years and Gill always counted her the greatest blessing God had given him. Her life had been a hard one and the sanctity of it had often been a cause for complaint by the female members of the congregation who did not understand the difference between true piety and standoffishness. Elizabeth was extremely discreet in the affairs of the church and always gave her husband the support he needed. For well over twenty years she had to suffer being bedridden for various periods each year with difficult pregnancies or hazardous miscarriages, besides having to nurse her sickly infants. Of the very many children born to Elizabeth, only two reached adulthood. These were John, who became a goldsmith, and Mary, who married her father's publisher George Keith. Mary was received into fellowship in her father's church as a believer in April 1744 but it was not until March 1751 that John, with two others, 'gave a satisfactory account of ye work of God upon their souls' and was accepted into membership.

During her last days, Mrs Gill could often be heard in prayer, crying, 'Let me go; oh let me go to my Father's house.' Two verses of Scripture were ever precious to her at this time, 'Them that sleep in Jesus will God bring with him,' and 'Casting all your care upon him, for he careth for you.' No doubts or fears seemed to trouble her final days in any way and she continually testified to feeling the Lord's presence but confessed that she was too weak to describe her experiences in detail. Her last words were to say that she had comfort in the Lord but not always in the same form, confessing that 'The covenant is sure.' A period of delirium followed these words after which Elizabeth slept until she suddenly thrust out her arms and cried 'Lord! Lord!' and died.

As old age took her toll of Gill's health, his flock realized that they might soon be without their beloved pastor. After Gill had ordained new deacons in February 1770 a group of members met with the deacons to discuss how Gill's memory could be best kept fresh amongst the church members after he had gone. The second topic of discussion was what measures should be taken to renovate the chapel buildings and add a porch, and whether a mortgage should be raised to cope with the extensive alterations and repairs. The whole account must be told in full as the two projects have become hopelessly confused by recorders of Gill's life who have written obviously not aware of the church records.[2] The anecdote they seem to delight in telling is that Carter Lane took out a very high mortgage for the sole reason of financing a very expensive painting of their beloved pastor. Invariably, no mention is made of the renovation work, nor of the fact that sales of the mezzotints were designed to help pay the workers' wages.

On 19 March Brother Robinson presented the conclusion of the private gathering to the church meeting for consideration. The proceedings, which are as follows, were then entered into the Church Book:

> It was the Unanimous Request of the Brethren then prest[3] and Application was then made Agreeable thereunto to our worthy and hon. Pastor that he would Indulge them by Setting to have a Painting Drawn of his Person to be hung up in the Vestry from the great love and regard they have for the Original. And the Doctor was then pleased to Intimate his readiness to Indulge them therein.
>
> And accordingly the same has been Executed and that it had been thought expedient likewise to have a Mizzotinto Print taken therefrom and the which was Now in hand. But as the same would be attended with a considerable expense it was thought proper to lay the same before them, and to know their Minds. At the same time it was intimated that there would be a Necessity of Borrowing some Mony on a Mortgage on the place in order to pay the Workers bills for the Repairing and Beautifying the same. And therefore it was proposed to their Consideration whether they would approve of the Expenses Attending the Drawing and painting the Picture as also the Copper plate Engraving, paper and Printing of the same be added and thereunto, also in consequence thereof the said Picture

and Copper plates become the Property of the Church and the produce Arising from the Sales of the Print be also placed to the Church's Credit by the Officers of the Church. The which motion being seconded, it was desired that Every one present would speak their Minds freely before it was put up to the Vote and Every Member then present having separately signified their Approbation it was put up to the Vote and it was Unanimously Agreed that the said Expense of painting and Engraving be defrayed by the Church and to be Included in the Amount of the Sum to be Borrowed for the Repairs and of the Meeting and that they both became the property of the church.

The church then took out a mortgage 'on said Meeting House and buildings thereto belong' of £250 and the sale of Gill's likeness started.[4]

That Gill was ready for death was clear to everyone who knew him. Typical of this man of the pen, Gill, on realizing that his home-call would not be postponed for much longer, began to write down his dying thoughts.[5] The question he put to himself was: 'Wherein lies this readiness and preparation for death and eternity?' Spurgeon was always irritated by Gill's mannerism of asking a question and then saying first at great length what the answer was not, before going on to state what the correct answer was.[6] This is the very method that Gill uses in his final days, when one would think the urgency of the occasion would have moved him to answer his own question directly. Gill was a teacher of note and knew what false teaching there was on almost every point of doctrine. He thus always strove to sweep away the dust and cobwebs of wrong thinking before he applied true scriptural reasoning to the topic. Here Gill sweeps away the garbage that clutters even the righteous man's thoughts of death.

Some have thoughts of a well-spent life, Gill explains. He advises his readers to drop such litter at once. Who has lived a well-spent life according to God's standards? It is better for the believer to do as Paul did and count all that is past as dung and spend more time on looking at the prize of our high calling in Christ and his righteousness. Others think comfortably of how they have always striven to be just and rendered to others what was their due. They believe they can thus die with a good conscience, being in debt to no one. All very well and good, says Gill, but what about your debts to God? The best preparation for death is to know that we have Christ as our surety and know that he has cleared our debts, blotted out our arrears and written off our liabilities. There are also those who pride themselves on their generosity to the poor and on always being fervent in almsgiving. Gill reminds such that they might give all their goods to the poor and have not charity or true grace and so be unfit to die. Others say they trust in God's mercy, forgetting that God is a consuming fire to those who have not turned to his Son for that very mercy. 'We have made our peace with God', a further group says, never having bothered to ask themselves if God is at peace with them. No external righteousness whatsoever is of any use to man at death. If he has not found a better righteousness, he will never enter into the Kingdom of Heaven, says Gill with his dying thoughts.

What then makes a man ready for death? First, regeneration. As soon as man is born again, he is ready to die and not before. Second, sanctification. The work of grace and holiness must be in man, transforming him from one degree to another. This is the oil in the wise virgin's lamp that makes a believer ready when the Bridegroom comes. Third, the righteousness of Christ imputed. No man will be admitted to the marriage feast without the wedding garment. God will look for the pure white mantle Christ puts on us when the great day comes. Fourth, being washed in the blood of Christ. Until we are washed clean of all guilt and condemnation we are too dirty for heaven. Fifth, spiritual knowledge of Christ and true faith in him. We must know in whom we have believed and be persuaded that he is able to keep us until he calls us.

Gill then goes on to advise his readers to meditate much on death and its comforts and ask God why his chariot is so long in coming. But they must learn also to wait with their lamps burning, knowing that they do not wait in vain who wait on the Lord. Six things ought to console us. Death frees us from sin and sorrow. It is a going home to our Father's mansion where we belong. It is to be with Christ for ever. We shall be reunited with all our loved ones in Christ. God will gather in all the saints that ever lived. Last but certainly not least, the death of the saints is precious in the eyes of the Lord and what is precious to God should not deter us.

For Gill, experiencing the certain signs of death that were upon him, his main thought was to be with Christ and to be raised, and fashioned like his glorious body, putting off the corruptible and putting on the incorruption. At this very thought he can only say, 'Thanks, therefore, to God, who giveth us the victory through our Lord Jesus Christ.'

The chariot was indeed tardy in coming to John Gill as the marks of death were on him for almost a year before that end came which is the true commencement of life. At the end of 1770 Gill, now seventy-three years of age, realized he had not long to live and informed his church that they should look for someone to take over the pastorate, suggesting that they approach Benjamin Francis (1734-1799). This minister was the pastor of a growing church at Shortwood, Gloucestershire, which dearly loved him but could not afford to keep him. It is said that Francis' congregation was composed of the most materially destitute of believers who lived in a radius of thirty miles around the chapel. Though Francis was pastor of the church from 1758-1799, he only experienced one year in which church membership was not substantially increased and his chapel had to be enlarged three times to admit them all. Gill's deacons, however, ignored his wish to have Francis take his place in the vain hope that their beloved pastor would regain strength.

By 1 April 1771, however, Gill was growing noticeably weaker. This caused some disquiet amongst a number of young people in the congregation who felt that as their pastor could now only preach once on Sundays, he should at least take on a young co-pastor to assist him as a son would his father, or as Timothy helped Paul. The church was gradually reaching the stage, they argued, when all the 'hearers' i.e. the unconverted and non-members, were being 'drawn off'. Twenty-two of them, supported by two deacons Button and Warne, who eventually left the church after Gill's death, thus conveyed their views to Gill in a letter, arguing that the deacons were not answering the needs of both members and hearers. Unusual for such a letter was the fact that ten sisters signed the letter first, this being always the prerogative of the brethren.

This move strengthened Gill's determination to resign as he realized that the time was more than ripe to hand his mantle to a younger person. His reply was read out to the full church on 29 April.

Dear Brethren and Sisters,
    When I consider my Advanced age, and the growing infirmities of it, which render me uncapable of performing the Duties of my office, as they ought to be performed; and when I consider how many Members have been dropping off by Death one by one, and few or none coming in their stead, and others disposed to remove elsewhere, and more still cold and indifferent, together with a decrease of the audience; when, I say, I consider those things, I Judge it most eligible, <u>with your leave</u> to resign my office as Pastor of the Church and then you will be at full liberty to chuse another who may have greater strength of Body and more Vigour of mind to exercise it.
    That Christ gives pastors to churches is Certain, but that he gives Co-pastors is not so certain: a Co-pastor, you seem to be desirous of, is an Officer the Scripture is entirely Silent about; and which is much the same thing, as if a Man should take to himself another wife; whilst his first wife is living; or rather, as if a Woman should marry another man, whilst she is under the law, dominion and power of her former husband: The instance of Timothy serving with the Apostle Paul as a Son with a father is not the case; for they were neither of them pastors of any particular Churches much less Co-pastors; the one was an apostle, the other an Evangelist both extraordinary Ministers; the one accompanied the other in his travels into different Countries and was sent by him into different

parts, but stayed not long in any place: It would therefore, be more clear and Unexceptionable, for me by Consent to lay down my Office as Pastor, when your way will be plain and open to chuse another, and when you come to such a choice, may you be directed to chuse one who is sound in the faith, studious and diligent in his work and exemplary in his life and conversation; and may you have one to preach the Gospel to you as faithfully as I have done, according to the best of my lights and abilities; I can't say, I wish he may serve you, as long as, I have, for perhaps that may be but to his disadvantage and yours, but I wish he may serve you with greater success.

There my dear friends, are my best wishes for you,
Who for the present am, but not long expected to be
your Pastor, Elder and Overseer

John Gill

This letter caused great alarm amongst the members, the great bulk of whom could not imagine being separated from their beloved pastor. They told the deacons that they could not 'entertain the least thought' of Gill resigning and stressed that they wanted him to 'continue being pastor of this church till the Lord shall remove him to the Kingdom of Glory above'. The deacons were urged to write to their pastor explaining that his resignation was the very last thing they wanted. Accordingly, the following letter was drawn up and unanimously approved by the members at a full church meeting on the Lord's Day, 5 May 1771.

Revd and Dear Sir,
    We the Church of Christ under your Pastoral Care having at our last Church Meeting read your letter of the 29th Ult. and now in consequence of the vote then passed, being assembled in full Meeting and having again read the same, and Considered it, have come to a Resolution upon an answer, which youl please to receive as follows.
    Permit us, Dear Sir, to tell you how deeply We are affected at your Letter, from this Consideration, that We apprehend, you have mistaken the true meaning of ours of the 1st April. It appearing that you understand us, as desiring to have a Co-Pastor with you, Whereas We did not point out (or at least did not mean to point out) any thing as our Desire, either Co-Pastor or Assistant, but only to crave your Advice and Assistance, in that which might be most likely to terminate in the Glory of God, your Comfort, and our own profit, and that of the rising Generation, being desirous to prefer

your judgement in that Matter to our own. We greatly fear that you apprehend an Abatement in our affection and love towards you, That we are not Conscious of, We think it Impossible that our love should be easily removed from him who has instrumentally been made so useful to our souls, but we trust our hearts are knit as the hearts of one man towards you, as the Servant of Christ, and as our Father in the Gospel of our Lord Jesus.

Another grieving Circumstance is, that if the Church is willing, you seem inclined to resign your Office as our Pastor. This impression is extremely alarming to us, and is what can by no means find a place in our Thoughts, it being our fixed Desire, and Continual Prayer, that you may live and die in that endear'd Relation; We say with united Voice, how can a Father give up his Children, or affectionate Children their Father? Dear Sir. We beseech you to think and look upon us as your Children, either begotten again unto the Gospel of Christ, through your Instrumentality, or built up in the faith of that Gospel; We desire to say and Testify, that in this Sense you are our Father, and We beseech You not to cast us off, but bear us upon your Heart, and Spiritual Affections all your Days and Let us be recommended to God through your Prayers, with a Who knows? but the Lord may visit us again with the Light of his Countenance, and make us to break forth, on the Right hand and on the left, to the Glory of divine Grace, to the Comfort and Joy on your Soul, and the Refreshing and Rejoicing the hearts of many; This we trust is the fervent Prayer of every one of us.

There were a number of differences accompanying this letter in comparison with that of 1 April. It was now emphasized that a full meeting had taken place and that the fifty-eight signatories were unanimous in their support of Gill. This time the three deacons were listed first followed by the brethren, according to normal church meeting practice, one of the 1 April signatories being absent. Of the sisters who signed the letter of 1 April, half of them did not sign on 5 May and were thus absent at that meeting.

Again Gill expressed the desire that Benjamin Francis should succeed him but his deacons and church members were determined not to give up their beloved pastor until the Lord called him. They thus took no action concerning Francis, though several of the younger members left the church in protest. The deacons did not tell Francis about Gill's wish until two years after their pastor had first expressed it. By that time Gill was dead and Carter Lane was busy looking for a new shepherd.

Gill's very last preaching wish was to expound the song of Zachariah, going on through Luke until he came to the *Nunc Dimittis* in Chapter Two. Then, he felt, it would be his time, like old Simeon, to depart in peace.

God's planning runs on different lines to our hopes and ambitions and Gill never progressed beyond the final verses of the first chapter. But what better finish could Gill have had? His last words were on the central theme of the gospel and of that spirit of evangelism that had been with him throughout his fifty-one years in the ministry. 'To give knowledge of salvation unto his people by the remission of their sins, through the tender mercy of our God; whereby the dayspring from on high hath visited us, to give light to them that sit in darkness and in the shadow of death, to guide our feet into the way of peace.'

During these months Gill was wracked with violent pains in his stomach and he lost his sense of taste, eating merely out of duty. Middleton records how 'He bore his visitation with great patience, composure, and resignation of mind to the divine will; without uttering the least complaint; without ever saying to God, What doest thou?'[7] A fortnight or so before his death, Gill's nephew of the same name,[8] who was a pastor himself, asked his uncle how he was feeling. How many would have taken the opportunity to moan in self-pity. In answer, Gill preached a regular sermon to his dear one, outlining his hope in the Lord, saying:

> I depend wholly and alone upon the free, sovereign, eternal, unchangeable and everlasting love of God; the firm and everlasting covenant of grace, and my interest in the persons of the Trinity; for my whole salvation and not upon any righteousness of my own, nor any thing in me, or done by me under the influences of the holy Spirit; nor upon any services of mine, which I have been assisted to perform for the good of the church; but upon my interest in the persons of the Trinity, the person blood and righteousness of Christ, the free grace of God, and the blessings of grace streaming to me through the blood and righteousness of Christ; as the ground of my hope. These are no new things with me; but what I have been long acquainted with; what I can live and die by. And this you, may tell to any of my friends. I apprehend I shall not be long here.

To other enquirers, Gill was more brief. When one visitor asked him of his well-being, shortly before he passed away, Gill merely replied, 'I have nothing to make me uneasy,' and quoted a verse from Isaac Watts:

> He rais'd me from the deeps of sin,
> The gates of gaping hell;
> And fixed my standing more secure
> Than 'twas before I fell.

This again showed how steadfast to the last Gill was in stressing the need for a better covenant, bringing with it a better hope and a better righteousness which he faithfully believed God had made with him. Thus when the time came for John Gill to depart and be with his Lord, he went without a sigh or a groan, but with a look of inward joy and peace on his face and the words 'O my Father! my Father!' on his lips. Blessed are they that die in the Lord!

Although there had been some dissatisfaction at Carter Lane during the last two years of Gill's life, the great bulk of the membership had kept very close to their pastor whom they adored. After he was gone, they were truly like sheep without a shepherd. A fitting funeral celebration was planned, rather dampened by the discovery that Gill wished to have no funeral sermon preached with the usual obituary. Augustus Toplady, one of Gill's closest friends, offered to take the service but the church declined on the grounds that Toplady was an Anglican. Though grateful for the offer and display of affection, they believed it would be more fitting for a Baptist to take the service. After much deliberation, the church decided not to follow their pastor's wishes and invited Dr Samuel Stennet and Benjamin Wallin to preach burial sermons in the chapel and at the graveside. Churches all over Britain and a number in America reserved days for remembrance services with sermons preached, paying due tribute to Gill's achievements. This was the very thing that Gill had striven to avoid but John Rippon wrote that such were the number of sermons preached and published that never before and never since had such a lamentation gone up in the English-speaking world that a great man had fallen in Israel.

Before all this could be carried out, however, there was very strong opposition from Gill's children and in-laws who naturally desired to honour their dear one's last wishes. The church, in their enthusiasm to give Gill a fitting burial, had quite left their pastor's family out of their plans. Nevertheless, as soon as the church members had discussed all the funeral arrangements, including settling all ensuing bills from church funds, they sent messengers to John Gill Junior's home at Camberwell to make the family acquainted with their decisions. When the messages arrived there, it seems that the news of the church's activity had gone before them. They were thus surprised to find that Mr John Gill Junior refused to see them, telling them through Mr George Keith, his brother-in-law and his father's publisher, that he would not comply with their wishes and would not receive their charity as the family was quite well off enough to meet all the funeral expenses themselves. The three deacons who had been chosen as messengers, however, had also been instructed to tell the Gills that they would be quite happy to have them specify all funeral arrangements if they would rather do so themselves. As Mr Gill, as the head of the family, would not speak to the messengers, misunderstandings arose and some friction. Dr Stennet, however, spoke with both parties and, as a result of his skilled intervention, they then quickly came to an agreement concerning the order of events on the day of the funeral.

A burial ground at Bunhill Fields was chosen as Gill's last resting place as the family already possessed a tomb there, next to that of William Anderson who had been converted under Gill's ministry. The church members and hearers assembled at noon on 23 October at Carter Lane Chapel and found their place of worship suitably adorned. For the occasion, the pulpit and clerk's desk at the chapel had been hung with black cloth and the gallery was draped with black baize all along the front. The party then boarded a 'vast train' of coaches, which had been organized by Deacon Button, and then proceeded at funeral pace to the Turnpike at Newington where they joined the procession coming from Camberwell led by the Gill family. Black cloaks had been prescribed for the brethren and the sisters wore black scarves and hoods which Button had also procured. Bands and gloves were worn by all. Even the poorest of the church members wore full mourning as it had been agreed at the planning meeting that the church funds should cover costs arising from clothing and coach fares for those who could not afford them.

Once at Bunhill Fields, Dr Stennet preached briefly to the mourners and then informed them that he would speak to them again at a special memorial service on the following Sunday afternoon at Carter Lane. The funeral procession then moved on to the graveside where Pastor Wallin spoke on Zechariah 11:2: 'Howl fir-tree, for the cedar is fallen!' Wallin described Gill's usefulness as that of no ordinary saint but a chosen vessel of the Spirit to enlighten many eyes and subdue many hearts to the sceptre of Jesus. As Hervey and Toplady had already expressed, Wallin predicted that futurity would look back on Gill as one whose testimony was the finest of his age. Wallin also emphasized how, like David of old, Gill started to fight the Lord's battles whilst yet a stripling with great success yet he never thought himself too great to remain an ordinary, diligent and faithful shepherd feeding the same flock for over half a century. Wallin also pointed out to the crowds around the tomb that though gifted in literary powers, Gill never dealt in abstract speculation in his writings but kept to his main themes of God's salvation through Christ by the agency of the Holy Spirit, teaching the absolute necessity of conveying the whole counsel of God to sinners. Thinking of Gill's work as a defender of the faith, Wallin outlined how Gill was a man who spoke to the enemy in the gate and whom the adversary feared.

These old Particular Baptist preachers never neglected a chance to drive gospel truths home and Wallin had a message for Gill's family, Gill's faithful flock and those who had been hearers only and were still not converted. After outlining the gospel that Gill had taught his flock, Wallin confessed openly how great would be his hearers' condemnation if they disregarded those truths and died in their sins. He thus boldly proclaimed, 'How often, Sir, did your late teacher urge the importance and necessity of repentance towards God and faith in the Lord Jesus Christ; and art thou still in a state of rebellion, and without a real or visible subjection to the Redeemer? Take heed, lest his extraordinary abilities, labour, and faithfulness, aggravate thy conscience in the last and great day, when all they shall perish who obey not the gospel!' He went on to preach passionately, 'O friend, I beseech thee, take warning, if thou hear not that gospel published by this herald of life, and which continues to be proclaimed in thine ears by surviving preachers of the word; if thou believe not in the Lord Jesus Christ, thou must shortly go down to the dust without hope! There is no exchange for thy soul, unless thou partake in the redemption of Jesus, who having put away sin by the sacrifice of himself is sat down at the right hand of the Father, and is able to save them to the uttermost that come unto God by him.'

Gill was thus laid to rest in Bunhill Fields in the company of such great Dissenters as John Bunyan, Thomas Goodwin, John Owen, Isaac Watts and Daniel Neal. Dr Stennett, who was to be buried in the same cemetery twenty-four years later, composed the Latin inscription for Gill's tomb:

IN HOC CŒMETERIO
CONTDVNTVR RELLIQVIÆ
IOANNIS GILI, S. T. P.
VIRI VITÆ INTEGRI
DISCIPVLI IESV INGENVI
PRÆCONIS EVANGELII INSIGNIS
DEFENSORIS FIDEI CHRISTIANÆ STRENVI
QVI
INGENIO ERVDITIONE PIETATE ORNATVS
LABORIBVSQVE PERMAGNIS SEMPER INVICTVS
ANNOS SVPRA QVINQVAGINTA
DOMINI MANDATA FACESSERE
ECCLESIÆ RES ADIVVARE
HOMINVM SALVTEM ASSEQVI
FERVORE PERPETVO ARDENTE
CONTENDIT
IN CHRISTO PLACIDE OBDORMIVIT
PRIDIE ID. OCTOBRIS A. D. MDCCLXXI.
ÆTATIS SVÆ LXXIV.

A. M. Light gives the translation as:

'In this Sepulchre are deposited the remains of JOHN GILL, Professor of Sacred Theology, a man of unblemished reputation, a sincere disciple of Jesus, an excellent preacher of the gospel, a courageous defender of the Christian faith; who, adorned with piety, learning, and skill, was unwearied in works of prodigious labour for more than fifty years. To obey the commands of his Great Master, to advance the best interest of the church, to promote the salvation of men, impelled with unabated ardour, he put forth all his strength. He placidly fell asleep in Christ the 14th day of October, in the year of our Lord, 1771, in the 74th year of his age.'[9]

Benjamin Francis put his feelings on the occasion to words:

To part with thee — our ever watchful guide —
To part with thee prompts our succeeding tears,
Excites our sorrow, and our fear alarms.
No more we see thy venerable face
In sacred Zion, at her solemn feasts,
Exciting pleasure, reverence and love.
No more we hear thy heart-reviving tongue,
Touch'd with a coal of bright celestial fire,
Unfold the wonders of redeeming grace!
No more new streams of truth divine we taste,
From thy unwearied and exhaustless quill!
Thy learned pen, incessantly employ'd,
For half an age, in thy great Master's cause,
Thy hand has chang'd for never-fading palms;
And thy vast labours in the gospel field,
For fifty-five revolving suns, receive
The bright reward of an immortal crown.

13.
The widowed church

Typical of the many sermons preached in remembrance of Gill's ministry was 'A grain of gratitude being a sermon occasioned by the death of that venerable, learned, pius and judicious divine the Rev. John Gill D. D.' by Thomas Craner. An admirer and friend of Gill, Craner preached on 2 Samuel 3:38: 'And the king said unto his servants, Know ye not that there is a prince and a great man fallen this day in Israel?' Concerning Gill's learning, he said, 'How many voluminous writings, especially his expositions both of the Old and New Testaments, shew that he was such a workman, as I think, I may venture to say, without any disparagement to any either dead or living, who have done excellently, that he has excelled them all.'

Of Gill's theology, Craner told his hearers, 'How wisely, how accurately was he wont to distinguish between the law and the gospel; he did not blend law and gospel together, nor was he yea, and nay, but did rightly divide the word of truth, giving to every one their portion in due season. He did not give the saint the sinner's portion, making the hearts of the righteous sad, nor did he give the sinner the saint's part, but the gospel-trumpet by him gave a certain distinct sound, which shewed he was a great man.'

It was, however, Gill's skill as a preacher that charmed Craner the most. 'He was blessed with ready utterance and great volubility of speech, so that he was apt to teach. With what gravity and majesty had he used to stand and feed the church of God! How did his listening audience hang as it were upon his lips, while evangelical truth did sweetly drop from his mellifluous tongue! What an amazing measure of spiritual experience was he favoured with, as rendered him capable of speaking a word in season to weary souls.'

In order to prepare the members for the memorial service, they were given exact details as to how they ought to behave — details which are rather puzzling to the modern mind. The congregation was to come as early as possible so that they could file in through the vestry door. This strange command was possibly so that the members could see the place where their pastor had gathered his thoughts and sent up many a prayer, before opening the Word of God to his flock and so remind the congregation of their pastor's work for the care of their souls throughout the previous fifty years. The men, who were to enter first, were asked to place themselves as near as possible to the Table Pew and the ladies were to group themselves behind them in the middle of the chapel, as near to where the men were standing as decorum allowed. Stennet then preached on 2 Timothy 4:7-8. A church meeting was announced for the following day to discuss the 'present state of widowhood'.

At this 'well-attended meeting' the church decided that members should wear full mourning for two months and then half-mourning for a further month. They also determined that for the period in which they were without a pastor no members would leave the church to worship elsewhere. It was also decided that the deacons would intensify their activities amongst the members and strive to keep them together through a programme of intense house visitation 'for the purpose of cultivating brotherly love and spiritual affection'.

The weeks that followed revealed an admirable pattern of activity in the church. Days of fasting and prayer were held apart from the normal meetings and one business meeting after the other was arranged. The financial offering of the members was enormous. During an August church meeting it had been announced that the church funds stood at a mere £11 5s 6¼^{d}. Now the church quickly raised money to pay off the enormous funeral expenses accrued by their numerous poor, two collections were made in one day for the local charity school and no less than £50 was donated to the Particular Baptist Fund. Some of the most faithful and successful ministers in the Baptist churches came gladly to preach where the great Gill had so successfully laboured, but for several months no one was found who felt called to take up Gill's mantle. Then at the church meeting called on 10 February 1772 the members heard startling and welcome news. It was announced that Rev. B. Francis, who had been supplying the church from time to time and had been Gill's choice all along as his successor, was seeking the Lord's will concerning becoming their pastor. It seems that he had not been asked directly; possibly the church thought him too established in his own church to ask, but others had hinted that he was now interested. Francis was sent messengers to find out his mind on the matter and he requested time to think and pray about the call. The March church meeting went by and there was still no response from Francis but at the April meeting the word was passed on that he was still considering the offer but there was so much that spoke both for and against that he required more time to discern the will of the Lord. On 22 June

Francis at last gave the impatient church his decision. He was unable to take up the call. Raymond Brown quotes how Francis explained this to Caleb Evans: 'The thought of parting with my dear people, and of the unhappy consequences that may follow, dissolves my heart, and almost overpowers my spirits ... I do not expect to be more happy ... than I am at present: they love me exceedingly, as I also do them.'[1] On hearing the news of Francis' decision, a member reported that a Mr John Fawcett, who had been supplying at the chapel and who was pastor of a church at Wainsgate, should be contacted as it had been rumoured that he was now looking for a new church.

Fawcett was born in 1739-40 (o.s.) at Lidget Green, Bradford, in the West Riding of Yorkshire and was probably converted under Whitefield who preached on John 3:14 there in 1755. At that time Fawcett was in fellowship with the Church of England and later joined the Methodists, but at the age of nineteen became a member of Bradford Baptist Church. He eventually accepted a call to pastor the Wainsgate church in 1765. The church was extremely poor and could only afford to pay their pastor the meagre salary of £25 per annum. After getting to know the Carter Lane congregation, Fawcett initially accepted the call to the pastorate there. When returning home, he sold off a great deal of his furniture and books in preparation for moving south. The story goes that he had already heaped his remaining belongings onto the cart to take them to London when his love for his impoverished church compelled him to change his mind concerning London and to stay with his Yorkshire flock. He later took up a larger work at Hebden Bridge, not far from Wainsgate, to which his first flock were able to follow him.[2] Fawcett has achieved fame for his great assistance in fostering the education of many a Baptist minister, not the least of these being John Sutcliff of Olney. He was also the author of 'Blest be the ties that bind' and made a name for himself with a rhyming couplet composed when his hearers begged him to stick more to Gill in his teaching. His words were:

To be brief, my dear friends, you may say what you will,
I'll ne'er be confined to read nothing but Gill.

After the summer of disappointments at Carter Lane, the autumn brought fresh expectations. A very young man by the name of John Rippon came to preach and, after a number of services lasting into December, some of the members asked him to consider becoming their pastor. On seeing that interest in him was growing, these members urged the church to vote on the matter. This time the sisters were especially encouraged to indicate their thoughts on young Rippon and every sister immediately raised her hand. This was not a formal vote but Rippon was now asked to preach continually for several months.

At a meeting on Tuesday 4 March 1773 a formal vote was taken although only 68 members were present. 33 sisters voted for Rippon and 4 against. Of the brethren 21 voted for Rippon and 10 against. This left a majority of 40 in favour of Rippon. Now the same procedure started as in the case of Francis. Rippon needed time. In his plea for this, written on 7 March, it is obvious that the youth was tormented by the thought of stepping into the very large shoes of his predecessor whom he describes as the 'pius, learned and truly valuable Pastor Dr Gill whose praise is and will be no doubt in the churches to the latest posterity, and for whose memory and labours I have the most sincere veneration'. Nevertheless Rippon promised to assist the church until he had reached a final decision. At last, on 1 August 1773 it was announced to the church that Rippon had answered the call in the affirmative and a messenger was chosen to contact Rippon's home church for a transfer as they believed that only a full member of their own church could be elected as their pastor-elder.

Just as the majority of the members were feeling that all problems had been solved, a shadow fell on the church. Throughout the church members' display of enthusiasm for Rippon, the fact that their three elected and ordained deacons were not of one mind with the bulk of the membership seems to have escaped them. These men felt that Rippon was far too young, immature and unsure of his theology to take on the responsibilities of a pastorate. They also felt that normal church order and discipline had been lost in the anxiety and concern that comes when hopes are often dashed and time goes by with no signs of progress. Thus the autumn of 1773 started with new divisions in the church and the deacons pressed for another vote which was taken on 11 October. It seemed as if history would repeat itself and the call of Rippon would break the church as did Gill's call. This time the deacons and 16 members dissented from the majority but by 13 December, when yet another meeting was called, the opposition had grown to 13 sisters and 17 brethren which was almost half of the number who usually turned up at the meetings. Nevertheless, as the church formally numbered some 150 members, the 30 dissidents were still in the minority.

Meanwhile those who could not accept Rippon as pastor, led by deacons Joshua Warne and John Button with George Keith supporting them, were making plans to form a new 'church state'. It appears that they had hoped to eventually absorb the whole of the Carter Lane congregation into it, thus preserving the unity of the local church but shutting out Rippon. Towards the end of 1773, as the voting was against them and they could not hope to win more than 35-40 members over to their convictions, Button and Warne realized they would have to go their own way. It was now that the remaining members, led by John Rippon, showed the most gracious and brotherly conduct one could expect to a body of people who had disagreed with them. The church decided to dismiss the dissidents with their blessing and with the assurance of their continued fellowship. It was furthermore decided that as the departing members had contributed an estimated £100 towards paying off the chapel mortgage, this amount should be given back to them. As several of the dissidents were trustees of Carter Lane, this decision also made the transfer of trusteeships much easier. Not content with this gesture which might be described as businesslike rather than generous, Rippon urged the church to pay their friends a further £200 to help them build a church. This was a magnanimous proposal, especially considering the fact that the congregation was now in debt to the sum of £650.[3]

Needless to say, the separatists accepted these proposals with grateful thanks and, on receiving the news, Warne and Button replied in the same brotherly spirit: 'Wishing you grace, mercy and peace with the abundance of the blessings and presence of Christ the Head of the church to gather with the income of the blessed spirit by which you may be built as a spiritual house, an holy Temple in the Lord unto all well pleasing.'

The Carter Lane church wasted no time sending the new church 'a kind and favourable answer' telling them officially that they no longer laid claim on them as members of the Carter Lane church but as a sister church 'of the same faith and order'. From now on both churches experienced a ministry which brought them grace upon grace.

14.
Three hundred years on: the Modern Question brought up to date

Very soon after Gill's death, the Lord's saying that no prophet is accepted in his own country became true of John Gill. Whereas those Baptists that later gathered under the name of 'Gospel Standard Baptists' and many Anglican and Dissenting evangelicals continued to look on Gill as a 'father in Israel' and honoured his name, the greatest opposition to the teaching displayed in the large number of works that he authored (hence the nickname Dr Voluminous) has come from within the Baptist denominations who formerly professed to be as Calvinistic as Dr Voluminous himself.

In 1971 Olin C. Robinson, striving to explain this U-turn in the Baptist churches, felt moved to write:

> The world into which John Gill cast his systematic theology had grown weary of systems. Men were beginning to seek simple statements of faith and to draw away from the formidable systematic dissertations of Calvinistic scholars. Man was being viewed with more optimism. A more moderate Calvinism was arising, stemming partly from the tradition of Richard Baxter, wherein some were assured of absolute salvation, but the rest were not necessarily damned. Men were gradually ceasing to view themselves with 'that profound sense of worthlessness which leads to the Augustine-Calvinist position'.[1]

'If only Gill had been more moderate in this sense,' Robinson sighs, 'then the whole denomination might have followed him.'

Robinson put his finger on the sore spot that is still troubling Gill's critics of the present age, three hundred years after his birth. The robust doctrines of Calvinism are being watered down by a new form of ethically, rather than theologically, motivated evangelicalism which maintains that the old Calvinism was not evangelical enough and went too far in its teaching concerning the total inability of man to comprehend spiritual things.

It all started when Andrew Fuller (1754-1815), pastor of Gill's old church in Kettering, became dissatisfied with the theology he mistakenly believed was prevalent in Particular Baptist churches[2] and began to wrestle with Gill's works which he found difficult to understand. He was also highly dissatisfied with his own home church which had seen no conversions in ten years. Somehow he blamed this lack of carrying out the Great Commission on Gill's influence. Explaining his difficulties with Gill to Dr Ryland on 13 November 1809, Fuller explains that he was brought up on Bunyan, Gill and Brine but came to realize that Bunyan had a different view of the free offer of salvation to sinners than Gill. Although Fuller outlines Bunyan's view, he does not state Gill's but it is obvious that he interpreted Gill's position as anti-evangelistic. He goes on to say that he had formerly adhered to Gill's view and had thus 'very little to say to the unconverted; at least, nothing in a way of exhortation to things spiritually good, or certainly connected with salvation'. Fuller further states that, as a result of following Gill, he 'supposed there must be two kinds of holiness — one of which was possessed by man in innocence, and was binding on all his posterity — the other derived from Christ, and binding only on his people'.

By 1775 Fuller was despairing of finding anything to help him in contemporary Particular Baptist works though he had turned to the unorthodox teachings of John Johnson of Liverpool (1706-91) for assistance. It was not, however, until Fuller turned to the Independent pastor Abraham Taylor that he began to develop that system of doctrine which has come to be known as Fullerism. Taylor was a vowed opponent of Gill, and though professing to be a Calvinist, he leaned very strongly to the Arminian side.[3] He had written a pamphlet on 'The Modern Question'[4] which impressed on Fuller's mind that the preaching of John the Baptist, Christ, and the Apostles was 'addressed to the ungodly'. This was refreshing and enlightening to Fuller who seems to have believed the strange, unchristian doctrine that there was no gospel for the unconverted. Fuller was then further influenced by a Particular Baptist pastor called John Martin (1741-1820)[5] who argued that non-submission to the righteousness of God was 'owing to wilful ignorance, pride, prejudice, and unbelief', a remark that Gill would have fully endorsed.

Fuller's account of his dependency on Martin is most puzzling and provides further evidence that Fuller was confused in his theological appreciation of Gill. Martin was a second Toplady in his enthusiasm for Gill's teaching and took every opportunity to hear him in the few years before he died. Martin supplied regularly for Gill and after his death occasionally took over the Carter Lane pastoral duties until a substitute was found. He is invariably linked with Gill as being of one mind in doctrine. On reading Martin, however, Fuller realized that his own understanding of submission to God was at fault although he had been a baptized, professing Christian for some years. Fuller now became thoroughly convinced that his former views had been 'anti-scriptural'. Nevertheless, instead of looking to his own heart as the reason for his own 'wilful ignorance, pride, prejudice, and unbelief', he blamed Gill for providing him with his unscriptural views and thus turned from the teacher he thought he had followed hitherto. If he had consulted Gill, he would have found that he, too, believed as Martin that man's lost state was due to his own wilful unbelief. There is abundant evidence to prove that Fuller had little knowledge of Gill's system, but as Gill's name was attached to the basic beliefs of the Particular Baptists as a whole and Fuller found himself alienated from Particular Baptists because of their rejection of a universal atonement, he automatically made Gill the centre of his criticism associating him with Hyper-Calvinism.

Now if Fuller had formerly *denied* that a rejection of the standards God sets is due to wilful unbelief and *affirmed* that God had two standards of holiness, he had every reason to thank God for showing him the folly of his ways. Anyone, however, familiar with Gill's works might wonder how Fuller could have blamed them for his own going astray. It seems that poor workers really do blame their own tools. If Fuller had used these tools well and read Gill at all closely, he would have recognized that saint's exemplary zeal for evangelism, and his stress on repentance and belief and on God's unchangeable standards of holiness. He would have also realized that, unlike the state in his own dead church, Goat Yard and Carter Lane experienced a great number of regular conversions and baptisms and at least forty-five years of great blessing, allowing for the fact that this decreased in Gill's last eighteen months or so before his death owing to his declining health.

Fuller came into contact with the Johnsonians[6] during his membership, and later pastorate, of Soham Particular Baptist Church in Cambridgeshire.[7] Fuller's pastor, Mr Eve, had been influenced by Johnson and another member of this church, Robert Aspland.[8] Building on Johnson's modalistic[9] doctrines, Aspland went on to proclaim himself an outright Unitarian, founding the Unitarian Academy which he advertised honestly as training '*popular* rather than *learned* ministers'. Eve, too, had to leave because of his fruitless ministry and shaky theological foundation.

Those who deny particular atonement have often confused Gill's doctrines with Johnson's although they are as different as the gulf between truth and error can make them. The Baptist historian A. C. Underwood has perpetuated this confusion by writing of both men as if they shared identical beliefs.[10] He even links John Brine with Johnson although Brine combated and refuted Johnson's wild speculations repeatedly! The meagre evidence given is that both Gill and Johnson could not accept the doctrine of a universal atonement. Following upon this, it is deduced that they were thus in complete agreement with each other as to why! The evidence would indicate that Fuller confused Johnson's views with those of Gill as his caricature of Gill's doctrines matches those of Johnson more closely. Fuller's teaching concerning natural abilities (one could equally call it 'natural light'), his constant analysis of theological data into what is 'proper' and thus 'real' and what is 'improper' and thus figurative could indicate the influence of the Cambridge Platonists.[11] Arthur Kirkby suggests that Dr John Edwards, whose book *Veritas Redux* Fuller told Ryland in his 1809 letter was 'good', was a Cambridge Platonist. Whether that is so or not, there is much of the Platonist in Fuller's theory of reality and his reading of Dr Edwards is a certain sign of his confused thinking in the early years of his ministry. Robert Hall of Arnesby had told him he must read the great Edwards, meaning Jonathan Edwards of New England. Fuller misunderstood this advice and thought he meant Dr John Edwards of Cambridge.[12]

According to Prof. Michael Haykin, in a recently published work, one of the greatest factors which led Andrew Fuller and his closest associates away from what the author terms 'False Calvinism', was the teaching of the New Divinity School, influenced by the Grotian Moral Government Theory.[13] This theory denies that the law is a reflection of God's essential nature, that Christ was the Sin-Bearer, that the atonement of Christ is a necessary revelation of the righteousness of God, and that Christ's death was the penalty of a broken law and a sacrifice through which God is reconciled to the sinner. It sees the entire work of redemption as a gigantic metaphor or sham demonstration of justice to serve as a moral deterrent. This view is more in keeping with Socinianism than with the Reformed Faith. Indeed, Grotius propagated it to serve as a demarcation border between the two areas. Modern Grotians use it as a bridge to make it appear as if the opposite banks are in the very same country. Grotianism uses typical Reformed vocabulary such as 'substitution' and 'satisfaction' which make it appear orthodox to the unwary. On deeper examination, one finds that Grotian substitution is neither vicariously penal nor redemptive, but a figurative substitution for both truths. The term satisfaction refers to the airy-fairy doctrine of a 'satisfaction of benevolence', whatever that may be.

Whatever the true reasons were for Fuller's change in principles, he began to view Gill's teaching as the great obstacle which had allegedly hindered the church from experiencing true Calvinism for over half a century. He thus determined to rid the world of such an obstacle and clean up the Reformed faith, reintroducing what he called 'strict Calvinism'. Fuller's 'strict Calvinism' was founded on the belief that Calvin never taught that a limited atonement and Christ's eternal covenant love for his elect were part of his creed and outlined in his works.[14]

This confusion of belief concerning what Gill actually taught, and what entails being a Calvinist, perhaps explains why those who have inherited and followed Fuller's teaching have a prejudice against what they call 'Gill's system' which they never question. This prejudice is enhanced by the fact that Fuller's followers see him, to echo Haykin, as 'a theological genius' and '"the greatest theologian" of the nineteenth century'.[15] Thus, though they often complain about Gill, they rarely bother to quote him at any length, believing the 'fact' of his erroneous teaching to be a settled matter. When they do look into Gill, they often find quotes which completely refute their narrow view of him. Instead of modifying their picture of Gill and dropping their prejudices, these critics choose to raise a great cry, claiming that they have found yet another ground for disapproval of their arch-foe. They conclude that Gill had not only a faulty systematic theology but one that was self-contradictory at best![16]

This nonchalant manner of dismissing Gill is as unscholarly as it is superficial. A few examples must be given. Gill always sought to exhaust the entire meaning of a text in exposition and strove to give all its possible interpretations usually starting with the least probable and finishing with the interpretations he thought best.[17] Many of his critics, unfamiliar with such methods of exposition, use his commentaries as an inexperienced schoolboy uses a foreign language dictionary, picking out the first entry in a list of possible meanings for his translation. This is seldom a successful method. Similarly these critics pick out his first entries, ignore the rest and then proclaim that Gill is guilty of weak exegesis.[18] Others are so sure that Gill's alleged High-Calvinism must have preached his church empty that they state this dogmatically in their books, though a simple check in the contemporary documents and statistics available would show that Gill maintained one of the largest Baptist churches in the kingdom for many decades.[19] Others are certain that Gill is a heretic, but as they have no primary evidence at hand to support their theories, they 'prove their point' by quoting secondary sources or give examples of other writers whom they feel Gill has influenced negatively.[20] By far the bulk of criticism levelled at Gill is really a harsh criticism of John Brine. This stalwart Baptist minister was one of Gill's first converts at Kettering. In many ways he was a less eloquent, less learned shadow of the mentor whom he loved and followed. Fullerites seem to feel that when Brine speaks, he is merely Gill's mouthpiece, thus on reading Brine, they find, or rather think they find, ammunition against Gill proving that he was intolerant, against preaching to sinners and had a tendency towards Antinomianism.[21] They do not listen to Brine carefully enough. Brine constantly appealed to orthodox and moderate Calvinists alike to stop arguing on minor points of doctrine to the neglect of the greater business of preaching the gospel and wrote a book called *Motives to Love and Unity amongst Calvinists*[22] pleading for mutual toleration. The book went unread and Brine has been labelled a one-sided 'Hyper' ever since. Brine also wrote fervently against Antinomianism but his critics rarely acknowledge this fact.[23]

Interestingly enough William Anderson, James Fall and Henry Scoffield were also converted through Gill's ministry and became useful 'Gillite' preachers. Their exemplary lives and zeal for the conversions of souls are seemingly never referred to by the anti-Gill lobby to assist them in gaining a more balanced picture of Gill's faith and practice. William Anderson's case is worthy of note because after preaching at Goat Yard with a view to becoming a candidate for the ministry and receiving the church's approval and valediction, he took over the church at Glasshouse Street in May 1743. Ivimey comments that this church was 'in a very low and weak state, but by the blessing of God on the ministry, it soon became large and prosperous'.[24] Another case in point is Samuel Wilson (1702-1750), a close friend and co-worker of Gill of whom the Goat Yard pastor said, 'He came forth with clear evangelical light, and with great warmth, zeal, and fervency of spirit; and like another Apollos, with a torrent of eloquence, being mighty in the scriptures; *which made him exceedingly popular.*'[25] Jones tells how Wilson's 'popularity increased, so that at the close of his ministry, *the church was in a very prosperous condition*'.[26] Wilson clashed with Dr James Foster of Paul's Alley. Whilst the latter was giving his Socinian lectures at the Old Jewry, the former laboured at Tallow-Chandlers' Hall preaching Christ from the very same texts!

Typical of this disregard for original sources is the modern fashion amongst Gill's critics to base their findings on the works of fellow scholars rather than at least checking them in the light of Gill's works. Thus Michael R. Watts in his standard work on *The Dissenters* calls Gill a High-Calvinist and links him with those he accuses of Antinomianism. The reader looks in vain, however, for evidence given from Gill's works but Watts refers to Peter Toon's hyper-critical book *The Emergence of Hyper-Calvinism in English Nonconformity* as his source. The twenty pages Watts cites, however, again give no doctrinal evidence from Gill's works. In these pages Toon merely assumes that Gill is a Hyper-Calvinist because he wrote a preface to Richard Davis' hymnbook, edited Skepp's *Divine Energy*, published some choice works of Crisp with a critical analysis and wrote a preface with Brine for Witsius' classic *Economy of the Covenants*.

This is a most odd list of presumed '*enfants terribles*' indeed. Toon defines a Hyper-Calvinist as one who does not believe evangelism is necessary,[27] yet Davis evangelized through eleven counties, founding churches wherever he went. He trained weavers, carpenters, tailors and farmers to go out into the highways and byways to bring sinners to Christ. In so doing, he earned the animosity of many sleepy pastors in an eighty-mile radius of his Northamptonshire church who woke up to find that Davis was doing their evangelistic and pastoral work for them. Gill was indeed influenced by Davis, whom he knew well, but not in the way Toon suspects. In his preface to Davis' hymn-book, Gill praises his 'very powerful and evangelistic Ministrations' with his zeal for soul-winning.[28] Toon also defines a Hyper-Calvinist as one who does not offer God's grace to those for whom it is not intended but Tobias Crisp (1600-43) stressed that, as nobody could tell who were candidates for grace, he had to bring the gospel to all. William Twisse, the Puritan, said that the reason Crisp's opponents spread rumours of Antinomianism etc. about him was that so many were converted under Crisp's ministry and so few under theirs.[29] Though James Hervey disagreed with Crisp on a few minor points that had nothing to do with Hyper-Calvinism, he outlined his love for the author in many letters to John Ryland, viewing his works as 'a reservoir for the spiritual nourishment of his people'.[30] Gill did form a friendship with Skepp in the two years before the latter died but their time together was spent in studying rare Hebrew texts rather than points of evangelistic approach. The historian Ivimey, though always ready to criticize Hyper-Calvinists, gives a very positive picture of Skepp, calling him an 'excellent servant of Christ', emphasizing that many were converted and edified under his ministry.[31] Anyone linking Witsius with Hyper-Calvinism cannot have read the pure gospel which is revealed in the pages of his great work on the covenants. One wonders why Toon picked out Gill's and Brine's names from the list of six men who penned the very short preface to Witsius. Walker, Hall, King and Gibbons all joined Gill and Brine in recommending Witsius as having a 'deep, powerful, and evangelical spirituality and savour of godliness'. Hardly the stuff that Antinomian Hyper-Calvinists are reputed to be made of! Hervey had received Witsius from John Ryland Senior and was very conscious of the value of any literary recommendation by Gill and Brine. When Ryland wrote his *Descant on the Oath of God*, Hervey asked him to have it approved by the two 'master builders in Israel', Gill and Brine, first, comparing them with the just judge in Isaiah 2:1-5 who does not 'judge after the sight of his eyes, neither reprove after the hearing of his ears: but with righteousness'.[32] It is interesting to note that Toon admits that Gill's very intimate friends were John Ryland and Augustus Toplady. The aged Ryland looked sadly upon the emphasis of Andrew Fuller and the two Robert Halls in making the Modern Question the centre of their teaching and said, 'The devil threw out an empty barrel for them to roll about, while they ought to have been drinking the wine of the kingdom. That old dog, lying in the dark, has drawn off many good men to whip syllabub, and to sift quiddities, under pretence of zeal for the truth.'[33]

On the other hand Ryland was impressed with the sanctified life of Brine and the deeply practical divinity of Gill but what he says of the two men does not smack of Hyper-Calvinism in the least. Linking the two Ryland says, 'Mr John Brine entertains us with most nervous and manly reasoning on all branches of doctrinal and practical religion, and teaches us the most intense personal holiness by his own example. Dr Gill leads us into an ocean of divinity, by a system of doctrinal and practical religion, and by a judicious and learned exposition of the Old and New Testament.'[34] It is obvious that Ryland preferred Brine and Gill's all-round approach to the whole body of divinity than the one-sided entrenched emphasis on human duties which became the main topic of the Modern Question enthusiasts. None of this, of course, points to Hyper-Calvinism but a balanced approach to doctrine in general. Ryland's support of DeFleury and antagonism towards Huntington show that he was not what critics usually take to be an Hyper-Calvinist.[35] Nobody, whom one can take seriously, has ever thought of labelling Toplady, the author of 'Rock of Ages' as a 'Hyper'. It is thus legitimate to ask why Toon did not link Gill with his closest friends to prove that he was no 'Hyper'. Such a series of 'proofs' that Toon gathers to help him clothe Gill in false feathers is the stuff that destroys good reputations and creates myths but is hardly material which serves any positive objective purpose.

Severe as this exposure of anti-Gill teaching may seem, a scrutiny of the works of Gill's numerous modern, and supposedly evangelical, traducers has left me with no other explanation for their unfounded, ill-argued views. Even university Ph.D. theses with Gill as their topic show a high degree of blatant prejudice backed up with exclamation marks rather than documentation. Typical of these is Robert E. Seymour's *John Gill, Baptist Theologian*, Edinburgh, 1954. Seymour claims that 'absolutely nothing of Gill's pen is known today' and that his work is 'virtually valueless'. He accuses Gill of 'twisting interpretations of Scripture to a predetermined point of view' and of having 'a venomous tongue and an uncontrollable temper'. He views Gill's defence of the Reformed faith as 'a storm of pointless protests' and tells us that Gill lived a life completely cut off from his fellow men as 'Day after day he arose at dawn and remained with his books until dark.' Not a shred of evidence is given for any of these harsh criticisms, of which this is only a tiny sample, though this is a doctor's thesis.[36] Thus, though criticism of Gill's teaching is, at the present time, indeed vast, it is a remarkable fact that very little of it is centred around sound, scholarly, Bible-centred analysis and obviously stems from a personal unwillingness to accept Gill's orthodox teaching concerning the total inability of man to understand spiritual things. Gill's enemies invariably attempt to combine what they believe are the best parts of Calvinism and Wesleyanism and reject what they believe is the worst which is invariably the doctrine of Christ's efficacious atonement. As the old Particular Baptists say, such critics attempt to drive a Calvinistic bus on Arminian wheels. They are then perturbed when Gill refuses to be their passenger in such an accident-prone vehicle.

Fuller criticized writers such as Gill, Hervey, Marshall and the Marrow Men[37] for their teaching that faith was a gift of God and argued that one must see faith rather as a response to one's inner sense of duty. In the context, he is defending writers of the New Divinity school who, because of their allegiance to the Moral Government Theory of Grotius, believe that reason and an awareness of duty can accept the fitness of believing in Christ. Fuller does not entirely drop the use of the word 'gift' in relationship to faith but emphasizes dutiful reception rather than God's decree to give.[38] The gift of grace is always, for Fuller, sequential to the asking. Before man grasps out and takes hold of salvation, no gift is possible. This was, of course, putting the clock back to the Anglican Latitudinarian teaching of the days before Gill's reforms. It also makes such conversions as Paul's impossible as no feast was spread (to keep to Fuller's imagery) before the Apostle and no request was made by him to partake of it. He was struck blind that he might be given the gift of better sight.

Fuller was convinced that those who stressed that faith and salvation were gifts rather than man's presumed knowledge of his inborn duties, also believed that evangelism was not necessary. Thus, as evangelism is obviously commanded by God, preachers such as Gill, Hervey, the Erskines and the Marrow Men must have no idea of evangelism. This is a preposterous idea, which can be immediately rectified by reading the works of these men. This is why, however, critics always maintain that as Gill believed that faith was a gift, he could have had no interest in evangelism. They argue, in the face of Gill's massive volumes to the contrary, that he taught that because God saves those whom he wishes to save, his human servants play no part in this work. We thus find the principal of Rawdon College, A. C. Underwood, writing that Gill 'never addressed the ungodly'.[39] This biography has perhaps succeeded to some degree in showing that such a position, which is echoed uncritically through the pages of numerous modern Fullerite and Arminian works, is as blatant a misconception as was ever held.[40]

Radical as Fuller's opposition against Gill was, his modern cohorts have taken the battle further and have become even more entrenched in answering the Modern Question rather than preaching the whole gospel properly. Fuller, I believe, was genuinely guilty of misunderstanding Gill and blamed him for his own previous failings. He thus rejected the very man who could have put him on the right path. His followers, with a few exceptions, understand Gill all too well and, though they disagree with him, their quotes from Gill reflect his adherence to orthodox Calvinism.[41] These modern opponents, however, claim that Gill's five-point orthodoxy is not the orthodoxy of the Bible. They thus do not style themselves 'strict Calvinists' any longer (this would bring them too close to the Five Points which they reject), but 'Moderate Calvinists' or 'Evangelical Calvinists'. Gill is now called by them, not a High Calvinist but a Hyper-Calvinist. Such a person they define as one who 'couples a belief in the Five Points of Calvinism with a denial of the doctrine of the free offer of the Gospel'.[42] The name 'Calvinist' used by these 'Moderates' seems to be merely kept up for tradition's sake, showing that most of these people had their roots in Particular Baptist churches. The name no longer has a doctrinal meaning.

'Modified Calvinists' reject the doctrine of limited atonement, and many of them even reject the total depravity of man. The latter argue, following Grotius and Fuller, that sin has not marred man completely in all respects as all the natural abilities which Adam possessed are still there. He is only fallen in the moral exercise of his will. When man again exercises his will positively in recognizing and responding to his Christian duties on hearing the gospel, man is restored to his former pre-Fall Adamic position[43] as nothing else needs to be changed. We thus hear such Moderate-Calvinists calling themselves Four-Point or Three-Point Calvinists, again showing that the name 'Calvinist' has little relevant meaning. This is why traditional Five-Point Calvinists of today refer to their 'modified' brethren as 'Fullerites', seeing in them no Calvinists at all. Some, less politely, call them 'Mongrel Calvinists' to stress the mixed nature of their doctrines. Dr Henry Cole, Calvin's translator, called them 'illegitimate Calvinists' as he felt the great Reformer could never have fathered them. The Fullerites, in their turn, do not refer to the five-point men as 'Calvinists' but as 'Gillites' or, more critically, the 'High and Dry'. Their most favourite title is, however, that of 'Hyper-Calvinist'. A more sinister development seems to be taking place. Slowly but surely, evangelical writers are awakening to the fact that what the 'moderates' call 'Hyper-Calvinism' is indeed traditional Calvinism at its most orthodox. This is causing the anti-Gill lobby to revise its terminology. It is now becoming popular for critics of the five-point system to call the traditional Calvinist school 'Hyper-Orthodox' and themselves 'Orthodox'. In cookery lessons at school, we learnt that the poshest names on the menu were always reserved for re-hashed left-overs from other dishes! This 'posh' name, however, shows that Gill's enemies are gradually being frank about their own theology and dropping the name of Calvinism completely. As nowadays when buying a Hamburger at certain restaurants, one is in danger of finding no meat in it, so those who now offer us Calvin Pie have left out the five most fundamental ingredients!

Though modern Fullerites, who really ought to be called Hyper-

Fullerites (more Fullerite than Fuller), challenge Gill's doctrines on almost every point, they major on the fact that he did not believe that every sinner is naturally able to exercise duty-faith savingly.[44] The only trouble with the sinner, in their view, is that he *will* not be saved. They then develop their own logic and argue that if a person stresses God's sovereignty in salvation more than man's duty-faith, he must, of necessity, believe that good works bear no relevance to faith and are thus superfluous to salvation. Though they would not dare criticize Gill's moral life, as it was so obviously exemplary, they, illogically enough, teach that what they call 'Gillism' leads to Antinomianism i.e. the teaching that the believer need not pay attention to what they call 'the moral law' which is, for them, a highly modified version of the Mosaic Law excluding its condemning and commanding function and the promises.[45]

The inhabitants of the so-called Moderate Calvinist house are quite divided amongst themselves regarding their criticisms of Gill, though all are united in believing that criticized he must be! Some denounce Gill for turning the heads of his hearers and readers from the traditional Baptist faith but others are equally sure that he merely ploughed in old furrows and stopped reform and progress in the Baptist churches. Coupled with this censure is invariably the criticism that Gill merely appealed to simple country folk and the labouring classes,[46] but others say that Gill, being 'high and dry', could only appeal to half- fossilized academics.[47] It is argued that Gill turned from the old Baptist ways because they were paved too much with law rather than with grace, whereas others are equally certain that Gill was entirely legalistic and there was no room for grace in his theology.

What has happened to Gill can be paralleled with how critics have treated my favourite poet William Cowper. This great evangelical writer loved to be out and about in storms and wrote nearly all his poetry in the winter time, a season he loved. He could be often found playing battle-door and shuttle-cock in the garden, training with his dumbbells and skipping ropes or swimming across the Ouse in all weathers. The *Gentleman's Magazine* wrote of him as a fine sportsman. Against these facts and influenced by his own conception of a 'romantic poet', Hazlitt wrote that Cowper was frightened of a drop of rain and confined himself to his easy chair and parlour fire. Generations of critics have since built up a theory of Cowper as a timid 'fair weather poet' merely on this quite untruthful 'aside' of Hazlitt's without bothering to check the facts for themselves. Such a snowballing of criticism, as this biography has shown, has gathered in size and momentum in Gill's case ever since Arminians of various descriptions[48] chose to call Gill's Calvinism 'Antinomianism', 'Superlapsarianism', and 'Hyper-Calvinism',[49] to stick to the more theological terms of abuse. Abraham Taylor, whose works turned Fuller from Gill, trumped all critics and displayed his great command of epithets by calling Gill's orthodox Christian faith 'a filthy dream', 'a rude, ignorant, horrible blasphemy', 'invented by one of the vilest and lewdest heretics'.[50]

This is one of the major reasons why the reforms which Gill worked out to the great spiritual benefit and organizational stability of the Particular Baptist churches have been rendered null and void in the mainline Particular Baptist and Strict Baptist churches of today and why modern Baptist leaders, on writing about Baptist church life in the eighteenth-century, never even mention Gill who played a major formative role in the denomination both theologically and socially.[51]

This biography has emphasized that Gill's teaching was built soundly on the true gospel doctrines of sin, salvation and a Christian's duty to evangelize. The 'gospel' the Fullerites replaced it with, and proudly boasted was 'A Gospel worthy of all Acceptation', was a dogma with a lower view of the sovereignty of God and Christ's divine love for his church, and a higher view of man than the good news of the Bible. It was a gospel which sought to preach moral principles and moral reform on the basis of a metaphorical, platonic, view of sin, salvation, atonement and the imputation of Christ's righteousness, and was thus a gospel which could only lead to doubt as to whether Christ truly and historically died the Just for the unjust.

A serious outcome of the modern anti-Gill school, three hundred years on, is not merely that it inevitably has become an anti-Calvinism school in rejecting the Five Points.[52] It has also become an anti-Calvin movement and a movement antagonistic to the Reformed doctrine of Scripture. Modern Fullerites argue that Gill is different to Calvin in a way that shows he is 'more Calvinistic than Calvin himself'.[53] In enforcing their polemic on their readers, they tend to make Calvin himself less Calvinistic to highlight the difference. Many typical examples are to be found in Peter Toon's novel little book mentioned above. Toon is confident that Gill, whom he believes followed Joseph Hussey (1659-1726) closely,[54] is one of the founders of Hyper-Calvinism. Yet nearly all Gill's words quoted remove all force from Toon's argument and, contrary to his aim, reveal Gill as a most orthodox traditional Calvinist, fully grounded in a belief that Scripture is the inspired Word of God. Calvin, however, is portrayed, perhaps unwittingly, as an ancient prototype of Karl Barth with strong Modernistic tendencies.

Toon explains that 'God was on trial' in the days of Gill and Brine, 'And it is against this background of rational enquiry that we must set the Hyper-Calvinist doctrine of God.' He then looks at what he believes Gill and Brine accept as the source of knowledge of God, considering their hermeneutical principles and doctrines of divine revelation. As evidence Toon lists seven statements of Gill's which are chiefly concerned with the all-sufficiency of the written Spirit-given Word. Each of these statements is thoroughly biblical and thoroughly evangelical. Toon then concludes:

> Gill also had definite views about the inspiration of the Bible. He held that its penmen wrote as they were directed, inspired and guided by the Holy Spirit. Not only the general message and substance of the Scriptures but the very words of the original languages also were suggested in such a way as to correspond with the individual style of the author.[55]

Such teaching is the very marrow of the Reformed Christian doctrine of Scripture and certainly does not deserve to be put under the heading 'Hyper-Calvinist doctrine', but this is where Toon surprisingly puts it. Gill, however, is surely in full agreement with Calvin who goes to great length in his *Institutes* to show that 'the authority of Scripture is founded on its being spoken by God',[56] and it is obvious in the context that he is speaking of the whole canon of Scripture as given to the church. The *Westminster Confession*, which has always been thought of as being 'as Calvinistic as Calvin', echoes this view in affirming that the Scriptures were 'immediately inspired by God ... at the time of writing'. If this view is, however, not truly Calvin's, but rather a Hyper-Calvinist's view, and therefore wrong, what, according to Toon, do 'Moderate Calvinists' accept as Calvin's doctrine of Scripture? His answer is as surprising as it is alarming. Toon says: 'Calvin held that the primary authority of Scripture rested in the work of the Holy Spirit making the words of Scripture become for the individual reader or hearer, the words of the living God ... Also Calvin never enunciated the doctrine of the *literal* inspiration of Scripture although he held a very high view of its authority through the work of the Holy Spirit.'[57]

Here no appeal is made to Calvin's works for authority but rather to a misquote of a quote from H. Clavier borrowed from François Wendel's biography of Calvin. It is of interest to note that Clavier, in his *Études sur le calvinisme* (the work Wendel quoted from), is not criticizing 'literal inspiration' at all in connection with Calvin as Toon suggests, but *'extreme literalism'* which is usually associated with the 'typewriter-method' of inspiration, a view which Gill rejected as vigorously as Calvin.

Anyone reading Toon's words with any kind of theological training behind him will immediately see the Modernistic, but also Neo-Pentecostal, view expressed here. The Bible is simply a λογος 'as written' but only becomes a ρημα or the true Word of God when applied effectively and savingly to the heart of the hearer or reader by the Holy Spirit. Both Calvin and Gill, however, stressed that the Scriptures were Spirit-inspired on being written by the penmen who were given this canonical task.

The obvious conclusion of holding such a doctrine of Scripture is that it can never be looked upon as the objective Spirit-breathed Word but only as a subjective insight on the part of the one who receives the ρημα. Thus the Word has no objective authority but is to be interpreted according to the situation of the one who professes to receive a word of Scripture as 'the Word of God'. This is the arbitrary stuff that Modernism and Liberalism are made of but it is a far cry from the *Institutes* and the teachings of Gill.

Almost all opposition to Gill is based on a refusal to take God's Word literally in the orthodox Reformed manner outlined by Calvin and Gill. Wherever one scrutinizes Fullerite claims to be biblical one discovers mere references to the subjective moral influence of a Bible word on the recipient coupled with a highly metaphorical interpretation of the scriptural doctrine it is based on. Thus sin, the sinner's debt to the law, the imputation of sin to Christ, Christ's righteousness imputed to the believer, the atonement, Christ's redemptive death, the work of the Holy Spirit, in fact all the major doctrines of Christianity, are mere figures of speech and imagery resulting in the believer never knowing what he ought objectively to believe.[58]

Whenever a single doctrine is emphasized as the vital nucleus of the gospel, other, equally vital aspects, are lost. Modern Question preaching has failed for this very reason. Its initial aim was praiseworthy, to emphasize man's responsibility before God. The reasons given for doing this were more questionable. It was the conviction that those Christians such as Brine who emphasized the sovereignty of God would become too cock-sure of their election and thus live a life of licentiousness. It was also a fear that the doctrines for which Gill stood would lead men to give up preaching repentance, in fact, give up preaching to sinners altogether. Actually Brine's contemporaries praised him for the exemplary nature of his life and Gill was praised for the full gospel he preached to sinners. Equally true is the fact that such scandalous lives as the Modern Question people assumed that their brethren would live were few and far between amongst God's Reformed evangelical ministers and, morally speaking, there does not appear to have been any general difference in godliness between those who tended to major on God's sovereignty and those who felt called to emphasize man's responsibility.

As matters developed and the Modern Question enthusiasts distanced themselves from their chosen enemies, their one-sided approach led them onto almost secular paths. The theological aspect of salvation retreated for them into the background and salvation became gradually a matter of morals. In fact, one can safely say that the movement became a kind of Society for the Upkeep of Moral Duties for the Unsaved, manned by a staff with a strong proselytizing fervour. The more the emphasis was placed on morals rather than doctrine, the more rational became the movement and the more intent were they at discerning and describing man's supposed moral capacities. The Moral Government Theory came to their assistance as did the theories of the New Divinity School, thus influencing them in believing that a residue of moral awareness of man's saving duties to God had not been eradicated by the Fall. We therefore soon find the Modern Question movement proclaiming man's abilities rather than his responsibilities. This turn of events caused them to change their former semi-theological belief in the naturally known duty of man to repent savingly to a mere philosophically moral appeal to man to exercise his will and accept Christ as if he had never apostatized. Then the movement applied the remnant of theological thinking they had left in the background to affirm that when man morally refused to receive Christ, he would be damned for this act. If they had kept their theology central to their faith, they would have realized that man was damned already in his fallen state and Christ had come to redeem his Bride through payment of his vicarious sacrifice. This was the very point, however, that Fullerites and Hyper-Fullerites rejected or interpreted merely metaphorically.

History was now left with a Modern Question movement standing on one leg as a need for legal repentance was eclipsed by the evangelical call to love Christ and obey the gospel. This leg was to follow the first. As Fuller maintained that the law as a covenant of works and a giver of life had been annulled by God for both saint and sinner alike, the need for a law work in the life of the sinner became superfluous. Neonomianism now came to the assistance of the movement. Belief must be followed by repentance and this should be proved to God and the church by sincere obedience to the gospel resulting in evangelical righteousness. This view, of course, is Antinomian to the core. We thus have a modern moral movement which came into being through affirming human responsibility and the need for repentance for breaking the law of Moses coupled with an abhorrence of Antinomianism, now freeing itself from its foundation and taking off as a balloon, no one knows where. Fullerites have become Hyper-Fullerites and Fuller himself would not recognize them as his children.

This has not happened in a corner but has been universally noticed. It has moved Reformed evangelical leaders to check and re-check the facts of their faith. A great upheaval is taking place in the churches and in the Christian press in an effort to get back to basics. Sadly tempers are being lost and theological swearwords, as one *Evangelical Times* writer put it, are being verbalized on all sides as brother wars with brother.

There are roughly two ways taken by modern evangelicals to attempt to get back to normal. The first is to admit that both sides have a point and they should get round the conference table and see what unity can be obtained. Here, however, the danger is that both sides may drop the remnant of biblical doctrine which they retain and unite in a common humanism or philosophy of life, believing unity is more precious than doctrine which divides. This is the way the Ecumenical Movement has taken, the results of which are enough to frighten any converted man away. The next solution taken by well-meaning men is to say that it is not necessary for both sides to come halfway in meeting each other. It is suggested that there can be unity on full terms with a full acknowledgement and acceptation of each other's views. All one brother has to say to another is, 'If you do not complain about my favourite doctrine, I will not complain about yours. Are we not brothers in the faith?' The Bible says, 'Can two walk together less they be agreed?' A modern ombudsmen has a fine way out of this predicament. He affirms that 'There are two lines found in Scripture, one that declares man's helplessness through being dead in sin and yet that he is responsible to turn to God, and the other, that the Lord is sovereign to save.' This is sound theological thinking. The only difficulty is that if what the writer of these words says about Hyper-Calvinists is true and what is obviously the case amongst Fullerites is taken into account, neither of these sides can now accept the truth of his statement regarding the biblical view of God's work and man's responsibility. Faced with this dilemma the writer makes a most extraordinary statement in his eagerness to unite evangelicals in a common faith. He declares regarding salvation, 'The idea that God did half and man did half is utterly false.' So far, who could disagree? He then goes on to say, 'God doing all and man also doing all is the teaching of the Bible'.[59] Here many readers must have almost fallen from their chairs. The writer attributes this quote to 'Rabbi' John Duncan who is famous for speaking in paradoxes and aphorisms, not all of which are readily understood. Many have taken this saying to mean that 'the Man doing all' is a reference to the Incarnate Lord who did all that the law required of him out of love for his church. This interpretation, even if it was not John Duncan's meaning, has the advantage of reflecting Scripture. The writer however cannot mean this in the context and is clearly suggesting that salvation is not only of the Lord but it is equally and fully of man. It would be appropriate to remember that John Duncan also wisely said, 'In preaching these doctrines never go beyond what can be proved by the express words of the Bible.' Elevating man to an equal role in the act of salvation with God hardly seems scriptural and shows what difficulties modern evangelicals are making for themselves in trying to find a solution to modern church disunity and doctrinal chaos.

There is a far better pattern for unity which can be placed before the Hypers of both sides, indeed before every professing Christian today, with spiritual profit. This is the full gospel as preached and lived out by John Gill. In presenting Gill's life as he lived it and outlining the doctrines which he lived by, my fervent aim is to show how Gill's critics on all sides have failed both to recognize and appreciate the scriptural nature of his teaching concerning the law and gospel. The Modern Question movement has taken gifts of God which are part and parcel of the Covenant of Grace and placed them in the Covenant of Works, making them available not only to the elect but to all sinners in general. In so doing, and in claiming that Christ's atonement was for all men, irrespective of any special covenantal relationship to Christ, they have revealed themselves as Universalists at heart and not as Calvinists who believe in a particular atonement. They thus empty sovereign grace of much of its sense content and lay the emphasis on the need for displays of legal self-righteousness in following the 'moral law' of naturally perceived duties. This is an insult to the righteousness of Christ which is the only righteousness worthy to obtain our salvation. The Modern Question ought not to ask whether man has known duties which he can exercise savingly or not. The all-important question is, 'Whose righteousness saves us?' Salvation is of God in Christ and is not a question of human duties but a question of Christ being obedient to death to save his Bride. This fact is underlined time and time again in Gill's works.

On the other hand any 'Hyper' blowing himself up in his own pride, feeling he must be something special for God to have elected him, or anyone of that ilk feeling he can live as he pleases because his salvation is secure, will find, on looking at Gill's works, that the Master in Israel proves a very strict teacher and warns such Hypers who claim to be his pupils that they have got their lesson quite wrong and are probably amongst those who cry 'Lord, Lord' yet were never converted.

When Gill took over the pastorate of the Goat Yard church in Southwark, London, he did so at a time when the Baptist churches were split asunder by faulty teaching concerning the Sonship of Christ, the person of God, the scope of the Fall and the nature of the atonement. In opposing these heresies, Gill taught both the sovereignty and grace of God in salvation and not only the need for repentance but also the need for a turning away from sin to the Saviour of sinners who was true God. Though Gill stressed the inability of man to do anything of himself which was pleasing to God, he, nevertheless, also emphasized the responsibility of man in placing himself in the spiritual mess he was in. In other words, Gill brought together the very doctrines which were dividing the churches asunder, as his contemporaries were, on the whole, tending to emphasize either the human or the divine element in a life of faith. As we have the very same situation today, it would pay us to have a new look at Gill.

I have thus portrayed John Gill as the Reformed and reforming pastor he really was, trusting that this will be to the glory of God. It has been demonstrated how Gill served the Baptist cause in an unparalleled way and made the Baptists a movement to be respected by all denominations for its soundness of doctrine and true evangelical fervour. Gill, however, was not only the theologian of the Baptists. He provided all evangelicals with a body of divinity second to none for the depths of its insight into the Word of God and the breadth of its application to all sorts and conditions of men. Gill's sermons, tracts, commentaries and doctrinal writings are therefore classics of the church universal, standing side by side in importance with works such as Augustine's *City of God*, the *Institutes* of Calvin, the sermons of Latimer, Luther's 95 Theses, Bunyan's *Pilgrim's Progress*, and Owen's *Death of Death*. We neglect this testimony of a great saint at our peril.

Appendix I:
The full gospel and the free offer

Curt Daniel in his thesis *Hyper-Calvinism and John Gill* defines Hyper-Calvinism as: 'that school of Supralapsarian "Five Point" Calvinism which so stresses the sovereignty of God by over-emphasizing the secret over the revealed will and eternity over time, that it minimizes the responsibility of Man, notably with respect to the denial of the word "offer" in relation to the preaching of the gospel of a finished and limited atonement, thus undermining the universal duty of sinners to believe savingly with the assurance that the Lord Jesus Christ died for them, with the result presumption is overly warned of, introspection is overly encouraged, and a view of sanctification akin to doctrinal Antinomianism is often approached'. This he summarizes in the words, 'It is the rejection of the word "offer" in connection with evangelism for supposedly Calvinistic reasons.'[1]

Daniel goes on to argue that the only 'tangible thing which differentiates' between what he calls 'Hypers' and High Calvinists, is the non-use or use of the word 'offer' with reference to preaching the gospel.

If Daniel's definition is accepted as a true statement of what a Hyper-Calvinist is then it is plain that those who speak of a 'free offer', or even 'an offer' in connection with preaching the gospel cannot possibly be Hyper-Calvinists, but those who never let such words pass over their lips are to be at once suspected of being such. This indeed is Daniel's procedure throughout his book. Using the phrase 'free offer' as his distinguishing shibboleth, he combs through an enormous list of works, judging their authors' orthodoxy by their use of the term. This results in some surprises. Tobias Crisp, who is seen by many Arminians as the Arch-Hyper, is pronounced 'clean' as he uses the correct words. Arthur Pink, however, is judged a Hyper because though he seems to argue for a free offer at times, he is at other times against it. Daniel actually believes that Pink has done more for the Hyper-Calvinist cause in writing than any one else since John Gill.

Daniel's definition could be taken seriously if all shared his view as to what a Hyper-Calvinist is, and if all meant the same thing when they used the all-important words 'free offer'. Daniel obviously believes that his definition of Hyper-Calvinism is a scientific, experimental definition such as Boyle's Law or Archimedes' Principle which cannot be subject to varying interpretations. This is, of course, not so, as the many free-offer authors whom Daniel quotes understand many different things by the term. Nevertheless, he lets them through his net because he measures them by the use of a word rather than any narrow definition of it. Some he mentions would accept the word 'offer' (as the Marrow Men) but not the word 'free'. Others such as John Murray have no scruples about using the term 'free offer' but mean something very different to what the Marrow Men meant by their shortened term. Fuller uses the phrase 'free offer' but would disagree with Boston and Murray as to what the term means. Perhaps, to make things easier, this is why Daniel, who has used the term 'free offer' throughout the first 766 pages of his work, suddenly frees the word 'offer' from its governing adjective and speaks only of an 'offer' when defining Hyper-Calvinism on page 767 — so as to envelop as many as possible under the protection of his orthodox 'offer' umbrella. Daniel criticizes 'Hypers' harshly and often for not defining the gospel more closely to show whether they are orthodox or not. He, however, uses no definition of the gospel at all to prove what is orthodox but is satisfied when he sees that the word 'offer' is used. Orthodoxy for him has become shibbolethism.

Daniel is not alone in this as it is becoming more and more common, one might even say popular, in evangelical circles to put brethren on trial for not using the words which would absolve them from suspicion.[2] This is an alarming state of affairs considering that preachers such as John Gill emphasized putting the whole counsel of God into the gospel preached, whereas many other evangelicals with an abhorrence of all so-called Hyper-Calvinists do not believe in preaching the whole counsel of God to sinners out of fear of probing too deeply into God's secret will. It will be necessary to look at some of these various uses of the term 'offer' to see if they contain the full gospel or even adopt any common understanding of the term whatsoever.

John Murray, writing in his *The Atonement and the Free Offer of the Gospel*, bases his appeal for a free offer on Christ's words in Luke 24:47: 'Repentance and remission of sins should be preached in his name among all nations, beginning at Jerusalem.' He concludes from this verse that 'unto all the nations' bespeaks universality. And since repentance is redolent of the gospel, the universality of the demand for repentance implies the universal overture of grace.

Murray points out that Christ gave the commission after emphasizing that he was to suffer and rise again. He thus concludes that 'The universal demand for repentance and the unrestricted overtures of grace involved must be grounded, according to our Lord's own express teaching, in the atonement.' There is some ambiguity here. Is he saying that as repentance is commanded of all, grace will be provided so that all might repent through the merits of a universal atonement? Is Murray offering grace to all mankind who automatically become partakers of it as they come under the universal call to repent? Is this Murray's gospel which he freely offers?

It is here that Murray begins to differentiate radically as to the nature and scope of the gospel. He has shown us his piece-dyed fine worsted, now he tailors it down to size to make a suit that will fit him. He maintains that there is 'a certain universalism belonging to the redemptive events that lays the basis for and warrants the universal proclamation. In other words, the extension in proclamation cannot be divorced from the question of extent.' The key words here to note are 'a certain universalism' and 'extent'. Murray is preparing the way for a two-gospels theory, one gospel being universal and the other of limited extent, neither of them being, however, the gospel that he freely offers.

One design of the atonement, according to Murray, is that the non-elect receive universal, indiscriminate, benefits from Christ's redemptive work as (1) Christ is in control of the world as a dispenser of good; and (2) Christ enables believers to 'do good to all men' so that order, equity, benevolence and mercy can reign on earth. This gospel for the non-elect is an essential element of the gospel of salvation. Thus Murray can conclude that 'There is *a* gospel of salvation proclaimed to all without distinction.' This is the gospel of God's universal love to mankind.

It must be queried whether such a gospel can really be called a gospel of salvation. This is also Murray's thought which leads him to argue that the atonement 'has an entirely different reference to the elect' leading to a 'radical differentiation'. Though the non-elect accrue benefits from the atonement they are not atoned for as the atonement was not designed for them. There is, Murray tells us, a 'differentiation' in God's love. He loves mankind universally and beneficially but loves his elect with a higher love savingly.

Murray must have realized that he was making it more and more difficult for his readers to understand what a 'free offer' of the gospel had to do with all this. Which of Murray's gospels is to be offered freely? The indiscriminate gospel of God's love to all mankind or the discriminate gospel to the elect? Taking the limited application of the gospel first, Murray accepts that it is the true doctrine but does not make this the contents of his 'free offer' arguing that the term has nothing to do with offering the possibility or opportunity of salvation but with salvation itself.

Secondly, as if to make the issue more complicated still, he says that 'It is not the general love of God to all mankind, the love manifested in the gifts of general providence, that is offered to men in the gospel.'

Thus the gospel which is to be freely offered is not the gospel of election, nor the gospel of universal love. Murray, however, has a third point — one might call it a third gospel. Sinners, he tells us, are not asked to believe that God or Christ loves them with a differentiating love. The gospel simply demands that they come to Christ and commit themselves to him. He argues that as Christ *is* salvation it is *Christ* who must be offered. This is the gospel which is to be offered to all men. Murray takes this step because he believes that 'It cannot be declared to men indiscriminately that, in the proper sense of the term, Christ died for them.' In teaching, however, that the free offer is an offer of Christ, Murray has not explained who Christ is or what Christ's work is. He has not introduced Christ to the sinner. It is all rather like the men who go round the blocks at voting time calling out through their megaphones, 'Vote for Joe Brown' when the hearers have no idea who Joe Brown is or what party he represents.

This view of the 'free offer' obviously raises more questions than it answers. It does not tell us, for instance, what place in the gospel repentance plays, although it is the gospel of repentance that led Murray on to his 'free offer' theology. Must repentance precede faith and what is meant by 'offering Christ', indeed by 'coming to Christ'? If a description of Christ's work is not at least part of the contents of the gospel offered, what sense is there in proclaiming an unknown Saviour?

Murray seeks to answer some of these questions in his essay *The Free Offer of the Gospel* presented before the fifteenth General Assembly of the Orthodox Presbyterian Church in 1948.[3] The real point of dispute concerning the free offer, he argues, is, 'Can it properly be said that God desires the salvation of all men?' Murray concludes that whereas this is the case with the *revealed* will of God, it is not the case with the *decretive* or secret will of God. The 'free offer' issue now becomes even more complicated. We are not only presented with three gospels but with two different and contradictory wills of God. Murray seems to be arguing that, leaving the Fall aside, God would wish all to be saved, but in view of the Fall and his subsequent will to save at least some, though none deserve it, God now only desires his elect to be saved. This point would be acceptable to most Calvinists but Murray draws conclusions from it hardly warranted by his premise. He believes that the gospel of salvation must be offered universally to all mankind in accordance with God's *original* desire for all to be saved and not his decreed desire to save some. In order to prove that his deduction is correct, Murray quotes Matthew 5:44-48:

> But I say unto you, Love your enemies, bless them that hate you, and pray for them which despitefully use you, and persecute you.

That ye may be the children of your Father which is in heaven: for he maketh his sun to rise on the evil and on the good, and sendeth rain on the just and on the unjust. For if ye love them which love you, what reward have ye? do not even the publicans the same? And if ye salute your brethren only, what do ye more than others? do not even the publicans so? Be ye therefore perfect, even as your Father which is in heaven is perfect.

This passage, Murray argues, 'tells us something regarding God's benevolence that has bearing upon all manifestations of divine grace'. He backs up this conclusion with quotes from Acts 14:17; Deuteronomy 5:29; 32:29; Psalm 81:13ff. and Isaiah 48:18; Matthew 23:37; Luke 13:34 and Ezekiel 18:23,32; 33:11. All these passages, however, merely imply that God shows benevolence (Murray's word) to the just and the unjust and that he has no delight in the death of the wicked. If this is the free-offer gospel, it falls far short of the full gospel of salvation in God's effectual call of the elect and thus it may be *a* gospel but it is not the full gospel.

Next, Murray deals with Isaiah 45:22: 'Look unto me, and be ye saved, all the ends of the earth: for I am God, and there is none else.' At last Murray has found a text which has to do with salvation and that on a worldwide scale. Two things must be noted, however. Rather than salvation being *offered* here, God is *commanding*. The people are ordered to assemble (v. 20), tell, bring (v. 21) and look (v. 22). They are told what will happen if they obey, and what will happen if they do not. Those that disobey will be ashamed and confounded (vv. 16, 24) and those that obey will be saved (vv. 17, 22). Here we have a clear testimony to the fact that God's call to the world is a discriminating call. Furthermore, the entire message of these chapters in Isaiah is to show that God upholds his elect and he has called them by their name to be his (43:1; 44:1). They shall be saved for ever and their enemies will be condemned. Murray argues that the universality of the command (he is suddenly writing about commands and not offers) is apparent from the expression 'all the ends of the earth'. He concludes that this illustrates 'the will that all should turn to him and be saved' and adds, 'While, on the one hand, he has not decretively willed that all should be saved, yet he declares unequivocally that it is his will and, impliedly, his pleasure that all turn and be saved.'

Apart from being very complicated metaphysics, this argument wrenches the text from its context. From Isaiah 40 onwards, starting with those moving words, 'Comfort ye, comfort ye my people, saith your God'. we are faced with the inner mysteries of the gospel, revealing the love of God for the church for whom he allowed his Son, the Suffering Servant (42:1) to die out of pure love. In other words, the whole witness of these chapters is diametrically opposed to Murray's exegesis. The gospel which is here expounded is one of discerning, discriminating love, a gospel which Murray refuses to accept as the gospel which is to be offered freely to all.

Murray's final, and for him conclusive, evidence concerning the scriptural nature of his 'free offer' is 2 Peter 3:9: 'The Lord is not slack concerning his promise, as some men count slackness; but is longsuffering to us-ward, not willing that any should perish, but that all should come to repentance.'

Murray does not believe that the 'us' in this verse refers to the church Peter is writing to but to sinners in general. God, he argues, is long-suffering with those outside of the church. This would clash somewhat with verse 15 where Peter says the long-suffering of our Lord is salvation and that this should encourage the church to persevere and be steadfast. Murray, however, argues that 'us-ward' is not a reliable reading and should be rather 'on your account'. He accepts that 'us' would refer to Peter and the church but feels that if the words 'your account' are used, they would be more open to a universal interpretation. Such a phrase could include any reprobates among those hearing the letter read. Murray thus concludes that 'God there stretches out his hand without a difference to all, but lays hold of those, to lead them unto himself, whom he has chosen before the foundation of the world.'

This conclusion is fraught with difficulties. Firstly, it is always unwise to base a doctrine on linguistic speculation as to whether the AV is a worse translation than, say, the ARV. Secondly, the text certainly does not say that God stretches his hand out to all, yet refuses to take hold of some. If God refuses to take hold of some, he must refuse to offer them his hand. Thirdly, even if this picture of God could be accepted, it would show not only a discriminating God but also an arbitrary God. This discriminating, arbitrary God would be saying to one and the same person at the same time, both 'come' and 'depart from me for I have never known you'. This is certainly not the gospel Murray tells us he wishes to have offered to every man. It is a 'gospel' with a most questionable view of God, besides being a 'gospel' that cannot possibly be found in the texts Murray uses.

The question once again arises as to whether Murray is arguing for a universal grace to match the universal call to repentance and remission of sins, or a discriminating, saving grace. He seems to be fluctuating perma-nently between these two opinions. In his closing words, however, he comes down firmly on the former proposition and says: 'The full and free offer of the gospel is a grace bestowed upon all. Such grace is necessarily a manifestation of love or lovingkindness in the heart of God. And this lovingkindness is revealed to be of a character or kind that is correspondent with the grace bestowed. The grace offered is nothing less than salvation in its richness and fulness.' This is an expression that would please the most ardent Arminian and quite does away with the doctrine of election and the fact that God saves some put passes by others. Murray, however, claims to be a Calvinist. One can only question why he sticks tenaciously to a phrase, the defence of which leads him to empty the gospel of its most important features, according to orthodox Calvinists, in order to make it acceptable to a mass audience. Once the self-contradictory way Murray has chosen is embarked upon, it opens the door to more and more difficulties. His argument that one must offer Christ but not Christ's message is one of them. Curt Daniel, in his work *Hyper-Calvinism and John Gill*, views this interpretation of the gospel as being typically Antinomian. He says of Saltmarsh, whom he believes is both a Hyper-Calvinist and an Antinomian, 'With typical Antinomian boldness of expression Saltmarsh wrote, "The Gospel is Christ revealed. The Gospel is Christ himself"',[4] obviously believing that a preacher who is not prepared to outline his gospel further is not preaching the 'free offer'. Later Daniel quotes Murray's summary of the gospel as 'offering Christ' and links him with Saltmarsh.[5] The fact is, as soon as one starts offering a gospel freely that is void of content and avoids controversial points, one is in danger of being regarded as a heretic by all sides.

The last court of appeal for many a contender for the free-offer terminology is usually Andrew Fuller. This writer has, however, very little to say about the free offer in comparison to the frequency with which he is quoted. At times Fuller uses the term to mean nothing more than preaching certain tenets of the gospel. In Letter V written to Dr Ryland in January 1803, Fuller refers to Calvin and the Synod of Dort as teaching 'the death of Christ as affording an offer of salvation to sinners without distinction', yet explains this in the words of the Synod and in terms of promises concerning 'whosoever believeth in Christ crucified shall not perish, but have eternal life' and the 'command to repent and believe, ought promiscuously and indiscriminately to be published and proposed to all nations and individuals to whom God in his good pleasure sends the gospel'. Here, though he has the opportunity were he an enthusiastic 'free offer' man, Fuller makes no such allusions and seems to merely refer to preaching the gospel, even limiting the word 'indiscriminate' to mean 'to whom God in his good pleasure sends the gospel'.[6] Here Fuller does indeed come very near to Gill. He appears also to agree with Gill concerning the non-universal scope of the gospel as he says: ' I allow it to be the revealed will of God that every man who hears, or has opportunity to hear, the gospel, should return to him by Jesus Christ; and whosoever so returns shall surely be saved. But I apprehend, let us understand by the *will* of God in this place what we may, we can never make it applicable to all men universally.' Fuller's reason for saying this is the same as Gill's in his rejection of the term 'universal offer'. It does not take into account the fact that millions have died without the gospel and there are still millions living without it.[7]

Nor does Fuller teach that God loves all alike in any way. In his *Reply to Philanthropos*, he is quite definite on the fact that there is a limitation of design in the death of Christ and grace is thus displayed discriminatingly. Fuller, however, qualifies this statement, stressing that such Scriptures which deal with a limited application of the gospel are for believers only.[8] This is paradoxical as Fuller's main argument concerning Hyper-Calvinists, or False-Calvinists as he called them, in 'The Gospel Worthy of All Acceptation' was that they preached the gospel to believers only. Here Fuller is claiming virtually the same doctrine for himself! This is no one-off slip of the pen as Fuller stresses his point over the following pages time and time again, arguing concerning propitiation that, 'He is "set forth to be a propitiation, through faith in his blood," Rom. iii. 25. He cannot, therefore, one should think, be a propitiation to any but believers.' Fuller drives this point home by an ingenious piece of exposition of 2 Corinthians 5:14: 'For the love of Christ constraineth; because we thus judge, that if one died for all, then were all dead.' Of Paul's words, he says: 'It does not appear to be the desire of the apostle to affirm that Christ died for all that were dead, but that all were dead for whom Christ died.' Lest even this could be misunderstood, Fuller goes on to explain that Paul does not mean that Christ died for all dead men but that those he died for were dead. It would seem that Fuller here is not writing, as he usually does, about a universal atonement but a limited one. Christ died for those whom he intended to save. This, however, is, according to Fuller, a gospel to believers only and not part of the gospel to sinners. This explains why Fuller places election and particular redemption in the secret will of God which ought not to be offered to sinners indiscriminately and thus not preached to them.[9] Here he differs radically from Gill who argued that the full gospel, including election and particular redemption, must be addressed to all as the Spirit leads and the reception or rejection of it alone distinguished the living from the dead. Realizing that those who used the term 'offer' were limiting the contents of the good news, Gill — as Richard Davis, the great evangelist, dropped the term because it confused the all-important issue.

Fuller is, in fact, developing a two-gospel theory based on what he believes is God's secret will as opposed to his revealed will. How can one know that God is thus at sixes and seven with himself because of his conflicting revealed and secret wills when his secret will is secret? Fuller does not tell us. It suffices for him, as also Murray, that God's revealed will is to *call, command and invite* sinners to himself. Murray, however, goes beyond Fuller here, stating that salvation and the necessary grace that goes with it is *offered* to all sinners. Fuller merely speaks of God *calling, commanding and inviting* sinners. He can thus conclude, 'that, however difficult it may appear to us, it is proper for God to exhort and invite men to duties with which he has not determined to give them a moral ability, or a heart, to comply; and for which compliance he has made no effectual provision by the death of his Son'. Here Fuller uses the same self-contradictory language as Murray. Just as Murray teaches that God holds his hand out to those whose hand he will not grasp, Fuller has God demand of individuals what he makes sure they cannot perform. There are two differences, however. Though this is called the 'free gospel' in Murray's jargon, it is not the gospel that is offered to every man in Fuller's system. Fuller, too, has a third gospel, the gospel of duty-faith. This is, for Fuller, the free gospel of the universal offer of salvation which guarantees that every sinner is warranted in believing that salvation is possible for him. The second difference between Fuller's and Murray's gospels reveals the dominant factor in Fuller's duty-faith teaching which is based on natural theology. Fuller strictly denies that in offering the gospel to all, those are being offered the gospel who cannot possibly accept it. In his *Change of Sentiment* he argues: 'If there were not sufficiency in the atonement for the salvation of sinners, and yet they were invited to be reconciled to God, they must be invited to what is *naturally impossible*.[10] The message of the gospel would in this case be as if servants who went forth to bid the guests had said, "Come," though, in fact, nothing was ready if many of them had come.'[11] What Fuller is actually saying is that fallen man is naturally able to appropriate the gospel savingly.

In his 'The Gospel Worthy of all Acceptation', Fuller points out that man is aware by the exercise of his natural abilities and his contact with the law that he has a natural duty to exercise faith savingly and, indeed, a natural ability to do so. This faith is directed to Christ who demands it of every man as his duty. Fuller can thus say, 'If faith in Christ be the duty of the ungodly, it must of course follow that every sinner, whatever his character, is completely warranted to trust in the Lord Jesus Christ for the salvation of his soul.'[12]

This doctrine is highly rationalistic and Pharisaic in origin. It virtually teaches that nature points the way not only to a Creator, but to a Saviour. Furthermore, it implies that following the moral law introduces to Christ the one prepared to do his duty savingly, and the sinner is assured that he has the natural abilities to follow this course, should he but be willing to use them.[13] 'No natural impossibilities' regarding man's salvation became a slogan with Fuller.[14] Strange, in Fuller's emphasis on the efficiency of the moral law to put a man on the right way to salvation, is that he hardly mentions the promises which pointed Abraham and the Jewish fathers to the Christ who was to come.

Here we are back to the moral grace and moral suasion of the English Deists of the pre-Gill era. Theirs was the gospel of the 'rational proposal of duty' which would enable a man to turn from sin to Christ and become a duty-bound Christian. In John Gill's eyes, such belief was as false a view of duty as it was of faith, and could in no way be a gospel worthy of being offered freely. Those who have been introduced to the law certainly have a duty to keep towards it as Gill constantly emphasized. Needless to say, one can only have a duty towards the law when the law is given. Paul says in Romans 7:7-8: 'I had not known sin, but by the law: for I had not known lust, except the law had said, Thou shalt not covet ... For without the law sin was dead.' Similarly, one can only have a duty to faith when faith is given. When faith comes, however, one has no faith in one's own ability to exercise faith savingly. One's duty is then first and foremost not to the law, nor to faith itself, but to Christ who is the end of the law and the giver of faith and the only One able to save.

It is plain that Scripture teaches man's duty to repent. It is equally plain that Scripture teaches that man has no natural abilities to do so. He is dead in trespasses and sins. If he could repent, there would be life in him. The usual New Testament method of preaching was to turn the conscience of the sinner to the law he had broken and preach the need for repentance and the need for faith in the Saviour who had kept the law for him. Thus we find in Scripture that all sinners are called to repentance (Mark 2:17; Luke 5:32 etc.) Hence repentance must be preached to all nations (Luke 24:47). Now the point is, are sinners to be *offered* repentance, are they to be *invited* to repent, or do we as God's ambassadors *command and call* people to repent? Scripture nowhere refers to offering repentance though we read of God *granting* repentance (Acts 5:31; 11:18; 2 Timothy 2:25). We also read of God *leading* sinners to repentance (Romans 2:4). The Christian's calling and duty in evangelization is to follow Christ's example and *call* and *command* sinners to repentance (Matthew 9:13; Luke 5:32; Acts 17:30).

Where is the sinner called upon to exercise duty in keeping the law? Ecclesiastes 12:13 says: 'Fear God and keep his commandments: for this is the whole duty [word implied] of man.' This is also implied in Luke 17:10 where we read, 'So likewise ye, when ye shall have done all those things which are commanded of you, say, We are unprofitable servants: we have done that which was our duty to do.'

The question now is, how does the sinner know he ought to repent? Does it come from an inner recognition of duty? Through an innate knowledge of responsibilities? Through a reason which is just as sharp after the Fall as before? No. Scripture makes it clear that fallen man is not aware of any such duties or responsibilities, nor has he any 'natural abilities' to live a perfect, law-conforming life.[15] He does not know Christ to repent and exercise duty-faith in him. If fallen men had known Christ, whom to know is life eternal, they would not have crucified the Lord of Glory.[16]

We notice then that the command to exercise duty applies to the law but it is used by Fullerites to mean a duty to exercise saving faith in Christ which belongs to grace. How then does a sinner repent, or more biblically, how do the elect repent so that they may receive the remission of sins and faith in Christ? Not by having their sense of duty appealed to. This would be merely appealing to their pride. Repentance is plainly and simply given by God (Acts 5:31). God grants repentance (Acts 11:18). God's goodness leads to repentance (Romans 2:4). God does all this by working in man a godly sorrow for his sins (2 Corinthians 7:10). Is this gift of repentance conditional on man's display of duty-faith or is it discriminating according to God's will? It is surely discriminating as 2 Timothy 2:25 shows: 'If God *peradventure* will give them repentance.' The word μηποτε here surely means it is up to God's will.

But now the Fullerites will say, 'It is all very well you talking about duty to the law, but we talk about the duty of sinners in respect of saving faith. Sinners are no longer under a law which is life, if obeyed.'[17]

Here Fullerites are denying the work of the law to show up man's sin and God's eternal standards and to pronounce him unsavable if left to himself. The law is shown to man as a life-earning pattern which he cannot possibly keep. The promises point to a Messiah to come who will keep it for us. Until he comes into the life of the sinner, he is still under the law which is life *if* obeyed and still under the penalty of death because he does not obey it. The law thus cannot give man life but death. Only dead men, according to the Scriptures, can be made alive again, born again. Fullerites jump over all this and invite sinners to exercise saving faith before the law has been allowed to do its work. They wish to revive men before they are diagnosed as dead. In emphasizing man's abilities and natural powers, Fullerites brush aside man's total inability and powerlessness to comprehend both his own state and the gospel — however modified.

The big question now is, does the Bible invite all men indiscriminately and everywhere to believe as Fuller maintains? No, says the Bible. Repentance must come first. Belief is always dependent on repentance. Repent ye and believe the gospel (Mark 1:15). When God grants repentance we may talk of belief but not before.

Where does this belief come from? Is it for all to grasp at, spurned by a knowledge of their duties? No. Belief comes solely through God's sovereign will. We read in Isaiah 43:10: 'I have chosen you that you might know and believe me and understand ...' Belief comes through Christ (John 1:17) and is the work of God (John 6:29). The non-elect may have this gospel declared to them — but only to their confounding: 'A work which ye shall in no wise believe, though I declare it unto you' (Acts 13:41). Only those who are chosen can know and understand what faith in Christ is. This is made obvious in 2 Thessalonians 2:13 where we read: 'God hath from the beginning chosen you to salvation through sanctification of the Spirit and belief of the truth.'

Sinners cannot possibly have any inkling of responsibilities towards saving faith as God has withheld these truths from them as fallen creatures. Their natural, fallen abilities are of no help whatsoever. When they are granted repentance, faith, justification and sanctification — then they know how to live the Christian life.

Thus the command to exercise duty-faith can only be given to those who have a faith to exercise dutifully and a knowledge of their duties towards God. This faith is God's gift to his elect. It is not offered and then given when God sees that the sinner is ready to accept it. It is given with the same divine authority and sovereignty that God uses when he grants repentance. It is this gift of faith and this alone that justifies and thus distinguishes between believers and unbelievers. In preaching duty-faith, the duty to exercise faith savingly, Fuller is again, in reality, preaching to believers only. He is preaching salvation to the already saved.

Graham Harrison censures Gill on the issue of duty-faith arguing that 'Gill and his friends laboured under the philosophical delusion that if faith is a gift, it cannot be a duty.' Here the confusion lies with Harrison. Gill was quite clear in his mind that the Christian had a duty to the God who had granted him faith and few spoke so much of the duties of the faithful as Gill. In his sermon on 'The Just Ruler found in Christ', Gill lists the duties of a Christian in respect to Christ as a ruler of men, and the church as the people of God and his obligation to work hard for the enlargement of Christ's Kingdom.[18] This is all in keeping with Gill's biblical duty-faith teaching that with the grant of faith comes the obligation to exercise it. What Gill could not believe was that the duty of the evangelist was to preach that sinners were duty-bound to exercise savingly a faith of which they knew nothing and of which they had nothing. He would not preach to the unsaved as though they were saved but he preached to save sinners.

Fuller was obviously influenced in his emphasis on duty-faith on the sinner's side rather than the gift of faith from God's side by his reading of American followers of Hugo Grotius (1583-1645), the Dutch rationalist and Moral Government theorist. An American author by the name of Anderson had reacted strongly against this rational, moral government theory as taught by Joseph Bellamy (1719-1790) of the so-called New England School, who criticized Walter Marshall, the Marrow Men[19] and James Hervey for believing that faith is a unilateral gift of God. To the Moral Government people, God's moral will can be known through nature by reason. It is difficult to find a true distinction in their teaching between man's ability to exercise moral duties and his ability to exercise faith. Fuller sided against Anderson and with the Moral Government theorists in the debate, arguing that 'The gospel is a feast freely provided, and sinners of mankind are freely invited to partake of it. There is no mention of a gift, or grant, distinct from this, but this itself is a ground sufficient.'[20] Here we see that strange mixture of Bible knowledge and rationalism which was so much part and parcel of Fuller's system. It seems that Fuller is not so much denying that faith is a gift but that this gift is only given where it is offered and accepted by the action of the sinner exercising his natural moral duty. It is as if every man is born with a natural understanding of how things should be. The onus of acceptance lies with man rather than the initiative in giving lying with God. In his effort to emphasize man's ability to react responsibly, Fuller is ignoring God's sovereignty in having mercy on whom he will have mercy. Fuller is also attributing abilities to man which he lost at the Fall. He is also following Hugo Grotius and not the scriptural view of man.

Fuller measures himself against Walter Marshall from time to time and is indeed comparing himself with a giant. Marshall's *Gospel Mystery of Sanctification* is one of the classics of Christian doctrine, which explains the full gospel of salvation in minute detail to the praise of God. Marshall uses 'free offer' terminology as freely as Fuller, yet he uses it in quite another context. The free offer to Marshall is the conferring of the right and duty to receive Christ's salvation as one's very own. With this right and duty comes the gift of salvation itself.[21] This gift of salvation, joining the sinner to Christ in a mystical union, is to be found fully in the sovereign active will of God in which the object of salvation is initially passive. Marshall says,

> Thus we are passive, and then active, in this great work of mystical union; we are first apprehended of Christ, and then we apprehend Christ. Christ entered first into the soul, to join Himself to it, by giving it the spirit of faith; and so the soul receives Christ and his Spirit by their own power; as the sun first enlightens our eyes and then we can see it by its own light. We may further note, to the glory of the grace of God, that this union is fully accomplished by Christ giving the spirit of faith to us even before we act that faith in the reception of Him; because, by this grace or spirit of faith, the soul is inclined and disposed to an active receiving of Christ.[22]

In his use of the term 'offer' Marshall never distracts from its sacrificial meaning of Christ offering himself for his church. If this meaning was universally kept to, there would be no misunderstanding concerning the term and thus no harm done in using it, but rather much good. Marshall's use of the term in relation to Christ's gift of himself in giving his imputed righteousness to his elect is, however, seen by many modern evangelicals as being 'typically Hyper-Calvinist' as it emphasizes God's sovereignty against man's responsibility. In so doing, however, they make nonsense of the term 'Hyper-Calvinism' and turn their backs on the biblical doctrine of the gospel mystery of sanctification.

Thomas Boston in his meticulous notes on *The Marrow of Modern Divinity* used by Fuller obviously believes in the free offer of the gospel and interprets Edward Fisher's emphasis on preaching the gospel to all in this way. He, however, distinguishes between an authentic and inauthentic gospel offer. Boston sees the authentic gospel offer as being the 'deed of gift or grant' given by God the Father, 'moved by nothing but his free love to mankind'[23] to whosoever receives it. He leans in this interpretation on the findings of the Synod of Dort, using the very same quote as Fuller above. This gospel must be broadcast to all but it is not a gospel of universal redemption, nor even of universal atonement but the divinely ordained means of reaching the elect for whom Christ died. When this deed of gift or grant comes to a sinner 'to whom it doth not belong particularly, that man hath no warrant to believe on Jesus Christ'. Pardon, however, which is preached to the elect is preached to them by God's messengers because it has already been granted. This is the point where Fuller is not in harmony with Fisher and Boston. Fuller believes that pardon comes when faith is exercised. The Marrow Men believed that pardon comes to whom pardon has been granted. It is a gift emanating purely from the will of God who has decided before the foundation of the world who will be saved.

If Fuller disagreed with the Marrow Men then it is not surprising that he disagreed with James Hervey. He preached the free offer in the sense of the Marrow Men a generation before Fuller reintroduced the duty-faith preaching of Toland, Tindal and Tillotson who were a generation older than Hervey. Of *The Marrow of Modern Divinity* Hervey says:

> It is a most valuable book; the doctrines it contains are the life of my soul, and the joy of my heart. Might my tongue or pen be made instruments to recommend and illustrate, to support and propagate such precious truths, I should bless the day wherein I was born. Mr. Boston's Notes on the 'Marrow' are, in my opinion, some of the most judicious and valuable that ever were penned.[24]

In his sermon on Ezekiel 18:27 which he called 'The Way of Holiness' Hervey emphasizes that:

> The Holy Ghost, in all his operations, and with all his graces, Christ sends to whomsoever he pleases. He gave this inestimable blessing to Saul the persecutor and blasphemer: he gave this inestimable blessing to many of his murderers and crucifiers: he still confers the heavenly gift on his enemies; *yea, on the rebellious also.* And the promise, the free gracious promise, *is to you, and to your children, and to all that are afar off, even as many as the Lord our God, by the preaching of his gospel, shall call.*

Hervey did not mention Saul, Christ's crucifiers and other rebels without due thought. He did so to emphasize that God grants salvation without any preparatory steps on the part of those to whom salvation is granted. It is while we are rebels that the gift comes to us. It was in the very moment that Saul was breathing out fire and slaughter against the will of God that he experienced God's converting will in his own life.

In summing up what preachers of the past have understood by the 'free offer', it is obvious that the term is no use whatsoever as a means of distinguishing extremists from the orthodox as those who stress God's side in salvation and those who stress human responsibility and those who stress both all use the term. It is also used by those who would deliberately shut out much of the gospel from their preaching, feeling that it is unsuitable for unconverted ears. Even those who feel that the free offer is for believers only use the term as do those who preach to sinners as if they were saints. All who use the term the 'free offer' limit its scope to some extent, just as many limit its contents. If we could define the free offer as merely indicating Christ's call to take the gospel to all the world, it would be a meaningful, usable term, though not a biblical one. Similarly, if we could define it as referring to Christ's substitutionary and redemptive death on the cross alone, we would have a basis for using the word which is descriptive of the gospel and has the advantage of being a biblical term. This would, of course, still present difficulties for those, as Fuller, who believe that the atonement did not virtually and vicariously redeem anyone but merely made redemption possible.

What must be obvious from this study is that it is presumptuous indeed to declare that such a mighty preacher of the full gospel as John Gill must be an extremist and a Hyper-Calvinist — even an Antinomian — because he feels that the term 'free offer' leads to so much misunderstanding that it should be dropped. This is a display of honesty and common sense which should be respected.

Gill's *Declaration of Faith* is a faithful testimony to the gospel which Gill taught. In that statement and Gill's comments on it one word occurs frequently: the word 'duty'. Here is meant however, not Christian duties expected of non-Christians as in the duty-faith teaching, but the duties of Christians to take the whole gospel to all mankind. Of Gill's summary of what he believed and preached in his 1729 *Declaration*, John Rippon says: 'This form of sound words, containing the substance of his early creed, he maintained, without deviation, to the very end of his days; and few are the formulas which have at any time been more closely united with *duty*. The term and the thing are remarkable, in this confession — and no man was more fond of either in their proper place, and fairly understood.'[25]

In expounding 2 Timothy 1:13: 'Hold fast the form of sound words',

Gill, following Paul, reduces the sum of the gospel under two heads, repentance towards God and faith towards our Lord Jesus Christ (Acts 20:21). He also accepted as a pattern for preaching Romans 8:29-30, outlining the doctrine of effectual calling, predestination, justification and glorification. These are doctrines which many who use the words 'free offer' remove from their message to sinners, believing that they are for believers only. Cotton Mather, in criticizing the duty-faith teaching of his day, outlines how such preaching leaves out predestination and election which are two of the most comforting doctrines to sinners that the gospel affords. He put the weak effects of preachers in his own day down to a refusal to expound this gospel. As he himself was one of the most successful preachers and pastors America ever had, one cannot say that preaching election frightened the people from the churches.[26] Attempts have been made to show that Gill was unsuccessful in drawing souls to Christ through preaching such 'Hyper-Calvinistic doctrines', but the statistics speak for themselves. Gill's church membership was for a long time one of the largest of any Baptist church in Britain.[27]

Keeping to the same text, Gill goes on to outline that within the pattern of sound words which was committed to Timothy to preach was the proper deity and unity of the Godhead. For Gill the modern evangelical doctrine that Christ had a different will to his Father concerning salvation would have been damned as the heresy it is.[28] That this teaching is being propagated today by those who feel Gill is a Hyper-Calvinist shows how ridiculous these 'theological swearwords'[29] have become and how meaningless the accusation when applied to Gill.

Next Gill emphasizes that part of the gospel is the eternal love of the Triune God to his elect and Christ's surety arrangements for them. He stresses the total depravity of man and his total inability and impotence to do anything spiritually good of himself. He includes particular redemption, satisfaction for sin by Christ's sacrifice, free and full pardon by his blood, justification by his imputed righteousness, regeneration and sanctification by the powerful and efficacious grace of the Spirit of God, the final perseverance of the saints to eternal glory as the free gift of God and much, much more. Similar long lists of all that a preacher should teach are to be found in Gill's commentaries on Galatians 1:23, 2 Corinthians 1:19 and in his remarks on Proverbs 15, Acts 10, Mark 16 and a number of his other works. Few preachers have stressed as Gill what the full scope of the gospel is and the need to preach it. The gospel to Gill is the sum total of all that the Father, Son and Holy Spirit have done and do and reveal in the Word. Not a jot or tittle must be left out.

For Gill Christianity was Christ, but he did not merely appeal to his hearers to accept Christ as if all knew inherently who Christ was. For Gill the gospel revealed Christ as 'really and proper God, and truly man; that he is the Son of God, and the Mediator between God and men; that he is the Messiah, who is actually come in the flesh; that he died and rose again the third day; is ascended into heaven, and sits at the right hand of God, and will come a second time to judge the world in righteousness; and that by his obedience and sufferings, and death, he has become the Saviour of sinners, and that none can be saved but by him'.[30] Many similar descriptions of the Christ who is to be preached to all men are to be found throughout Gill's works where he stresses time and time again the need to preach the whole counsel of God. In *The Watchman's Answer to the Question What of the Night*, Gill deals with the general decay in church growth of his day (1750). The answer lies chiefly in the work of gospel ministers, he finds, who he obviously suspects of holding back vital doctrines in their 'popular' preaching. He tells these preachers that 'They should watch, and stand fast in the faith, and quit themselves like men, and be strong; and they should not conceal any thing that ought to be known, or keep back that which is profitable, but declare the whole counsel of God. Their work is to warn sinners of their evil ways, and of the danger they are in by them; to shew them what an evil and bitter thing sin is, and that the wrath of God is revealed from heaven against it; that the wages of sin is death eternal; and that destruction and mercy are in all their ways, in which they will issue, if grace prevent not; and to convince them of the worth of their precious and immortal souls, and that nothing can be given in exchange for them.'[31] This is preaching the gospel properly.

Daniel's response to Gill's repeated emphasis on the whole gospel as seen in all the doctrines of grace shows what a dilemma he is in, trying to sift the evidence as to which side of orthodoxy Gill is on. Starting by airing doubts as to whether Gill preached the full gospel or not on page 384 of his thesis, by the time he has noted how comprehensive Gill's gospel is, he ends on page 395 by suggesting that whereas Gill would have accused others (Daniel's supposition, not Gill's own statement) such as Whitefield, Edwards, Doddridge etc. of *subtracting* essential tenets, they might have thought that Gill was *adding* superfluous tenets. Thus Daniel is fearful that Gill includes too much in his good news for sinners rather than too little! In his efforts to label Gill as a Hyper at all costs, Daniel always wants to have it both ways in his criticism. To drive this badly documented criticism home, he also resorts to sheer speculation. In particular his repeated assertions that Gill stood in opposition to the Evangelical Awakening and opposed Whitefield are without any basis whatsoever. Gill, with other Dissenters such as Risdon Darracot, was one of the unsung pioneers of the Evangelical Awakening as testified by such Anglicans as Toplady, Hervey, Middleton, Venn, Hawker and Doudney. There is no evidence to suppose that Gill opposed Whitefield who was joint friends with Gill's friends Hervey and Toplady. There is certainly much evidence to show that

Gill worked hand in hand with Anglicans, Congregationalists and Independents as supplied in this biography. Nor did Gill allow the matter of baptism to harm his fellowship with his Anglican brethren in the revival.[32] This is in stark contrast to Andrew Fuller who risked splitting the Particular Baptist Missionary Society over the matter of closed and open communion in which he argued that only those baptized in adult years could be members of the Serampore church, thus shutting out members of the local church who came from Anglican, Congregational, Independent, Lutheran and Reformed backgrounds. Though Fuller admitted that John Berridge lived a life marked by 'the beauty of holiness — of holiness almost matured', he still could not accept those from other denominations as 'real Christians'.[33]

The modern idea that Gill opposed Whitefield[34] seems to go back to a quote from W. T. Whitley in his *Calvinism and Evangelism in England especially among Baptists*, in which the historian writes: 'In the very years when Gill shut himself in his study to expound the New Testament, George Whitefield was preaching several times daily to thousands of people on Newington Common and Blackheath and Kennington Common.' The point drawn from this quote is that as Gill was a non-offer man, he could not support Whitefield's kind of evangelism and thus felt that Whitefield's mass evangelism to sinners was wrong. It also suggests that Gill left preaching to others whilst he wasted his time in his study instead of evangelizing.[35]

Gill was a pastor and not an itinerant evangelist. He had a flock to look after and though Whitefield preached daily throughout the country, visiting some areas but once, Gill kept up a solid teaching ministry to the same flock for over fifty years. Whitefield had his thousands, Whitely tells us, but Gill had at least his hundreds and, over a period of very many years, he probably reached over a thousand a week with the gospel.[36] The idea that Gill sat in his study whilst other preachers were doing the work of an evangelist is quite wrong as Gill's commentaries were products of his pulpit work. They grew out of the five or so preaching activities he had a week at his own church besides his preaching and lecturing activities in other churches and lecture halls. James Hervey cautioned Whitefield and Wesley about overestimating itinerant work and he agreed with Gill that the calling of a teacher-pastor to a certain flock was a true gospel calling and not to be underestimated in comparison with itinerant work.[37]

One of the main dangers of using the phrase 'free offer' is that its users invariably become embarrassed as to what they should include in the offer and to whom it should be free. This, just as invariably, leads them into metaphysical speculations in their eagerness to analyse the will of God concerning to whom and what is to be preached. Robert Hall, in his article on John Foster's essays published in the *Eclectic Review*, complains of those who 'choose rather to strike into the dark and intricate by-paths of metaphysical science, than to pursue a career of useful discovery'.[38] This danger is nowhere more evident than in the writings of free-offer enthusiasts who with greater or lesser surgical skills strive to dissect the mind of God into its desires and decrees; original intentions and subsequent intentions; revealed will and secret will; original design and modified design; special love and universal love; common grace and saving grace. Particularly the Fullerite dissecting of man into his supposedly non-fallen and fallen elements, and his presumed natural and moral abilities is to be questioned.[39] This is all very interesting mental gymnastics (a term used by the philosophers and theologians of the Enlightenment school for such thinking), and has its place, no doubt, in special works, but it is not the work of an evangelist to speculate in this way. His business is to preach the whole gospel where and to whom he is sent. He does not bring the same message to all men, as to some it comes as a message of death and damnation alone and to others it accomplishes a raising from the dead. This was the view of John Gill.

The gospel preached can be likened to the Apostles' fishing expedition in John 21. Without Jesus to guide them the would-be fishermen caught nothing. When they cast out their net in accordance with Christ's will, it was filled. The disciples did not know where the fish were or which fish they should catch. They did what they were told and they were successful. The Bible is full of advice as to how the gospel should be preached. Sinners must be called, commanded, even beseeched to repent and turn from their evil ways. God commands all to repent and grants repentance to some who would not otherwise repent. It is presumptuous to believe that we can offer, in God's name, that repentance and that turning. This would be foolishly thinking that we can take God's initiative in salvation. It would be casting the net on the wrong side of the ship.

Perhaps, to preserve the bonds of peace, we should have no quarrel with those who use the term 'free offer' yet preach the full gospel, though they may be unwise to use the term as it is ambiguous to the point of being quite misleading. It is another matter, however, with those who have broken the peace themselves and say that saints such as John Gill are Antinomians and Hyper-Calvinists because they do not use the term 'free offer'. This erroneous position must be condemned. By their fruits God's servants are known and not by the way they coin phrases or stick to shibboleths. Anyone who studies the life and teaching of John Gill will find that he remained as close as few have ever remained to the gospel pattern from his conversion to his death. It would thus be better to drop the phrase altogether than use it to condemn a great fisherman and to confuse the issue concerning where and when and for what fish the gospel net has to be cast out.

When Robert Hall Senior wrote his *Helps to Zion's Travellers*, he was perhaps over-careful in warning of the 'stumbling block' of emphasizing election and predestination, but he was very true to the gospel when he said, 'If any should ask, Have I a right to apply to Jesus the Saviour, simply as a poor, undone perishing sinner, in whom there appears no good thing? I answer yes; the gospel proclamation is, Whosoever will, let him come.'[40]

As shown in the chapter *The pastor in the pulpit* and in this appendix, this is a sentiment that fully expressed Gill's mind, whatever his reservations were in using the expression 'free offer'.

Appendix II:
John Gill on linguistics and Hebrew vocalization

During the late eighteenth and early nineteenth centuries, the Grimm brothers in Germany, famous for their collection of fairy tales, following Rasmus Kristian Rask in Denmark, began to see how inter-related languages were and how each language had grown apart from the next through definable laws of sound shifts which made it comparatively easy to spot relationships in languages and subsequently easier to learn foreign languages. One of these sound shifts is the movement from 'c' as in 'Carl' and 'cornet' to 'ch' as in 'Charles' and 'h' as in 'horn'. Most modern English-speaking people will find it easy to relate 'Carl' or 'Karl' to 'Charles' but may not realize that the word 'horn' is, linguistically speaking, the same word as 'corner' or 'cornet', being related to Latin 'cornu' which means 'a horn' as in the English loan-word 'cornucopia', a horn of plenty. In the same way a 'p' in a word, through the course of time, can develop into an 'f' or even a 'v' so that the Latin 'pater' is obviously the same word as English 'father' and German 'Vater'. These words also show that 't' and 'th' signify variants of the same sound as are also 'b' and 'v' as seen in German 'ich habe' and its English equivalent 'I have'. The sound signified by 'ch' often becomes a mere aspirate or drops out completely at the end of a word, so the German 'ich' is obviously an earlier variant of the English 'I'. The same can be said for a final 'n' which often drops out in the development of a word. Many English verbs had an 'n' ending which has now dropped, such as O.E. grasen = to graze. On comparing words in different languages, one soon spots that the sounds depicted by 's' and 't' are inter-related as in the English 'Water' and the German 'Wasser'. Once these consonantal and corresponding vowel changes are mastered, language learning becomes a joy and not the tiresome business of learning paradigms and glossaries merely by rote. These studies were carried out within Indo-Germanic languages, it being commonly thought at this period that Indo-Germanic languages such as Dutch and Hindi, and Semitic languages such as Arabic and Hebrew belonged to different families and were not related.

The interesting point is that Gill had already published a 325-paged treatise dealing, amongst other things, with sound shifts in 1767, half a century before Jacob Grimm entered the field. Furthermore, Gill did not confine his interest in sound shifts to the Indo-Germanic languages but established a linguistic relationship between that language group and the Semitic languages as his comparison of Greek and Hebrew shifts in pronunciation and sounds show. Gill also demonstrated that the sound shifts within the Indo-Germanic languages had exact parallels within the Semitic languages as in the Hebrew 'Ish' and 'Ishah', meaning 'man' and 'woman', and the word for 'women' in the Chaldee and Syriac of Onkelos which is 'Ittetha'. Modern research, based on the findings of such pioneers as Gill and Rask, has moved on in leaps and bounds since those days. Socio-Pragma-linguistics, as also Noam Chomsky's ingenious work in generative and transformational grammar, have shown that though languages have surface structures determined by local factors such as culture, religion, work, politics etc., the deep structures of almost all the world's languages are the same. With the recognition of these sound shift laws and a shared underlying language structure, the story of Babel receives new significance. Sadly, however, linguistic research into the growth and development of the Hebrew language has scarcely brought anything new to light since Gill's discoveries.

Gill made his findings in a roundabout way. He lived in the infant period of Higher Criticism when learned men began to feel they had to apologize for admitting that they believed the Bible. Just as the theory was spread that the Messianic message of the Old Testament was a 'later gloss', so Bible critics maintained that the Hebrew texts of the Bible which had survived had quite lost their original form which would be now meaningless even if it were produced. They maintained that the original texts were only written in consonantal form without the vowels which were added as a 'later gloss', at a venture by Massoretic scribes in Tiberias (dated variously between five hundred and a thousand years after Christ), to help pronunciation. They are said to have done this not knowing what that pronunciation was or whether they were using the correct vowel sounds or not. This view is, of course, a complete overstatement as witnessed by modern Israeli newspapers which carry unpointed text. Nobody would accuse today's Jewish readers of getting their facts wrong because they were reported without vowel signs. James Hervey used to preach from his unpointed Hebrew Bible, being guided by linguistic laws he had learned off by heart which made vocalization unnecessary.

Vowels, however, are essential meaning carriers for many as exemplified in the difference between asking someone to 'run' or 'ruin' one's business. That little 'i' makes all the difference! If, in a letter containing the words, 'Will you please run my business?' the vowels were suddenly to disappear and the receiver merely read 'Wll y pls rn m bsnss?' one might or one might not understand what was being asked.[1] Critics now argued that Hebrew written vocalization, or pointing as it is called by Hebraists, was never part of the original biblical texts. They thus deduced that a reconstruction of the Hebrew Bible was impossible as no one had the foggiest idea what the surviving conglomeration of consonants (called 'radicals' by Hebrew scholars) signified.

Knowing all this, Gill still argued for the historicity of a Hebrew pointing on grounds of archaeological and documentary evidence, sound shifts and the internal testimony of Scripture, especially the words of the Lord Jesus Christ in the Greek text. As biblical Hebrew was rapidly becoming a dead language by the time of the return of the Exiles from their Babylonian captivity, it is not surprising that evidence points to a use of vowel signs after that period to vouchsafe pronunciation by non-native speakers or by Jews who had forgotten their mother tongue. Other Semitic languages, closely related to biblical Hebrew also had vowel signs long before this period. If there were no such things as vowel points until centuries after Christ, Gill argued, how was it that Samaritan coins dated before Christ were decorated with Hebrew pointed script?[2] He also made very much of the Lord's saying in Matthew 5:18: 'Till heaven and earth pass away, one jot or one tittle shall in no wise pass from the law, till all be fulfilled.' Here, Gill points out, the Lord refers to two letters of the law. He mentions the yohd ($\prime$), which is the smallest consonant in Hebrew, pronounced like 'y' in 'you' and the *keraia* (κεραια) or tittle which, Gill explains, is the Hebrew point or dot used in vocalization.[3] Gill did not argue that the 'dot' system in his Hebrew Bible (which has the Massoretic vocalization which we have today) was the original one but rather that it was based on several ancient Semitic pointing systems.

What has all this to do with the Lord's words? A great deal. Expositors had thought traditionally that Jesus was merely referring to every little part of the law. Preachers invariably translated Christ's meaning as 'not a dot on an "i" will disappear from the law', which was not far wrong but not quite right. Using his knowledge of sound shifts, Gill showed that the Hebrew word H_{iriq} (חיריק), which Gill transcribes as 'Chirek', meaning a vowel point, is the very same word as the Greek κεραια used by Christ for our A.V. 'tittle'. Here we have both the 'ch-k' shift as in Charles and Karl and the fact that a k and ch at the end of a word tends to be dropped as in the 'ich-I' shift. Thus Jesus was referring to the very letter that later critics said did not exist until centuries after Christ. He was saying that not one consonant or vowel would disappear from the law.[4] In other words, the Hebrew text with which Jesus was familiar was a pointed text — a text with vowels. Incidentally, the Greek (κεραια) is related to the English word 'horn' ('h' and 'k' are interchangeable as we have seen, and a final 'n' often drops out) and there are three main traditions of vocalization — nobody knows just how old they are — the Babylonian, the Palestinian and the Tiberian which use various kinds of 'horns' to denote vowel signs, moving from the Babylonian ä which looks like a forked deer's antler, through the Palestinian or Samaritan å which looks like a cow's horn, to the Tiberian vowels which are mainly mere dots. The Tiberian vowels are the ones that are used in our present Hebrew text and show the latest development. The Samaritans, during or shortly after the Exile, used the yohd, which also looks like a horn, as a vowel sound as well as a consonant. This is very similar to 'y' in English which is a consonant in the word 'yellow' but a vowel in the name 'Tommy' or the word 'boy'.

Gill went even further in his argumentation concerning Hebrew pointing by arguing that even those vowels that did not appear in contemporary forms as being dots were in fact conglomerates of dots. He pointed out that a Qamats(ㅜ) pronounced like an 'a' in 'card', and a Patah (⸗), pronounced like an 'a' in 'cat', were really conglomerations of dots fused into lines. This may seem rather far-fetched and the idea appears to have been dropped by modern Hebraists who, on the whole, keep clear of modern linguistic findings. This phenomenon is, however, quite common in Indo-Germanic languages. The Swedish 'ä', for instance, with its two dots indicating an 'e' is now written by many Swedes as 'ā' and has, in fact, become the normal cursive form.

With the discovery of the Mescha Stele in 1868 which is dated around 835 B.C. and more recent discoveries of early eighth century ostraca, it has become obvious that various forms of vocalization were used at a very ancient date. Isaiah texts which have been discovered at Qumran, and which are centuries older than the Massoretic texts, are vocalized in varying degrees. It is interesting to note that where various readings have occurred through copying texts, it is mainly because of one consonant being erroneously read for another or that consonants have been carelessly interchanged. There is very little evidence of faulty interpretation due to vocalization and where this does occur the change in meaning is negligible.[5]

Gill, working backwards through history, studied an enormous amount of Hebrew literature to prove his point. Starting with works around the year 1037, the date Higher Critics argued Ben Asher and Ben Naphtali had 'invented' the vowel signs, Gill showed that they were already in general use at the time and there were even printed vocalized versions of the Bible. Gill quotes writers from those days who stressed that vocalization was of divine and ancient authority. He then shows how there was a book written on the importance of Hebrew pointing around 929 by a Saadiah Gaon and that in 900 writers testified to an MS being kept at St Dominia in Bononia which had vowel points and was said to have been written in Ezra's day. It was presented to the monastery at that early date because of its antiquity. Gill then goes on to quote writers from the eighth century and earlier who speak of 'the excellency and elegance of the vowel points' and shows that the fifth-sixth century discussions concerning the Ketib and Quere readings of the Babylonian Talmud must have been based on a pointed text. Coming to the year 385, Gill shows how Jerome used vocalized texts as he complained that he could not read the tiny dots by candlelight. Fifteen years further back in history, Gill refers to a Hebrew rules book by Rabbi Ase, the head of the Sura Academy, with a special section on the vowel points. Next Gill calls upon the Rabbot, the Jerusalem Talmud, references to Origen's *Hexalpa* and his commentary on Matthew, as evidence. He demonstrates that Irenaeus knew of 15 different vowel letters in the Hebrew and Clement of Alexandria refers in 190 to the Hebrew accents and points in his *Stromateis*. The Targums of Jonathan and Onkelos, which predate Christ's incarnation, are quoted as evidence for early pointing as also the works of Josephus. The year 40 B.C. brings Gill to the works of Rabbi Nechuniah Ben Kanah who is quoted as saying of the Hebrew script, 'Letters are like to the body, and points to the soul. For the points move the letters as the soul moves the body.' Gill then mentions how, as far back as 277 B.C., Ptolemy Philadelphus, King of Egypt, told his officials to place a vocalized Hebrew Bible in his library. Finally Gill follows Bishop Usher's theory that Ezra repointed the Hebrew text of the Jewish Bible on their return from Babylon around 454. Thus Gill can conclude that the Hebrew pointing goes back to the dawn of the Old Testament in its written form.

References

Chapter 1   Introduction

1 Otherwise called the Arminian Baptists.
2 See Rippon's *The Life and Writings of John Gill, D. D.*, p. 27.
3 It is customary to refer to the eighteenth-century Anglican Bible-believing ministers as 'Evangelicals' and Bible-believers in general as 'evangelicals'.
4 Written 18 January 1755.
5 Taken from Rippon's *Life and Writings of the Rev. John Gill, D.D.* and passim.
6 See Glossary.
7 Hervey died in 1758.
8 *History of the English Baptists, vol. 3,* London, 1830, p. 272.
9 Diary entry for Sunday 13 December 1767, *Works*, p. 4.
10 John Collet Ryland, *The Beauty of Social Religion*, circular letter, Northamptonshire Baptist Association, 1777, p. 7.
11 See Lloyd-Jones' Preface to J. H. Alexander's moving book, *More than Notion*, containing biographies of several generations of Huntingtonians.
12 This was included in subsequent editions of Gill's commentaries.
13 From Toplady's contribution to the 1772 biography, *Sermons and Tracts*, vol. I.
14 See John R. Broome, *Dr John Gill*, p. 10.
15 Nettles, *By His Grace and for His Glory*, p. 131.
16 I do concede that modern Fullerites misunderstand Fuller and Ryland. Fuller, for instance, admitted that Gill did not take part in the 'Modern Question' debate and Ryland exonerates Gill from the more extreme charges of Hyper-Calvinism. See Fuller's *Works*, vol. iii, p. 422, also Ryland's *Memoir of Mr Fuller*, Button & Son, 1818, p. 6. n..
17 *Biographia Evangelicala*, vol. iv, p.458.
18 *Task*, Book VI, lines 751-758.

Chapter 2   The world of 1697

1 See the chapters on eighteenth-century language and literature in J.H. Whiteley's book *Wesley's England* for numerous examples of the changes taking place.
2 Author not known.

[3] With the subtitle *The Gospel a republication of the Religion of Nature*, Matthew Tindal (1637-1733).

[4] John Toland (1670-1722).

[5] Tillotson's works distinguish themselves from the sheer rationalism of the other works mentioned. In many ways he strove to expound the Bible evangelically as his sermons show, yet he emphasized too much the abilities of man rather than the grace of God. In this his teaching was very similar to that of much Baptist teaching after Gill's death.

[6] Tillotson's emphasis.

[7] Taken from *The Works of the Most Reverend Dr John Tillotson*, London, 1704, p. 5.

[8] See Culross' *The Three Rylands*, p. 25.

[9] See Watts' *The Dissenters*, pp. 164-168.

[10] See J. Jackson Goadby, *Bye-Paths in Baptist History* for a wider discussion of Baptist title-bearers.

[11] See B. R. White, *The English Baptists of the 17th Century*, pp. 114-116.

[12] *Mr Russel of White Street*, BQ, 28, 1980, p. 380.

[13] In the days of Abraham Booth's presidency over the Jamaica Coffee House club, we find that the pastors' subscription had to be raised by 16 shillings because of the large amount of tobacco the brethren consumed.

[14] *A History of British Baptists*, p. 130.

Chapter 3   The birth of an infant prodigy

[1] See Glossary for o.s.

[2] Encyclopaedia of Religious Knowledge Vol. II. p. 874.

[3] A Summary of the Life, Writings, and Character of the late Reverend and Learned John Gill, D.D., *Sermons and Tracts*, 1772.

[4] Taken from Neal, *History of the Puritans*, vol. iii, Klock & Klock reprint of Tegg 1837 edition, 1978, p. 565. It is interesting to note that no distinction is made here between the local church and the Church universal and invisible. There is a hint of this, however, in Article 47 but again, this reference is to the same kind of Baptist 'compact and knit city' and would not apply to other Dissenting churches. As few Baptist creeds took the matter of the universal church into account, this made their inter-local-church-fellowship a matter of great difficulty.

[5] According to Geoffrey F. Nuttall, the Little Meeting revised its church covenant in 1768 barring the 'unbaptized' i.e. those who had not entered into church membership through believers' baptism, from the Lord's Table. *Northants, and the Modern Question*, p. 120.

[6] The 1772 biography, p. v.

[7] Taken from Gill's preface to Davis' *Hymns Composed on Several Subjects*, London 1748.

[8] *A Brief memoir*, p. 8.

[9] Grants were divided into three classes. On 13 May 1718, Gill was ordered a 'first class' grant of £9. 8s 72^d. As the total amount of money available was divided between the 19 candidates, this would explain the odd amount. Another undated entry says that Gill received the largest grant amongst 99 candidates from England and Wales. This may be a reference to the 13 May entry. On 19 August 1719 Gill was given a further grant of £5. This is again entered in the full 1719 list of recipients. The entry for 4 August 1724 shows Gill at the head of the list of members of the Fund Committee. In that year Gill's church contributed £28 to the fund. Evidence from Crosby's *Journal* suggests that Gill received further personal grants, even as a pastor, which were paid him at Crosby's discretion.

[10] These remarks are to be found in Crosby's *Journal* p. 144 ff. which is a direct continuation of Stinton's *Journal* in the same volume.

Chapter 4 Making his calling and election sure

[1] Goadby, in his *Bye-Paths in Baptist History*, quotes the necessary qualifications for the deaconesses of the Broadmead Church, Bristol, p. 239 ff.

[2] My attention was brought to this by a review of Patricia Craford's book *Women and Religion in England 1500-1720* by Michael A. G. Haykin in *The Baptist Quarterly*, Vol. XXXV, No. 7, July 1944, pp. 359-360. Isaac Marlow had objected to women taking any vocal part in worship (he was thinking of singing) but in his work *Answer to Marlow's Appendix*, Keach maintains that though women must not take on themselves ministerial authority, they ought to publicly be able to testify in disciplinary cases, give an account of their conversion, and declare how the Lord was pleased to work on their hearts. Keach maintained that as singing was in this category it was fitting for the sisters to sing in public worship.

[3] Crosby also appealed to a smaller group of Particular Baptist ministers who met at Blackwell's Coffee House. These appear to have worked subordinate to the Hanover Coffee House fraternal.

[4] Crosby's *Journal*, p. 161.

[5] Ernest Payne published the relevant passages dealing with the ordination of deacons from the Goat Yard and Carter Lane church book in an article entitled *The Appointment of Deacons*, BQ, NSV XVII, 1957-58, pp. 87-91.

[6] Crosby's *Journal*, p. 168.

[7] A number of further letters were sent by Crosby to the coffee-house which did not affect matters. These can be read in Crosby's *Journal*.

[8] Crosby's *Journal* p. 175.

[9] For a full account see Crosby's *Journal* p. 180 ff.

[10] Always called Skeep by Crosby in his *Journal* and the Church Book.

[11] *The Metropolitan Tabernacle: Its History and Work*, p. 40.

[12] Ivimey gives the exception of a Bristol church that traditionally elected a co-pastor. See vol. iv, pp. 283-289.

[13] There were exceptions regarding statements of faith. The London Particular Baptist Board demanded that its members be Calvinists and the Western Association required their members to sign the 1689 Confession from around 1733 onwards. In 1782, for instance, the Kent and Sussex Association headed their Association Letter with a brief statement of faith.

[14] The fact that Goat Lane was originally pewless and had always a fair pewless space perhaps explains the extraordinary high claims concerning how many people the chapel originally could hold. Early claims refer to between 1,200 and 2,000 people. It is obviously easier to pack great numbers into a chapel void of seating than in one filled with pews.

[15] Elizabeth Stinton, Susan Keach, Rachael Carter, Mary Boyd, Rebecca Crosby, Benjamin Stinton, Susan Stinton and Elizabeth Fisher were all disciplined for not 'filling up their places in the Church', but there was a coming and going between the two churches by members of these families for many years afterwards. See Ivimey's account of the two churches in vol. iii of his *History of the English Baptists*.

[16] Crosby, *History of the English Baptists*, vol. iv, p. 395.

[17] *Bye-Paths in Baptist History*, J.J. Goadby, London, 1871, p. 351. Goadby gives a detailed account of the 'union' policies of the coffee-house fraternals and their authority in the churches.

[18] Cf. the Caffynite Controversy, 1686 until early part of eighteenth century.

[19] In 1731 the General Baptist Assembly decided that no member 'should preach, write, or urge in discourse such controversies about the doctrine of the Holy Trinity, which shall be unto the disturbance of the Churches'. In other words, everyone could believe as he wished, providing he kept quiet about it.

[20] The more Gill gained influence in the churches, the more the Particular Baptists took care to distinguish themselves from the General Baptists until the coffee-house 'union' was

abolished and the Calvinists formed their own separate body in 1723/24 which became known as the Baptist Board.

[21] Various attempts were made to start new fraternals at the Gloucester, Blackwell's and Cole's Coffee Houses and also at the King's Head in St Swithin's Alley. These clubs apparently were open to all Dissenting ministers who met on Tuesdays around a common meal provided by a wealthy member of Currier's Hall. Dr Sayer Rudd, the Particular Baptist pastor, took over the leadership in 1730 but was asked to leave less than four years later because of his Arian beliefs. See Rippon's *Brief Memoir*, p. 117. Roger Hayden in his *English Baptist History & Heritage* (Baptist Christian Training Programme) mentions on p. 75 Donald Turner's view stated in his *Compendium of Social Religion* (1758) that Particular Baptist ministers should be called to the 'church in general', but Hayden argues that Gill's view was the complete opposite i.e. that a pastor 'may not act ministerially in any other congregation' than his own. This was not quite Gill's position. Though he was suspicious of associations, which is Hayden's topic here, Gill was enormously influential in the work of the Baptist Board founded 1723/24 for convinced Calvinists only and in the work of the Particular Baptist Fund. The Baptist Board worked closely with the Presbyterian and Independent boards and became part of the Three Denominations representing the churches before the Crown.

[22] *The English Baptists of the 18th century*, pp. 47-48.

[23] *A History of British Baptists*, p. 178.

[24] The breaking away of what came to be the Maze Pond church.

[25] See Elias Keach's *The Glory and Ornament of a True Gospel-Constituted Church* and Benjamin Keach's *The Gospel Minister's Maintenance Vindicated*.

[26] *The English Baptists of the 18th Century*, p. 48.

[27] For instance, a poor widow was given a shilling a day as a pew-opener in the galleries at Carter Lane to help her overcome her poverty and be usefully occupied.

[28] Church statistics from this period are difficult to evaluate as they were drawn up according to widely different criteria. It was still common amongst some churches merely to list male members, others listed pew-owners, regular communicants etc. See Ivimey, vol. 3, pp. 278-279 for Ryland's statistics. Mr Stephen Pickles has drawn my attention to the fact that if one adds up the numbers of the eight churches Ryland lists, they give an average membership of 76 and not 50 as Ryland suggests. Ryland also omits the membership of Eagle Street, Prescot Street and Unicorn Yard.

[29] See Pamela Russel's *Mr Russel of White Street*, BQ, XXVIII, 1980, p. 373-383.

[30] *John Gill: Baptist Theologian*, pp. 300-301.

[31] Rippon's *Life and Writings of the Rev. John Gill, D.D.*, p. 20.

[32] This baptistery was for many years the only building of its kind in London. It was enlarged and new dressing rooms added in 1717 and registered under the Toleration Act. Ivimey mentions that there was also a baptistery at Paul's Alley, Barbican, but this would hardly have attracted orthodox Calvinists.

[33] The neglected baptistery had been repaired under Stinton's orders in 1717 and he had organized the building of the chapel. The local bishop had insisted that it should be officially certified under his authority.

[34] See *Dr John Gill's Confession of 1729*, Seymour J. Price, BQ, IV, 1928. Price, quite contrary to the facts, looks on Gill as a 'true Baptist' because he feels that Gill shared the usual Baptist scorn for creeds. Price also says that were Gill alive in 1928 he 'would refuse to be bound by his own credal expression. Possibly he would turn to the Declaration of Principle as printed in the Constitution (1926) of the Baptist Union and there find all that is needful to say.' Suffice it to say that Gill was bound by his own confession for fifty years until his death during which period many unionistic 'confessions' came and went without tempting Gill in the least from his own.

[35] Ivimey, vol. 2, p. 91.

[36] See Goadby, *Bye-paths of Baptist History*, p. 121.

[37] See Arnold H. J. Baines, *The Signatories of the Orthodox Confession of 1679*, BQ, vii, 1957-8, pp. 35-42, 74-86, 170-178. It is not at all clear whether Ivimey was ignorant of the authorship or not. The fact that he, as a 'moderate Calvinist', finds so much with which he agrees in the creed, shows how successful the Arminians were in their endeavours.

Chapter 5   The Goat Yard Declaration of Faith

[1] Most Baptists nowadays prefer to speak of 'confessions of faith' or 'declarations of faith' rather than 'creeds', but the terms are used here as synonyms for variety's sake.

[2] Thus the 1646 confession declares in the provocative nature demanded of the Christian witness of the time: 'If any man shall impose upon us anything that we see not commanded by our Lord Jesus Christ, we should, in His strength, rather embrace all reproaches and tortures of men, to be stripped of all outward comforts, and if it were possible, to die a thousand deaths, rather than do anything against the least tittle of the Word of God, or against the light of our own consciences.'

[3] See Glossary.

[4] See Glossary.

[5] *History of British Baptists,* p. 201.

[6] See Glossary.

[7] Lumpkin, *BCF,* p. 17.

[8] Winthrop S. Hudson obviously does not believe this to be generally the case. See his *Who were the Baptists?*, *BQ*, vol. xvii, 1957-8, pp. 53-55.

[9] See Olin C. Robinson's *The Legacy of John Gill*, BQ, xxvi, 1971, p. 122, also Seymour J. Price, *Dr Gill's Confession of 1729*, BQ, iv, 1928, p. 371.

[10] Their own works confute them. See the articles by Robert Oliver and Robert Sheehan in *Foundations*, 7,8,9, 1981-82. These authors argue that churches who adopted Gill's and Huntington's views declined and that their brand of Calvinism was not accepted by other pastors. The truth is that 'Gillism' spread far and wide amongst all denominations. Oliver contradicts his own negative image of Gill, Huntington and the Particular Baptists in matters of church growth by saying that Huntington had an 'immense following' and Gadsby, a Particular Baptist if ever there was one, was 'heard gladly' and he 'combined a prosperous pastorate with an extensive itinerant ministry' founding no less than forty new churches! It is interesting to note that Gadsby was greeted by packed churches in London where Oliver maintains that Particular Baptist outreach had waned. This would suggest that where the doctrines of Huntington and Gadsby were not preached, those churches declined. Sheehan agrees with Oliver in arguing that Gill, Huntington, Styles etc. were 'Hyper-Calvinists' who caused evangelism to wane, but his examples refute his argument as these were highly successful ministers who preached to thousands. Gill was certainly the most well known and effective Baptist pastor in the London of his day, as was Independent Huntington in his. Gadsby was the most successful preacher in the North and, though Spurgeon was attracting thousands not far off, Styles and Wells in London could still fill their churches though faced with such 'competition'! According to Ryland's statistics mentioned above, Gill, at Goat Yard's lowest level of membership, had considerably more members than 'moderate' Stennett, another leading London minister. Stennett edited Alvery Jackson's *The Question Answered*. See Ivimey, vol. iii, p. 271.

[11] See Rippon's biography of Gill, p. 14.

[12] *Further History of the Gospel Standard Baptists*, vol. 5, p. 289. I am grateful to Mr Stephen Pickles for pointing this out to me.

[13] See John R. Broome's booklet entitled *Dr John Gill* for a most positive appraisal of Gill's faith and teaching. Also *What Gospel Standard Baptists Believe*, Gospel Standard Trust Publications.

[14] See especially Chapter XXVI.

[15] They believe that the covenant of works has been done away with for saint and sinner alike and that the law was never meant to be a bringer of life, could it be kept.

[16] Chapter X, Article 3. Curteis, whom this author previously followed in his criticism of the 1677 declaration, gives Chapter X wrongly as declaring 'Infants dying in infancy are regenerated,' as if the Particular Baptists believed in the salvation of all those who die in infancy. See *Dissent in its Relation to the Church of England*, p. 244.

[17] Here it is admitted that infants are 'in Adam' but it is claimed that this status brings with it mere physical death but not eternal punishment. The Scriptures teach, however, that the words 'death reigned from Adam' and 'for as in Adam all die' refer to the spiritual and penal death which those who are 'in Christ' will not experience. In other words, being 'in Adam' is no guarantee of eternal life but being 'in Christ' is. See Rom. 5:14; 1 Cor. 15:22.

[18] Kiffin has been described as 'the father of Particular Baptists'. See B. A. Ramsbottom's excellent little book *Stranger than Fiction: The Life of William Kiffin*, Gospel Standard Trust Publications, 1989.

[19] See 'Concerning immediate Revelation' and 'Concerning the Scriptures' in *A Concise View of the Chief Principles of the Christian Religion, as Professed by the People called Quakers*, quoted in full by Neal, vol. iii, pp. 569-571.

[20] Stinton/Crosby *Journal*, p. 130. Crosby lists all of Stinton's pleas for extending the sources and scope of the fund, including his argument that Presbyterians would think the Particular Baptists uncharitable, it would give offence to 'several worthy and generous gentlemen' and stop fellowship with churches who have become mixed in doctrine 'for the public good'.

[21] Pp. 121-123. Crosby gives quite a different rendering in his Appendix to vol. 3 of his *History of the English Baptists*.

[22] Modalists maintain that the whole of the undivided divine essence is in either the Father, the Son or the Holy Spirit, according to the mode in which God is revealing himself at the time. There are thus, in their unscriptural view, no three persons in the Trinity but they *could* accept the above-quoted definition.

[23] *Church History Research & Archives*, second reprint, 1979, vol. iii, pp. 116, 280, iv, pp. 328-342.

[24] This is not a general recommendation of Tertullian's concept of the Trinity. In Apol. xxi he uses the phrase 'produced from God' of the Incarnation and in Adv. Prax. he refers to Christ as 'part' of the divine Substance. His imagery of the Father being the sun and Christ being a beam from the Father is not always helpful in explaining the unity of the Godhead. Hence even Tertullian has been accused of Subordinationism, though in the context he is merely trying to explain the phrase 'My father is greater than I' (John 14:28). Elsewhere, however, he refers to the pre-existent, eternal immanence of the Son in the Father so, as Schaff suggests, perhaps Tertullian's figurative language should not be taken too strictly in view of the specific problems he was seeking to solve at the time i.e. Patripassianism. See Schaff's *History of the Christian Church*, vol. ii, p. 555.

[25] *The Story of the English Baptists*, p. 153.

[26] *A History of the English Baptists*, p. 146.

[27] The numerous Scripture references Gill gives have been omitted.

[28] P. 81.

[29] See Goadby, op. sit. pp. 29-34, 106-107.

[30] *Works, The Reality and Efficacy of Divine Grace*, Letter X, vol. II, pp. 546-547, n. See also *Works, II*, p. 438. Fuller argues that man is totally depraved in his will but not in other natural abilities. Even this view is modified, however, as he at times suggests that man is not 'totally unable to believe in Christ', suggesting that man has a will to do so, if he would only use it.

[31] See comments on Fuller's limited view of the Fall in the next chapter.

[32] See Glossary.

[33] See Glossary.

[34] See the chapters on the Sonship controversy and the separation of the Gospel Standard churches in *Historical Sketch of the Gospel Standard Baptists*, S.F. Paul, 1961. J. C. Philpot

played a major role in combating this heresy amongst the Baptists.

[35] See his work *The Question Answered. Whether saving faith in Christ is a duty required by the moral law of all those who live under the Gospel revelation* (1752). Nowadays the 'Modern Question' would be called 'The Modernist Question 'as its theology is basically that represented by Karl Barth believing that there is an Esau and a Jacob in every man until either the one is cancelled out by the other through either rejecting or accepting the gospel. The true state of man after the Fall and before hearing the gospel is not given due attention.

[36] *Works*, Vol. VI, 1833, p. 144.

[37] See Underwood, p.170 for the full story.

[38] Jones, *Bunhill Memorials*, p. 60.

[39] *Picking up a Pin for the Lord*, p. 167. Naylor is commenting on John 5:34 and argues that Gill limits the words 'but these things I say, that ye might be saved', to the temporal preservation of the Jews only. This is, however, only one of several interpretations Gill gives, referring the bulk of his arguments to salvation in a spiritual sense.

[40] Pp. 91-92.

[41] Justification through the imputed righteousness of Christ was held, of course, by the Puritans including Baptists Bunyan and John Noble (1660-1730) and Presbyterian Cotton Mather. Judging by the words Edward Wallin (1678-1733) preached at Noble's funeral, he too believed the doctrine, as did all sound men everywhere as it is the doctrine of the New Testament. Not only the Arminians but the so-called 'Evangelical Calvinists' or 'Moderate Calvinists' dropped preaching this christocentric doctrine for a more man-centred evangelism in the eighteenth century.

[42] See James Hervey's eleven letters to Wesley on the subject in the various editions of Hervey's works. Also Owen op. sit. p. 113. and the various articles on the righteousness of Christ in Wesley's *Journals*. Also my BLQ essay, *Whose Righteousness Saves Us?*

[43] Gill's contribution to the debate on baptism will be discussed further in the chapter entitled 'Defender of the faith'.

[44] Even the 'Modern Question' adherents differed widely in their doctrine of baptism. Fuller had a very 'closed' High Church view of the matter, whereas Dr John Ryland had an 'open' view which was far less ritualistic than his friend's. Ryland wished the churches founded by Carey to practise open communion as they were supported by many Anglicans. Fuller protested strongly at this, regarding Anglican Evangelicals as 'less than Christian'. Fuller won the day and the Indian missionaries complained that they had to drop sweet fellowship with other Christians so as not to rock the home boat.

[45] Gill did practise the laying on of hands at the ordination of his deacons in the same service in which hands were laid on him. His first new members were also welcomed by his laying hands on them. This practice may have been due to the presence and influence of his fellow 'elders' and was quickly dispensed with.

[46] See Louis Benson's *The English H'ymn* and J. J. Goadby's *Bye-paths of Baptist History* for a full discussion of this topic.

[47] They argued that singing was neither a gospel, nor a church ordinance.

[48] *A History of the Baptists*, vol. ii, pp. 548-550.

[49] Early adherents of Source Criticism demonstrated their lack of serious scholarship by declaring that the original text of several psalms had been mutilated as it no longer rhymed. They even suggested rhyming endings in order to 'restore' the original text. This unscholarly practice was used in leading European universities until way into the 1970s! It was an Evangelical of the Church of England, Bishop Lowth, who first described the Hebrew synonymous, antithetic and synthetic forms of parallelism. See his *De sacra poesie Hebræorum*, 1753, or *Lectures on The Sacred Poetry of the Hebrews* (translated by G. Gregory), 1839. It is interesting to note that 1753 was also the year that Jean Astruc published his notorious *Conjectures* which ushered in destructive biblical criticism and unfounded speculations on the Hebrew O.T. text.

[50] See *Lectures on Hebrew Poetry*. p. 393 ff. for a refutation of the 'similarity of terminations'

theory.

[51] Michael Watts in his *Dissenters,* p. 310, says that the anti-singing faction was excommunicated by Keach, but no sources are given for this information. According to Brown, p. 48, Marlow left London for Leominster.

[52] Many church historians follow Ivimey (vol. 2, pp. 431-432) in claiming that Maze Pond were guilty of 'disusing' singing in their services. This is quite false. They did not 'disuse' singing but refused to jump on the new bandwagon and start singing.

[53] *John Gill: Baptist Theologian*, p. 266.

[54] *The English Baptists of the 18th Century*, Raymond Brown, Gen. Ed. B. R. White, Tyndale Press, pp. 92-93.

[55] See Rippon, pp. 38-39.

[56] *A Discourse on Singing Psalms as a Part of Divine Worship*, London, 1734, p. 21.

[57] P. 5.

[58] *Institutes*, Book II, Chap. 7.

[59] See Goadby's rather unbalanced account of the three-day conference in *Bye-paths in Baptist History*, pp. 213-216.

[60] See *Sermons and Tracts* vol. I, sermons on Rom. 3:31, Deut. 10:5. See also Gill's essay *Of the Law of God* in vol. i., BDD.

Chapter 6   The voice of the Beloved

[1] Underwood, Abbey, Overton etc. call Whiston 'William Whiston' but he is recorded by Ivimey as 'Matthew Whiston'.

[2] *The English Church in the 18th Century*, pp. 202-204.

[3] John Brine published a 406-paged octavo volume against Foster's teaching in 1746.

[4] See J. C. Philpot's extensive series of articles on Gill's Song in his *Reviews*, vol. i., pp. 377-407.

[5] Hervey's *Works*, 1837, *Theron and Aspasio*, Letter IX, p. 380.

[6] S of S 1:2. The quote is from Jones' 1854 Preparatory Address to Doudney's edition of Song of Solomon.

[7] Crosby was obviously influenced by Gale. See his remarks on Gale's book *An History of the notion of original sin*, p.369. Chap. IV of *A Short Confession or a Brief Narrative of faith* which Crosby appended to his fourth volume maintains that original sin 'does not destroy our liberty which we had naturally', which became the slogan of later Fullerites.

[8] *Works*, Vol. II, *The Reality and Efficacy of Divine Grace*, p. 546 ff. Fuller apparently argues in this way as he believes that man could not be held responsible for sinning or for rejecting Christ unless he had a natural awareness.

[9] See Chap. X, 'John Gill and Eternal Justification' in *Picking up a Pin for the Lord.* Naylor argues that Gill was 'confused' in his doctrine of Christ's eternal love for his bride (p.179). Naylor himself, however, confuses the issue by arguing *in time* for what Gill places *before* and *outside* of time. Naylor's arguments are all of the 'what-came-first-the-chicken-or-the-egg kind. He stresses the apparent human side of the picture i.e. that justification appears to be linked *in time* to an exercise of faith as if the latter sparks off the former. Gill's sound theology stresses God's side, i.e. that both faith and justification are direct gifts of God planned before time as an expression of his love.

[10] Deuteronony 32:2.

[11] John 15:16.

[12] Not merely here but in scores of places elsewhere, some of which will be pointed out in this biography.

[13] Revelation 22:20.

Chapter 7   The defender of the faith

[1] From *An Elegy on the Death of the Rev. John Gill, DD*, John Fellows, London, 1771.

[2] I Peter 1:10-11.

[3] See John 5:39, 46, and Luke 24:27, 44.

[4] See, for instance, Abbey and Overton on Collins in their *The English Church in the Eighteenth Century* and Wesley Bready's *England Before and After Wesley*.

[5] From September 1737 to February 1738 several church meetings were called to discuss how James Hart should be disciplined for 'occasional conformity' at a church of another faith and order.

[6] Mentioned in chapter five when dealing with the 1729 Declaration of Faith.

[7] See a brief discussion of Watts' views of Scripture in relation to worship and his ideas concerning hymn-singing in my *William Cowper: Poet of Paradise*, pp. 197-8, 228-30.

[8] See Gill's *S.&T.*, vol. 3 pp. 512-555.

[9] See Glossary.

[10] Charles Hardwick, *A History of the Articles of Religion*, Cambridge, 1859. p. 90.

[11] Schwenkenfeld's teaching is still looked upon as a 'continuation of the Reformation' by certain British Baptists and Charismatics such as the Apostolic Church and is still very widespread amongst evangelicals on the Continent.

[12] The distinction between Particular and General Baptists seems to have been little understood by the Establishment. Baptists were Baptists!

[13] See Lumpkin, p. 339 'Of Reprobation' from the 1691 *A Short Confession or a Brief Narrative*. See also Lumpkin p. 330 'Of Children dying in Infancy', Article XLIV of The Orthodox Creed and Lumpkin p. 265 'Of Effectual Calling', Chap. X. of the Second London Confession. Especially Article X. of the Standard Confession of 1660, Lumpkin p. 228 for the teaching that I Cor. 15:22 and Matt. 19:14 apply to 'holy innocents'.

[14] Gill maintained that neither Whiston nor Foster his 'Baptist' pastor were baptized as believers.

[15] Tindale, one of the greatest of British Reformers, argued for immersion but regarded those who declared that a baptism was null and void unless every part of the body became wet were destroying the spiritual meaning of baptism. See *The Work of William Tindale*, S. L. Greenslade, Blackie, 1938, 'Selections from his Works', p. 143.

[16] Underwood, the Baptist historian, obviously favours this sacramental development arguing that they 'alone preserve the full sacramental value of believers' baptism as a means of grace', *A History of the English Baptists*, p. 268 ff.

[17] See C. H. Curteis, Lecture IV, The Baptists in his *Dissent in its Relation to the Church of England*, 1872, p. 211 ff. for traditional criticisms of Baptist ritualism and Charles Hardwick, *A History of the Articles of Religion* for Anglican quarrels with (Ana)Baptist doctrines.

[18] That this belief is still maintained by some Baptist bodies is seen by the more recent republication of D. B. Ray's book *Baptist Succession: A Handbook of Baptist History*, Church History Research & Archives, Tennessee, 1984.

[19] It is argued that as both these methods of baptism are invalid, Smyth could not have been the father of British Baptists. See *Baptist Succession*, D .B. Ray, p. 133.

[20] See J.J. Goadby on marrying outside of a Baptist church in *Bye-Paths in Baptist History*, pp. 264-270, 304-310.

[21] This, of course, occurred some time after Gill's death but is given as an example of General Baptist thinking. The BMS took upon itself, as a para-church movement, the same 'rights' as the old coffee-house fraternals of Gill's days.

[22] See Fuller's articles on the subject in vol. iii of his *Works*, especially his letter to Ward, pp. 503-506, where he argues that Ward, in admitting his Anglican and Lutheran co-workers to the Lord's Supper would be admitting those who were not 'real Christians'. See E. Daniel Potts' article 'I throw away the guns to preserve the ship': A Note on the Serampore Trio, *BQ*, XX, 1963-64, for an excellent discussion of the problem.

[23] See *C. H. Spurgeon and the Baptist Missionary Society* 1863-66, BQ, 1982, 29(7), pp. 319-328. This first stage in Spurgeon's controversy with the down-graders is, strangely enough, left out of modern debate regarding the reasons for the controversy.

[24] Op. sit. p. 121.

[25] *Ibid*, p. 121.

[26] *The Dissenter's Reasons for Separating from the Church of England*, London, 1763, pp. 18-19.

[27] Taken from the fifth edition 1763.

[28] Indeed, those of Gill's persuasion, such as William Rushton in his excellent book *Particular Redemption*, have taken their own churches to task for 'Establishment' thinking in the wake of the new evangelicalism of his day. See Letter Four, 'Observations on the Effects of the Errors and Perverted Gospel', pp. 101 ff.

[29] See Appendix I on the 'free offer' which shows how Gill was second to none in preaching the whole gospel.

[30] Collected Letters CLVI, *Works*, p. 878.

[31] There is some confusion of terminology amongst Baptists, some objecting to the word 'plunge' and 'taken out' or 'come out', preferring 'immersed' and 'raised' as the only correct words to describe baptism. I am following Gill, who used a variety of words to describe the ordinance, closely.

[32] References are to Gill's last work on baptism in his *Body of Divinity*, Book III, Chapter I, Of Baptism.

[33] As in Henry Jessey's church at the split up in 1640 on the question of sprinkling versus dipping.

[34] See John 8, Romans 4, Galatians 3.

[35] P. 78. E. Littleton in his excellent little autobiography gives several beautiful examples of children called by grace whom he considered as sure candidates for baptism.

[36] See R. E. Seymour's *John Gill: Baptist Theologian*, pp. 239-260. Seymour deals critically 'as one Baptist to another' with Gill's doctrine of baptism.

[37] Lumpkin, p. 228.

[38] See Article XLIV of the Orthodox Creed of 1678 and Article X in the 1689 Confession and also the confessions of the English Amsterdam Baptists in Lumpkin's *Baptist Confessions of Faith*, pp. 124-142 (especially p. 127).

[39] See W. E. Spears' *The Baptist Movement in England in the late Seventeenth Century as reflected in the work of Benjamin Keach*. This is a very positive, enthusiastic analysis of Keach's life and work and is excellent in its thorough examination of its subject. P. 164 ff deals with Keach's views on infant baptism.

[40] See 'Of Baptism', pp. 310-312.

[41] *Ibid*. p. 310.

[42] See Watts p. 265. and Ivimey Vol. iii, pp. 228-233.

[43] The story is told with fine humour by Jay in his autobiography, BOT, pp. 329-333.

[44] Gill signed himself 'overseer' in his letters to his church.

[45] *Bye-Paths*, p. 233.

[46] To all intents and purposes, Jessey was a Particular Baptist but I have refrained from calling him such as most modern Particular Baptists seem unwilling to accept open communion ministers as being true Particular Baptists.

[47] Watts mentions nineteen Baptist ministers who were ejected in 1660-62, most of whom practised open membership i.e. open communion. See pp. 160-161.

[48] *History of the Metropolitan Tabernacle*, p. 39.

[49] Vol. iii, pp. 288, 293.

[50] Crosby with other eighteenth-century sources spells Rudd's name 'Rhudd'.

[51] See Neal, *History of the Puritans*, vol. i, p. 42 and also vol. iii, pp. 329-416 entitled *History of the Baptists*.

[52] Formerly in Sheer's Alley, now extinct.

[53] John Russel applied to become a member of the Baptist Board in 1742 but, although supported by his church, was rejected because of doubts concerning his character. His son Joseph, who took over John's pastorate for a while, was, however, disciplined for drinking and John's other son Joshua was disciplined for 'drinking to excess, and of using prophane language'.

[54] *Mr Russel of White Street*, pp. 380-382.

[55] P. 2.

[56] Sadly inner-Baptist controversy concerning closed or open communion has taken the emphasis away from these men's sermons and doctrinal works and the personal testimony of their Christian lives. As later generation Particular Baptists, one could also mention the testimonies of J. C. Philpot, John Warburton, John Kershaw and William Gadsby who are more well known, perhaps because of their proximity to more modern times and the fact that their biographies are still readily available. The Baptist Standard Bearer, Inc. is reprinting Gill and Brine and Pastor Terry Wolever of Springfiels, MO, is reprinting Kinghorn's works.

[57] *Biographia Evangelica*, vol. IV, pp. 458-59.

[58] Op. sit., p. 225.

[59] Taken from John Brown's *Memoirs of Mr. Hervey*, p. 234.

[60] Lines 604-611.

[61] *Baptist History*, p. 442.

[62] *Reviews*, vol. ii, pp. 299-300.

[63] Thomas Yeoman F.R.S. (c. 1704-81) was a leading civil engineer and expert in electricity, a member of College Lane Baptist Church, Northampton.

[64] Isaac Mann Collection, Letters 1742-1831, N.L.W. 1207 D.

Chapter 8 The good news of God's everlasting love

[1] See Rippon p. 27. Johannes Albert Fabricius (1668-1736) listed Gill's *The Prophecies of the Old Testament, respecting the Messiah, considered and proved to be literally fulfilled in Jesus*, written against Collins and Chandler together with most of the literature in this controversy in his bibliographical work *Salutaris Lux Evangelii* (1731).

[2] See the Lessing 'Fragments' *Das Christentum der Vernunft* and *Über die Entstehung der geoffenbarten Religion* (written probably in the 1750s) and especially his *Erziehung des Menschengeschlechts* (1780).

[3] Olin C. Robinson in his BQ article entitled *The Legacy of John Gill* says on page 121, 'Much of the pamphlet answer to Taylor is devoted to a vindication of Crisp.' This is not merely an exaggeration, it is factually quite wrong. Crisp is mentioned in one sentence along with Richardson on page 8 and nineteen lines refer to him along with Hoornbeek, Witsius and Chauncey on pages 9-10. Thus Crisp is dealt with on little more than half a page out of 62 pages.

[4] In 1755 Gill published Dr Crisp's *Works* in two volumes, adding a Memoir and explanatory notes dealing with the passages so often criticized. Hervey argues, however, that these passages 'are not contrary to the pure Word of the Gospel, but to our pre-conceived and legal Ideas'. See Hervey's Letters LXXXIV, XCIII and passim in *Letters to the Right Honourable Lady Francis Shirley* for a fine defence of Crisp.

[5] See Ivimey, vol. 3, pp. 47-56 for an anti-Crisp discussion of the work of the assembly. See also Goadby, pp. 213-216 giving full details of the Lorimer's Hall Association meeting.

[6] Op. sit. p. 150.

[7] See Book III, Chapter XIV of Calvin's *Institutes* (especially pp. 80-81) where a detailed study of the relationship between justification and good works is made. It is interesting to note that writers who are Neonomian in doctrine tend to accuse those such as Crisp, Gill and Huntington, who maintain that the Mosaic Law is eternal, of Antinomianism. Of course, they

are Antinomians in Neonomian eyes as they have not only another gospel but another law. The question is which law is used by God to judge man and pronounce his Son righteous: the Old Testament Law or the New Law of the Neonomians without the Old Law's commanding and condemning power? Which gospel does God use to display his salvation: the gospel of free grace whereby Christ has fulfilled the law on our behalf or the gospel of righteousness under the so-called New Law which man must work out for himself though converted?

[8] See *Calvin: His Life and Times*, Thomas Lawson, pp. 16-17.

[9] See Brown's *Memoirs of the Life and Character of the late Rev. James Hervey*, A. M., 1822, p. 31.

[10] This is a dig at Taylor for changing his views. With the outbreak of the Modern Question theology, diverting the attention in doctrine from what God does to what man is capable of doing, a number of Independents, followed by Particular Baptists, shifted their emphasis. It is obvious that once man's side of salvation is emphasized it is more difficult to maintain that justification is an eternal decree of God.

[11] Galatians 4:6.

[12] Gill argues, however, that faith is a uniting factor in fellowship with the brethren.

[13] This doctrine is as unpopular today as it was in Gill's days. See 'Sin borne away', *Evangelical Times*, April 1994, p. 19. A letter by D. Hunter points out clearly how weak the preaching of the gospel must be without this life-giving factor.

[14] 2 Timothy 1:9.

[15] Ephesians 1:3; 1 Peter 1:4.

[16] Hebrews 2:11.

[17] See also Louis Berkof, *Systematic Theology*, pp. 450 ff. Berkof speaks of an organic, vital, mediated, personal and transforming union.

[18] Taylor's Arminian tendencies have been denied recently by Robert Oliver, in his *A Highly-Biased Biography BOTM*, Issue 376, but modern research is coming round to the opinion that Taylor took the 'wrong' side in the Arminian-Calvinist controversy (see Alan Sell's *The Great Debate*, Walter, 1982, pp. 79, 85,. His contemporaries such as John Gill and John Brine were convinced of this and Brine wrote *A Refutation of Arminian Principles in 1743* against the very views that Taylor had pioneered. Gill combated Taylor's Arminian views on election and good works in *God's Everlasting Love to His Elect* (1732) and *The Necessity of Good Works unto Salvation Considered* (1738). It was Taylor, of course, who helped Fuller change his views concerning the Fall and redemption and Taylor who turned radically from the Five-Point Calvinism of his own father, Richard Taylor. It would be an anachronism to call Taylor a Fullerite as, in many ways, he is the father of Fullerism, but he cannot be called a traditional Calvinist as he was certainly Arminian in his doctrine of election, atonement and good works.

[19] Jeremiah 31:3.

[20] 1 John 4:16.

[21] Malachi 3:6; James 1:17.

[22] Romans 5:6.

[23] John 17:2, 23.

[24] Deuteronomy 10:15.

[25] Psalm 149:4; Jeremiah 32:41; Zephaniah 3:17.

[26] Hebrews 11:6.

[27] Romans 11:27-28.

[28] 1 John 1:8.

[29] Ecclesiastes 7:20.

[30] 1 John 3:9.

[31] Prof. Donald MacLeod addressed this doctrine some years ago and his subsequent writings show how his development of this doctrine has taken him away from traditional Calvinism. See his *Paul's Use of the Term 'The Old Man'*, Banner of Truth Magazine No. 92, pp. 13-19, *Behold Your God*, Christian Focus Publications, 1990. See also *The Death of Confessional Calvinism in Scottish Presbyterianism*, Prof. David J. Engelsma, The Standard Bearer, Vol.

68-69, 1992. In the Banner article, MacLeod bases his argument on the supposition that he has discovered a new interpretation which has been missed since biblical times, and the relevant texts have been wrongly translated by the AV scholars.

[32] Psalm 89:30-33.

[33] Song of Solomon 4:7.

[34] Numbers 23:21.

[35] Recorded by Crosby, iv, pp. 354-355. See Crosby's *Journal* for Stinton's full reasons for opening the fund to wealthy Arminians and liberals, p. 30 ff.

[36] Recorded by Rippon, *Memoir*, pp. 36-37. Spurgeon may be referring to the same incident or a similar one when he says that great effort was made to silence Gill by a number of his free-will enemies and he was often cautioned by his own people to be less rigorous when preaching the truth. He says of his 'eminent predecessor', 'Dr. Gill, was told, by a certain member of his congregation who ought to have known better, that, if he published his book, *The Cause of God and Truth*, he would lose some of his best friends, and that his income would fall off. The doctor said, "I can afford to be poor, but I cannot afford to injure my conscience."' Spurgeon then added, 'and he has left his mantle as well as his chair in our vestry'. See *C. H. Spurgeon Autobiography,* vol. ii. p. 477.

Chapter 9   A saint is slandered

[1] Grace Publications, 1986, p. 114.

[2] *Ibid*, p. 112.

[3] Grace Publications, 1992.

[4] P. 145.

[5] *Ibid*, p. 147.

[6] See Ivimey's *History of the British Baptists*, Vol. 3, p. 449 for full statement. Ivimey is otherwise very critical of Gill.

[7] My emphasis. *Ibid* p.147.

[8] *Historical Survey of English Hyper-Calvinism*, Issue 7, Nov. 1981, p. 8 ff.

[9] Engelsma, no Gillite by any means, in the book quoted above believes that orthodox Calvinism has no room for a 'free offer' but a call to repentance and faith must go out to all who come under the sound of the gospel.

[10] *Cause of God*, p. 170.

[11] Oliver may be using another text to the one Nettles refers to. Though I have checked a number of versions, I cannot find one referring to Gill's argument on p. 315 but the passage is always on p. 170 as given by Nettles.

[12] *Ibid*.

[13] *Ibid*.

[14] Oliver gives the word 'revelation' here.

[15] S.o. Note Gill has 'redemption'.

[16] *The Presentation of the Gospel amongst 'Hyper-Calvinists'*, Issue 8, May 1982, p. 28 ff. *The Presentation of the Gospel amongst Hyper-Calvinists: A Critique*, Issue 9, Nov. 1982, p. 42 ff.

[17] *Works*, vol. iii, p. 344. As so often, Fuller de-theologizes such passages to make them fit into his doctrine of a universal invitation to believe.

[18] Commentary on Acts 8:22, Vol. 8, p. 215. Sheehan gives vol. 5, p. 861 of his edition.

[19] 2 Corinthians 5:20, vol. 8, p. 791 f. Sheehan gives vol. VI, p. 310.

[20] Olive Tree, 1967.

[21] My italics.

[22] Toon takes a general snobbish attitude to those whom he considers 'Hyper-Calvinists', believing that they are lacking in intelligence. In his *EQ* article *The Growth of a*

Supralapsarian Christology, XXIX, 1967, p. 25, he argues that the theology of Thomas Goodwin would become 'a dangerous mode of thought in the hands of less intelligent men'.

[23] Op. sit. p. 86.

[24] *Ibid*, p. 146.

[25] *Ibid*, p. 147.

[26] *A History of the Baptists*, vol. ii, p. 561.

[27] John Dogget's review of *Picking Up a Pin for the Lord, ET*, Aug. 1993, p. 20.

[28] See Calvin's reply to the accusations brought on by the publication of his *The Eternal Predestination of God* in *Calvin's Calvinism, The Secret Providence of God*. The quote is from p. 266.

[29] Vol. VIII, § 113 Predestination, p. 553.

[30] *Ibid.*

[31] *The Doctrine of Predestination*, p. 118.

[32] Vol. II, p. 206 of the 1979 Eerdmans two-volumed edition. See Wesley's 'Predestination Calmly Considered', *Works*, vol. 14, pp. 319-320 for Wesley's own typical 'translation' and exposition of this passage.

[33] Gill strongly denies that he teaches any such thing in 'Truth Defended', *Sermons and Tracts*, vol. iii, p. 422, Primitive Baptist Reprint.

[34] Op. sit. p. 176. Naylor refers to a similar passage in *Sermons and Tracts*, vol. II, p. 489 f. A puzzling factor is that though Naylor gives a lengthy quote from the version used by this author with exactly the same reference, the quote varies considerably in its wording.

[35] Op. sit. pp. 175-6. The full quote is found in *Body of Divinity*, Vol. I, p. 334. Naylor gives p. 294 in his footnote and suggests that Gill was 'unsure'of his exposition.

[36] Often νυν (now) is used as an illative strengthener for αρα (therefore), i.e. 'Therefore now' could be a strengthened 'therefore' meaning 'We can thus conclude'. The word νυν is thus often logical and not temporal as seen in I Corinthians 5:ll meaning 'now you see' or 'now you understand'. At other times νυν can even mean 'now' in the sense of 'hitherto' or 'up to now' cf. I Corinthians 3:2. Naylor's rendering is rather unusual to say the least.

[37] Op. sit. p. 165. 'Gill insisted that faith, understood as assent to the facts of the gospel, is an exercise demanded by God from all who hear; we ought to believe what we are told.' This is also the view of Seymour who says in his *John Gill: Baptist Theologian*, p. 211 'Similarly, Gill interpreted all general exhortations to faith merely to an external assent to the truth of Christian doctrine.' This point is dealt with in the next chapter.

[38] Op. sit. p. 336.

[39] *Sermons and Tracts*, vol. i, p. 490.

[40] See *Sermons and Tracts*, vol. ii, p. 492 and *Body of Divinity* pp. 332-333.

[41] Op. sit. p. 332. Also *Sermons and Tracts*, vol. ii, p. 491.

[42] Op. sit. Book III, Chapter XI, p. 53.

[43] See Calvin's argument in The Eternal Predestination of God, *Calvin's Calvinism*, p. 98.

[44] Ibid, p. 43.

[45] Ibid, Chapter XIV, p. 72.

[46] Ibid, Chapter XI, p. 42.

[47] Ibid, pp. 39-40.

[48] Op. sit. p. 338.

[49] Vol. II, p. 38.

[50] See *Offer*, vol. ii, pp. 214-277, especially pp. 256-258.

[51] The difference between the moral law as seen by Chandler and the moral law as seen by Grotius is that the former finds it is a universal absolute to which God himself must bend, whereas the latter sees the moral law as an abitrary and temporary display of God's revelation at a given time for a given purpose. Both, however, believe that man is basically aware of 'the fittness of things' i.e. what is expected morally and rationally of him and what he ought to do about it.

[52] 'The Moral Nature and Fitness of Things Considered', *Sermons and Tracts*, vol. iii, pp. 488-489.

[53] *Works*, p. 7.

[54] *Body of Divinity*, vol. i., pp. 338-339.

[55] *Dr John Gill and his Teaching*, 1971. pp. 5-23.

[56] *Ibid.* 8-9.

[57] See Fuller's *Works*, vol. ii. p. 335 where Fuller criticizes Anderson for challenging Bellamy's view in his *Scripture Doctrine of the Appropriation which is in the Nature of saving Faith*. Fuller argues, 'The gospel is a *feast freely provided*, and sinners of mankind are *freely invited* to partake of it. There is no mention of any *gift* or *grant*, distinct from this, but this itself is ground sufficient' (p. 338). Gill would answer that Christ's sheep, to whom has been granted faith, come to be fed when they hear his voice and they see the feast.

[58] Op. sit., p. 17.

[59] *Baptist Theologians*, pp.91-92.

[60] See 'The Necessity of good Works Unto Salvation Considered', *Sermons and Tracts*, Vol. 3, p. 492.

[61] See Fuller's *Works*, vol. ii, p. 422. and Ryland's *Memoir of Mr Fuller*, Button & Son, 1818, p. 6 n..

[62] See Rippon's *Life and Writings of the Rev. John Gill, D.D.*, Gano Books, 1992, pp. 43-48.

[63] *The Cause of God and Truth*, Section XXXII, p. 34 ff.

[64] *A defence of some important Doctrines of the Gospel by several Ministers*, vol. II, p. 512.

[65] *The Doctrine of God's Everlasting Love*, 732, The Baptist Standard reprint, pp. 57-58.

[66] *Ibid*, p. 58.

[67] For a candid discussion of Mather's views on the subject, see *The American Pietism of Cotton Mather: Origins of American Evangelism*, Richard Lovelace, 1979, Chapter Two.

[68] See my article 'God's Hiawatha', *ET*, May 1995.

[69] Naylor, p.149. Naylor, of course, uses 'high-Calvinism' as a synonym for Hyper-Calvinism.

[70] See letter quoted in Ryland's *The Life and Death of the Reverend Andrew Fuller*, Button, 1818, p. 36 ff.

[71] See Fuller's *Works*, vol. ii, p. 378 where Fuller argues for the natural and moral abilities of sinners to exercise duty faith and a denial of the biblical doctrine that they cannot of themselves comprehend and apprehend spiritual things.

[72] The *Strict Baptist Historical Society Bulletin*, No. 20, 1993, p.7. The dots are Oliver's.

[73] *The Free Offer*, p. 15. Note that Gill is criticizing 'universal offers' which does not carry the same meaning as 'free offers'; the former referring to a universal offer of the full gospel, which must then, of course, include election and predestination, warranting such salvation *for all at all times*, whereas the latter is normally understood as 'preaching the gospel freely to *all as the Spirit leads*'. This is the clear teaching of the Synod of Dort which refers to 'affording an offer of salvation to sinners without distinction' adding 'to whom God in his good pleasure sends the gospel'. The former gives every man a mandate over his own salvation and is thus not preaching the gospel at all. The latter is preaching the gospel properly. The 'universal offer' theory, if held by a professing Calvinist, would mean that he sincerely believes that God offers salvation to some to whom he will not give it. If this is not a blasphemous thought, it is difficult to conceive what is. As the word 'offer' is highly ambiguous and modern evangelists often give the word a free-will connotation bordering on the 'universal offer' theory, it is perhaps best to use a more biblical and apt phrase. The idea that Gill did not earnestly plead with sinners to repent cannot have been obtained from Gill's works and contemporary testimony. It obviously belongs to the category 'mistaken rumour'.

[74] See Curt Daniel's *Hyper-Calvinism and John Gill* where the author assumes that all those who deny the 'free offer' are Hyper-Calvinists. His 'free-offer' candidates, however, had quite contradictory views as to what the 'free offer' entailed and a number of them demonstrably preached a less free and more restricted gospel than Gill. Others mentioned as

'free offer' men spoke traditionally of 'offer' but avoided the epiphet 'free' which is not given due note. Those who plead for a 'free offer' will find that most of the saints who have spoken of 'offering Christ' have been most particular as to whom Christ should be 'offered' i.e. whether universally, freely, indiscriminately or discriminatingly. See Appendix II on the Free Offer. See also Gill's Introduction to Davis' hymn book, the other major passage where Gill discusses the word 'offer'. Here Gill explains that Davis dropped using the word because of wrong connotations applied to it.

[75] *Sermons and Tracts*, III, pp. 117-118, Primitive Baptist Library reprint.
[76] See Glossary for term 'Sensible Sinners'.
[77] My emphasis.
[78] *The Cause of God and Truth*, Baker Bookhouse Reprint, 1980, Section X, p. 15.
[79] Gill's words.
[80] See Fuller's 'Reply to Mr Button', *Works*, vol. ii, p. 422 n.
[81] *Works*, vol. ii, p. 345.
[82] See Chapter Five on the Goat Yard Declaration.
[83] Gill is dealing with the false teaching that this verse implies that every man could come to Christ if he only exercised his will.
[84] *The Cause of God*, Section XXX, p. 33. Gill's emphasis.
[85] Fuller sees his own difficulty thus arguing that whereas man's reason is intact, his reasoning is defective.
[86] *Ibid*, p. 109.
[87] *Works*, vol. ii, p. 357.
[88] P. 33.
[89] *Baptist Theologians*, p. 9.
[90] Collingridge, vol. iii, pp. 604-605.
[91] *Hyper-Calvinism and John Gill*, p. 618.
[92] *The Free Offer*, p. 15.
[93] Op. sit. p. 146.
[94] Gill wrote a pamphlet under that title.
[95] See Toplady's appendix to *The Life and Writings of the Late John Gill, D.D.*, John Rippon, D.D., Gano Books reprint, 1992.
[96] Pp. 114-115. Hoad is referring here to the Strict Baptist churches.
[97] *The Necessity of good Works Unto Salvation Considered*, p. 510.
[98] *Ibid*, pp. 494-495.
[99] See Michael Haykin's book *One Heart and One Soul* on the subject. For an analysis of Grotius' views see entries in Hastings, Schaff-Herzog and Berkof as also A. M. Peski's *Waarom Grotius als Oecumenisch Theoloog Mislukken Moest*, Nederlands Theologisch Tijdschrift, 38 (4), 1984 pp. 290-297 and E. J. Kuiper's *Hugo de Groot en de Remonstranten*, NTT, 38 (2), 1984, pp. 111-125.
[100] Op. sit., Book III, Chapter XI, pp. 53-54.
[101] *Sermons and Tracts*, vol. ii, pp. 116-117.
[102] Op. sit. p. 92.
[103] Op. sit. p. 106.
[104] Op. sit. p. 5.

Chapter 10 The pastor in the pulpit

[1] See Wright's *The Life of Augustus M. Toplady* for details of Gill's influence over the author of Rock of Ages.
[2] The list of subscribers to the various editions of Gill's works reveal a large number of Anglican readers.

3 *Biographia Evangelica*, vol. 4, pp. 454-455, *Sermons and Tracts*, vol. 1, pp. xxxiv-xxxv.

4 The Banner of Truth Trust, p. 47.

5 From the short biography appended to Rippon's *Life and Writings of Dr. John Gill*, pp. 138-139.

6 This short excurse is highly necessary as so many of Gill's critics say that his congregation had so shrunk that they had to leave Goat Yard for far smaller premises. The Carter Lane chapel was more extensive in all respects and, unlike Goat Yard, was fully pewed even in the galleries.

7 *S & T*, vol. i., pp. 377-432.

8 *Ibid*, p. 405.

9 *Ibid*, p. 383.

10 *Ibid*, p. 384.

11 The picture Spurgeon gives of Gill in his various descriptions of the preacher seem to have given rise to this myth that tells us that 'all the stories told of Dr Gill are somewhat grim' (*History of Metropolitan Tabernacle*, p. 43.) This is far from the case as even Spurgeon's own stories of Gill illustrate.

12 Taken from a longer extract in Ivimey's *History of the English Baptists*, vol. 3, pp. 277-278.

13 My emphasis.

14 Op. sit. p. 156.

15 Naylor's emphasis.

16 See his funeral sermons on the deaths of Elizabeth Gill, John Brine, Joseph Stennett, John Davenport, Mrs J. Smith, Mrs Button, Martha Gifford, William Anderson, Edward Wallin, Aaron Spurner, Edward Ludlow, Benjamin Seward, James Fall, Mary Fall, Anne Brine, Samuel Wilson etc..

17 See Gill's sermons at the ordinations of George Braithwaite at Devonshire Square in 1734, Walter Richards in 1752, John Davis at Waltham Abbey in 1764, John Reynolds at Cripplegate in 1766 etc..

18 Ivimey, vol. 3, pp. 274-275.

19 Though Ivimey argues that Gill correctly defines evangelical repentance and saving faith, he still misses the application that sinners cannot escape wrath if they neglect so great a salvation.

20 Ivimey was obviously not a 'Gillite' but he uses his sources faithfully often recording either positive or negative accounts of Gill according to what documents he was using at the time.

21 Ivimey, vol. iii. pp. 455-461. See especially the words preached at Edward Ludlow's burial, p. 458.

22 See Naylor pp. 156-58 for a most biased attempt to ridicule Gill's preaching and pastoral abilities.

23 Newman's *Reminiscences of Ryland*, p. 80.

24 Ivimey calls her Miss Eleanor in his index to vol. iii.

25 Gill's sermon was preached on 4 June and published in the same year, under the title A *Sermon Occasioned by the Death of Elizabeth Gill who Departed this Life May 30th 1738 having entered the 13th Year of her Age*.

26 Ephesians 2:9.

27 Ephesians 1:3-4.

28 John 10:10.

29 Acts 9:15.

30 Acts 13:2.

31 Galatians 1:1.

32 Op. sit. p. 165.

33 *Ibid*, p. 171.

34 Matthew 11:28.

35 John 6:37.

36 *Hyper-Calvinism and John Gill*, p. 453.

314

37 *Dr John Gill and his Teaching*, p. 22.
38 *S & T*, vol. II, p. 414.
39 *Ibid*, pp. 295-296.
40 *S & T*, vol. II, p.126.
41 *The Seceders*, vol. II, pp. 207-208 (letter to Fanny Philpot).

Chapter 11 Laying the axe to popery's roots

1 Rippon's phrase 'the moral law as the rule of their conduct' used here is also widely open to misinterpretation. Gill's position was that the believer is under the law to Christ, which means that Christ's eternal law-fulfilling righteousness was also his standard. He did not mean by the term that the Ten Commandments were the only rule to be followed in attaining Christian holiness. This latter interpretation is sadly very prevalent nowadays.
2 Op. sit. pp. 103-104. The emphasis is Rippon's.
3 Spurgeon tells this story in his *Commenting and Commentaries*. Gill's portrait hung in Spurgeon's study.
4 *Works*, Sprinkle, 1987 reprint, p. 506.
5 *Ibid*, p. 506.
6 So states Philip Schaff in his *Encyclopedia of Religious knowledge*, vol. iv, p. 2509.
7 See Toplady's article *Arminianism charged and proved on the Church of Rome*, and Hervey's Eleven Letters against Wesley's attack on the imputed righteousness of Christ
8 *Journals*, entry for June 1766.
9 *Ibid*, 5 February 1786.
10 My emphasis.
11 *Works*, vol. ii, p. 344.
12 Wesley accused Toplady, Gill's friend, of saying 'The sum of all is this: one in twenty (suppose) of mankind are *elected*; nineteen are *reprobated*. The *elect* shall be saved, do what they will: the *reprobate* shall be damned, do what they can.' 'The Consequence Proved', Wesley's *Works*, vol. 14, p. 406. This was one of several base attempts by Wesley to dirty Toplady's name, as, needless to say, Toplady said no such thing. See Toplady's More Work for Mr. John Wesley; or a Vindication of the Decrees and Providence of God, from the Defamation of a Late Printed Paper, Entitled 'The Consequence Proved', *Works*, pp. 729-762.
13 Op. sit. pp. 163-164.
14 Psalm 51:5; 58:3; Isaiah 48:8.
15 *Works*, vol. 14, pp. 412-428.
16 My emphasis.
17 *Sermons and Tracts*, vol. iii, pp. 83-100.
18 *Body of Divinity*, vol. ii, pp. 883-913. This work was not published until 1769.
19 Wesley's work was originally published anonymously and Gill only learnt that Wesley was the author after writing against it.
20 *Ibid*, p. 883.
21 *Ibid*, pp. 883-884.
22 Op. sit. vol. iii, pp. 89-90.
23 See Mr Wesley's Letter, *Hervey's Works*, pp. 472-80, also Romans 4, John 8:56.
24 Wesley gives his quote as *Dialogues*, vol. 1, p. 43, Dublin edition. In my edition, Edinburgh 1837, this quote is in Dialogue II. Hervey begged Wesley to cease from quoting the Dublin edition in his criticism of Hervey as it was faulty in many respects. Wesley, though the English and Scottish editions were available to him and though he had received a MS from Hervey, continued to use the Irish edition which made it almost impossible for people to check his arguments.
25 *Theron and Aspasio*, Dialogue II, p. 157.

26 Wesley's Works, vol. 13, *Remarks on Dr. Erskine's Defence of Aspasio Vindicated*, pp. 122-123. See biographies of Hervey by Ryland, Brown etc., for descriptions of Hervey's glorious end.

27 Letter CXXX, *Works*, p. 856.

28 *A Dialogue Between a Predestinarian and his Friend*, *Works*, vol. 14, p. 404.

29 Wesley's interpolation.

30 This was Wesley's usual policy against those who wrote on the perseverance of the saints. James Hervey wrote of this doctrine in his *Theron and Aspasio* and was immediately condemned by Wesley for supporting predestination. Hervey had not written at all on the topic apart from quoting a verse of Scripture which Wesley believed Hervey was using to indicate predestination. Hervey never wrote on predestination because he felt he was out of his depth on the subject. He did, however, warmly write on the perseverance of the saints. See Hervey's letter to Lady Shirley (LXXIV) where he complains of Wesley's action and says, 'A Reader, ten Times less penetrating than He is, may easily see, that this Doctrine (be it true or false) makes no Part of my Scheme; never comes under Consideration; is purposely and carefully avoided.' Hervey felt this was all part of Wesley's campaign to 'put the wolf's skin on the sheep' and have Hervey discredited.

31 Gill quotes the Article as VII in his essays, whereas it is Article XVII.

32 See Arthur W. Pink's *An Exposition of Hebrews* for a splendid balanced exegesis of this difficult chapter.

33 Wesley's interpolation.

34 *Works*, vol. XIV, pp. 406-411.

35 See Toplady's defence in 'More Work for Mr. John Wesley or A Vindication of the Decrees and Providence of God, from the Defamation of a Late Printed Paper entitled 'The Consequence Proved.''', *Works*, pp. 729-762.

Chapter 12   The work accomplished

1 Hosea 13:14; 1 Corinthians 15:55.

2 Even Timothy George, whose account of Gill is the most positive in many years, writes, giving Horton Davis' *Worship and Theology in England, 1690-1850*, Princeton, 1961 as his source, 'At his death the church he had served for so long voted to raise a mortgage and go into debt in order to pay for a portrait of their beloved pastor, from which small prints were provided for every member of the congregation.' Op. sit. p. 95.

3 Original spelling retained.

4 Just how well the prints sold is not recorded but if every member bought just one, and obviously more people would have been interested in having a picture of Gill than the mere membership, sales must have gone a long way to paying off the debt. They were still being sold in 1773 when Rippon obtained £21 for prints sold to help balance off the church debts at the end of that year.

5 Dying Thoughts, *S & T*, vol. iii. pp. 562-567.

6 *Commenting and Commentaries*, A Chat about Commentaries, p. 15.

7 *Biographia Evangelica*, vol. vi, p. 457.

8 Rev. John Gill was also a pastor for over fifty years, serving mostly in St Albans. When he died in March 1809 aged seventy-nine, his funeral sermon was preached by John Sutcliff of Olney. Mary Gill, Dr Gill's daughter, had been in membership with her cousin's church since May 1764.

9 *Bunhill Fields*, p. 118.

Chapter 13   The widowed church

[1] *The English Baptists of the 18th Century*, p. 11. Evans (1737-91) succeeded his father Hugh as pastor of the Broadmead church and principal of the Bristol Academy in 1781.
[2] See J. Gadsby's *Memoirs of Hymn-Writers and Compilers*, p.53 ff. for a brief biography of Fawcett. Gadsby mistakenly thought Gill was still alive in 1772.
[3] This amount was quickly halved in the first few months of Rippon's ministry, though there were now barely 90 active members in the church. £21 was raised by selling some of Gill's engravings.

Chapter 14   Three hundred years on: the Modern Question brought up to date

[1] *The Legacy of John Gill*, Olin C. Robinson, *BQ*, XXVI, 1971, pp. 111-112.
[2] His own church practised a form of Johnsonism which was seen as heresy by the traditional Particular Baptists.
[3] Answering the Modern Question in the affirmative is a true form of Arminianism as it leaves the onus of salvation to man's awareness of his spiritual duties which the Reformed Faith declares have been extinct since the Fall. Calvinism emphasizes God's intention to save through his loving gift of his Son. See Allan Sell's *The Great Debate*, p. 79 and Geoffrey Nuttall's *Northamptonshire and the Modern Question*.
[4] See Glossary.
[5] That Fuller confesses to being influenced positively against Gill by Martin is one of the many puzzles in understanding Fuller's turn from Calvinism. Martin could not accept Fuller's view of the limitation of depravity to the will and argued that one cannot speak of duties to believe savingly in reprobate when the Bible says faith is a gift to the elect only. Fuller seems to have misunderstood Martin as much as he did Gill.
[6] *Works*, vol. i, p. 14. See Glossary.
[7] Ted Wilson has recently given a brief history of this church, outlining its struggles and triumphs in *Grace*, January 1995.
[8] See Raymond Brown's excellent *The English Baptists of the 18th Century*, *BHS*, Tyndale Press, 1986 pp. 108-109, 162 for details of Aspland's career.
[9] See Sabellianism in Glossary.
[10] *A History of the English Baptists*, Carey Kingsgate Press, 1961, p. 135.
[11] See Arthur Kirkby's PhD thesis, *The Theology of Andrew Fuller and its relation to Calvinism*, Edin., 1956. Fuller sees the great historical acts of Christ's life and atoning death as being 'figurative' i.e. reflecting ideals that lay behind them but are not identical with them.
[12] Kirkby argues that Jonathan Edwards influenced Fuller far less than is generally held. He also argues that Fuller was more influenced directly by Calvin's works than is generally held. Kirkby also shows that the special 'Fullerite' flavour of Fuller's theology is the teaching that in matters of belief fallen man 'could if he would'. Op. sit. p. 160.
[13] See *One Heart and One Soul*, EP, 1995, pp. 139 ff, 300 ff. Haykin teaches that Grotianism is of the very substance of Evangelical Calvinism. Haykin surprisingly links John Sutcliff and David Brainerd with Grotianism through the New Divinity School. Here Haykins' evidence is weak in the case of Sutcliff and non-existent in the case of Brainerd. The latter had great difficulty in preaching penal substitution to the Indians as they had no legal or commercial culture to provide forms of expression for it. Nevertheless, he stuck to the penal and commercial language of the Bible. If he had been a Grotian, this would have been the first phraseology he would have abandoned as Grotians do not believe in the idea of sin being a debt to the law and Christ being a ransom paid. See Sect. IV, 'Second difficulty in converting the Indians, viz. to convey divine truths to their understanding, and to gain their assent to them as such'. Brainerd's *Journal*, Edwards *Works*, vol. ii, BOT, p. 425 ff. (esp. 427). On the other

hand, Andrew Fuller rejects 'commercial' and penal language repeatedly in his works, thus showing that he is a true Grotian. See Hastings, Schaff-Herzog and Luis Berkof for entries on Grotius.

[14] See William Cunningham, *The Reformers and the Theology of the Reformation*, BOT, 1979, p. 398 ff. for a discussion concerning the scope of the atonement in Calvin's teaching. The question of Calvin's relationship to the Modern Question is merely an academic one as Calvin did not address himself to a question which was not yet raised. Calvin's position on the scope of the atonement, when comparing his views expressed in his *Institutes*, *The Eternal Predestination of God* and *The Secret Providence of God* with those on his John and I John commentaries, might suggest a shift of opinion. Gill's doctrine remained demonstrably constant.

[15] See Haykin op. cit. especially p. 127. This must be a misprint as Fuller died in 1815 and wrote his major works before the turn of the century.

[16] See Fuller's *Works*, vol. ii, 'The Gospel Worthy of All Acceptation' for several criticisms of Gill on this count. See also *Picking up a Pin for the Lord*, pp. 162, 166, 167. Naylor often finds Gill 'at odds with himself', where Gill is at odds with Naylor's view of him. See also R. J. Sheehan's article 'The Presentation of the Gospel Amongst "Hyper-Calvinists"', Foundations, Issue No. 8, 1982, p. 29 with footnote. Other typical examples are to be found in John Ryland's *Memoir of Fuller*. Dr Ryland who, unlike his father John Ryland Sen., followed Fuller's view of Gill, quotes texts from Gill which completely repudiate Fuller's false claims, yet this does not stop him from claiming that he adheres to Fuller's criticism of Gill in all points. See p. 5 where Ryland states that Gill never even wrote on the Modern Question subject and p. 6. where he stresses that Gill taught that Adam's pre-Fall faith was faith in Christ in contradiction to what Hyper-Calvinists taught.

[17] See Spurgeon's comments on Gill's method in Commenting and Commentaries, p. 15.

[18] See Naylor, op. sit. p. 167. The author gives Gill's first entry on John 5:24, ignores the 'but' which follows it with the various other interpretations and proceeds as if it were the only interpretation given, even arguing that this 'utterly dominated' Gill's thinking. Naylor decontextualizes Gill in a number of his arguments against him. Erroll Hulse, referring to 2 Peter 3:9, which he does not expound, lines Gill up with exegetes who practice 'carnal reasoning' and 'hack and hew texts into their own mould'. Most unfairly, Hulse compares Gill's exposition of 2 Peter 3:9 with Spurgeon's exposition of Isaiah 1:18. One can only wonder what the point of such a comparison is meant to be. If Hulse had compared Spurgeon's exegesis with Gill's of the same passage, there would have been sense in the comparison and Hulse would have found some very moving comments not found in Spurgeon, good as the latter may be. Spurgeon speaks of God's invitation going out to 'that poor soul yonder who shivers in his shoes, because he fears that he has committed the unpardonable sin'. Gill speaks of those 'seeing their sins in their dreadful colours, and with all their aggravating circumstances, were ready to conclude that they were unpardonable; and, seeing God as an angry Judge, dared not come nigh him, but stood at a distance, fearing and expecting his vengeance to fall upon them ... when the Lord was pleased to encourage them to draw near to him.' See Hulse's *The Free Offer*, p. 15. Gill's *Commentary* vol. v, pp. 7-8, vol. 9, pp. 609-610.

[19] See Erroll Hulse's *The Free Offer* p. 15 and Michael Haykin's *One Heart and One Soul*, *passim* for such undocumented allegations. After maintaining that so-called Hyper-Calvinism stunts evangelistic activity, Haykin mentions that the gospel in Olney was pioneered by Richard Davis. He refrains from stating, however, that Davis is thought to have been the one who, with Hussey, pioneered Hyper-Calvinism in Britain. This will be referred to again as this chapter proceeds.

[20] A prime example is to be found in Naylor's PPFTL. Naylor argues on p. 147 that 'Among the Baptists of the period, John Gill was, without doubt, the most prominent exponent of high Calvinism [Naylor has explained that High-Calvinism is the same as Hyper-Calvinism].' What follows are quotes from Ivimey, Wayman, Brine and Whitefield but one looks in vain for evidence for Naylor's statement from Gill's pen until over a dozen pages later there is a

reference to Gill's effort to give up smoking and his remark to his daughter that keeping the ordinances does not grant salvation. Could this be a sign of Hyper-Calvinistic Antinomianism to Naylor?

[21] An objective study of Brine will show that he is in no way the man of straw critics make of him and he was far more independent of Gill than his opponents care to admit.

[22] Its full title was *Motives to love and Unity among Calvinists, who differ in some points: A Dialogue between Christophulus, Philalethes and Philagathus Wherein is contained an Answer to Mr Alvery Jackson's Question Answered*, London, 1754.

[23] See Brine's *An Antidote Against a Spreading Antinomian Principle*, London, 1750.

[24] Ivimey, vol. iv, p. 228.

[25] Emphasis mine. *Sermon Occasioned by the Death of the Revd Mr Samuel Wilson*, preached 14 October 1750, London, 1760.

[26] My emphasis. *Bunhill Memorials*, p. 380.

[27] See Toon's *Definition of Hyper-Calvinism*, p. 144 ff.

[28] *Hymns Composed on Several Subjects And on Divers Occasions*, London, 1748,

[29] See Benjamin Brook's *The Lives of the Puritans*, Vol. ii, pp. 471-475.

[30] Letter VII, p. 14. Collection of letters appended to *The Character of the Rev. James Hervey, A. M.*, John Ryland, London, 1791.

[31] See *History of the English Baptists*, vol. iii, 363-366.

[32] Op. sit., Letter VII, p. 14.

[33] Newman's *Reminiscences of Ryland*, p. 78.

[34] *Ibid*, p. 166.

[35] See my *William Huntington: Pastor of Providence* for a discussion of this clash of views.

[36] See pp. 294, Abstract, 140, 283, 149, 278.

[37] Those influenced by Edward Fisher's *The Marrow of Modern Divinity*, with notes by Thomas Boston. This book was used widely, especially in Scotland, to create a biblical balance between legalism on the one side and Antinomianism on the other. The author (Fisher's authorship has been challenged) maintained that the law is only *a* rule of life not *the* rule of life. Christians must also follow the law of faith and the law of Christ. This became the main stand of the Gill-Huntington theological tradition and was criticized as being 'unevangelical' by Fullerites who stress that the law is the sole rule of the Christian life. See also Fuller's Works, vol. II, p. 335 ff. Anderson, with whom Fuller disagrees, was attacking the theories of Bellamy. The fact that many modern Calvinists accuse the Marrow Men of opening the doors to Amyraldianism does not affect my argument here as Fuller certainly connected the Marrow Men more with the Gill-Hervey school than with that of Moïse Amyraut. The suspicion has probably arisen because those who speak of an 'offer' nowadays are very often Amyraldians so that critics go to the extreme of believing that anyone using the term must be an Amyraldian. This modern trend also neglects to see that the word 'offer' is used quite differently by today's Amyraldians i.e. in the sense of Dort and the Westminister Confession, 'to present Christ' or 'to set forth the gospel'.

[38] *Ibid*, p. 338.

[39] *A History of the English Baptists*, 1945, p. 135.

[40] See, for instance, Eric W. Hayden's *A History of Spurgeon's Tabernacle*, p. 4. Hayden merely quotes Underwood and builds on his unfounded statement, apparently quite unaware of the works and teaching of the man whose life and service he is supposed to be describing.

[41] One might differ in opinion as to whether Gill's view of church ordinances is 'orthodox' or not.

[42] Defined by Robert Oliver, *Historical Survey of English Hyper-Calvinism, Foundations*, No. 7, 1981, p. 8.

[43] The question at once arises, 'If man's natural abilities are all intact, how is it that a saved, restored son of Adam still experiences physical death and the decay of his physical, mental and rational capacities?' This question has often been asked Moderate Calvinists by the author who has invariably received the answer that man is a moral being and fell as such and

thus needs to be restored in the realms of morals only. This seems a far cry from the gospel of salvation in the Bible which is obviously to the whole man who is wholly fallen.

[44] See Robert Oliver's *Historical Survey of English Hyper-Calvinism, Foundations*, Issue No. 7, Nov. 1981, p. 8 ff. See also Oliver's *The Significance of Strict Baptist Attitudes towards Duty Faith in the Nineteenth Century, The Strict Baptist Historical Society Bulletin*, No. 20, 1993. Oliver refers to Brine here, whom, if it were possible, he finds worse than Gill. Arguing that 'Brine was possibly the most entrenched of the eighteenth century Particular Baptist High Calvinists', he, nevertheless says that Brine considered the duty-faith issue was a matter on which Calvinists could agree to differ. Oliver is arguing that it is the denial of duty faith which makes an 'entrenched High Calvinist'. Brine is not 'entrenched' in the matter at all but he is still, in Oliver's eyes, an 'entrenched High Calvinist'. It seems true that once a dog has a bad name, it sticks!

[45] This topic is discussed further in Chapter 9.

[46] See *The Legacy of John Gill*, Olin C. Robinson, *BQ*, XXVI, 1971.

[47] An odd opinion expressed by Toon in his book on Hyper-Calvinism is that whereas Hyper-Calvinists were only of average intelligence, only the very intelligent could read them with safety!

[48] Fullerism is a form of Arminianism as it teaches an atonement which is universal in scope though limited in its final application. Here John Wesley and Andrew Fuller were in complete harmony of doctrine.

[49] Armitage says for instance, 'He was so high a superlapsarian, that it is hard to distinguish him from an Antinomian.' *A History of the Baptists*, vol. ii, p. 561. See also Peter Naylor's *Picking up a Pin for the Lord* for a thoroughly negative assessment of Gill's presumed Hyper-Calvinism.

[50] Taylor's anti-Gill works are discussed in Chapters 8 and 9.

[51] See, for instance, Ernest A. Payne's *The Free Church Tradition in the Life of England* in which the author emphasizes Fuller's importance in 'challenging Noncomformity' but never once mentions Gill.

[52] See Glossary.

[53] See Naylor's PPFTL, p. 145.

[54] Hussey, a Congregationalist minister, who wrote *God's Operations of Grace: but No Offers of Grace* (1707). There is very little evidence to show that Gill was influenced by Hussey in any way.

[55] Pp. 104-106.

[56] *Institutes*, Book 1, Chap. VII, p. 68.

[57] Op. sit., p. 116. Toon argues, where my dots are, that Gill thought arguments from prophecy, miracles and what Toon calls 'other things' (what 'other things'?) are of primary importance rather than secondary. This is not Gill's argument. Gill argues that miracles and prophecy fulfilled confirm the validity of the Scriptures.

[58] See Fuller, *Works*, vol. II, pp. 681, 682, 688 and 690 where he argues that imputation, Christ's being made sin for us, sin as a debt and Christ's redemption are not to be understood literally but metaphorically. See also Fuller's rationalistic arguments against the vicarious, penal, redemptive death of Christ in *The Gospel Worthy of All Acceptation*.

[59] See *ET*, July issue, p. 11.

Appendix I: The full gospel and the free offer

[1] *Hyper-Calvinism and John Gill*, p. 767.

[2] See *Evangelical Times, Preaching the Gospel Properly*, John Legg, November 1994.

[3] Republished by Banner of Truth Trust in vol. 4 of the *Collected Writings of John Murray*, 1982.

[4] *Hyper-Calvinism and John Gill*, p. 388.

[5] *Ibid*, p. 410.

[6] *Works*, vol. II, p. 712.

[7] See 'Reply to Philanthropos', Fuller's *Works*, vol. ii, pp. 497-8 and the section entitled 'The gospel call and duty faith' in Chapter 9 of this biography.

[8] *Works*, vol. II, p. 494 ff.

[9] *Works, The Gospel Worthy of All Acceptation*, vol. ii, p. 374.

[10] Fuller's emphasis.

[11] *Works*, vol. ii, p. 709.

[12] *Works*, vol. ii, 'Concluding Reflections', p. 383.

[13] See 'Every man is bound cordially to receive and approve whatever God reveals', *Works*, vol. II, pp. 347-352; 'Whether Faith is required by the Moral Law', vol. II, p. 483; 'On Faith being a Requirement of the Moral Law', p. 539 ff.

[14] See *Works*, vol. II, pp. 345, 374.

[15] I Corinthians 2:14 ff.; Romans 1-3.

[16] John 17:3; I Corinthians 2:8.

[17] *Works*, vol. II, pp. 375-76. See especially, 'God requires nothing of fallen creatures as a term of life. He requires them to love him with all their hearts, the same as if they had never apostasized.'

[18] *S & T*, vol. II, p.47.

[19] See Glossary.

[20] *Works*, vol. ii., p. 338. See pp. 335-338.

[21] *Gospel Mystery of Sanctification*, Evangelical Press, 1981, p. 52.

[22] *Ibid*, pp. 57-58.

[23] See *The Marrow of Modern Divinity*, Edward Fisher, ed. Thomas Boston, Philadelphia, undated, p. 126 ff.

[24] Extract from a letter to William Hogg.

[25] *Life and Writings of the Rev. John Gill, DD*, John Rippon, Gano Books, 1992, p. 20.

[26] See Cotton Mather's *Free Grace*, Boston, 1706. Needless to say, Mather has been accused of Hyper-Calvinism but his works and gospel testify against the accusation.

[27] The records of the Midland Association show that Benjamin Beddome's church had 180 members in 1751, though the rest of the churches had far fewer at this time. Gill's church records show he had 235 members in 1757. Beddome, who perhaps came nearest to Gill in church members, however, has been traditionally placed nearer Gill than Fuller, an argument that would again prove the folly of believing that those sharing Gill's theology emptied their churches.

[28] See *Banner of Truth Magazine*, July and August-September 1994, 'Preaching the Gospel to Sinners' I and II by David Gay. Gay says in Part II, 'Jesus said that he often desired that which God, clearly, had not decreed.' Just as the duty-faith teaching of Toland etc. led to a separation of the persons in the Godhead, and eventually to Deism and Arianism, so this modern Hyper-Fullerism (more Fullerite than Fuller) is shifting the faulty doctrine of the two conflicting wills of God (the revealed and the secret; the desired and the decreed) to a distinction between the wills of the Father and his Son.

[29] See 'Preaching the Gospel Properly', John Legg, *Evangelical Times*, November 1994 for the use of the term 'theological swearword'.

[30] *The Cause of God and Truth*, p.31.

[31] *S&T* I, pp. 38-39.

[32] See Middleton's and Toplady's tribute to this in *Biographia Evangelica*, vol. 4, pp. 458-9. Another Particular Baptist who worked closely with Anglicans, especially Whitefield, in the revival was William Steele (1690-1769), a pastor at Broughton in Hampshire and father of Anne Steele, the hymn-writer.

[33] See *Works*, vol. iii 'Thoughts on Open Communion' and 'Strict Communion in the Mission Church of Serampore', pp. 503-515. Fuller's point is that if a Baptist has church fellowship

with a non-Baptist, he ceases to become a Baptist. Apart from the illogical nature of such a statement one would have thought that having fellowship as Christians in Christ is the point of church fellowship. One wonders whether Fuller really believed that the Church Universal and Church Triumphant in heaven is for Baptists only. When the press complained that the Serampore church had been forced to change their church constitution through Fuller's injunction, Fuller denied in a letter to the *Instructor* that this was so and made it appear that it was a decision of the Serampore church alone. The church, however, had broken their own church constitution concerning open communion so as not to break friendship with a rather tyrannical Fuller. See 'I Throw Away the Guns to Preserve the Ship: A Note on the Serampore Trio', E. Daniel Potts, *BQ*, XX, 1963-64. Potts shows how Fuller doubted the Christian character of Paedobaptists, including even Jonathan Edwards, and doubted whether Wesley was even a good man and approved of those who felt he was 'a dishonest man' and a 'crafty jesuit'. Gill's criticism of Wesley was never personal but always doctrinal.

[34] See *Dr. John Gill and his Teaching*, Graham Harrison, p. 27, and *Hyper-Calvinism and John Gill*, Curt Daniel, p. 372.

[35] Seymour must be guilty of the greatest exaggeration in this respect. On page 278 of his *John Gill: Baptist Theologian* he says, 'John Gill's life was so consumed in writing that he had little time left for anything else. He spent most of his ministry in his study. Day after day he arose at dawn and remained with his books until dark.'

[36] Combining references to his preaching to a packed church at Goat Yard, his Great East-Cheap lectures etc.

[37] Gill's critics appear to be tarring him with a brush meant for others. The Eagle Street church, for instance, entered into their Church Book on 23. 11. 1760 that a brother and sister were rebuked for 'communicating at the Tabernacle with Mr Whitefield'. This is all the more telling as the Eagle Street pastor, Andrew Gifford, was an admirer of Whitefield and published his sermons.

[38] Robert Hall's *Miscellaneous Works*, London, 1846, p. 428.

[39] See Fuller's *Works*, vol. II, footnotes pp. 546-547.

[40] *Helps to Zion's Travellers*, Bristol, 1781, p. 117.

Appendix II: John Gill on linguistics and Hebrew vocalization

[1] This is merely because the syllable structure and irregular stress and rhythm of the English language makes it difficult to work out vowelization. Hebrew is so regular in its structure that vowelization poses hardly any problems to trained readers and writers.

[2] Studying and collecting coins was quite a hobby amongst Baptist ministers of the time. Andrew Gifford, now pastor of Little Wild Street, London, had one of the best collections in the country which was eventually bought by George II.

[3] See Hebrew Pointing in Glossary.

[4] Hebrew texts have been found since 1947 (Dead Sea Scrolls) which have been dated from several centuries before Christ to at least two centuries after Christ. These texts such as the Isaiah scroll, written possibly at the time of Christ and the, probably later, parchment of The War of the Sons of Light against the Sons of Darkness have no pointing. Thus the last word has still not been said on the issue.

[5] See *Second Thoughts on the Dead Sea Scrolls*, F. F. Bruce, Paternoster Press, 1961, esp. p. 61 ff., *The Old Testament and Modern Study*, H. H. Rowley, Oxford, 1961 and *The Archaeology of Palestine*, W. F. Albright, Pelican Books, 1949.

Bibliography

Gill's Works Used

Answer to the Birmingham Dialogue Writer, An, London, 1737

Ancient Mode of Baptizing by Immersion, Plunging, or Dipping into Water; Maintained and Vindicated, The, 1726

Body of Divinity (3 vols), Subscription, 1769

Cause of God and Truth, The, Baker Book House, 1980

Christ the Ransom Found, Sermon Occasioned by the Death of Mr John Davenport, London 1754

Discourse on Singing Psalms as a Part of Divine Worship, London, 1734

Dissenters Reasons for Separation from the Church of England, The, London, 5th edit., 1763

Dissertation Concerning the Antiquity of the Hebrew Language, Letters, Vowel-Points and Accents, A, London, 1767

Divine Right of Infant Baptism Examined and Disproved; Being an Answer to a Pamphlet, Entitled A brief Illustration and Confirmation of the Divine Right of Infant Baptism, London, 1749

Dr. Gill's Sermon Occasioned by the Death of the Revd Mr. James Fall, London, 1763

Doctrine of Justification by the Righteousness of Christ, London, 1756

Doctrines of God's Everlasting Love to His Elect, and their Eternal Union with Christ, The, The Baptist Standard Bearer, 1987

Doctrine of the Trinity Stated and Vindicated, The, London, 1752

Essay on the Original of Funeral Sermons, Orations, and Odes, etc., An, London, 1729

Exposition of the Old & New Testaments (9 vols), Baptist Standard Bearer, 1989

Faithful Minister of Christ Crowned, A. Being a Sermon Occasioned by the Death of the Rev. Mr. William Anderson, London, 1767

Form of Sound Words to be held fast, London, 1766

Infant Baptism, Part and Pillar of Popery, London, 1765

Mutual Duty of Pastor and People, The, London, 1734

Necessity of Good Works unto Salvation Considered, The, London 1739
Preface to Hymns Composed on Several Subjects and on Divers Occasions, Davis, Richard, London, 1748
Reply to a Defence of the Divine Right of Infant Baptism by Peter Clark A.M. Minister of Salem in a Letter to a Friend, London, 1765
Sermon Occasioned by the Death of the Revd Mr Samuel Wilson, Preached October 14, 1750, London, 1760
Sermon Occasioned by the Death of Elizabeth Gill, London, 1738
Sermons and Tracts, The, (3 vols), Primitive Baptist Library, 1981
Song of Solomon, Sovereign Grace Publications, 1971
Truth Defended. Being an Answer to an Anonymous Pamphlet intitled Some Doctrines in the Supralapsarian Scheme impartially examined by the Word of God, London, 1736
Vindication of a Book Entitled The Cause of God and Truth, A, London, 1740

Biographies of Gill and Tributes Paid

Broome, John R., Dr. *John Gill*, Gospel Standard Publications, 1991
Coxon, Francis, *Christian Worthies* (2 vols) Gill in vol. 1, Zoar Publications, 1980
Craner, Thomas, *A Grain of Gratitude. A Sermon Occasioned by the Death of that Venerable, Learned, Pious and Judicious Divine The Revd John Gill D. D.*, London, 1771
Fellows, John, *An Elegy on the Death of the Revd John Gill, D. D.*, London, 1771
George, Timothy and Dockery, David, *Baptist Theologians*, Gill in Chapter 4, Broadman Press, 1990
Harrison, Graham, *Dr. John Gill and His Teaching*, Evangelical Library, 1971
Middleton, Erasmus, *Biographia Evangelica* (4 vols) Gill in vol. 4, Subscription, 1784
Rippon, John, *Life and Writings of the Rev. John Gill. D.D.*, Gano Books, 1992
Spurgeon, C. H., *The Metropolitan Tabernacle: Its History and Work*, Passmore & Alabaster, 1876, Gill biography in Chapter Four.
Wallin, Benjamin, *The Address Delivered At The Interment in The Burial-Ground at Bun-Hill, October 23, 1771*, London, 1771

Other Biographies and Autobiographies Containing information on Gill and Related Subjects

Brown, John, *Life and Character of the Late James Hervey*, Ogle, Duncan & Co., 1822
Culross, James, *The Three Rylands*, Elliot Stock, London, 1897
Dallimore, Arnold, *Spurgeon*, The Banner of Truth Trust, Edinburgh, 1985
Doudney, David Alfred, *Retracings & Renewings*, W. Mack, London, 1880
Ella, G. M., *William Huntington: Pastor of Providence*, Evangelical Press, 1994
Ella, G. M., *William Cowper: Poet of Paradise*, Evangelical Press, 1993
Fuller, Thomas Ekins, *A Memoir of the Life and Writings of A. Fuller*, J. Heaton & Son, 1863
Fuller, A. G., *Life of the Rev. Andrew Fuller*, Religious Tract Society, Undated
Fullerton, W. Y., *C. H. Spurgeon*, 1920

Haykin, Michael A., *One Heart and One Soul: John Sutcliffe of Olney, his friends and his times*, EP, 1994

Hervey, James, *Letters* to the Right Honourable Lady Frances Shirley, eighteenth century, undated

Jay, William, *The Autobiography of William Jay*, The Banner of Truth, 1974

Lawson, Thomas, *Calvin: His Life and Times*, London, undated

Martin, Hugh, *Benjamin Keach*, Independent Press, 1961

Murray, Iain (ed.), *C. H. Spurgeon: Autobiography* (2 vols.), The Banner of Truth Trust, 1973

Murray, Iain, *The Forgotten Spurgeon*, The Banner of Truth Trust, 1986

Newman, William, *Rylandia: Reminiscences*, London, 1835

Pike, G. Holden, *The Life and Work of Charles Haddon Spurgeon*, Banner of Truth Trust, 1991

Ramsbottom, B. A., *Stranger Than Fiction: The Life of William Kiffin*, Gospel Standard Trust Publications, 1989

Ryland Junior, John, *The Life and Death of the Rev. Andrew Fuller*, Button and Son, 1818

Ryle, J. C., *Christian Leaders of the Eighteenth Century*, Banner of Truth Trust, 1978

Wright, Thomas, *The Life of Augustus M. Toplady*, Farncombe, 1911

Baptist History and Confessions

Armitage, Thomas, *A History of the Baptists* (2 vols), Baptist Heritage Press, 1988

Baptist Record Society, *The Records of a Church of Christ in Bristol 1640-1687*, 1974

Beasley-Murray, G. R., *Dopet idag och i Morgon*, Westerbergs, 1967

Brown, Raymond, *The English Baptists of the 18th Century*, Baptist Historical Society, 1986

Bunyan, John, Exhortation to Unity and Peace, *The Whole Works of John Bunyan*, vol. ii, ed. George Offer, Blackie and Son, 1862

Carlile, J. C., *The History of the English Baptists*, James Clarke, London, 1905

Christian, John T., *A History of the Baptists* (2 vols), Bogard Press, Texas, undated

Clifford, John, *The English Baptists: Who They Are and What They Have Done*, London, 1881

Cramp, J. M., *Baptist History*, Elliot Stock, London, 1871

Crosby, Thomas, *The History of the English Baptists* (4 vols), Church History Research, 1978

Donat, Rudolf, *Das wachsende Werk*, Oncken, 1960

Goadby, J. J., *Bye-Paths in Baptist History*, Elliot Stock, London, 1871

Gosden, J. H., *What Gospel Standard Baptists Believe*, Gospel Standard Societies, 1993.

Hayden, Eric W., *A History of Spurgeon's Tabernacle*, Pilgrim Publications, 1971

Hayden, Roger, *English Baptist History & Heritage*, BU, 1990

Hoad, Jack, *The Baptist*, Grace Publications, 1986

Hulse, Erroll, et al, *Our Baptist Heritage*, Chapel Library, 1993

Hulse, Erroll, *Baptism and Church Membership*, Carey Publications, 1989

Ivimey, Joseph, *A History of the Baptists* (4 vols.), London, 1814

Krajewski, Ekkehard, *Leben und Sterben des Züricher Täuferführers Felix Manz*, Oncken, 1962

Littel, F. H., *Das Selbstverständnis der Täufer*, Oncken, 1966.

Lumpkin, William L., *Baptist Confessions of Faith*, Judson Press, 1959

Naylor, Peter, *Picking up a Pin for the Lord*, Grace Publications, 1992

Nettles, Thomas J., *By His Grace and For His Glory*, Baker Book House, 1990

Nowén, Sven, *Varför Döper Vi?*, ÖM:s Förlag, 1964

Paul, S. F., *Historical Sketch of the Gospel Standard Baptists*, Gospel Standard Publications, 1961

Payne, Ernest A., *The Baptist Union: A Short History*, Carey Kingsgate, 1959

Ray, D. B., *Baptist Succession*, Church History Research, 1984

Sheehan, R. J., *C. H. Spurgeon and the Modern Church*, Grace Publications, 1985

Spurgeon, Charles Haddon, *The Downgrade Controversy*, (collected materials which reveal his viewpoints), Pilgrim Publications, Texas, undated

Underwood, A. C., *A History of the English Baptists*, Carey Kingsgate, London, 1961

Vedder, H. C., *A Short History of the Baptists*, Baptist Tract and Book Society, 1898

Warns, Johannes, *Baptism*, Paternoster Press, 1962

White, B. R., *The English Baptists of the 17th Century*, Baptist Historical Society, 1983

White, B. R. , (ed.), *Association Records of the Particular Baptists of England, Wales and Ireland to 1660*, (Index by Howard, K. W. H.) Parts 1-3, Baptist Historical Society, 1971-1977

Whitley, W. T., *Calvinism and Evangelism in England especially among Baptists*, London, the Kingsgate Press, 1933

Whitley, W. T., *A History of British Baptists*, Kingsgate, London, 1932

Yoder, John H., *Täufertum und Reformation im Gespräch*, EVZ-Verlag, Zürich, 1968

General Church History and Creeds

Abbey/Overton, Charles/John H., *The English Church in the Eighteenth Century*, Longmans, Green & Co., 1887

Arbeitskreis Taufe und Gemeinde Rheinland, ad hoc 2: z.B. *Taufe: Ein Kapitel Kirchenreform*, Burckhardhaus-Verlag, 1970

Balleine, G. R., *A Layman's History of the Church of England*, Longman's, Green & Co., 1923

Balleine, G. R., *A History of the Evangelical Party*, Longmans, Green & Co., 1911

Barth, Karl, *Det Kristna Dopet*, Westerbergs, 1949

Bettenson, Henry (ed.), *Documents of the Christian Church*, OUP, 1967

Bicknell, E. J., *The Thirty-Nine Articles*, Longmans, 1957

Bready, J. Wesley, *England: Before and After Wesley*, Hodder and Stoughton, 1939

Carpenter, S. C., *Church and People 1789-1889* (3 vols) , SPCK, London, 1933

Carter, C. Sydney, *The English Church in the Eighteenth Century*, Church Bookroom Press, 1948

Cornish, Warre F. , *A History of the English Church in the Nineteenth Century*, (2 vols.), Macmillan, 1933

Cragg, G. R., *The Church and the Age of Reason*, Penguin Books, 1960
Cullmann, Oscar, *Nya Testamentets Lära om Dopet: Vuxendop och Barndop*, Svenska Kyrkans Diakonistyrelses Bokförlag, 1952
Curteis, George Herbert, *Dissent in Relation to the Church of England*, Macmillan, London, 1906
Hardwick, Charles, *A History of the Articles of Religion*, Cambridge, 1859
Harrison, Archibald, W., *The Evangelical Revival and Christian Reunion*, Epworth, Press, 1942
Hart, A. Tindal, *The Curate's Lot*, John Baker, London, 1970
Hart, A. Tyndal, *The Eighteenth Century Country Parson*, Wilding & Son Ltd, 1955
Hartman, Olov, *Dopets gåva förpliktar*, Svenska Kyrkans Diaonistyrelses Bokförlag, 1950
Hendry, George S., *The Westminster Confession for Today*, SCM Press, 1960
Jeremias, Joachim, *Barndopet under de fyra första århundradena*, EFS-Bokförlag, 1959
Jones, J. A., *Bunhill Memorials*, James Paul, London, 1848
Light, Alfred W., *Bunhill Fields*, Farncombe, London, 1915
Moorman, J. R. H., *A History of the Church in England*, Black, 1958
Payne, Ernest, A., *The Free Church Tradition in the Life of England*, SCM, 1944
Plummer, Alfred, *The Church of England in the 18th Century*, Methuen, London, 1910
Poole-Conner, E. J., *Evangelicalism in England*, FIEC, London, 1951
Overton, John H./Relton, Frederic, *The English Church 1714-1800*, Macmillan, London, 1906
Simon, John S., Robert Culley, *The Revival of Religion in England in the Eighteenth Century*, London, undated
Thomas, W. H. Griffith, *The Principles of Theology*, Church Room Book Press, 1945
Wakeman, Henry Offley, *An Introduction to the History of the Church of England*, Rivington's, 1914
Walker, Williston, *A History of the Christian Church*, (revised ed.), Clark, 1958
Watts, Michael R., *The Dissenters*, Clarendon Press, 1978
Whiteley, J. H., *Wesley's England*, Epworth Press, 1945
Wood, A. Skevington, *The Inextinguishable Blaze*, Paternoster Press, London, 1960

Collected Works

Bunyan, John, *The Whole Works of*, (3 vols.), ed. George Offer, Blackie and Son, 1862
Fuller, Andrew, *The Complete Works of the Rev. Andrew Fuller*, Sprinkle Publications, 1988
Hervey, James, *The Works of the Rev. James Hervey*, Thomas Nelson, 1837
Owen, John, *The Works of John Owen* (16 vols), The Banner of Truth Trust, 1968
Toplady, Augustus Montague, *The Works of Augustus Toplady*, Sprinkle Publications, 1987
Wesley, John, *Works*, (16 vols), London, 1812

Doctrinal Works

Calvin, John, *Calvin's Calvinism*, SGU, trans. Henry Cole, D. D., 1927

Calvin, John, *Institutes of Christian Religion* (2 vols.), Eerdmans, 1979

Brine, John, *An Antidote Against a Spreading Antinomian Principle*, London, 1750

Dale, James W., *Classic Baptism*, Bolchazy-Carducci, 1989

Dale, James W., *Johannic Baptism*, Bolchazy-Carducci, 1993

Dale, James W., *Judaic Baptism*, Bolchazy-Carducci, 1991

Engelsma, David, *Hyper-Calvinism & The Call of the Gospel*, Reformed Free Publishing Association, 1980

Fisher, Edward, *The Marrow of Modern Divinity in Two Parts*, Philadelphia, undated

Girardeau, John L., *Calvinism and Evangelical Arminianism*, Sprinkle Publications Reprint 1984

Huehns, G., *Antinomianism in English History*, 1951

Hussey, Joseph, *God's Operations of Grace: But No Offers of His Grace*, London 1707, reprint Primitive Publications, abridged, 1973

Murray, John, *Christian Baptism*, Presbyterian and Reformed, 1977

Nichols, J. B., *Evangelical Belief*, RTS, 1899

Niesel, Wilhelm, *The Theology of Calvin*, Westminster Press, 1956

Owen, John, *A Display of Arminianism*, Calvin Classics 2, 1989

Ringgren, Helmer, *The Messiah in the Old Testament*, SCM Press, 1956

Sell, Alan, *The Great Debate: Calvinism, Arminianism and Salvation*, Walker, 1982

Shed, W. G. T., *Calvinism Pure & Mixed*, The Banner of Truth Trust, 1986

Toon, Peter, *Hyper-Calvinism*, The Olive Tree, 1967

General History

Dewar, Canon M. W. (ed.), *An Exact Diary of the Late Expedition of His Illustrious Highness the Prince Orange, 1689*, Reprint Focus Christian Ministries Trust, undated

Edwards, William, *Notes on European History* (6 vols), Rivingtons, 1948

Hill, Christopher, *The Century of Revolution 1603-1714*, Abacus, 1975

Lecky, William E. H., *Rise and Influence of the Spirit of Rationalism*, Longmans, Green & Co., 1910

Lecky, William E. H., *A History of England in the Eighteenth Century* (7 vols.), London, 1899

Macaulay, Thomas B., *The History of England From the Accession of James II*, Everyman, 1917

Thomson, J. M., *Lectures on Foreign History, 1494-1789*, Blackwell, 1951

Trevelyan, G. M., *English Social History*, Reprint Society, 1948

Trevelyan, G. M., *England Under the Stuarts*, Methuen, London, 1928

Wolf, John B., *The Emergence of the Great Powers 1685-1715*, Harper, 1950

Miscellaneous

Benson, Louis F., *The English Hymn*, Hodder and Stoughton, 1915

Bihlmeyer, Karl, *Die Apostolischen Väter* (Original texts), J. C. B. Mohr, 1956

Engnell, Ivan, *Gammaltestamentlig Hebreiska*, Svenska Bokförlaget, 1960
Gadsby, John, *Memoirs of Hymn Writers, Gadsby*, Bouverie Street, undated
Hulse, Erroll, *The Great Invitation*, Evangelical Press, 1986
Ireson, Tony, *Northamptonshire*, Robert Hale, 1954
Kenyon, Sir Frederic, *The Story of the Bible*, John Murray, 1949
Lowth, Robert, *Lectures on the Sacred Poetry of the Hebrews*, London, 1839
Philpot, J. C., *Reviews by the Late Mr. J. C. Philpot*, M. A., Frederick Kirby, 1901
Rosenthal, Franz, *A Grammar of Biblical Aramaic*, Otto Harrassowitz, 1968
Sambrook, G. A., *English Life in the Eighteenth Century*, Macmillan, 1940
Spurgeon, Charles H., *Commenting and Commentaries*, Kregel Publications, 1992
Underdown, David, *Pride's Purge*, Oxford, 1971
Wake, Archbishop, *The Apostolic Fathers*, Routledge, undated
Würthwein, Ernst, *Der Text des Alten Testaments*, Deutsche Bibelgeselschaft, 1973

Encyclopedias, Lexica and Dictionaries

Abbot-Smith, G., *Manual Greek Lexicon of the New Testament*
Bagster, Samuel, *The Analytical Greek Lexicon*, Bagster, undated
Bauer, W., eds Arndt, W. F. and Gingrich, F. W., *A Greek-English Lexicon of the New Testament*, Chicago Universits Press, 1957
Compton's Interactive Encyclopedia, 27 vols, CD-ROM, 1995
Davidson, Benjamin, *Analytical Hebrew and Chaldee Lexicon*, Bagster, 1967
Douglas, J. D. (ed.), *Dictionary of the Christian Church*, Paternoster Press, 1974
Gesenius, Wilhelm, *Hebräisches und Aramäisches Handwörterbuch über das Alte Testament*, Springer-Verlöag, 1962
Elwell, Walter, A. (ed.), *The Marshall Pickering Encyclopedia of the Bible*, 2 vols., Marshall Pickering, 1990
Grolier's Academic American Encyclopedia, 21 vols, CD-ROM, 1995
Hastings, James, *Dictionary of the Apostolic Church*, 2 vols, Clark, 1915
Hastings, James, *A Dictionary of the Bible*, 5 vols, Clark, 1936
Hastings, James, *Dictionary of Christ and the Gospels*, 2 vols, Clark, 1906
Hastings, James, *Encyclopedia of Religion and Ethics*, Clark, 12 vols, 1908
Liddell, Henry George and Scott, Robert, *A Greek- English Lexicon*, Clarendon Press, 1890
Microsoft Encarta, Funk and Wagnall, 29 vols, CD-ROM, 1995
Schaff, Philip (ed.), *Schaff-Herzog Encyclopaedia of Religious Knowledge*, Funk & Wagnalls, 894, 4 vols.
Smith, William and Wace, Henry (eds), *A Dictionary of Christian Biography*, 4 vols, John Murray, 1900
Thayer, Joseph Henry, *A Greek English Lexicon of the New Testament*, Clark, 1930

Magazine Articles

Abreviations:

Banner of Truth Magazine	BOTM
Baptist History and Heritage	BHH
Baptist Quarterly	BQ

British Reformed Journal   BRJ
Evangelical Quarterly   EQ
Evangelical Times   ET
Journal of Ecclesiastical History   JEH
Nederlands Theologisch Tijdschrift   NTT
Observer   O
Strict Baptist Historical Society Bulletin   SBHSB
Transactions of the Baptist Historical Society   TBHS

Amey, Basil, Baptist Missionary Society Radicals, *BQ*, 26 (8), 1976, pp. 363-376
Anonymous, Antinomianism, *BOTM*, 259, 1985, pp. 23-28
Baines, Arnold H. J., The Signatories of the Orthodox Confession of 1679, *BQ*, vol. xvii, 1957-8, pp. 35-42, 74-86, 170-178.
Baird, Allen, Amyrauldianism: Historical and Contemporary, *BRJ*, Issue No: 9, Jan-March 1995, pp. 17-27
Beckwith, Frank, Dan Taylor and Yorkshire Baptist Life, *BQ*, IX, pp. 297-306
Champion, L. G., Baptist Church Life in London, *BQ*, 18, 1960, pp. 300-304
Champion, L. G., The Letters of John Newton to John Ryland, *BQ*, 27(4), 1977, pp. 157-63
Champion, L. G., The Theology of John Ryland, *BQ*, 28(1), 1979, pp. 17-29
Clark, Sydney F., Nottingham Baptist Beginnings, *BQ*, XVII, 1957-58, pp. 162-69
Clipsham, E. F., Andrew Fuller and the Baptist Mission, *Foundations* (Am), 10 (1), 1967, pp. 4-8
Clipsham, E. F., Andrew Fuller: Fullerism, *BQ*, XX, 1963
Ella, G. M., A Gospel Unworthy of Any Acceptation, *Focus*, No. 8, Winter 1993/94
Ella, G. M., John Gill and the Cause of God and Truth, *ET*, April, 1994
Foreman, H., Baptist Provision for Ministerial Education, *BQ*, XXVII, pp. 358-61
Hayden, R., Particular Baptist Confession 16, *BQ*, XXXII, 1988, pp. 403-17
Hudson, Winthrop S., Westin, Gunnar, Who were the Baptists, *BQ*, xvii, 1957-8, pp. 53-60
Hughes, G. W., Robert Hall of Arnesby 1728-91, *BQ*, X, 1940-41, pp. 444-47
Jewson, C. B., Norwich Baptists and the French Revolution, *BQ*, xxiv, 1963-66, pp. 209-215
Kirkby, A. H., Andrew Fuller: Evangelical Calvinist, *BQ*, XV, 1954, pp. 195-202
Kuiper, E. J., Hugo de Groot en de Remonstranten, *NTT*, 38 (2), 1984, pp. 111-125.
MacGregor, James, The Free Offer in the Westminster Confession, *BOTM*, 82-83, 1970, pp. 51-58
Manley, K. B., John Rippon and Baptist Histography, *BQ*, 28 (3), 1979, pp. 109-208
Martin, H., The Baptist Contribution to Early English Hymnody, *BQ*, XIX, 1961-62, pp. 199-207
Namier, Prof. L. B., The Church in the Eighteenth Century (review article), *Observer*, 1. Sept., 1936
Nicholson, J. F. V., The Office of 'Messenger' amongst British Baptists in the Seventeenth and Eighteenth Centuries, *BQ*, xvii, 1957-8, pp. 206-225
Nuttall, G. F., Northamptonshire and the Modern Question, *JTS*, NS, XVI, 1965, pp. 101-23

Nuttall, G. F., Baptists and Independents in Olney, *BQ*, XXX, 1983, PP. 26-37

Nuttall, G. F., Calvinism in Free Church History, *BQ*, 22 (8), 1968, pp. 418-428

Oliver, R. W., John Collet Ryland, Daniel Turner, *BQ*, XXIX, 1981, pp. 77-79

Oliver, R. W., By His Grace and For His Glory (Review/Nettle, *BOTM*, 284, 1987, pp. 30-32

Oliver, R. W., Historical Survey of English Hyper-Calvinism, *Foundations* (Engl), 7, 1981, pp. 8-18

Oliver, R. W., Significance of Strict Baptists Attitudes to Duty-Faith, *SBHSB*, 20, 1993, pp. 3-26

Parker, T. H. L., Calvin's Doctrine of Justification, *EQ*, XXIV, 1952

Payne, E. A., Baptists and the Laying on of Hands, *BQ*, XV, 1954, pp. 203-215

Payne, E.A., The Appointment of Deacons, *BQ*, xvii, 1957-8, pp. 87-91

Payne, E.A., More about Sabatarian Baptists, *BQ*, XIV, pp. 161-66

Payne, Earnest, Abraham Booth, *BQ*, 26 (1), 1975, pp. 28-42

Payne, Earnest, Carey and his Biographers, *BQ*, 19, 1961, pp. 4-12

Payne, Earnest, The Downgrade Controversy, *BQ*, 28 (4), 1979, pp. 146-158

Peski, A. M. van, Waarom Grotius als Oecumenisch Theoloog Mislukken Moest, *NTT*, 38 (4), 1984, pp. 290-297

Price, S. J., Reparing a Baptist meeting House, *BQ*, V, 1930-31, p. 28

Price, S. J., Sidelights from an Old Minute Book, *BQ*, V, 1930-31, pp. 86-96

Price, Seymour, Dr. John Gill and the Confession of 1729, *BQ*, IV, 1928, pp. 366-371

Robinson, O. C., The Legacy of John Gill, *BQ*, XXVI, 1971, pp 111-125

Richards, Thomas, Some Disregarded Sources of Baptist History, *BQ*, NS 17, pp. 362-379

Rupp, Gordon, Salters' Hall 1719 and the Baptists, *BTHS*, V, 1916-17, pp. 172-89

Russel, Pamela, Mr. Russel of White Street and His relatives, *BQ*, XXVIII, 1980, pp. 373-383

Sellers, I., The Old General Baptists, *BQ*, XXIV, 1971, pp. 30-38, 74-85

Sheehan, R. J., The Presentation of the Gospel Amongst Hyper-Calvinists, *Foundations* (Engl), 8, 1982, pp. 28-39

Sheehan, Robert J., The Presentation of the Gospel amongst Hyper-Calvinists: A Critique, *Foundations* (Engl.), 9, 1982, pp. 42-46

Sparkes, D. C., The Test Act of 1673 and its Aftermath, *BQ*, XXV, 1973, pp. 74-85

Sparkes, D. C., The Portsmouth Disputation of 1699, *BQ*, pp. 59-75

Stanley, Brian C. H., C. H. Spurgeon and the Baptist Missionary Society, *BQ*, 29 (7), 1982, pp. 319-328

Taylor Bowie, W., The Hollis Family and Pinner's Hall, *BQ*, I, 1922-23, pp. 78-81

Taylor Bowie, W., William Carey, *BQ*, VII, 1934-35, pp. 167-74

Thomas, Roger, The Non-Subscription Controversy Amongst Dissenters in 1719: the Salters' Hall Debate, *JEH*, IV, 1953, pp. 162-86

Toon, P., The Growth of a Supralapsarian Christology, *EQ*, XXIX, 1967

Toon, Peter, English Strict Baptists, *BQ*, 21, 1965, pp. 30-36

Weeler Robinson, H,. A Baptist Student: J. C. Ryland, *BQ*, III, 1926-27, pp. 25-33

White, B. R., How Did William Kiffin Join the Baptists?, *BQ*, XXIII, 1969-70, pp. 201-7

White, B. R., Open and Closed Membership, *BQ*, XXIV, 1972, pp. 330-34
White, B. R., Thomas Crosby, Baptist Historian I, *BQ*, 21, 1965, pp. 154-168
White, B. R., Thomas Crosby, Baptist Historian II, *BQ*, 21, 1966, pp. 219-234
White, B. R., John Gill in London 1719-1729, *BQ*, XXII, 1967, pp. 72-91
Whitely, W. T., The Influence of Whitefield on Baptists, *BQ*, V, 1930-31, pp. 30-36
Whitley, W. T., Seventh Day Baptists in England, *BQ*, XII, 1950, pp. 252-58
Young, Doyle L., Andrew Fuller and the Modern Missionary Movement, *BHH*, 17 (4), 1982, pp. 17-27

Original Handwritten Documents and Unpublished Theses

Daniel, Curt, *Hyper-Calvinism and John Gill*, Edin. Ph. D. 1884, (published privately, Dallas, 1984)
Goat Yard / Carter Lane Church Book 1719-1808, Metropolitan Tabernacle
Isaac Mann Collection 1742-1831, National Library of Wales Reference N.L.W. 1207 D., micro film, Angus Library
Journal of the Affairs of ye Antipedobaptists beginning with ye Reign of King George whose Accession to the Throne was on the First of August, 1714, Benjamin Stinton and Thomas Crosby, Angus Library
Journal of ye Proceedings of the Managers for Raising and Setting ye Funds, A, (2 vols) 1717 f., Angus Library
Kirkby, A. H., *The Theology of Andrew Fuller and its relation to Calvinism*, Ph.D., Edin., 1956
Seymour, R. E., *John Gill. Baptist Theologian*, 1697-1771, Ph. D., Edin., 1954
Spears, W. E., *The Baptist Movement in England in the late Seventeenth Century as reflected in the work and thought of Benjamin Keach, 1640-1704*, Ph.D., Edin. 1953

Index of Persons and Places

Index of Topics and Institutions

Index of Works Quoted

Index of Scriptural References

40:, p. 275,
42:1, p. 275,
42:2, p. 166,
43:1, p. 275,
43:10, p. 281,
44:1, p. 275,
45:20-24, p. 275,
48:8,
48:18, p. 275,
53, p. 42,
53:5-6, p. 79,
54:5-17, p. 211-212,
55:1, p. 156, 211,

Ezekiel
18:, p. 220,
18:20, p. 230,
18:23, p. 275,
18:24, p. 229,
18:27, p. 284,
18:32, p. 275,
24:13, p. 212,
33:, p. 220,
33:11, p. 275,

Job
14:4, p. 218,
14:5, p. 227,
17:9, p. 223-224,
30:, p. 191,
30:24, p. 191,
34:21-22, p. 148,

Jeremiah
31:3, p. 308,
32:41, p. 308,

Ecclesiastes
7:20, p. 308,
12:13, p. 280,

Zephaniah
3:17, p. 308,

Daniel
9:26, p. 79,

Hosea
13:14, p. 315,

Habakkuk
2:4, p. 232,

Zechariah
11:2, p. 345,

Malachi
3:6, p. 308,

New Testament

Matthew
1:21, p. 79,
5:18, p. 293,
5:26, p. 80,
5:44-48, p. 274,
7:7, p. 195,
9:2, p. 166,
9:13, p. 280,
11:25-26, p. 81,
11:28, p. 202, 313,
12:43, p. 233,
19:, p. 72,
19:13, p. 72,
19:14, p. 71, 121, 305,
20:28, p. 218,
22:28, p. 218,
22:36-40, p. 181,
23:37, p. 275,
24:44, p. 235,
26:33ff, p. 140,
28:19-20, p. 115,

Mark
1:15, p. 281,
2:17, p. 280,
16:, p. 286,
16:16, p. 228,

Luke
5:32, p. 280,
12:55, p. 99,
13:3, p. 211,
13:34, p. 275,
17:10, p. 280,
22:29, p. 228,
24:27, p. 305,

Glossary

Act of Uniformity: The first of many such acts enrolled on the statute-book was in 1549 when Edward VI's Parliament made the new Prayer Book the only legal service book in England. It became a breach of both common and ecclesiastical law for ministers not to abide by the ruling. This was followed by another act in 1552 referring to the amended and extended Prayer Book. Punishment for non-users was made more severe. This act was renewed by Elizabeth I in 1559, after Mary's reign. The most notorious Act of Uniformity was that passed by Charles II's Parliament in 1662 as the Prayer Book had been extended by some 600 items which were thought necessary to make the Church of England thoroughly reformed. The legalizing of the 'black rubric' concerning kneeling at communion and the addition of the black-letter saints' days caused a great stir amongst many of the more Puritan ministers, though the words 'real and essential Presence' were altered to 'corporal Presence'. In fact, the Act of Uniformity was a triumph for the catholic element in the Church of England and signalled the end of the Puritan era. There was a mass resignation of church benefices by the Puritan clergy and many were ejected because they refused to accept the ruling of the act. In all, some 2,000 clergy lost their churches, these being mainly those of Presbyterian, Independent and Baptist convictions who had received benefices during the Commonwealth period. The Church of England lost some of her very best men and the ejection marked the birth of true Nonconformity. There was also an element of politics mixed with doctrinal views in the ejection as the act demanded an oath of allegiance to a Stuart who many ministers regarded as more a Frenchman than Englishman and a potential servant of Rome.

Amyraldianism: Named after the French Pastor Moïse Amyrald (1596-1664) (Moses Amyraldus), who taught that God's original plan was to send Christ into the world to die for all men but, as he then foresaw that no one would believe, he had second thoughts and elected some to salvation through his own sovereign will. The story of the elect is thus one of divine compromise. Amyrald was given a professor's chair at Samur in 1633 but was twice accused of heresy and twice acquitted.

Arianism: The heresy taught by Arius (d. 336), a presbyter in Alexandria who maintained that what is begotten must be created out of nothing and therefore 'there was a time when the Son was not'. Christ was thus the first of the Father's creations, created in order that he, in turn, might create the world. This teaching was rejected at the Council of Nicea in 325, chiefly through the work of Athanasius (c. 296-373) who explained that the Scriptures teach the eternal Sonship of Christ and, though human sons are born in time and thus have a temporal beginning, Christ is eternally begotten of the Father outside of time, having no beginning and thus coeternal.

Baptist Historical Society: The BHS was founded in 1906 to encourage an awareness of Baptist history and doctrines and has produced a number of books on the history of the Baptist churches in Britain, besides organizing many regular summer schools and lectures throughout the years. Seven volumes of *Transactions* and thirty-three volumes of the *Baptist Quarterly*, the society's official organ, have also been published. Several office-bearers in the society such as Drs B. R. White and Raymond Brown have greatly enriched research into the life of John Gill.

Baptist Missionary Society: Successors of The Particular Baptist Society for Propagating the Gospel among the Heathen. Founded in 1792 through the efforts of William Carey (1761-1834), supported by the Northampton Association. Carey's missionary zeal and strategy was reflected in his booklet *An Enquiry into the Obligations of Christians to use Means for the Conversion of the Heathens* and he found great support for his endeavours in his fellow missionaries William Ward and Joshua Marshman with whom he formed the famous Serampore Trio. A trio of firm friends John Sutcliff, Dr John Ryland and Andrew Fuller manned the home base. In 1891 the society amalgamated with the General Baptist Missionary Society, the Bible Translation Society and the Baptist Zenana Mission and changed its name to the above.

Clarendon Code: Statutes passed by the Cavalier or Pensioner Parliament, which first sat in 1661, including the Corporation Act of 1661, the Act of Uniformity of 1662, the Conventicle Act of 1664 and the Five Mile Act of 1665. The Code's aim was to remove from the ministry, national and local government and the armed forces all those who would not subscribe to the order of service and doctrines of the Church of England. The Code was named after Edward Hyde (1609-74), Charles II's Lord Chancellor, also known as Lord Clarendon, who appears to have had little to do with the acts.

Conventicle Act (1664): An act making it illegal for anyone to take part in a religious assembly or service other than one held according to the practice of the Church of England.

Convocation: The ancient gathering of clergy in the Archbishoprics of Canterbury and York to discuss disciplinary, doctrinal and liturgical matters. It was the Convocation of 1531 that forced the Church of England to throw off papal supremacy, the 1571 Convocation which drew up the Doctrinal Canons, i.e. the Thirty-Nine Articles, the 1604 Convocation which drew up the Disciplinary Canons and the 1662 Convocation which drew up the Ritual Canons or Book of Common Prayer. Convocation rarely sat after 1717 in the eighteenth century but was revived in middle of the nineteenth century by the efforts of Henry Hoar and Bishop Samuel Wilberforce. The present General Synod has taken over most of the functions of Convocation.

Corporation Act (1661): One of the Clarendon Code acts requiring all those holding civic office to renounce the Solemn League and Covenant, to swear not to take up arms against the Crown and receive communion from the Church of England.

Council of Dort (1618-19): Otherwise called the Synod of Dort. Sat in the Netherlands in the town of Dordrecht (Engl. Dort) to work out the doctrinal standards for the Dutch Reformed Church which were adopted as the standards for succeeding Reformed or Calvinistic churches in a number of other countries including Germany, Britain and North America. The synod was called as the followers of Arminius, also named Remonstrants, had been campaigning for the freedom of the human will yet they wished to put the church under State supervision. The findings of the synod ruled that a true Reformed church must hold to the Five Points of Calvinism, namely total depravity, unconditional election, limited atonement, irresistible grace and the perseverance of the saints. (See entry under Remonstrants.)

Five Mile Act (1665-6): An act forbidding Nonconformist ministers to live or visit within five miles of his former parish or church area. This was mainly aimed at ejected ministers who were now Dissenters because of refusing to take the oath of allegiance to the king and Established Church.

Five Points of Calvinism: The five tenets of Calvinism drawn up at the Synod of Dort in 1618/19 to combat the five tenets of Arminianism put forward by the Remonstrants in 1610. They are particular predestination, limited atonement, natural inability, irresistible grace and the perseverance of the saints. The so-called Moderate Calvinists reject limited atonement and natural inability and replace them with an atonement efficacious for all and limit man's inability to the moral sphere and sphere of the will.

Hebrew Pointing: A short half-vowel or shewa pronounced like the 'e' in 'the' is rendered in Hebrew by two dots under each other; three dots in the form of a triangle with a pointed base is called a Seghol and is pronounced like 'e' in the word 'pen'. Two dots side by side are called a Şereh and pronounced as 'e' in 'prey'. One dot, which is always followed by a yohd is called Ḥiriq Gadol, pronounced like a long 'i' in 'marine' and one dot under the consonant is called a Ḥiriq Qaṭan and is pronounced like a short 'i' as in 'sit'. Gill spells Ḥiriq 'Chirek' but this does not matter as there are many ways of transcribing Hebrew.

Imputation: The New Testament word for imputation, λογιζομαι, has as its basic meaning 'to put to a person's account either favourably or unfavourably', 'to reckon as being such' or 'to lay to one's charge'. The Bible teaches that in Christ's redemptive death our sin was imputed to him and his righteousness to us (II Corinthians 5:21; Romans 4:5-11; 22-25). Because Christ paid the penalty of sin with his penal suffering and vicarious substitution, God no longer imputes sin to the believer (Psalm 32:2; Romans 4:8 ff.) but looks on the believer as having received the righteousness that Christ gained for him and bestowed on him as a free gift (Romans 5:13 ff.).

Johnsonism: The highly speculative beliefs held by the followers of John Johnson (1706-1791) of Liverpool who wavered between Arminianism and Hyper-Calvinism and often burst the boundaries of both. He held modalistic ideas of the Godhead, held unusual views concerning eschatology, gained the doctrinal enmity of both sides in the 'Modern Question' debate and expected his followers to distance themselves rigidly from other denominations. Johnsonism spread throughout the North of England, especially in the Yorkshire and Lancashire Associations, and moved to the Western Particular Baptist Association besides influencing other denominations. See Johnson's *The Faith of God's Elect*, 1754, and Brine's answer in *Some Mistakes in a book of Mr Johnson's of Liverpool* noted and rectified, 1755.

King's Bounty: This ought really to be called Queen's Bounty as it was Queen Anne under the influence of Archbishop Sharp (1691-1714) in 1704 who first set up a fund for the support of poor clergymen by using annates and church taxes amounting to some £16,000 formerly collected for the pope and subsequently for the use of the monarch. This was implemented by John Chamberlayne (1666-1723) and William Stevens (1732-1807), both associated with the Society for Promoting Christian Knowledge. Subsequently, this was also made available to the Three Denominations, and John Martin (1741-1820) became the king's distributor for the Baptists.

Mesha Stele: A stone inscription erected by Mesha, King of Moab, in the ninth century B.C. at Dibon, near the Dead Sea, otherwise called the Moabite Stone. It tells of Mesha's rule and victories, especially in relation to Omri and Ahab.

Modern Question: The belief that every man is naturally aware of his duty to believe savingly in Christ on hearing the gospel. Man is seen as lost when he refuses to believe in Christ savingly, whereas the Scriptures point out that man is damned because of his sinful nature and needs the gift of God's grace to save him.

Moral Government Theory: Based on the idea of Hugo Grotius, influenced by Abelard, that natural law as a part of divine law may be deduced *a priori* from the conception of human nature, and *a posteriori* from the fact of its universal acceptation. Thus the moral law is seen as an inherent part of human nature and is authoritative because it is a creation of God. The aim of preaching the gospel is thus first to make the hearer conscious of his natural ability to know and understand what God requires of him and secondly to appeal to his sense of duty which this is thought to kindle. The theory denies that the justice of God necessarily demands that all the requirements of the law be met. The atonement is thus merely a *nominal* display on God's part, not a *real* atonement. The sufferings of Christ are to be seen as a moral deterrent. Thus the sinner is frightened off committing future sins but there is no retribution for past sins, God merely relaxing his standards. Grotius wished by this theory to distance himself from the Socinians with whom he was accused of agreeing. In this he was completely unsuccessful. In full agreement with the Socinians, Grotius denied that the satisfaction of Christ was required by the nature and attributes of God and was thus a full equivalent of the penalty of sin. This heresy became very popular towards the end of the eighteenth century both in Britain (Fullerism) and New England (the New Divinity School) as the Reformed theological nature of the Awakening was gradually watered down.

Nazarite: Person who was either consecrated to God for life as in the case of Samson (Judges 13) or for a temporary period as in the case of Paul (Acts 18:18). A time in which various purifying rituals were observed. Nazarite vows included abstinence from strong drink, shaving one's head and beard and avoiding contact with dead bodies.

O.s./n.s. (old style/new style): The Julian or Old Style English Calendar was abolished in 1752 bringing with it two major changes. Eleven days had to be dropped to accommodate the difference to the New Style or Gregorian Calendar and 1 January was made the first day of the year instead of 25 March.

Puseyites: Those sympathetic with the views of Edward Bouverie Pusey (1800-1882) of Oxford. Pusey's views were Anglo-Catholic and High Church but he claimed that they were those of the Primitive Church. Unlike Newman who left the Anglican Church for Rome, Pusey remained a member of the Church of England though adopting Roman Catholic theology to a great extent, in particular, the Real Presence in the sacraments.

Remonstrants: The followers of Arminius, a lecturer at the University of Leyden. Their Five Points were formulated by Uytenbogaert, maintaining conditional predestination, salvation offered to all men freely, the capability of all men to be saved, free will can only be exercised properly after the reception of divine grace but can be refused at will beforehand and the possibility to fall from saving grace. (See entry under Council of Dort.)

Sabellianism: Called such after Sabellius who practised the heresy at the beginning of the third century. Sabellians insisted rightly on the unity of the Godhead but wrongly rejected the teaching of the separate persons of the Trinity, arguing that the Father, Son and Holy Spirit were mere modes or manifestations of the true God. One of the first to spread this heresy was a man by the name of Praxeus whom Tertullian (c. 160-215) accused of denying the persons of the Godhead. In his work entitled *Against Praxeus*, Tertullian said, 'Praxeus did two bits of business for the Devil in Rome. He drove out prophecy and brought in heresy, he put to flight the Paraclete and crucified the Father.' The logical consequences of Sabellianism as taught by Praxeus was that God the Father died on Calvary, hence he and his followers became known as Patripassians.

Salters' Hall Conference: In 1719 Presbyterians, Congregationalists and Baptists, known historically as The Three Denominations to distinguish them from the Anglican Church, met at Salters' Hall, London, to discuss a joint statement of faith concerning the Trinity. As a basis for discussion, the first Article of the Church of England was put forward: 'There is but one living and true God, everlasting, without body, parts, or passions, of infinite power, wisdom, and goodness, the Maker and Preserver of all things, both visible and invisible. And in unity of this Godhead there be three Persons, of one substance, power, and eternity, the Father, the Son, and the Holy Ghost.'

This move was thought necessary as Arianism and Socianism were spreading rapidly amongst Dissenters and the resulting divisions were splitting the churches into fragments. Of the 110 London Dissenting ministers who met on 19 and 24 February, only a small minority were Baptists. With a narrow majority of four votes the proposition was rejected on the grounds that 'no human compositions, or interpretations of the doctrine of the Trinity, should be made a part of those articles of advice'. Of those voting against a declaration of faith in the Trinity seventeen were Baptists, of those approving the motion fifteen were Baptists. Most of the 'nay men' amongst the Baptists were General Baptists, only three Particular Baptists refused to sign.[1] This does not mean that all the non-subscribers amongst the Baptists were Arians or Socinians but their refusal to sign may also have reflected the general disinterest in drawing up creeds amongst the Baptists. Baptists were also hyper-sensitive regarding Article I of the Church of England as it had been specifically drawn up to protect the church against anti-Trinitarian teaching amongst Continental Baptists which was quickly being spread in England. At a second meeting at Salters' Hall on 3 March, the defeated faction (mainly Congregationalists and Particular Baptists), joined by a number of other sympathizers, drew up a statement affirming their belief in the Trinity.

Sensible sinners: A common phrase used in John Gill's day and in the previous century to describe the state of the sinner after the Holy Spirit has begun to work on his soul. Bunyan described in his *Come and Welcome to Jesus Christ* how 'The truly coming souls are those sensible of their need of salvation by Jesus Christ; and, moreover, that there is nothing else that can help them but Christ.' Gill taught that there is no general awareness in sinners of gospel truths but the Holy Spirit makes those whom he is about to save 'sensible' of their situation so that they are able to respond to the gospel call.

Socinianism: Based on the ideas of Lelio Sozzini (1525-62) and his nephew Fausto (1539-1604) it began as a denial of the deity of Christ and the belief in an annihilation of souls who were not faithful to him. It gradually developed into a highly structured rationalistic, humanistic philosophy. Socinianism spread rapidly throughout Poland due to Fausto's work there and after the Counter-Reformation in 1638, it spread throughout Europe, including the British Isles, influencing the development of Latitudinarianism, Arianism and the Cambridge Platonists and also the rationalistic schools of Isaac Newton and John Locke. Presbyterianism and the General Baptists were highly influenced by the movement; Congregationalists and Particular Baptists, on the whole, withstood infiltration. There is no doubt that it was Reformed Calvinistic teaching that served as an antidote against this poisonous doctrine.

Socinians were more radical in their approach to the person of Christ than the Arians, arguing that Christ did not exist before the creation and thus could not possibly be the Creator as stressed by traditional Christianity. He was merely a man born in time. To them, the Holy Spirit was a mere divine influence and in no way a person of the Trinity. They taught that man was not essentially sinful and could avoid sin but needed no expiation or atonement, forgiveness always being guaranteed to all men by God's loving-kindness. Thus Christ has no office as Saviour but was merely used of God to demonstrate a perfect way of life. Socinians believed that baptism was only to be practised by first generation Christians, demonstrating their break with pagan culture, and was in no way a seal of divine grace.

Solemn League and Covenant (1643): A document drawn up by Alexander Henderson and accepted by the general assembly of the Church of Scotland and ratified by the English Parliament during the Civil War paving the way for a religious alliance between Scotland and England on Presbyterian lines. Mutual acceptance of the document by the two countries led to the calling of the Westminster Assembly resulting in the Westminster Confession being drawn up.

Sonship controversy: Arose among the Particular Baptists, after being introduced by Joseph Hussey amongst the Independents, concerning the eternal generation of the Son of God. The doctrine that Christ was 'eternally begotten of the Father' had been challenged in these circles and J. C. Philpot defended the doctrine in a row of articles starting with his letter published in the *Gospel Standard* magazine in 1844. Others in the churches were prepared to accept that Jesus was the Son of God as regards his human nature but not the Son of God as regards his divine nature. Their views were propagated in the *Gospel Herald*. Another Particular Baptist magazine, the *Earthen Vessel*, decided to adopt an open position and published articles both for and against the eternal Sonship of Christ, believing that it was not an essential doctrine and that the *Gospel Standard*'s stance was 'popish'. Soon 'Standard men', 'Herald men' and 'Vessel men' who had formerly shared sweet fellowship were now at loggerheads. The controversy reached new heights when some critics of the *Gospel Standard* position began to go to the extreme of arguing that Christ's human nature was pre-incarnate. J. C. Philpot referred to John Gill's book *A Dissertation concerning the Eternal Sonship of Christ*, 1768, as support for his defence of the traditional doctrine but his antagonists affirmed that Gill was now followed by a small minority of Baptists only. The Gospel Standard churches maintain in their fifth article of belief that 'though he (Christ) existed from all eternity as the eternal Son of God, the human soul of the Lord Jesus did not exist before it was created and formed in His body by Him who forms the soul of man within him, when that body was conceived, under the overshadowing of the Holy Ghost, in the womb of the virgin Mary'.

Test Act (1663): Passed by Parliament to rule that all those holding public offices, whether civil or military, should attend holy communion at an Anglican church, take the oaths of supremacy and uniformity and reject the doctrine of transubstantiation. The main aim of the act was against Roman Catholics but Dissenters of all kinds were brought under its jurisdiction.

Thirty Years War (1618-48): A pan-European war with the Protestant forces of Bohemia, Denmark and Sweden on one side and the Roman Catholic forces of Bavaria, Austria and Spain on the other. Other countries such as France changed sides repeatedly. Germany found herself the main battlefield as gradually the Swedish forces under Gustavus Adolphus and his model army of fierce Protestants, similar to Cromwell's, forced a peace which was signed on 14 October 1648 at Münster in Westphalia. At the peace talks, Lutheran, Reformed and Roman Catholic church boundaries were laid down and agreements were made regarding the powers of the nobility respecting the churches.

Toleration Act (1689): An act passed by Parliament after the Glorious Revolution led by William of Orange. Dissenters were allowed to have their own places of worship, providing they were registered, and appoint their own pastors and teachers who were required to take an oath of loyalty and accept a modified version of the Thirty-Nine Articles.

---

[1] Two if St Paul's Alley is not counted as a Particular Baptist church.